MW01061202

COMMUNITY AND CLIENTELE
IN TWELFTH-CENTURY TUSCANY

EX LIBRIS

OXFORD

UNIVERSITY PRESS

Community and Clientele in Twelfth-Century Tuscany

The origins of the rural commune in the plain of Lucca

CHRIS WICKHAM

CLARENDON PRESS · OXFORD
1998

Oxford University Press, Great Clarendon Street, Oxford OX2 6DP
Oxford New York
Athens Auckland Bangkok Bogotá Buenos Aires Calcutta
Cape Town Chennai Dar es Salaam Delhi Florence Hong Kong Istanbul
Karachi Kuala Lumpur Madrid Melbourne Mexico City Mumbai
Nairobi Paris São Paolo Singapore Taipei Tokyo Toronto Warsaw
and associated companies in
Berlin Ibadan

Oxford is a registered trade mark of Oxford University Press

Published in the United States by
Oxford University Press Inc., New York

British Library Cataloguing in Publication Data
Data available

Library of Congress Cataloging in Publication Data
Wickham, Chris, 1950–
[Comunità e clientele nella Toscana del XII secolo.   English]
Community and clientele in twelfth-century Tuscany : the origins
of the rural commune in the plain of Lucca / Chris Wickham.
p. cm.
Originally published in Italian by Viella libreria editrice, Rome,
1995. With slight modifications and a new bibliography.
Includes bibliographical references.
1. Lucca (Italy : Province)—Rural conditions.   2. Rural
population—Italy—Lucca (Province)—History.   3. Villages—Italy—
Lucca (Province)—History.
HN488.L82W5313   1998
307.72'0945'53—dc21   97–50496
ISBN 0–19–820704–2

1 3 5 7 9 10 8 6 4 2

Typeset by Graphicraft Typesetters Ltd., Hong Kong
Printed in Great Britain by Biddles Ltd., Guildford & King's Lynn

Acknowledgements

I am very grateful to Leslie Brubaker, Susan Reynolds, and Wendy Davies, all of whom read the whole text and substantially improved my arguments. Maribel Alfonso and Steven Bassett read, respectively, Chapter 8 and Chapter 3, and greatly improved them too. I benefited enormously from the unpublished thesis of Arnold Esch and from the research materials he so generously let me use, as will be quite clear from my footnotes; and also from the extensive experience that Franca Leverotti has of the demographic material for late medieval Lucca: the book would have been far less adequate without their help. Mons. Giuseppe Ghilarducci, archivist of the Archivio Arcivescovile di Lucca, facilitated my researches in every way, and indeed made them feasible, given my constraints of time, in the first place. The maps were drawn by the late Jean Dowling, one of the best cartographers; Susan Martin ably compiled the index. I am also grateful to Julia Barrow, Sandro Carocci, Paolo Delogu, Oretta Muzzi, Duane Osheim, Rosanna Pescaglini, Giuliano Pinto, Cinzio Violante, and, last but not least Enzo Matera and Matteo Sanfilippo, for discussions, advice, help, and bibliography, as well as to friends and colleagues, in Birmingham, Pisa, Florence, and Rome for an intellectual framework during my Lucchese researches of recent years. My stays in Lucca and Pisa in 1983 and 1987 to research this book, six months in total, were made possible by Small Grants from the British Academy.

Note to the English Edition

An Italian edition of this book was published in August 1995 by Viella libreria editrice of Rome, as *Comunità e clientele nella Toscana del XII secolo*. This is the English version of that text. It is almost unchanged, except that a couple of minor errors are silently amended, and some new bibliography is added to the footnotes. I have enclosed the latter in square brackets, to indicate that it has not had any effect on the main text. This new bibliography is almost entirely restricted to works on Tuscany; I have not in fact seen much other new work in this field in the last few years, outside Spain at least, but I decided anyway that there was no point in adding yet further to the long bibliographical footnotes in Chapter 8. The only exception (n. 69 of that chapter) is where a new debate has suddenly emerged, which needs to be recognized, even though it has not caused me to change my views as expressed here.

A word about terminology. I have extensively used several standard terms used by Italian historians, most of which I have kept in roman rather than italic type, on the grounds that too much italic for normal parts of a technical vocabulary is irritating to the reader. Four such terms need a brief gloss before we start.

The 'signoria' denotes a network of political and judicial dues and rights ('signorial rights') enjoyed by lords over either the land they themselves held or over the lands of all the landowners in a defined territory (see also Ch. 2 n. 8). It is the equivalent of the French seigneurie banale; I keep the French spelling when discussing that country in Chapter 8. The internal workings of one signoria, Moriano in the Lucchesia, are discussed in detail in Chapter 4, section 1.

I use the word 'castello' rather than English 'castle' throughout the text, because the word in Italian means not only 'fortification' but also 'fortified village': so, for that matter, did the medieval Latin words used in Italy for the same network of concepts, *castrum* and *castellum*. There is a substantial historiography on the impact of the building of castelli in Italy, the process called *incastellamento* by modern historians, which turns precisely on the different impact of that process on settlement patterns from place to place: see below, p. 7, and the references cited there.

'Consorteria' is another modern term, used for large extended families (sometimes many generations deep), which operated as single groups, sometimes with formally constituted political structures; in some cases these

consortial groups seem to have united families with no direct genealogical links at all.

Finally, the 'pieve' (Lat. *plebs*) was one of the principal elements of
medieval Italian ecclesiastical organization; it was the major subdivision
of the diocese, based on the pieval church at its centre. Its priest was
known as a pievano (*plebanus*). Pievi could have any number of subordinate churches in their territories, from one to thirty or more. They were,
however, the only churches at which baptisms could be performed, and
they were the centres to which tithes were due, until they were super-
seded, not without difficulty, by a parish system during the twelfth and
thirteenth centuries. They had some relationship and similarity to minsters in Anglo-Saxon and Anglo-Norman England. See further below,
pp. 75–81.

Other technical terms, principally those I have left in Latin, will be
explained in the text.

As to names, I have consistently translated the names of kings, emperors, popes, and marquises into English, while putting into Italian those
of counts, bishops, saints, and everyone else (thus Pietro di Giovanni means
Peter son of John, throughout). When Pope Alexander II is the same man
as Bishop Anselmo I of Lucca, this may look odd; but no system is perfect, and this one, at least, looks the least odd to me. The names of places
are less trouble, for in Tuscany only Firenze (Florence) has a currently
used English form; but it may be worth noting that the territories of the
various cities each have a name in Italian, mostly corresponding to the ad-
jectival form of the city, and I use these throughout—the Lunigiana and
the Lucchesia (irreg.), and the Pisano, Pistoiese, Fiorentino, Fiesolano,
Aretino, and Senese. These territories will, throughout, be the medieval
dioceses, not the modern provinces.

C. J. W.

Birmingham
January 1997

Contents

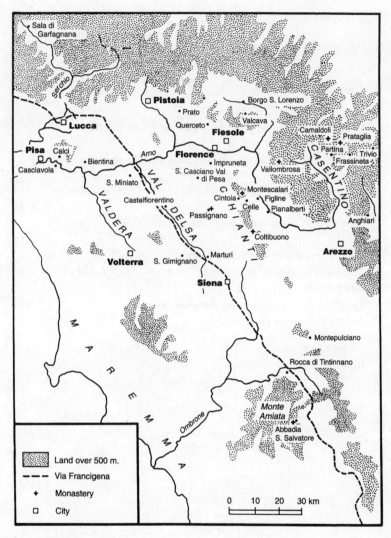

MAP 1. Tuscany

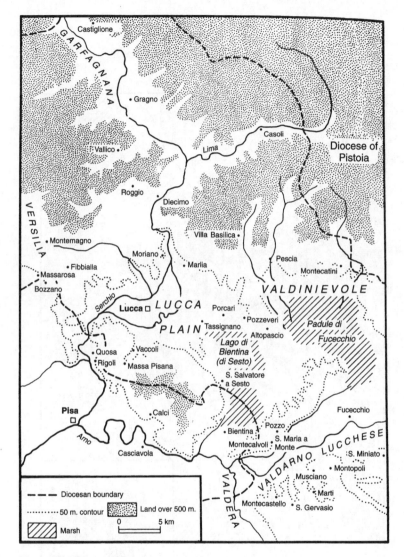

MAP 2. The Diocese of Lucca

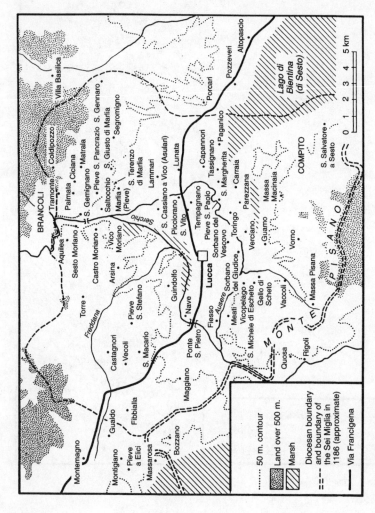

MAP 3. The Sei Miglia

Legend:

.... 50 m. contour

Land over 500 m.

Marsh

– – – Diocesan boundary
and boundary of
the Sei Miglia in
1186 (approximate)

—— Via Francigena

Labels on map:

BRANCOLI

Villa Basilica
Coldipozzo
Tramonte
Matrala
Ciciana
Palmata
S. Gennaro
S. Pancrazio
Pieve S. Gennaro
S. Giusto di Marlia
Segromigno
S. Gemignano
Saltocchio
Marlia (Pieve)
S. Terenzo di Marlia
Lammari
Aquilea
Sesto Moriano
Vico Moriano
Castro Moriano
Arsina
S. Cassiano a Vico (Asulari)
Lunata
Torre
Freddana
Serchio
S. Vito
Piciorano
Capannori
Tassignano
S. Margherita
Paganico
Carraia
Parezzana
Pozzeveri
Porcari
Altopascio
Lago di Bientina (di Sesto)

Pieve S. Stefano
Vecoli
Castagnori
S. Macario
Guindolfo
Nave
Ponte S. Pietro
Fiesso
Lucca
Tempagnano
Pieve S. Paolo
Sorbano del Vescovo
Sorbano del Giudice
Toringo
Verciano
Guamo
Massa Macinaia
COMPITO
S. Salvatore a Sesto

Meati
Vicopelago
S. Michele di Escheto
Gello di Scheto
Vaccoli
Vorno
Massa Pisana

Montemagno
Montigiano
Pieve a Elici
Massarosa
Gualdo
Fibbialla
Bozzano
Maggiano
Quosa
Rigoli

MONTE PISANO

0 1 2 3 4 5 km

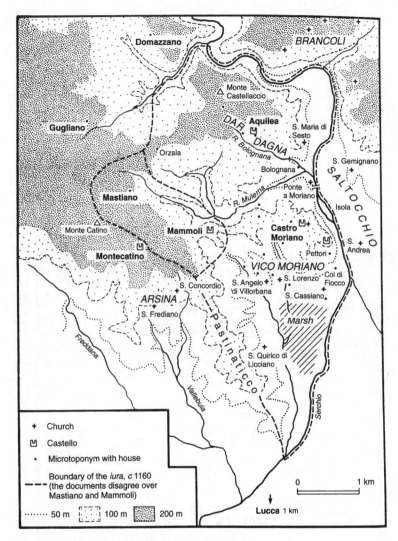

MAP 4. The Morianese in the Tenth to Twelfth Centuries

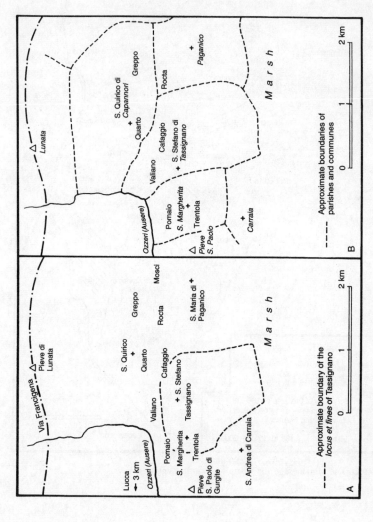

MAP 5: Tassignano and Capannori: A, 850–1050; B, 1150–1200

Map A (left panel):

Via Francigena

Pieve di Lunata △

Lucca
← 3 km
Ozzeri (Ausere)

S. Quirico +
Quarto
Valiano
Pomaio
S. Margherita +
Trentola
Pieve △
S. Paolo di
Gurgite

Greppo
Rocta
Cafaggio
S. Stefano +
Tassignano

Mosci

S. Maria di +
Paganico

M a r s h

S. Andrea di Carraia +

Approximate boundary of the
locus et fines of Tassignano

0   1   2 km

A

Map B (right panel):

Lunata △

Ozzeri (Ausere)

Pomaio
S. Margherita +
Trentola
Pieve △
S. Paolo

Carraia +

Valiano

Cafaggio
S. Stefano di +
Tassignano

Quarto +

S. Quirico di
Capannori
Greppo

Rocta

Paganico +

M a r s h

Approximate boundaries of
parishes and communes

0   1   2 km

B

I
Introduction

It is curious how little has been written in the last half-century in Italy about the early rural commune. In the period 1890–1930, the rural commune and its origins were a major issue of debate, the rustic counterpart to the fierce arguments about the commune in the city. The founders of the modern Italian historiography of the Middle Ages saw in the slow development of collective activity the basis for a future national identity; and, while of course they were most interested in the city, which had come to be the essential point of reference for any view of the pre-Risorgimento past, an understanding of the countryside was already seen as an inescapable prolegomenon to any clear analysis of urban society. The rural commune was the servile version of the uprising against (implicitly northern European) feudal lords that consuls and their allies achieved in the city (Salvemini, Caggese), or, alternatively, the demonstration that the social vivacity that produced the city commune and the *vita civile*, leading, in the end, to the Renaissance, was matched in the rural world and was all the stronger for these rural roots (Volpe). There were many other versions of the imagery; every scholar of the period found it important to have a view of the rural commune. Some stressed the Church as its driving force, some collective land; some the stimulus of the rural signoria, some the constricting bonds of signorial power, to be overthrown by class struggle; some the solidarity of serfs, some the economic advances of free peasants or small local aristocrats; some the pre-Roman roots of the commune, some its eleventh- or twelfth-century affirmation. They bickered interminably over these issues, especially in the decade preceding the First World War; they wrote rude reviews of each other's works, and came back with vigorous defences of their own positions, in *Studi storici* and the *Rivista italiana di sociologia*, in debates that renewed themselves yearly, and sometimes even more often.[1]

---

[1] My complaints follow the recent critical comments in S. Bortolami, 'Comuni e beni comunali nelle campagne medioevali: un episodio della Scodosia di Montagnana', *Mélanges de l'Ecole française de Rome*, 99 (1987), 555–8. For the major formulations of the authors cited, see G. Salvemini, 'Un comune rurale nel secolo XIII' (1901), in id., *La dignità cavalleresca* (Milan, 1972), 274–97; R. Caggese, *Classi e comuni rurali nel medio evo italiano*, i (Florence, 1907); G. Volpe, *Medioevo italiano* (Florence, 1961), 119–87. They will be discussed further in Ch. 8, along with other versions of the imagery. For the speed of debate see, e.g., Ch. 3 n. 69.

Looking back on these dead debates, two things strike the reader: their vivacity and their schematism. It is only too obvious now how exactly the arguments reflect the major lines of disagreement about the nature and future direction of the still infant Italian state. Socialism was, with Salvemini and Caggese and others, the most explicit of these over-arching theories, and indeed the most powerful; it is also the one whose memory survives best, as an image which subsequent historians still think worth accepting or contesting. But whereas, in the parallel debate on the city, Salvemini's class struggle model was explicitly opposed from the 1920s onwards by Ottokar and others, thus letting the pendulum return in the last two decades to a recognition that there were, indeed, socio-economic issues that divided *magnati* and *popolani*, the rural communal debate stopped dead. The eventual response to the socialist viewpoint was not, in the countryside, given by a rival global interpretation, but instead by a rival *methodology*, empirical research.

The rural communal debate was characterized by a supreme indiffer-ence to exact research methodologies. Examples could be plucked out of the documents at random and generalized to the whole of Italy—or the whole of Italy north of Rome—when, indeed, examples of real historical developments were used at all. (The exceptions, like Checchini on the Saccisica in the Trevisano or Volpe on Pisa or Luzzatto on Matelica in the Marche, still stand out; but they were exceptions.)[2] Part of the intel-lectual justification for this approach was undoubtedly the dominance of legal history as a methodological framework, for it was often taken as axiomatic that early medieval society, like contemporary society (at least as seen by lawyers), was a world of institutions, reasonably clearly laid out and generally understood at the time, even if they were not very well documented; it was, therefore, enough to find one reference to an insti-tution or to an official to be able to generalize it to a very wide social environment indeed. This is above all what Gianpiero Bognetti did in the last, and the most methodologically aware, contribution to the rural commune debate in its traditional form, published in 1926. Bognetti, indeed, went so far as to declare that the institutions of the commune were essen-tially unchanged from the pre-Roman period. This form of extreme con-tinuitism, of course, made it less necessary to adopt or adapt any form of class struggle imagery for the new developments of the years around 1100, an imagery that was anyway hardly fashionable in Italy in 1926 (though

---

[2] A. Checchini, 'Comuni rurali padovani', *Nuovo archivio veneto*, 18 (1909), 131–84; G. Volpe *Studi sulle istituzioni comunali a Pisa*, (2nd edn., Florence, 1970), 6–123; G. Luzzatto, *Dai servi della gleba* (Bari, 1966), 245–350; and, once more, Salvemini, 'Un comune rurale'.

continuitism is by no means an intrinsically conservative position, as Emilio Sereni demonstrated in the 1950s).[3] But Bognetti's substantial book was the last in the series, not so much because his vision came clearly to dominate the discussion, but because the nature of research on the subject changed. The substantive contributions to the debate that have been made since the 1920s have been much less ambitious, restricted to specific local areas, and without many pretensions to wider generalization.

Simeoni, publishing on the Veronese from 1921 onwards, was the first to write in this genre: he not only refused to generalize about rural communes but did not even cite the previous bibliography. And Simeoni, followed by Schäfer, writing on the Sottoceneri in the Ticino, established an empirical tradition that has lasted ever since. Some intensive local analyses of very high quality now exist. The Veneto is particularly well studied, thanks to Checchini, Simeoni, Fasoli, Castagnetti, and Bortolami; Lombardy pretty well, with the overviews of Bognetti in 1926 and Menant in 1993 (and one should not forget Romeo's study of Origgio in 1957, though it is very little concerned with communal origins); Tuscany more patchily, though with some major recent contributions—in particular, Odile Redon has published important studies on the Senese, and Dameron on the Fiorentino.[4] These provide real advances, even though they are relatively few in number; they have made it possible, indeed, for the rural commune to figure without embarrassment in major recent syntheses of central medieval history.[5] On this level, there might seem to be no problem: the issues have not, it is true, changed very greatly since 1930, but now we know, as was not known in 1930, more or less what we are talking about.

But it is at this point that one looks back at the authors of the early debates and regrets the loss of their vivacity. They thought that the

---

[3] G. P. Bognetti, *Studi sulle origini del comune rurale* (Milan, 1978), 1–262 (reacting in part against F. Schneider's *Origini dei comuni rurali in Italia* of two years previously, an equally brilliant mix of careful empirical observation and wild legalistic generalization). E. Sereni's *Comunità rurali nell'Italia antica* (Rome, 1955), a Marxist classic, is quite content to follow Bognetti, e.g. 505–12. I shall in this book be consistently critical of legal historians, so it seems fair to recognize from the start that not all legal history is schematic, and the tendency for some social historians to neglect it altogether is unfortunate. I intend to return to the issue elsewhere.

[4] See Ch. 8, pp. 219–29, for discussions; for the authors cited, see the bibliography.

[5] G. Tabacco, *Egemonie sociali* (Turin, 1979), 236–57; A. I. Pini, *Città, comuni e corporazioni* (Bologna, 1986), 63–108; A. Castagnetti, 'Il potere sui contadini', in B. Andreolli *et al.* (eds.), *Le campagne italiane* (Bologna, 1985), 219–51 (the only recent survey to be specifically focused on rural communes); P. Cammarosano, *Le campagne nell'età comunale* (Turin, 1974); C. Violante, 'La signoria "territoriale"', in W. Paravicini and K. F. Werner (eds.), *Histoire comparée de l'administration* (Munich, 1980), 333–44.

crystallization of rural identity alongside that of the city was *important*. We no longer have that sense of mission to see the past as a quarry of moral examples to support an interpretation of the present, and we are not, by and large, nostalgic about it; but it seems to me that, even if Caggese and the others discussed the rural commune for the wrong reasons, they had the right intuition. If one accepts that rural communes genuinely were new in Italy in the years between 1050 and 1250 (which now more or less everyone does), then their crystallization *was* the analogue to that in the city, and did represent a major change in the whole organization of rural activity and identity, the beginnings of the structures of rural government that still exist today. The changing social structures of the city have remained central to the interests of historians; those of the countryside (notwithstanding much sophisticated economic history) have not. They were not, however, less important, whether or not they were always as dramatic (and very often they were not, as we will see). Recent work on the early city commune has shown itself very sensitive to the necessary interplay between the analysis of individual local specificities and the wider generalization from those local specificities that is necessary to make the local analyses themselves comprehensible and meaningful; indeed it is evident that the nature of political power, particularly in the twelfth century, is more complicated an issue than it was once thought to be.[6] The same sort of methodology is necessary for the communes of the countryside. We need, in particular, to look as carefully as we can at the differences in experience between different individual communes or different regions, and then analyse why these differences existed. For, as with the city, rural communes did, despite enormous divergences in their nature, identity, and purpose, appear across the same wide arc of time, and with very similar structures; we have to understand why this was—why, that is, such different processes tended to produce such similar results. Only by this sort of movement from the particular to the general can we get beyond Caggese, who remains, despite the incoherence and the rhetoric of his work, the only historian who has tried to explain the rural communal movement as a whole.

At this point it may be a good idea to offer a brief definition of the concept 'rural commune', because the way the phrase is used in this book is not quite the same as the way it has been used by some other

---

[6] See, for example, R. Bordone, *La società cittadina* (Turin, 1987); R. Bordone and J. Jarnut (eds.), *L'evoluzione delle città italiane* (Bologna, 1988); and, for the problem of power, G. Tabacco, 'Gli orientamenti feudali', in *Structures féodales et féodalisme* (Rome, 1980), 219–40.

historians. 'Rural commune' (*comune rurale*) is a specifically Italian term, corresponding to the village *concejo* of Castile, the *consulat* of southern France, the *Dorfgemeinde* of the Germans, the organized *communauté rurale* of northern France, taking account of the inevitable differences between the specific historical experiences of each region.[7] The term most directly describes the widely documented institutions of rural local government of the late Middle Ages, which in Italy were generally called *communia* or *universitates*; and in Italy, these institutions, with their own statutes and quasi-autonomous leaders (consuls or *sindaci* or *podestà*), were a normal feature of the late medieval countryside. Historians tend to define the origin of rural communes as the origin of these rural institutions: the office of consul as representative of the village, the institution of the village assembly (maybe based on a collective oath), the written document (*breve* or *patto* or *franchigia*) by which the lord conceded freedoms to the village community. The 'commune' of the twelfth century onwards, at least in Italian (less so in French) is thus differentiated from the 'rural community' of the earlier Middle Ages; villages may have had some sort of communitarian organization before 1100 or so, but it was much less precisely characterized, for it had no institutional structures and no formal representatives. Such a definition is specific enough to make a further point clear: it is possible to have a rural commune, as it would now be defined, even without the word *commune* (or its synonyms, such as *communis populus*, *compagnia*, or *universitas*) appearing in the sources; consuls and organized village institutions are all that need be looked for, and indeed, in their absence, even a village described in a document as a *commune* is not necessarily a 'commune'.

This definition is probably by now that most in use among historians in Italy. It makes certain assumptions about rural communal origins, however. One such assumption (which I share, although not every historian has done) is that villages in Italy were indeed less systematically organized before 1100 than they were afterwards. Another assumption is that twelfth-century 'communes' can actually be described in institutional terms. This, however, I do not accept; it will, in fact, be a major contention of this book that communes were not, or often were not, as yet institutions. Twelfth-century villages had networks of explicitly characterized cooperative relationships, but these depended less on developed rules than on relationships between people: that is to say, they consisted of sets of

---

[7] The regional differences between these separate concepts will be further discussed in Ch. 8, pp. 192–219.

consciously regulated interactions between members of a social group, rather than being clear-cut institutions that existed independently of them. (One can for that matter say the same for the earliest city communes, though the point will not be argued at length here.) The institutions only developed in a subsequent phase of communal crystallization, closer to 1200 than to 1100. These, of course, are precise empirical claims; they will have to be substantiated through the study of local contexts, for only such a study will show how people really behaved in the twelfth century. But they make a definition of what I mean by 'rural commune' rather more complex than a reliance on institutional features would. Here, the term will describe structured and explicit collective associations, based on units of rural settlement; which will normally have leaders (often called consuls from the start), but not yet necessarily formally characterized representatives; and which certainly will have a collective consciousness and some control over their own affairs, but not necessarily yet a specific terminology (*commune* or *universitas*) or a clearly defined institutional framework. This definition (or, if you like, ideal type) should serve to distinguish twelfth-century collectivities from the less articulated communities that existed in (most of) Italy in the early Middle Ages, without attributing to them a legal precision that might as yet be inappropriate. It will be fleshed out further in the text.

In this book, I will look at one precise set of local contexts, those of some of the villages in the plain of Lucca, to see what people were actually doing, and what rural communes meant for them when these latter appeared in the course of the twelfth century. Then, at the end of the book, I will move from the particular to the general, setting these Lucchese examples against those discussed by other historians elsewhere in Tuscany and in Italy (and, indeed, elsewhere in Europe, where analogous developments were taking place in the same period), to see what light they shed on the communal movement as a whole. We probably do not yet have enough empirical analyses to make really wide-ranging syntheses possible: rural society was not only more diverse than that of the city, but also, of course, furnishes more examples for the simple reason that there were more villages than there were cities. But one can at least make an initial move towards such syntheses. Such an attempt seems to me to be worth while, for two reasons. The first is the traditional, but still unsolved, problem of explaining the origins of the rural commune itself (or, better: of rural communes in the plural). The second is in effect the same issue, but seen in reverse: the rural commune is one of those concepts whose consistency, at least in its outer form, across such a wide range of different experiences acts as an organizing device for the understanding of those multiplicities of experience themselves. The point has already been made for the castello and for the process of *incastellamento*, which have been very extensively studied in the last two decades;[8] the rural commune, though less fully analysed, has a similar potential. The different elements in these local experiences are relatively easily recognized —the signoria, the parish, the castello itself, common lands, settlement patterns, the influence of the city, the interests of local élites, the end of 'serfdom'; it is, however, how these different variables fit together in each individual case that needs to be better understood, and the process of the development of the commune is an analytical line that can help that understanding. For none of them can be seen on their own as the 'first cause' of the rural communal movement, as people variously tended to argue at the beginning of the century; but every one can be seen as one of the crystallizing agents for at least some communes, or for communes in at least one geographical space. One of the intentions of this book is to confront why and how these differences came to exist through detailed studies of the differences between villages in one specific area, the plain of Lucca.

The plain of Lucca and its surrounding hills, otherwise known as the Sei Miglia from the six-mile jurisdiction around the city that is known from the late eleventh century (and that still survives, little changed, in the two large and interlocking communes of Lucca and Capannori), is extremely well documented in the Middle Ages. There are over 1,500 documents for the eleventh-century diocese of Lucca, and over 3,500 for the twelfth; over three-quarters of these are for the Sei Miglia. And, although we will not look at them in detail here, the well-known eighth- to tenth-century sequence of Lucchese charters, nearly another 2,000 in number, gives our material a chronological perspective that most other cities do not have. The reason for choosing Lucca is above all this richness of documentation. It is certainly not because the territory is 'typical'. Nowhere is. But there are some very clear features that make the Sei Miglia Lucchese apparently quite atypical of twelfth-century Italy. These include, most notably, two sets of elements. First, the local weakness of private signorial powers and, conversely, a greater than average importance for the parish in local territorial organization, including that of

---

[8] For surveys see P. Toubert, *Les Structures du Latium médiéval* (Rome, 1973); A. A. Settia, *Castelli e villaggi* (Naples, 1984); C. J. Wickham, *Il problema dell'incastellamento* (Florence, 1985); and the articles collected in *Archeologia medievale*, 16 (1989).

the communes themselves. Second, a long-standing weakness of village identity, that makes the process of communal formation stand out quite clearly, but that, conversely, makes the social role of rural communes themselves apparently less great, and certainly less aggressive, than in many other parts of Italy.

These are important atypicalities, and they will be discussed in some detail in the book. But they are amply compensated for by the number of documents themselves. Many studies of rural communes have been based on relatively few texts, and principally on normative ones: *cartae libertatis*, other agreements between lords and communities, early statutes, and the like. But if, as I have proposed, early communes were not yet fully institutionalized, then they cannot be properly understood through normative texts. What one has to study, in fact, is not so much the commune as seen externally, through its formal regulations, but, rather, the people who composed it: one must see the 'institutions' socially, as part of the daily practice of the individuals and families that made them up. It follows that we must study as much as we can of the documented behaviour of all the inhabitants of each village, so as to be able to locate the importance of the slowly crystallizing commune for them, in the context of all the other things they can be seen to be doing. It is for this reason that it is necessary to choose places that are as widely documented as possible, and such places can certainly be found in the Sei Miglia Lucchese.

Even in Lucca, our documentation is not entirely satisfactory, it must be said. Before the surviving notarial registers start (which in the case of Lucca is not before 1220, and only fragmentarily for some decades yet), all our texts survive only in ecclesiastical archives, and thus only give us evidence for what was, or came to be, inside the purview of churches. Furthermore, documented activities are, as elsewhere in Italy, almost all land transactions: sales, gifts, leases, pledges, or litigation. I have discussed elsewhere, in a book on the Tuscan Appennines entitled *The Mountains and the City*, some of the problems of, and the possible methodologies for, using such a limited record to construct a wider social history, and for a fuller account of my interpretation of the issue I refer the reader to it. But the basic point can be summarized relatively briefly. Land was the principal source of wealth and status for almost everyone we will be looking at; and thus its alienation, or the alienation of its fruits, and the wider issue of what happened to it, can be assumed to have been of immense symbolic and practical importance to people. In principle, what happened to land ought at least to respect the essential framework of the other, often more interesting, but undocumented social activities of its owners or holders. (One does not, for example, readily transact business with enemies; and certainly not sell them something as important as land, if one can avoid it.) Land transactions ought to involve the same sorts of social networks that villagers had at their disposal in other contexts; and, with due weight given to the problem of the distortions implicit in the accidents of survival, they can be analysed in that light. Some patterns, as we shall see, can certainly be discerned in such analyses.[9]

The whole of the Lucca Plain contains several dozen villages, of widely differing depths of documentation; it would not be practicable to discuss all of them here. I will focus on two areas, which offer useful sorts of social contrast. They are the zone of Moriano in the low hills to the north of the city, which was part of the signoria (*iura*) of the bishop of Lucca; and the zone of Tassignano, Paganico, and Capannori in the plain to the east of Lucca, which was not subject to any form of territorial signorial control, and whose communes were as a result somewhat different from that of Moriano. I chose the two areas precisely because of the contrasts they offer in signorial control, for the signoria has traditionally (and rightly) been understood as a very important element in the formation of the commune; but also because of the richness both of them offer in their documentation. Each area, though quite small, has over 200 documents for the period 1050–1225, the time-span which I have researched most systematically for this book. I have in addition studied the texts for the areas of Marlia and Brancoli, to the east of Moriano, areas which I will use as comparisons for my principal research zones, though I will when necessary take examples from the rest of the Lucca Plain as well.[10] I cannot hope to have been systematic outside the areas I have looked at most carefully; it is indeed one of my main arguments that every village has a different social structure from every other. But I hope that I have looked at enough texts to be able to tell in which respects Moriano and the

---

[9] C. J. Wickham, *The Mountains and the City* (Oxford, 1988), e.g. 190–215, 254 ff.; see also, for methodological warnings (and Lucchese examples), A. Esch, 'Überlieferungs-Chance', *Historische Zeitschrift*, 240 (1985), 529–70.

[10] See App. 1, below, pp. 243–6, for greater details on Lucchese documentation. I have looked at all the surviving Lucchese charters up to the end of the 11th cent., although only about two-thirds of those for the 12th cent., which are largely unpublished; after 1200 I have only looked at those for specific villages. But for the 12th cent. I have benefited from the great kindness of Arnold Esch, who let me use his name index for the entire series of unpublished Lucchese charters across that century; as a result, I can be reasonably certain about the presence and absence of the people I have studied up to 1200 even in texts I have not directly consulted.

Tassignano area are similar to other parts of the Lucca Plain, and in which respects they are different, so as to be able to generalize further.

Even inside the relatively restricted ambit of a few villages, it is not my intention to reconstruct a general rural history of the Lucchesia in the eleventh and twelfth centuries. I shall focus on the changes in the social networks of individual villages (and villagers) that seem to have to do with the development of the rural commune and the slow crystallization of its institutions. I shall discuss, too, the changing patterns of territorial identity, of landowning networks (including those of city dwellers), and of clienteles, for in my view these changes relate very closely to the formation of communes. But the links between these arguments and wider problems of Lucchese society in the period 1050 to 1200/1225, to say nothing of those of economic and (urban) political development, cannot be discussed in detail here; the only format that would be able to include them all would be the French *thèse d'état* of 1,000 pages or longer, the sort of book I have neither the patience to write nor the publisher to put into print. And that would not, after all, be the point. The aim of this book is not to discuss the Lucchesia, but to discuss the origins of the rural commune (or: of rural communes) through a discussion of the Lucchesia. Only once we can understand the process in an empirical framework, from below, through the actions of the people who constituted it, can we begin to generalize. But generalization is the eventual aim of the book. In the last chapter, at least schematically, I will attempt to do precisely that: to look at Lucca and its neighbouring villages in the context of Italy, and Europe, as a whole.

2

Lucca and the Sei Miglia in the Eleventh and Twelfth Centuries

It is inescapable that one should begin a discussion of rural society in the Sei Miglia Lucchese with a discussion of the city; for Lucca has been dominant in its immediate hinterland in every way from the beginning of our documentation in AD 700 until the present day. I will start with Lucca, then, and its relationship to the economic structures of its surrounding plain. I will discuss the city commune and the nature of its political hegemony over its immediate hinterland, the Sei Miglia; the impact of the city food markets on the economics of land sales and leasing in the Lucca plain; and the consequences this had for the relationship between landlords and tenants in the twelfth-century Lucchesia. Discussion of all three of these themes, however brief and generic, is essential if we want to understand the background to the appearance of rural communes in Lucchese villages. The other purpose of this chapter is to offer an impression of the local dimensions of village society in the Lucca plain and how it changed; this I will do through the counterposition of two 'personal archives' that survive for two medium landowners from Marlia from about a century apart, *c.*1030–60 and *c.*1150–90. How these two differed will give an immediate image of the shifts in the social and economic environment of villagers that occurred across the same period. This too will, I hope, allow a greater intuitive understanding of some of the more detailed social processes I will be discussing later in the book.

i. City society and the agrarian economy

Lucca in the eleventh and twelfth centuries was a major political and economic centre, not only from the moment of its appearance as a city commune (in existence by 1119–20 at the latest), but also before.[1] Lucca

[1] The major secondary works on Lucca are: for the period up to 1100, H. M. Schwarzmaier, *Lucca* (Tübingen, 1972); and, for the 12th cent., A. Esch, 'Lucca im 12. Jahrhundert', a Habilitationsschrift for the University of Göttingen that is in the process of being published: I am grateful to the author for letting me use it. The former tends to concentrate on socio-political history, the latter on economic history. For the political history of the early commune, the principal recent discussion is V. Tirelli, 'Lucca nella seconda

had in fact been for centuries the principal city of the March of Tuscany, and retained this association up to the death of the Countess Matilda of Canossa, the last powerful marquis, in 1115, although it was by then weakening—the Canossa marquises when in Tuscany often found themselves in Florence and Marturi (modern Poggibonsi) as well.[2] It is far from clear what specific advantages Lucca drew from its status in the March, though the evident importance of judges and *causidici* in its political life throughout these centuries must in part be a result of it; judges seem more or less to have controlled Lucca's local affairs from at least the time of Marquis Hugh in the late tenth century.[3] The power of the marquises in the city, however, certainly had an effect on the institutional development of the diocese/county of Lucca, as we shall see.

As an economic centre, Lucca principally drew its importance from its position on the via Francigena, the road from France and northern Italy to Rome; its merchants and money-changers are readily visible from the late eleventh century onwards in our (few) public texts. The sparseness of reference to urban occupations in private documents does not allow us to say much more about the detail of the city's economic activities until the very late twelfth century; but the fact that from then on changes in notarial formulae suddenly show us a wealth of urban trades, and the fact that the first notarial registers in the 1220s show the full range of

metà del s. XII', in *I ceti dirigenti dell'età comunale* (Pisa, 1982), 157–231; still important, however, is the brief institutional survey in S. Bongi, *Inventario* (Lucca, 1876), ii. 293–309. For the commune and the bishops, the basic text is D. J. Osheim, *An Italian Lordship* (Berkeley, 1977); see also, now, V. Tirelli, 'Il vescovato di Lucca', in A. Spicciani and C. Violante (eds.), *Allucio da Pescia* (Rome, 1991), 55–146 [and, above all, R. Savigni, 'La signoria vescovile lucchese', *Aevum*, 66 (1993), 333–67; id., *Episcopato e società* (Lucca, 1996)]. I discuss the social relationship between city and country in more detail in 'Economia e società rurale', in A. Spicciani and C. Violante (eds.), *Sant'Anselmo* (Rome, 1992), 391–422.

[2] For the 11th-cent. marquises in Tuscany, see A. Falce, *Bonifacio di Canossa* (Reggio Emilia, 1926–7); A. Overmann, *Matilde di Canossa* (1895; Ital. edn., Rome, 1980), neither of them exactly masterpieces of synthesis; more recently, M. G. Bertolini, 'Bonifacio', *Dizionario biografico degli Italiani*, xii (Rome, 1970), 96–113; M. Nobili, 'Dominazioni marchionali', in *Atti della VIII settimana di studio* (Milan, 1980), 243–6; Schwarzmaier, *Lucca*, 253–60, 322–34. [See now, in general, P. Golinelli (ed.), *I poteri dei Canossa* (Bologna, 1994).] In the 12th cent., the marquises became more marginal to Tuscan affairs—the office itself was abolished in 1198—and they tended to restrict themselves to places like Marturi and S. Miniato, strategic but distinctly un-citylike centres. See F. Schneider, *L'ordinamento pubblico* (1914; Ital. edn., Florence, 1975), 232–3, 263; P. Scheffer-Boichorst, *Zur Geschichte des XII. und XIII. Jhts.* (Berlin, 1897), 60–91; D. von der Nahmer, *Die Reichsverwaltung in Toscana* (Aalen, 1965), 184–93. The March and its political structures need considerably more attention, along the lines of the programmatic surveys at the start of *Formazione e strutture*, i (Rome, 1988), a book of articles on central medieval territories.

[3] Schwarzmaier, *Lucca*, 317–34.

complex (and indeed international) economic transactions that we would expect to find in any active early thirteenth-century Italian city, must indicate that behind the fairly standard land transactions that survive in their thousands from the Lucchesia in the years 1000–1200 there was already a complex urban economy in operation. Lucca probably did not match Pisa as an economic centre after 1050 at the latest, and it did not have easy access to the sea except through Pisa itself (an attempt to create an alternative port at Motrone, on Lucchese territory, was never entirely successful; the geographical location was not particularly favourable, and the Pisans destroyed it too often). But it was still a first-rank city in Tuscany, and expanded fast, well beyond its Roman walls; a new circuit had to be built in the early thirteenth century.[4]

The consuls of the commune of Lucca are first recorded, casually, in 1119; by 1120 they were city representatives, clearly recognized by Marquis Conrad. The detail of the debate about their origins cannot be dealt with here. It is doubtless not insignificant, though, that the Lucchese consuls, like all those in Tuscany except for Pisa (and maybe Arezzo), are not documented before 1115, when Matilda died; her authority, even though her power was receding, was such that the affirmation of collective identity in Tuscan cities may not have led to the recognition of stable representatives before that date.[5] But the Lucchesi had run their own legal affairs for long before that, under the patronage of the marquis; and after 1080–1, when the citizens expelled Matilda's protégé Bishop Anselmo II, and accepted a charter of privileges from the Emperor Henry IV, the city became effectively independent of the marquises as well. The consulate of 1119/20 must, that is, have simply crystallized a reality that

---

[4] For urban economic activity in general, see Esch, 'Lucca', ch. 1; L. A. Kotel'nikova, *Mondo contadino* (1967; Ital. edn., Bologna, 1975), 55–64; Wickham, 'Economia e società rurale'. (Cf. A. Esch, 'Überlieferungs-chance', *Historische Zeitschrift*, 240 (1985), 536: 'Urkundliche Überlieferung macht das Mittelalter noch agrarische, als er ohnehin schon ist'.) For Lucchese international trade and the port at Motrone, *Tholomei Lucensis Annales*, ed. B. Schmeidler, *MGH, SRG*, NS 8 (Berlin, 1955), 37, 48, 136, 157; Bernardo Maragone, *Annales pisani*, ed. M. Lupo Gentile, in *Rerum italicarum scriptores*, 2nd edn., vi. 2 (Bologna, 1930), 50–2; A. Gchaube, *Handelsgeschichte* (Munich, 1906), 58–62, 349–51, 646–54; D. Abulafia, *The Two Italies* (Cambridge, 1977), 256–61. It should be observed, though, that in the documents of 12th-cent. Pisa the same repertoire of land transactions gives much more evidence for commerce than at Lucca.

[5] For first references to consuls, with previous bibliography, see T. Blomquist and D. Osheim, 'The First Consuls at Lucca', *Actum Luce*, 7 (1978), 31–8, which however misses the crucial 1120 diploma of Marquis Conrad, ed. G. Tommasi in *Storia di Lucca* (Florence, 1847), appendix, 5–6. For Arezzo and further bibliography on Tuscany see J.-P. Delumeau, 'Commune d'Arezzo', in *Les Origines des libertés urbaines* (Rouen, 1990), 325–46, and now id., *Arezzo. Espace et sociétés 715–1230* (Rome, 1996), 850–5.

had existed for over a generation—or, at least, have begun to do so, for
the legal position of the commune of Lucca, as elsewhere, remained uncertain for decades.[6] As we shall see in the case of Moriano, some rural
communities are already documented as acting collectively in the early
1120s; they were following an urban practice that certainly preceded the
recent appearance of the consulate. And the city commune was active in its
contado early, too. The Sei Miglia was already under urban control, as
we will see; by the 1130s the Lucchesi were prosecuting wars well beyond
its bounds, in the Valdinievole and the Valdarno (as well as carrying on
interminable frontier wars with Pisa, which had begun as early as 1004),
and by the end of the century, apart from some areas intermittently taken
out of their hands by the emperors, they controlled the whole contado
except for some parts of the far south.[7]

Twelfth-century Lucca needs a great deal of further study before we
can say as much as needs to be said about the political, social, and economic bases of the early commune. For our purposes, however, it is enough
to stress the hegemony it had in its immediate hinterland, the Sei Miglia,
for the villages nearest to Lucca are our principal subject-matter. I have
argued elsewhere that territorial signorie were weak in the twelfth-century
Lucchesia as a whole, and that most local aristocratic families maintained
a wide spread of landholding and scattered signorial rights across the whole
diocese, thus making it easy for the city to establish (or re-establish) itself
as a political force on the diocesan level, either by war or, more commonly,
by peaceful affirmation. I would link this, at least in part, to the hegemony the marquises had in this corner of Tuscany right up to 1080–1:
the tendency for rural lords slowly to establish local signorial bases, with
increasingly defined boundaries, which was general in the Po plain and
visible in many parts of Tuscany too—at least on the edges of dioceses,
at the margins of the influence of each city—began late for Lucca (as
for Pisa) and did not get very far.[8] In the Sei Miglia, however, there

---

[6] See on this point, among many, G. Volpe, *Medio evo italiano* (Florence, 1961), 87–118;
G. Tabacco, *Egemonie sociali* (Turin, 1979), 229–36; A. I. Pini, *Città, comuni e corporazioni*
(Bologna, 1986), 67–76.

[7] For the wars, see Tommasi, *Storia di Lucca*, 26–51; R. Davidsohn, *Storia di Firenze*,
i (1896; Ital. edn., Florence, 1956), chs. 9, 10; G. Volpe, *Pisa* (2nd edn., Florence, 1970),
chs. 3, 4—all three drawing liberally on the same basic sources, Tolomeo and Maragone.
For imperial interventions, see below, n. 10.

[8] Wickham, 'Economia e società rurale'; see further below, Ch. 4, App. [See now also
C. J. Wickham, 'La signoria rurale', in G. Dilcher and C. Violante (eds.), *Strutture e
trasformazioni* (Bologna, 1996), 343–409.] Here and elsewhere I will distinguish between
'territorial' signorie, networks of judicial and other rights based on defined territories
in which the lord did not usually own all the land, and signorial rights attached directly to

were almost no signorial territories at all. This is a point of considerable importance for any discussion of the rural commune, and deserves further emphasis.

In 1081 Henry IV's privilege to the Lucchesi explicitly states that a zone of six miles around the city should be kept free of *castelli*, and that it should not be left *sine legitima iudicatione*: that is to say, outside the judicial hegemony of the city. This is the first surviving reference to the Sei Miglia, which retained its territorial specificity inside the State of Lucca, right up to the present day. Its present boundaries are little different from those of 1186, in which year Henry VI issued a privilege to the Lucchesi that is the first text to make explicit how far the zone extended (see Map 3).[9] Henry VI further clarified the limits of urban jurisdiction inside it, a natural enough development in an age of judicial definition that had sharply increased relative to that of a century before: in 1186, the only exemptions from the remit of the city's courts in the Sei Miglia were the *iura* of the bishop over Moriano and Sorbano del Vescovo, that of the cathedral canons in Massa Macinaia, and the signorial rights held in respect of their private landowning by certain aristocratic families, most notably the Porcaresi and the Montemagno. It must be emphasized that these privileges were not themselves responsible for the creation of a compact territory subject to the jurisdiction of the city: emperors were not that powerful, at least after 1050 or so. (Their attempts at other times to abolish city jurisdiction in other parts of the diocese, such as the Garfagnana or the Valdinievole, were in the long run futile.)[10] But what we can see of the presence of signorial rights in the thousands of documents for the Sei Miglia confirms the picture as described by Henry IV and Henry VI in all but detail: city power in the area was, and remained, very real.

landowning or landholding ('signoria fondiaria'), which were almost always highly fragmented, indeed scattered across wide areas, following the standard Italian patterns of private property. The clearest set of definitions along these lines can be found in C. Violante, 'La signoria "territoriale"', in W. Paravicini and K. F. Werner (eds.), *Histoire comparée de l'administration* (Munich, 1980), 333–44, and id., 'La signoria rurale,' *Settimane di studio*, 38 (1991), 329–85; for further bibliography see C. J. Wickham, *The Mountains and the City* (Oxford, 1988), 105–8. Pisan parallels: Volpe, *Pisa*, 103–6; G. Garzella, 'Cascina', in M. Pasquinucci *et al.*, *Cascina*, ii (Pisa, 1986), 72–83, 102–3.

[9] *MGH, Heinrici IV Dipl.*, ed. D. von Gladiss (Weimar, 1952–3), n. 334; A. N. Cianelli, 'Dissertazioni', in *Memorie e documenti* (Lucca, 1813), i. 198–200, for Henry VI. The latter text does not mention the *iurae* of the church, but these had independent confirmation in the same years—see e.g. *MGH, Friderici I Dipl.*, ed. H. Appelt (Hanover, 1975–90), n. 910 (*a*.1185) for the bishop, n. 727 (*a*.1178) for the cathedral Canonica.

[10] For the attempts, see von der Nahmer, *Reichsverwaltung in Toscana*, e.g. 205–7.

The victory of the city even in the Sei Miglia was not painless, however. There were, for example, at least eight castelli in the area in 1081, despite Henry IV's diploma. The Lucchesi destroyed two of them, Vaccoli in 1088 and Castagnori in 1100, as well as the probably later construction at Vorno in 1150. These were in the context of the Pisan wars, however, and other castelli were left alone; with few exceptions (Moriano, Porcari, Compito) they were of minor political or demographic importance.[11] There are other references to signorial rights, too. In one case, a signorial territory was explicitly created by an emperor (that of the tiny castello of Coldipozzo, ceded to the Avvocati family by Barbarossa in the 1160s); three other territories seem to have been *de facto* developments, against the grain of city dominance—the Montemagno signoria in Mammoli, the lordship of Vorno, and the Porcaresi signoria over S. Gennaro on the eastern edge of the Sei Miglia.[12] The references to local *potestates* in individual villages of the plain that suddenly appear in the 1140s (though soon disappear again) may also indicate hiccups in the judicial control of the city; and one must not forget the long-standing coherence of the episcopal signoria in Moriano, documented already in the 1070s, and by no means always welcome to the Lucchesi (it is notably absent from the 1081 diploma; indeed, the Lucchesi would in 1081–2 besiege this castle too, this time without success).[13] But with the exceptions of these, and the other sets of rights recognized in 1186, the Sei Miglia had no signorie

---

[11] *Tholomei annales*, s.aa.; see further below, Ch. 3 n. 3. One consequence of this was that there was nowhere in the hinterland of Lucca closer than S. Maria a Monte that could be defined as in any way 'urban'. More urbanized castelli (often called *borghi*) did exist elsewhere in Italy; see below, pp. 214–15. Not all of my discussions of strictly rural communes fits them.

[12] Coldipozzo, Vorno, S. Gennaro, and other signorial references: see Wickham, 'Economia e società rurale', nn. 28, 34, 36. Mammoli: see below, Ch. 3 n. 39. The basic works on the episcopal and canonical *iurae* (above, n. 9) are Osheim, *Italian Lordship*; and G. Dinelli, 'Una signoria ecclesiastica', *Studi storici*, 23 (1915), 187–291, with P. J. Jones, 'An Italian Estate', *Economic History Review*, 2 ser. 7 (1954) 18–32.

[13] Local *potestates* in the Sei Miglia, outside known areas of signorial powers: ASL ii. 487 (*a.*1139), RCL 940 (*a.*1140), 1020 (*a.*1147), 1031 (*a.*1148), ASL ii. 587 (*a.*1148), RCL 1048 (*a.*1149); there follow only six other references in any texts I have seen for the rest of the century, RCL 1163–4, 1209, 1272, 1322, 1709, AAL Frat. Cap. 16 (*a.*1161). They all appear in penal clauses, and nowhere else. (For this aspect of local identity, see below, pp. 93–4, for the signoria of Moriano.) There is no doubt about the judicial powers ascribed to such *potestates* (they 'coerce' or 'dominate' their villages), and the formulaic context is matched exactly in known signorial centres such as S. Gennaro (RCL 1032–9, 1294, 1543–4, 1596); but that they were an important feature of local political structures seems unlikely, for they never appear in any other context than penal clauses, and they are very temporary. For comments on another possible local structure, the *iudicaria plebis*, see below, Ch. 3 n. 53.

that lasted long enough or firmly enough to appear in our documents. Indeed, even the signorial rights attached to Porcaresi or Avvocati or episcopal landowning, although ratified by emperors, rarely appear in private charters, and did not play an important part in the political structures of the twelfth-century Lucca plain. It is significant, for instance, that we can find very little trace of a signoria at Porcari itself, seat of the most powerful aristocratic family of the diocese;[14] and in Moriano, by far the best-documented signorial territory, the city had considerable powers, as we shall see. In practice, then, independently of imperial decisions, the city was politically and legally dominant in the Sei Miglia—as it had been, indeed, ever since our run of documents began in the eighth century. And even its potential rivals, the holders of signorial rights in the plain, all lived in the city by 1200 (the Porcaresi and the Montemagno had moved there only very recently, it is true, but did so with some enthusiasm: they were among the major faction leaders by the early thirteenth century at the latest). The city and its inhabitants were and remained the undisputed point of reference for its immediate hinterland.[15]

This political centrality of Lucca in the Sei Miglia was matched by an economic dominance, that operated on a number of levels. The first of these that matters for us here is that the city was an enormous agricultural market. In the late fourteenth century, roughly 55 per cent of the population of the area lived in the city and its immediate suburbs. Two centuries before, the percentage would have been somewhat less; although it can only be guessed at, 25 per cent would not seem to me unreasonable.[16] They had to be fed. Lucca must, of course, have had a

---

[14] For the content of signorial rights on the plain, see below, pp. 107–9, and Wickham, 'Economià e società rurale'. The most entrenched area of such rights in the Sei Miglia was Massa Macinaia and Vorno, for which see in particular *RCL* 1186, 1188, 1382, 1521, and below, p. 107. There are two references only to signorial powers in Porcari, *RCL* 1543, 1563, even though the castello was probably just outside the boundary of the Sei Miglia, and the second of these explicitly mentions the city's powers too.

[15] Porcaresi and Montemagno: *Tholomei annales*, s.aa. 1198–1209; G. Sercambi, *Le croniche*, i, ed. S. Bongi (Lucca, 1892), 12–17; cf. Bongi, *Inventario*, ii. 307. Outside the Sei Miglia, urban political and economic influence was certainly less, but remained strong all the same, as I have argued elsewhere: *Mountains*, 126–33 (for the Garfagnana); 'Valdinievole', in A. Spicciani and C. Violante (eds.), *Allucio da Pescia*, 279–96; 'Economia e società rurale'.

[16] For the figures, C. Meek, *Lucca* (Oxford, 1978), 22–6; for the general demographic context in that period, see Franca Leverotti's works cited in the bibliography, notably her important survey 'La crisi demografica'; I am indebted to her for advice and figures. The only pre-Black Death figures easily available are those derived from the 1331 collective oath from most adult male Lucchesi, urban and rural, to John of Bohemia, listed in ASL Capitoli 52; a cursory initial calculation indicates a city:Sei Miglia proportion of perhaps 45:55. (In 1971 it was 40:60; ISTAT, *11° Censim. generale*, iii. 9 (Rome, 1974), 16–22.) Only a total

market for the agricultural produce of the plain from the earliest times. From the mid-eleventh century, however, this market is mentioned quite often in documents; its core was the grain market of the *classo salaiolo*, which furnished the dominant grain measures for the whole Sei Miglia. (Wine and oil measures were often more local, particularly in the early twelfth century, but these too were largely taken over by the city by 1200.)[17] Already in the eighth century, inside a general framework of subsistence cultivation, the villages around Lucca showed a quantifiable tendency to specialize in certain crops, the plains having more grainfields and the hills more vineyards. By the twelfth century, however, the contrast is very sharp, with rents in particular dividing abruptly at the edge of the hill slopes: those on the plains being generally in wheat and millet or beans, those on the hills generally in wine and oil, with chestnuts coming in as one proceeds up the valleys into the mountains.[18]

This was, it must be emphasized, a difference in rent rather than in production: that is to say, in the needs of landlords rather than those of primary producers. Plains villages like Tassignano or Paganico, whose rents were uniformly in wheat and millet or wheat and beans throughout the twelfth and early thirteenth centuries, largely consisted of land termed *campus cum arboribus*, arable land cultivated promiscuously with tree crops, which after 1200 or so was often more explicitly glossed *campus cum arboribus et vitibus*; the wine remained part of subsistence cultivation and was not required as rent. Sometimes, the disjuncture between terrain and rent could be alarming: vineyards in Moriano rendered rents

survey of the documents for the period 1100–1300, a huge task, would give us earlier figures, but they were certainly lower for the city, which was expanding fast around 1200 in particular, as already noted. No systematic provision for urban food supply is visible in Lucca before the 13th-cent., incidentally, which may mean that the city was still small enough for market mechanisms in the Sei Miglia to function reasonably well (from the point of view of the city, that is; country-dwellers, who in Moriano at least were already at or beyond a Malthusian maximum by 1120—see Ch. 5 n. 1, may have thought differently). For these issues, see in general E. Fiumi, 'Sui rapporti economici,' *Archivio storico italiano*, 114 (1956), 18–68; Pini, *Città, comuni e corporazioni*, 102–8.

[17] *Classo salaiolo*: see refs. in I. Belli Barsali, 'La topografia di Lucca', in *Atti del 5° Congresso internazionale* (Spoleto, 1973), 485, 515 f.; and *RCL*, index, s.v. For local measures in Moriano, see below, Ch 4 n. 14. Outside the Sei Miglia, measures were generally local, not urban; indeed, this whole discussion of the economic weight of the city has less relevance further towards the edges of the diocese (though see Wickham, *Mountains*, 25, 137, for its considerable effect on the Garfagnana after 1150).

[18] For the 8th- and 9th-cent. background, see B. Andreolli, 'I prodotti alimentari', *Archeologia medievale*, 8 (1981), 117–26. See tables in Esch, 'Lucca', ch. 1, for local differences in rents (and ch. 2 for the dominance of oil and wine in Compito, a hill area to the south of the city comparable to Moriano in the north). For chestnuts, see e.g. *RCL* 1106, 1119, 1147 for Villa Basilica in the hills of the Valdinievole.

in oil in 1183, 1198, and 1202; in grain in 1194 and 1223. We cannot, that is to say, read production off from rentals at all accurately. But, in general, there were undoubtedly more vines and olives on the hills; and certainly far more *vinee* (vineyards), indicating a more specialized production than *campi cum vitibus*, than on the plain.[19] At the very least, the sharp difference between the plains rents and the hill rents indicates a clear awareness by landlords of the relative advantages of different terrains for different crops; and this awareness, one visibly orientated towards sale in the city markets, must have stimulated an already existing tendency towards cash crops. Indeed, the reliability of a market mechanism that worked not only for landlords but for peasants as well is the best way to explain the 'anomalous' rents in Moriano just cited. At the end of the Middle Ages, this would reach its height with the introduction of silk cultivation.[20]

The twelfth century is the first time since 850 that rents in kind are documented in large numbers in the Lucchesia. The basic reason for this is that rents from cultivators that had been, in the tenth- and eleventh-century *libellus* leases, almost exclusively in money, began from the late eleventh century to be transmuted into rents in produce; produce rents then dominate the *tenimentum* contract, the principal type of written lease given to cultivators during the century following. This fact is in itself a sign of the importance of the city market, for landlords began to wish to exploit it directly rather than leave their tenants to do so. The change to kind from money rent was given further impulse at the end of the twelfth century by the defensive reaction that landlords had to the serious price inflation of the period after *c*.1170, although in Lucca this reaction was merely an accentuation of a development nearly a century old.[21] Both

---

[19] Promiscuous cultivation in Tassignano and Paganico: e.g. *RCL* 1356, 1772, ACL H92 (*a*.1208), R49 (*a*.1214), random examples from huge numbers. 'Anomalous' Moriano rents: *RCL* 1492 (*a*.1183), 1795 (*a*.1198), ASL S. Ponziano 6 apr. 1202; AAL ++L76 (*a*.1194), ++S6 (*a*.1223). Compare G. Pinto, *La Toscana* (Florence, 1982), 188–92, for the rarity of specialized olive-groves in Tuscany, outside the Lucchesia, before the 15th cent.; and see, for Moriano in general, Ch. 3 n. 1.

[20] See T. W. Blomquist, 'Trade and Commerce in Thirteenth Century Lucca', University of Minnesota Ph.D. thesis 1966, 82–118, for silk. Cash crops and market reasoning are both, it is worth stressing, exemplifications of landlordly control over production—peasants will require more market stimulus than existed in the 12th cent. readily to risk cash cropping and the resultant weakening of subsistence agriculture. See, for a good argument along these lines, M. Barceló *et al.*, *Arqueología medieval* (Barcelona, 1988), 202–29.

[21] The reappearance of rents in kind might in part be due to a change in documentation: the 12th cent. is also the first time since 850 that leases to cultivators survive in large numbers from the Lucchesia, thanks to the development of the *tenimentum* contract (for which see Jones, 'Italian Estate', 24–5). But the rents from cultivators that are documented

aspects of the process testify to the importance of the commercial economy of the city in the Sei Miglia.

The twelfth century also showed a gradual tendency, evidenced in the documents, towards the ever more careful definition and specification of the terms of contracts. We find, for example, detailed apportionment of the responsibility for transporting products from the tenant holding to the landlord's house, barn, or warehouse (and sometimes a description of the meal to which the carriers were entitled), or a specification of the exact size of fields and of the types of measures used; these features are rare in earlier texts. Tenants were also protected in many leases from the 1060s, and in particular from the mid-twelfth century onwards, from natural and human disasters, *furor de celo et de terra*, or, more explicitly, *si wastata fuerit per oste de rex aut de marchione, vel si gelaverit aut tempestaverit.* Apart from the undoubted fact that the twelfth century was a rather more dangerous time for Tuscans than the relatively peaceful years of the March of the Canossa, these provisions display a greater concern for legal precision than did contracts of a previous period; this greater legalism is a general feature of the twelfth century everywhere.[22] They also, however,

from the years around 900 certainly tended to be in money; conversely, in the 12th cent., unlike earlier, Lucchese leases generally expected kind rents from non-cultivators as well— the expectations for rents in general had evidently changed. The issue has a large bibliography: see, as guides, Kotel'nikova, *Mondo contadino e città*, 26–64; Jones, 'Italian Estate', 27–9; Wickham, *Mountains*, 78 ff., 228 ff.; Esch, 'Lucca', ch. 1, who emphasizes (pp. 21–2) how hard it is to distinguish leases to direct cultivators, and who argues that many apparent leases to cultivators in the 12th cent. are in reality nothing of the kind. For the price inflation in Lucca, ibid. 18–19, 84–8; its intensity was local, but parallel inflations in 12th-cent. Europe had similar effects (cf. a classic English example, H. E. Butler (ed.), *Chronicle of Jocelin of Brakelond* (Edinburgh, 1949), 33). Simply raising rents was not an easy option when most leases were still perpetual. It should be added, as a general background observation, that most landowners in our period held according to absolute property rights, as in 'Vulgar' Roman law. Some substantial tracts of land were held by aristocrats in lease (*libellus*), notably from the bishop (see e.g. Wickham, *Mountains*, 16); these 'great *libelli*' tended to be renamed fiefs (*feuda*) after 1100 or so, and the bishop slowly lost control of many of them, but he took rents from them for a long time. There could be, as we shall see, many levels of letting and subletting between landowners and tenant cultivators; all in the 9th to 11th cents. could be expressed through the *libellus*, which was both the name for a document of lease and the term used for a particular form of hereditary lease-holding contract. It is the latter form that was replaced by the hereditary *tenimentum* contract in the 12th cent.

[22] Disaster quotes: AAL *E71 (*a.*1175), *RCL* 640 (*a.*1103); the first known to me is ASL ii. 201 (*a.*1066). Rents in the case of disaster were sometimes held over to the following year, or else commuted to labour-service or another product; they rarely were cancelled. Other examples of the legal precision of the century are a greater exactness in specifying the rights transferred in property (whether full ownership or rent-paying tenure or usufruct), a greater concern for rights of access (which often produced court cases, as in ASL S. Ponziano 10 giug. 1189, S. Giovanni 7 genn. 1193, Certosa 23 dic. 1200); and more detail in sanction clauses.

testify to a concern for accuracy that goes with a desire for the calculation of agricultural profit. There is, indeed, evidence that such profit was
calculated: Arnold Esch has shown that acquisitions of lands and rents
in the later twelfth century tended to produce a standard 4–6 per cent
profit per annum on initial outlay.[23] Although, as we shall see, land transactions were not yet a purely commercial operation, a commercial aspect
to the 'land market' was already in operation by the later twelfth century. Once again, the pattern is that of the economy of the city. Lucca
and its markets were not only influencing what was grown on the plain
and the hills around the city, but also the whole socio-economic context
that structured the relationship between landlords and tenants.

These developments had numerous consequences for our major focus
of interest, social relationships in the countryside. One was the well-known
tendency for city-dwellers to buy land in the countryside, as a firm and
reliable investment, and as a more status-producing location for wealth
than money on its own. (One tends to assume that land must have been
important for status, for in a strict commercial sense it was not the most profitable investment: 5 per cent is a reasonable average for landed property,
but usury tended to produce 20 per cent in this period, and international
trade at least that, allowing for risks.)[24] This, when added to the equally
well-known though socially distinct tendency for country-dwellers to
move into the city, led to sharp increases in urban property-owning in
the Lucchese contado, and in the Sei Miglia in particular, most notably
from the mid-twelfth century onwards. We will see examples of both
developments in the course of the book. But the concentration of ownership was not the only innovation relevant to us. The urban market is also
one of the contexts for an opposite but equally important feature of the
Lucchese countryside in our period: the extreme fragmentation of tenure.

The Lucca plain had always had a fragmented pattern of landholding.
This was true of most of Italy, and was a normal result of the rules of
partible inheritance, which were generally taken seriously in the peninsula: a man with three sons and nine fields tended to divide each field
into three. By no means all such divisions were real; and, even when they
were, at least where medium and large landowners were involved, the

[23] Esch, 'Lucca', ch. 1, 45–51, 77, 83–6, for the calculations and a general discussion.
[24] Usury at 20%: see, for example, *RCL* 156 (*a*.1035), 919 (*a*.1138), 1181 (*a*.1160), ASL
ii. 268 (*a*.1119). See the survey by A. Spicciani, 'I prestiti su pegno fondiario', in *Banchi
pubblici* (Genoa, 1991), esp. 652–7. For the general issue of mercantile vs. agrarian usury,
see V. Bonazzoli, *Il prestito ebraico* (Ancona, 1990), 62–4, 99–101. For international trade
profits, see Abulafia, *Two Italies*, 223–37.

practical result was often simply that each tenant paid a third of his former rent to each of the three sons. But in the long run land was divided and subdivided, and often bought and sold in very small portions. One example from the late eleventh century, taken at random, is the pledge by one Azzo di Fralmo in 1075 of land in Vaccoli: a third portion of three pieces of land (one with a house), and two fifteenths plus a twelfth portion of thirty-five other pieces of land (two with houses) and of the castello of Vaccoli itself. Single landlords could have dozens or even hundreds of pieces of land, which by now tended to be listed individually in documents rather than grouped into tenant holdings. Tenant holdings had themselves always tended to consist of scattered fields, but by the eleventh century even the terminology of the holding, the *mansus* or the *casa et res*, had largely disappeared. Azzo could have been describing his portions of three such holdings; but it made more sense by now to list them field by field. Anyway, the situation was doubtless already more complex; people had been buying and selling fractions of land (and thus, in effect, rent) in Vaccoli for generations, thus making it highly unlikely that Azzo's tenants only owed rent to his family. Indeed, they themselves had been letting and subletting land too: it is easy to find examples in the eleventh century of four or five levels of leasing, representing different levels of aristocratic dependence, non-cultivators leasing to cultivators, and cultivators leasing to each other, sometimes all at once. This sort of fragmentation was common in the period, and has often been described. It made aristocratic control of single villages nearly impossible; and it was no easier for churches, or, eventually, citizens, for they accumulated land parcels by the same sorts of transactions. It tended, too, to lead to the very considerable *de facto* independence of individual cultivators themselves, who, even if they did not own at least some land outright, could owe rent to many different people and at many different levels at the same time, making it hard for them to be subjected to anyone in particular. Only a small minority of peasants can be identified as really subject in the Lucchesia, in fact; the others had a relatively distanced relation to their landlords.[25]

---

[25] See, for fragmentation, E. Conti, *La formazione* (Rome, 1965), i. 133–217, *passim*; Wickham, *Mountains*, 231–5, 254–5; it would continue into the late 13th cent. in the Lucca plain, as D. J. Osheim shows, 'Independent Farmers' (in press). Azzo di Fralmo: *RCL* 408. Multi-level leasing: see, for example, ASL i. 77 (*a.*1032); AAL ++C75, AF33 (*a.*1065, Gemignani 141, 148); *RCL* 1383 (*a.*1178); and Esch, 'Lucca', ch. 1, 41–4. For subject tenants (*manentes*), see below, pp. 108–9.

This sort of pattern does not in itself have to have much relationship to a commercial environment. It can be found in parts of eleventh-century Tuscany far from city economies, and it gave rise in such environments to 'land markets' with very pronounced social connotations, with men (very rarely women) selling to each other to establish or maintain links of friendship or dependence, more often than to maximize profit. But when a commercial environment is also present, as it undoubtedly was in the Lucchesia by the late twelfth century, the fragmentation of tenure could lead to some very complex networks of transactions. Esch has argued that many people in that period were not so much buying land, as buying rents; and that the land market, thus separated from a traditional politics of property, was a genuinely commercial phenomenon.[26] And people can certainly be seen, by the end of the century, operating as buyers, lessors, and usurers with pledges in land, in an apparently entirely economic framework; we will see some examples later.

One particularly clear type of transaction that expresses a purely economic relationship, quite a common one in the period, is that in which a landowner pays money to a tenant (who is desperate presumably for cash in hand) in order to increase the rent on the land, or in which a tenant sells his tenure to another tenant who then leases it back to the first at a higher rent. So, when Ravignano di Barone of Marlia bought an episcopal tenure of a grainfield there from Guido di Ricciardino in 1197 for £6, and leased it back to Guido for 3 *stai* of wheat and millet, while Guido continued to pay the rent due to the bishop of 24 *stai* of wheat and barley, one can clearly propose that Ravignano was operating economically inside the land market, and, indeed, getting exactly the going rate, which Esch's lists show was 1 *staio* of grain for every £2 (40s.) in 1194–6.[27] Rents were thus indeed becoming separated as a phenomenon from the land from which they were paid. A clear indication of this fact is that, when people made pious donations at the end of their lives, they were beginning to give not (or not only) land, but portions of rents due from lands that remained in their family or went elsewhere. In 1214–15,

---

[26] Esch, 'Lucca', 83. For the social element to the land market, Wickham, *Mountains*, 252–4; id. 'Vendite di terra', *Quaderni storici*, 65 (1987), 355–77. 'Social' and 'economic'/'commercial' are used in this section to denote ideal-type opposites, along the lines of Marx's discussion of commodity fetishism in *Capital*, i, ch. 1. iv.

[27] Rent-increases for money: e.g. ASL S. Giovanni 24 febb. 1196 for S. Pancrazio; Guido and Ravignano: AAL ++R67 (*a.*1196, *recte* 1197); cf. the sales of rents to third parties, such as AAL *S54 (*a.*1223) for Capannori, and the full lists in Esch, 'Lucca', ch. 1, 47 ff. (table on p. 61 for 1194–6 figures),

for example, Ildebrandino di Cortefugga of Paganico gave to the monastery of Pozzeveri 1 *staio* of grain from his properties, and his father gave 2 *stai* of millet; the properties, however, were not alienated. Earlier, in 1133, Guglielmo di Sifredo gave to the cathedral chapter a field in Marlia and 16 *stai* of grain-rent from it, but the labour-service due from the tenants there he gave to S. Bartolomeo in Silice in the city suburbs. In 1183 Ciofforo di Rustico gave to S. Bartolomeo, among many other gifts, 8 *modii* of land in Paganico; but 4 *stai* of the grain-rent due from it went to laymen, either friends or kin. In a separate but analogous pattern, in 1151 Leuccio di Gualando willed to several churches not land, but debts from usurious loans on pledges of land in Moriano. Tenants already owed rents to many different people as a result of inheritance, land sales, and subletting; but these cessions dispensed even with the legal procedure of subletting, resting as they did purely on the apportionment of surplus produce.[28]

This sort of complexity was clearly the product of a commercial environment. But the existence of such purely economic transactions does not in itself weaken the existence and power of social relationships. What concerns us here, indeed, is not the commercial environment itself, which we can now take as read, but the social activities that were made possible by such an environment. I will dwell on only two aspects of such activities here. The first is the pattern of subletting. Esch is right to stress the economic aspects of this, and I have been following his analysis in that respect; but not all our documents make sense in strictly economic terms. Subletting can be an economic choice if it is the decision of the previous cultivator, or of someone who buys in from landlord or cultivator as Ravignano did in Marlia in 1197; but most subletting was an assignment from the top, from landholders to non-cultivators, of rents from cultivators that the former could perfectly well have collected themselves, and would have derived more profit therefrom if they had. The many levels of tenure that result can often be clearly recognizable as representing social relationships. This is most obvious when they are called fiefs or when they represent other forms of aristocratic or quasi-aristocratic tenure, such as the four levels of leasing of the tithes of Pieve S. Pancrazio recorded in 1032: here, bishops and others were establishing clienteles and entourages, and indeed doing so in a fairly traditional manner. But

---

[28] Examples, respectively: ACL Q123 (*a*.1214–15), *RCL* 900 (*a*.1133), AAL +I45 (*a*.1183), *RCL* 1073 (*a*.1151). Other gifts of produce: ASL SMFP 13 ott. 1189, S. Ponziano 28 ago. 1196, *RCL* 1795 (*a*.1198), all for Moriano.

what can we think when we find later, as we do in the episcopal entourage in 1200, relationships of military loyalty expressed in terms of the interest due from a loan, that could be liquidated by paying back the *capitale?* Or when in 1188 one episcopal dependant, Perfetto di Gerardo Mannaiola, ceded to his brother renders in grain, themselves held in fief from the bishop, due to the same Perfetto from six other city aristocrats and notables?[29] Here, the abstractions characteristic of the 'land market' become elements in very concrete social and political bonds. And this sort of argument can be extended to many others of the more orthodox transactions that survive for the twelfth century. Ravignano di Barone of Marlia may have reasoned as an economic entrepreneur, but his new tenant Guido di Ricciardino may have thought he was gaining a protector out of the transaction, and, if so, could well have been right. The motives are pure speculation in this instance, for we know too little about the parties; but we will see in other contexts how transactions that to the city entrepreneur on one side doubtless had a purely or largely economic value had a well-defined social reality to local groups on the other (below, pp. 124–5). The market did not, that is to say, destroy social relationships in the city and its hinterland, or even those social relationships expressed by the holding of land—no one who knows anything about city communal politics could imagine it for a moment; it simply contributed to the growing complexity of tenure and therefore of the *forms* of such social relationships, while at the same time allowing those who wished to play the market entrepreneurially the space to do so, for at least some of their transactions.

The second point that is worth further development here has already been mentioned: the complexity of these transactions did not contribute to the extension of the control of landlords over tenants. This is not, in Lucca, a period where concern for agricultural profit leads to the concentration of tenures and the 'rationalization' of rent-taking from given territories, as would be seen, for example, in the establishment of the *mezzadria* in some parts of late medieval Tuscany. Instead, after the establishment of kind-rents (itself, as we have seen, a rationalization of a kind, that is to say, in the direction of cash cropping), the way the economy moved was, rather, towards the dissolution of direct landowner–cultivator relationships and the ever more complex apportionment of

---

[29] ASL i. 77 (*a.*1032), which shows tithes leased by the bishop to a major aristocratic family, then to an important notarial family, then to a lesser family; AAL AE24 (*a.*1200), *M12 (*a.*1188). Note also the bishop's fiefs in Moriano in the 1110s, which were already of rents, not lands: below, pp. 85, 117–18.

surpluses.[30] One must not exaggerate this complexity; many rents, perhaps most, still went directly from cultivator to landowner in 1200 without any mediators. But few cultivators had a single landlord even in the eleventh century, and in 1200 the proportion was smaller still. The sort of aggressive hegemony that landlords had over peasants all over medieval Europe seems as a result to have been relatively weak in the Lucchesia in this period.

One source that illustrates the relative weakness of landlordly hegemony are the court cases between lords and tenants from the twelfth century. There are many of these, particularly in the years after 1170—for documents describing court cases increase considerably in number everywhere in Tuscany after that date. They show some differences from lord–tenant court cases in previous centuries. In the ninth century, such cases had had as their subtext the gradual extension of landlordly power over free neighbours and tenants, who became more and more subject as aristocratic and ecclesiastical control extended itself. Sometimes tenants protested in court, sometimes landowners established their just (or unjust) rights in court, in the face of peasant protests of a more informal kind; but the subtext was always the same.[31] These processes are less apparent in the Lucchesia in the twelfth century. Landlords did, for example, raise rents; but they paid money to tenants to buy the increases. Tenants were doubtless forced to this, by economic desperation or by more direct methods on the part of landlords; but the concern for the formalities of the economic transaction remain evident. And, in fact, the overall level of rent-taking in the Sei Miglia seems pretty similar at the end of the twelfth century to what it had been at the beginning. It may be for this reason that relatively few of the cases seem to derive from tenant reactions to landlordly pressure. There are certainly some; but, rather more commonly, cases show an opposite tendency: they consist of landlords trying to make individual tenants pay long-standing rents, which the tenants have been withholding for years, and sometimes decades. Rolanduccio di Guittone of Marlia, for example, was instructed to pay five years' back rent to Gerardino di Morettino in 1179 for land the latter had bought there: Rolanduccio had already ignored one previous judgment. Many such cases were, indeed, assigned in contumacy, the tenant not turning up in court at all—in one instance, in 1216, the bishop's

---

[30] For basic Tuscan background, see P. J. Jones, 'From Manor to Mezzadria', in N. Rubinstein (ed.), *Florentine Studies* (London, 1968), esp. 211–18.

[31] See B. Andreolli, 'Contratti agrari', *Studi medievali*, 19 (1978), 125–7, and, in general, C. J. Wickham, *Società degli Appennini* (Bologna, 1982), 18–28.

representative declared that the absent tenant had not paid anything for over thirty years.[32] We cannot easily tell how often tenants were in the right in cases like this, and how often landlords were. But for our purposes here the issue is less important than the degree of detachment shown by the tenants concerned, as shown, for instance, in their tendency not to appear in court to defend themselves. In the case of Ciofforo di Rustico's complex gifts of rents to S. Bartolomeo in Silice and others in 1183, cited above, we have a clear example of how this process was linked to the fragmentation of tenure: the various recipients disputed the will, and the 1183 tenant, Giovanni di Rolandino, ended up not paying the rent at all for many years, as a series of cases in 1211–14 show (in most of these, too, Giovanni did not turn up); the issue was not fully resolved until 1228. Giovanni was not a very dependent cultivator, and held a lot of land on lease—he may indeed not have cultivated directly at all. But undoubtedly direct cultivators could defy lords too, like Vitaletto of S. Terenzo di Marlia in 1193, an episcopal *manens* (or quasi-servile dependant; see below, pp. 108–9), who denied this status with its associated rent and servile obligations, despite a considerable amount of contrary evidence, but stated, among other arguments, that he held land from at least two laymen and three churches as well as the bishop.[33] Vitaletto was a member of the lowest

[32] Rolanduccio: AAL ++R30 (*a*.1179); the 1216 case: *M29 (*a*.1216). General rent stability in the century: Esch, 'Lucca', ch. 1, 25–39. Examples of 12th-cent. cases which seem to show tenants reacting to landlordly pressure include AAL *D20 (*a*.1192); ASL SMFP 29 mar. 1197, S. Nicolao 20 mar. 1199, S. Frediano 26 apr. 1200. Examples of cases which seem to show landlords trying to get tenants to pay rent as agreed in contracts include ASL S. Giovanni 30 dic. 1176, S. Nicolao 8 dic. 1180 (*recte* 1187), S. Giovanni 21 ott. 1188 (with 26 nov. 1188), S. Ponziano 25 genn. 1189, 10 mar. 1191, Spedale 28 dic. 1191, S. Giovanni 5 magg. 1195, 26 nov. 1196; AAL *K83 (*a*.1183), *R40 (*a*.1191). Not all these tenants were direct cultivators, but many were. We cannot be sure of the real situation in many of these cases, of course, or what real relationships of coercion or rejection were covered up by agreed contracts; I have also excluded other cases where the situation cannot even be guessed at. It may be added that this picture of relative tenurial independence is not an argument for harmony in the countryside; landlordship was, for instance, increasing quantitatively in the late 12th cent. as peasant owners were bought out by citizens (below, pp. 128, 149). Still, we do not have in the Lucchesia the collective battles over rents that are well documented elsewhere in the period (discussed most recently for the Fiorentino by G. W. Dameron, *Episcopal Power and Florentine Society* (Cambridge, Mass., 1991), 93–140); disagreements in the area seem more individual, and tenant resistance more passive. See further the valuable discussions of D. J. Osheim, 'Countrymen and the Law in Late-Medieval Tuscany', *Speculum*, 64 (1989), 317–37, who shows that such passive resistance in the Sei Miglia was unabated in the 14th cent.

[33] Ciofforo's gifts: AAL +I43 (*a*.1177), +I45, +I47 (*a*.1183); for Ciofforo's career, see Esch, 'Lucca', ch. 2. For Giovanni, see +E65 (*a*.1172), +82 (*a*.1180), +L14 (*a*.1183), +I50 ('sec. XIII'), +I32 (*a*.1211), +I45 (seven cases, *a*.1211–28); cf. +B8 (*a*.1220), +I33 (*a*.1222). Vitaletto of Marlia: AE90.

stratum of Lucchese society, but being a tenant of six separate landlords put him in a much more distanced relationship with his principal lord from that serfs are supposed to have. This sort of distance was essentially made possible by the general fragmentation of property characteristic of the eleventh, and, even more, the twelfth century in the Lucchese Sei Miglia. It was a major contributor, too, to a relative absence of tension in the Lucchese countryside in that period by Italian (and, still more, European) standards, which is a phenomenon to which I will return.

The land market and the fragmentation of rents in the twelfth century thus came together with the political hegemony of the city to produce one important consequence: the traditional patterns of coercion available to landlords elsewhere in Europe, and in Lucca too in earlier centuries, whether the economic threat of expulsion from the land or the direct military-judicial powers of signorial lordship, were here unusually weak. The consequences of this for the question of the twelfth-century politics of land we will see illustrated in the next section. But its consequences for the formation of Lucchese rural communes were even more considerable; for rural communes are widely thought to be a reaction to signorial lordship, and the latter was of little significance in the Sei Miglia Lucchese, or else restricted to powers over individuals. This whole issue essentially underpins the analyses in this book. It must be borne in mind when considering the more specific village studies that will be the subjects of later chapters.

ii. Marlia in the eleventh and twelfth centuries: a case study of two landowners

These patterns are all very well as background generalizations, but they are as yet only outlines. Some of the main trends in Lucchese rural society and its development should already be visible. But how they worked on the ground must be looked at more closely; for rural communes formed inside rural communities, and not in the abstract interstices of the land market. If we look at land transactions in the light of the activities of some reasonably well documented individuals, we can better understand what sorts of relationships to fellow villagers, to superiors, or to inferiors, people actually had in the eleventh and twelfth centuries. For this, we will look at two examples from Marlia, both medium landowners whose personal archives have at least in part survived, a little over a century apart: Moro di Petruccia (fl. 1029–53) and Gerardino di Morettino (fl. 1147–93), whom we have already seen trying to coerce a tenant in court. The contrasts between their social worlds are simply intended to serve

as an introduction to some of the essential differences between the structures of eleventh- and twelfth-century society; in particular to the changing ways in which people fitted into aristocratic clienteles and built up
networks of local support. Marlia's rural commune is, in fact, relatively
ill-documented, and the differences between these two figures will not in
any way represent a simple move towards communal or any other kind
of collective relationships; but they will at least give an indication of the
internal contours of the world in which communes formed, to set against
the external outlines that I have delineated so far.

Moro *presbiter*, son of Baruccio and Petruccia (he ascribes his filiation
to both in different texts), dealt in property together with his friend (and
almost certainly kinsman) Lamberto di Inghiza; the two appear in more
than twenty texts between the 1020s and the 1070s, one of the largest
groups of references for any inhabitant of the eleventh-century plain.[34]
Moro was a medium landowner, by which I mean one who owned (or
leased) enough lands and tenant houses to be able to survive without
having to engage personally in cultivation in more than a marginal way.
Moro personally, indeed, was certainly not a cultivator: he was important enough to be in the clientele of both the bishops and the Porcaresi,
and probably the Aldobrandeschi counts as well. He must have been, that
is, one of the most important notables living in the Marlia area in the
second quarter of the century: what is true for him is not necessarily true
for lesser inhabitants. But the boundaries of Moro's social world, at least,
are unlikely to have been surpassed by his poorer and less influential (as
well as less clearly documented) neighbours; Moro is in this respect as
good a place as any to start. I will discuss him in more detail than many
of the local figures in this book, so that the sort of evidence we generally have to go on in this period can be understood as well.

Most of the texts we have for Moro and his circle are sales to him, or
to his father, or to Lamberto di Inghiza, or to some combination of the
three. They therefore suffer from the commonest feature of personal
archives of this period: that people tended to keep texts that involved the

---

[34] The Moro archive consists of AAL ++R40, ++R41 (*a.*1029, Marchini 63–4), ++A23,
+N36, ++C75, ++R40, +C62 (AAL iii. 5–9, *a.*1032), ++M43, *M2 (AAL iii. 25, 38,
*a.*1034), +E48, *C20 (AAL iii. 80, 84, *a.*1041), ++D11 (AAL iii. 86, *a.*1042), +K100 (*a.*1046,
Pianezzi 21), ++D26 (*a.*1050, Pianezzi 97), *I84, *D64, *E34 (*a.*1053, Bertocchini 35–7),
+E40 (*a.*1071, Gemignani 262); with *RCL* 156 (*a.*1035), 183–4 (*a.*1042), ASL Arch. Guinigi
11 (5 ago. 1044), and some associated texts that mention the family: AAL *B22 (AAL iii.
74, *a.*1040), *RCL* 246 (*a.*1053), AAL +C87 (*a.*1058, Gemignani 28), ++A34 (*a.*1073,
Gemignani 308), ++B74 (*a.*1075). On personal archives, see Esch, 'Lucca', ch. 2, who dis-
cusses three 12th-cent. examples in detail.

acquisition of land, but not its alienation. Nor can we be sure how complete the collection is even as an archive of acquisitions; although most of the texts ended up in the Archivio Arcivescovile, presumably following an undocumented alienation by Moro or (less likely) his sons, some have found their way into the archives of the Capitolo or of the Guinigi (in the Archivio di Stato), and others yet may have been dispersed elsewhere; his sons, too, must have inherited the great part of his land.[35] But the sort of evidence the text collection offers us is fairly homogeneous, and certainly allows us to construct a picture of aspects of Moro's social activity—those aspects, as usual with charter material, that have something to do with the alienation of land.

Moro and Lamberto bought land for twenty-five years: a field in Marlia in 1029 for an unnamed price; three fields in 1032 for 5s.; a vineyard for 12s. and two fields for 3s. in the same year; portions of a house and thirteen fields (that is to say, of a *mansus*, a tenant holding, now dissolved into its component parts) for 52s. in 1034; half a house, a mill, and five fields in 1041 for 70s. (this was from Moro's mother, shortly before her death in the same year); 1/72 of the church of S. Venanzio di Marlia and small portions of two fields in 1042 (price unnamed); two fields in 1042 for 29s., one in 1044 for 10s., another in 1046 for 8s., another in 1053 (as a pledge) for 5s.; Lamberto also leased a field in 1050 for a small grain rent of 1 *staio* per year. The property they accumulated was bought for between 200 and 250s., the price of two or three tenant holdings or so.[36] All of it was in Marlia, although, judging by the microtoponyms in the charters we can locate, it was to be found in nearly every corner of the village territory, which was, at around 6 km.², a large one by Lucchese standards. They had to do with land outside Marlia as well, but only when they took pledges from aristocrats. Donnuccio Sirico of the Porcaresi pledged to Moro four houses in Sesto Moriano and Saltocchio (respectively 3 km. and 1 km. west of Marlia) for 40s. in 1035, for 20 per cent interest; these Moro pledged away to a third party in 1042, together with part of the church of S. Andrea in Saltocchio and of another house there, for 48s.—as Donnuccio Sirico was a guarantor for this charter as well, it is likely enough that S. Andrea too came from the Porcaresi.

---

[35] Moro had sons, for they are referred to casually in AAL ++B74 (*a.*1075), but they never appear as actors in any document; it is likely, then, that it was before they began to make their own charters that Moro alienated to the bishop the properties that brought his chapters to the archiepiscopal archive: most likely in the mid-1050s, when they begin to dry up, and when Moro became an episcopal dependant (see n. 38).

[36] See documents cited in n. 34.

Lamberto, finally, in 1071, after Moro's death in 1053/8, when Lamberto himself was at least 60 years old, took in lease part of the receipts from the pieve of S. Maria di Marlia and from S. Angelo di Matraia nearby, in the hills overlooking the village, from one of the Cunimundinghi—the latter being the family who held S. Maria and the neighbouring pieve of S. Pancrazio from the bishop.[37]

Moro and Lamberto were certainly local men. Many of their charters were explicitly written in Marlia, in a century when most documents were at least nominally registered in Lucca. The occasional tenure in Saltocchio, Sesto, and Matraia cannot detract from the fact that the overwhelming focus of their interests was in a single village. Marlia was, as I have said, a large sprawling village, with six churches already in the eleventh century, but it evidently held a certain social identity for men like Moro, whose lands were spread far across it but seldom outside it (see below, p. 61). Moro, furthermore, had a formal position in Marlia, for he was, at any rate at the end of his life, rector of the church of S. Terenzo in the castello there, a post that he held in benefice from the bishop, as also, probably, previously from the Aldobrandeschi, who ceded castello and church to the bishop in 1054–5.[38] Moro's family must have been locally important as landowners and landholders, and more prominent still as a result of the fact that three of the village's six churches, and two others, were at some time or another at least partly subject to them. The other major owners or lessees of Marlia lands and churches, and we know of several, were all diocesan aristocrats, without any local base. We can, I think, safely assume that Moro's circle was that of the most influential people actually living in Marlia in the mid-eleventh century.

One notable feature of Moro's dealings is the number of times they involve aristocrats. As has just been remarked, quite a number of aristocratic families did, indeed, own or lease land in the area: the

---

[37] RCL 156, 183–4, AAL +E40 (*a.*1071, Gemignani 262). In 1040 (*B22, AAL iii. 74), Moro was also the recipient, with two other people, of a vast gift from Donnuccio, of lands and castles all over the diocese; these properties in reality soon ended up in episcopal hands, and Moro seems to have been simply acting as an executor or intermediary for the Porcaresi.

[38] Moro as rector of S. Terenzo: AAL +C87 (*a.*1058, Gemignani 28). This is the first charter to refer to him as deceased; since the Aldobrandeschi cessions to the bishop, +G15, +O42 (*a.*1054), +O34 (*a.*1055, Manaresi 395), +I18 (*a.*1055) were only three years previously, it is likely enough that Moro was already rector before the bishop got the church. For the other churches, see below, p. 55. On the Aldobrandeschi in Marlia, see G. Rossetti, 'Pisa, Volterra, Populonia', in *Atti del 5° Congresso internazionale* (Spoleto, 1973), 298–306. (S. Terenzo, and the castello of Marlia, had already been leased by the Aldobrandeschi to the bishop in 996 (Barsocchini 1712), but it was a personal cession, to a member of the Cunimundinghi family, and had evidently reverted.)

Aldobrandeschi, who held the castle until 1054–5; the Porcaresi; the Cunimundinghi, who held the pieve from the early tenth century until into the twelfth; the 'Leoni' and the family who would in the next century be called the Avvocati, the two leading families of the professional strata of the city; as well as the bishops, and even the king. This led to a landowning pattern, and presumably a political pattern, of great complexity in Marlia. Moro was probably the Aldobrandeschi's priest in S. Terenzo; but he bought land from the Cunimundinghi, too, in 1034, and one of the latter family leased part of the pieve to Lamberto in 1071. Lamberto also leased land in 1050 from Ioco of Brancoli, a protégé of Marquis Boniface, and a substantial city-based landowner. Perhaps the closest of Moro's links was, however, with the Porcaresi. He took pledges from Donnuccio Sirico, as we have seen, as well as acting as an executor for him, and the latter underwrote Moro's own pledges; Donnuccio's collaborator Bonifacio/Bonizo di Contulino also witnessed for Moro and Lamberto, and Lamberto witnessed for him: a set of links that indicates a relationship of collaboration, rather than of clientele, at least in Marlia.[39]

In contrast, the Cunimundinghi were poorly represented in Moro's documents, for this family must have been by far the largest landowner in Marlia. Its known members appear as owners on land boundaries in half the charters in the century, for the most part between parties entirely unrelated to them; that only one transaction with Moro di Petruccia survives is thus remarkable, given the family's local importance.[40] This may

---

[39] See Schwarzmaier, *Lucca*, 110–12, 222–36, 288 ff., 309 ff., for the families. The Porcaresi were two families, one of whom was dying out at the time of Donnuccio Sirico's cessions to the bishop; the second family replaced them in almost exactly the same lands by episcopal cession in the third quarter of the century (ibid. 110–12, 234). Cunimundinghi leases of the pieve: Barsocchini 1266 (*a.*939), 1541–4, 1547–8, 1565, 1593, AAL ++K53 (*a.*1017), ++H43 (*a.*1018), +E41 (AAL iii. 73, *a.*1040), ++C74 (*a.*1062), ++B82 (*a.*1063), +E40 (*a.*1071, Gemignani 262). Moro and Lamberto dealt with the Cunimundinghi in AAL iii. 25 and +E40; with Ioco of Brancoli in ++D26 (Pianezzi 97), in the *sala* of Marquis Boniface (this text shows explicitly that the family was living in Lucca in 1050; although Brancoli was certainly a major centre of their landowning, and doubtless their area of origin, they held land all across the plain in the 11th and 12th cents.). Bonifacio di Contulino: AAL iii. 80 (*a.*1041), *RCL* 246 (*a.*1053).

[40] For the Cunimundinghi, see Schwarzmaier, *Lucca*, 222–7; Wickham, *Mountains*, 97–9, 128–9. I doubted there, following Schwarzmaier, the family links between the Gherardinghi, the Rolandinghi, the Soffredinghi, and the original Cunimundinghi; but the four names in Marlia and S. Pancrazio, at least, certainly denote the same family: AAL ++R40 (*a.*1029, Marchini 63), AAL iii. 80 (*a.*1041), +Q63 (*a.*1075); ASL ii. 146 (*a.*1103), *RCL* 671 (*a.*1106), 707 (*a.*1111), ACL Fondo Martini 32 (*a.*1131, Guidoni 50) are local examples of the surnames. Other Cunimundinghi charters for 11th-cent. Marlia, apart from those cited in n. 39, are: ASL Guinigi 10 (*a.*1020), AAL ++K61 (*a.*1027, Marchini 40), *RCL* 117 (*a.*1027), AAL ++N10 (AAL iii. 26, *a.*1034).

be an indication that there were two rival clientele structures in Marlia in the early eleventh century, one focused on the Aldobrandeschi and Porcaresi (and their churches), the other on the Cunimundinghi and their churches, with Moro and his circle clearly part of the former. Such a counterposition would only have ended when the Aldobrandeschi left Marlia in the 1050s and the first Porcaresi family died out in the 1060s; it is after this date that Lamberto is found for the first time as a tenant of the pieve of the Cunimundinghi. Such oppositions are commonplace in the period, of course; that they could be found at the level of village politics can be seen elsewhere in Tuscany—in the Casentino, for example. Rivalry expressed through mutually exclusive land transactions was not total in Marlia, for Moro bought from the Cunimundinghi once, and another family sold land to both the latter and Moro's family; but it is likely enough for all that.[41]

Moro's dealings with these families were sometimes, as we have seen, almost those of an equal; but he was not an aristocrat himself. It should be recognized that, in 1050, a clear legal division between aristocrats and non-aristocrats barely existed; when we use the words, we are as yet only speaking in terms of relative access to landed wealth and political power, in a continuum that stretched from counts to the poor free. But Moro was essentially restricted to a single village; he had no known direct dealings with the marquis, or for most of his life even the bishop; he and his family had no known formal military or civil role. And, in fact, Moro's charter collection has more documents in which he and his family transacted with other local owners than it has for transactions with the Porcaresi or the Cunimundinghi, people who certainly can be described as aristocracy. These transactions were rather more small-scale, often involving only two or three fields. They seem to be with people who have a social, rather than just an economic, relationship to Moro's family—one, that is, that was not restricted to land transactions; the same family groups tend to recur in the texts and many figure as witnesses to other transactions with Moro and Lamberto.[42] We know relatively little else about them: their other documents do not survive. Since it was churches that preserved documents, what this means is simply that, of the Marliesi alive around 1050, only Moro would give land (and thus charters) to the

---

[41] Cf. Wickham, *Mountains*, 210–15, 256–68.

[42] See documents cited in n. 34. For the issue of the definition of the aristocracy, see Wickham, *Mountains*, 285–92; compare, now, Delumeau, *Arezzo. Espace et sociétés*, 451–61, for another view, not incompatible with mine.

cathedral; perhaps just because he was a priest, but also quite possibly because of his link with Donnuccio Sirico, who, as a childless aristocrat, gave vast quantities of property to the bishop in the years around 1040.[43] This eventual link with the cathedral was perhaps the major difference between Moro and his neighbours; the landowning society of eleventh-century Marlia was not as a whole closely attached to any church whose archives still exist. But, as a result, we cannot be sure whether any of them were of a roughly equivalent economic or social standing to Moro. I have argued that Moro and his family were the principal local family, but there is no sign that any of his social circle were his clients (Moro kept no leases), or that any were losing ground to him locally (the scale of these transactions was, as already noted, pretty small). Perhaps the best conclusion is that Moro and Lamberto were the leaders of a medium landowning stratum, but that other members of it doubtless had inde-pendent links to the city aristocracy.

This is the sort of evidence that one has at one's disposal in the eleventh century—and, indeed, in the twelfth: it is restricted to the sort of rela-tionships that can be delineated by transactions for land that eventually ended up in the hands of churches, and it tends, too, to tell us about owners (in this case quite prosperous ones) rather than tenants. But the pattern in Marlia, when compared with those that have been analysed elsewhere in Tuscany during this period, can tell us slightly more. In the central Chianti and in the Casentino, systematic donations and sales to rural monasteries by particular groups in particular villages can illumin-ate reasonably clearly at least some aspects of the social structures of these villages, their local solidarities and their local oppositions—more clearly, indeed, than those in Marlia. For such villages, we do not so much have personal archives, like Moro's, but *monastic* archives, which show a firm relationship between (some) members of a given village and a monastery, expressed through many alienations, not just one. That the texts were preserved by a single monastery—Passignano or Montescalari or Coltibuono in the central Chianti, Camaldoli or Prataglia in the Casentino—gives us a field of vision restricted to the interests of that one monastery, of course; villages and social groups which did not cede land to the monastery remain in the shadows, for their documents do not sur-vive. None the less, such ecclesiastical associations throw a strong beam of light sideways on to a village society, that allows the shadows of the undocumented at least to be outlined, and creates at least an oblique image

---

[43] Major Porcaresi gifts to the bishop: AAL iii. 62–6, 74, 99, 100, 104 (a.1039–43).

of many social phenomena, such as local factional oppositions, that are not directly connected to the church at all.[44]

The Sei Miglia Lucchese in the eleventh century was different from this. For a start, it was far closer to the city; nearly all the churches that collected documents in the new era of gift-giving to churches that began in the Lucchesia in the 1020s were urban, not rural. And, because Lucca was a large city, there were many churches there that could, and did, receive gifts and other grants of land. In the Casentino, those social strata in a village in Camaldoli's orbit who did not give or sell land to that establishment did not alienate it to another monastery: by the eleventh century villages seem already to have associated themselves with religious houses in some sense as collectivities.[45] In the Lucchesia, however, this did not happen; there were so many churches with a certain prestige that villagers could be pulled in a number of different directions. This contrast was certainly not total. In fact, even in the Lucca plain, despite a greater tendency to disperse pious gifts among many recipients, some indications of more local associations can be identified through the distribution in the documents. Most surviving Marlia documents for the eleventh and twelfth centuries come from the archiepiscopal archive, indicating that their preservation was largely due to cessions (of different kinds, and from certain distinct periods) to the bishop; Tassignano and Capannori charters come very largely from the archives of the cathedral chapter (the Canonica) and from the rural monastery of Pozzeveri; Brancoli is documented principally through the archives of the extramural Lucchese houses of S. Ponziano and S. Maria forisportam. These were long-standing and continuous associations that were delineated at least in part by local relationships; the inhabitants of Marlia tended to look in different directions from those of nearby Brancoli. But these tendencies were not so developed that they can tell us very much about village *identity*; and there were other variables, too, that cut across the relatively straightforward relationships between villagers and churches that one finds in the mountains of the Casentino.

This difference did not so much result from differences in the social structures of the villages themselves. In the plains, as in the mountains, landowners on a medium and small scale, like their tenant neighbours,

---

[44] Wickham, *Mountains*, chs. 7, 9, for methodological points. Personal archives may have been commoner in the Lucca plain simply because there were more documents there: the city and its notaries were closer, and land transactions were even more frequent than elsewhere, as land was so fragmented. The very complexity of transactions may also have meant that documents were more likely to be preserved, at least for a time.

[45] *Ibid.* 210–12. For the new era of gift-giving, see W. Kurze, 'Monasteri e nobiltà', in *Atti del 5° Congresso internazionale* (Spoleto, 1973), 358–62.

generally had their fragmented holdings inside a single village, and looked
to a single local area to establish their identity. But they also looked to
patrons and landlords, and here differences are rather more visible.
Lucchese society was, like all city societies, dominated by aristocrats and
other substantial landholders, and this dominance spread into the immediate hinterland of the city, the Sei Miglia. The Casentino had aristocrats too, but the socio-economic hierarchy in a mountain valley was less
complex and articulated than it was in the villages closest to a city; in the
Sei Miglia there were more aristocrats, and they were (or could be) much
richer and more influential. Before the late eleventh century, most of
Marlia did not look to the bishop at all, but, rather, to three of the most
influential families of the diocesan aristocracy, in perhaps two opposed
groupings, as we have seen. (All the same, the aristocrats themselves had
episcopal associations, of varying kinds; indeed, it was this network that
brought the Marliesi into the episcopal orbit.) Similarly, the fact that most
cessions to the church from Capannori were to Pozzeveri ties in well with
local aristocratic interests, in this case the presence of much Porcaresi land
in that village, for the first Porcaresi family founded Pozzeveri in 1056:
village piety, not illogically, was largely directed towards the monastery
of the most influential local patrons.[46]

The Porcaresi were not the only aristocratic owners in Capannori,
none the less; other lords, as well as lesser local owners, alienated land
to other churches too. Large-scale landowning was fragmented, as was
all landowning, and did not necessarily result in the direct control over
local society that existed in much of eleventh- and twelfth-century Europe.
We have already seen two aspects of this, the local weakness of signorial
rights and the relative independence of many tenants. But this fragmentation also acted as a unifying force on another level, one that diminished
local political identity (Marlia vs. Brancoli) in favour of an identity that
extended to the whole of the Sei Miglia: for landholding by more than
one major family could be found in nearly every village in the hinterland
of Lucca, and each family held land in many villages, thus linking each
of them together. Furthermore, the families themselves in most cases lived
in the city, and focused their clienteles on the city as a result. Their pious
donations further reinforced these patterns: when aristocrats gave to
churches, which they did more enthusiastically than their non-aristocratic
neighbours, the churches would similarly end up with lands in many

---

[46] Pozzeveri: *RCL* 261 (*a.*1056). Porcaresi in Capannori: e.g. *RCL* 680, 682, 729, 1047, AAL
++M54 (*a.*1160), etc. The Capannori charters in *RCL* are largely cessions to Pozzeveri.

villages, intermingled with the lands of other churches. The clientele patterns that eleventh-century pious gifts reveal stretched across the entire Sei Miglia, and can only be fully analysed at that level, not at the level of the village: the scale of local political society was considerable, and was further extended by the fact that most of these churches, too, were in the city. This (very traditional) pattern of social links thus further reinforced the dominance of Lucca in the Sei Miglia, a dominance that we have seen to have been already enormous for other reasons over both the political and the economic activities of the plain.

This aristocratic network, however, seems to have diminished in the twelfth century, in favour of more local relationships. Not that it is easy to tell how. Indeed, one of the most difficult questions to answer in the current state of research on Lucca is exactly what happened to the aristocracies of the eleventh century during the social transformations of the twelfth. There are very few families that can easily be traced from the network of diocesan aristocrats and élite city judicial families of 1050 or so to the leading communal families of the thirteenth century. Certainly the latter were often their direct descendants, but exactly how can rarely be seen, in the absence of regular patterns of surnames, except in the case of a few highly privileged, visible, and atypical lineages such as the Avvocati and the Porcaresi. This ignorance is at least in part due simply to the relative absence of systematic studies of the families. But it is also true that, as family groups, the old aristocracies begin to fade from our documentation before 1100, only to re-emerge a century later with newly minted surnames and maybe newly established family relationships, in effect refashioned in their basic elements in the chrysalis of the *primo comune*—for the new communal politics, itself still inchoate before 1150, would provide hierarchies and points of reference for élite identity that were very different from the episcopal and marchesal clienteles of the eleventh century.[47] In particular, aristocratic landholding seems often to

---

[47] For the 11th-cent. aristocracies, see Schwarzmaier, *Lucca*; Wickham, 'Economia e società rurale'. Among the few studies of 12th-cent. Lucchese families one should single out those of Rosanna Pescaglini Monti, 'Le vicende politiche e istituzionali della Valdinievole', in C. Violante and A. Spicciani (eds.), *Pescia e la Valdinievole nell'età dei Comuni* (Pisa, 1995); ead., 'Le vicende del castello di Collodi', in *Atti del convegno* (Buggiano, 1989); ead., 'Nobiltà e istituzioni ecclesiastiche', in A. Spicciani and C. Violante (eds.), *Allucio da Pescia*, 267–77. For the restructuring of families during the early communal period see the important study by Jean-Pierre Delumeau of the Bostoli of Arezzo, 'Des Lombards de Carpineto aux Bostoli', in *I ceti dirigenti* (Pisa, 1982), 67–99. In Pisa, by contrast, aristocratic family structures seem to have shown more continuity: see, for example, G. Rossetti *et al.*, *Pisa nei secoli XI e XII* (Pisa, 1979); ead., 'Histoire familiale', in G. Duby and J. Le Goff (eds.), *Famille et parenté* (Rome, 1977).

have been quite mobile: in keeping with a political structure that in Lucca
had always been city based, it was more necessary to have a large amount
of landed resources in the abstract, as a basis for urban political transactions, than lands and local influence in any specific rural locality.

Local influence was not to be rejected, of course, when it was available;
we will see examples when we come later to Tassignano and S. Concordio
(see below, pp. 138, 164). Outside the Sei Miglia, in particular, the more
stable structures of local signorial territories were important for families
to hang on to when they could. But even in the mountains of the Garfagnana,
on the edge of the diocese, not all signorial power or landowning was
stably attached to single families across several generations;[48] and in the
Sei Miglia such stability seems to have been far less. The Cunimundinghi
are one example: in the eleventh century they were by far the dominant
landholders in Marlia and neighbouring S. Pancrazio, as well as the lessees
of the pievi of both villages, but in the twelfth century they become
harder and harder to trace on land-boundaries in the area. This may be
because we do not know their names in the new century, but the pieve of
Marlia, at least, was back with the bishop in 1164. Yet the family certainly
continued: among other places, they held Sala in the Garfagnana under
the new name of the *filii Guidi*, and sections of the Soffredinghi and
Gherardinghi families that were associated with them were landowners
in several places on the plain and in the city—they had not disappeared,
but merely shifted their identity and their landed base.[49]

It is not my concern here to discuss the changing nature of the
Lucchese aristocracy in detail; it is only relevant at all because it relates
to the problem of the political structures inside villages. Moro di Petruccia
was a client of local aristocratic families because they held land and
exercised political influence in Marlia; but none of them continued to do so
for long after his death. The shifting pattern of aristocratic landholding
and even family identity that seems to have been a feature of the twelfth

---

[48] Wickham, *Mountains*, 122–33.

[49] Ibid. 128–9 for the 12th-cent. Cunimundinghi; *MGH, Friderici I Dipl.*, n. 430, for
the pieve of Marlia in 1164. Greater stability was shown by major ecclesiastical landowners in the plain than by their lay counterparts; but the principal independent political
actor among the major churches of the diocese, the bishop, never held in the 12th cent. the
influence in Lucca that he had had in the 11th cent.—the office never entirely recovered
from its political eclipse in the two decades following Anselmo II's expulsion in 1080. See
in general Osheim, *Italian Lordship*; Barsocchini, i. 365–507; but the Lucchese episcopate
in this period awaits its political historian. [It has now found him: Savigni, 'La signoria
vescovile lucchese'; id., *Episcopato e società*.] Bishops did none the less exercise local patronage when they had it, as we will see at length for Moriano in Chs. 4 and 5.

century did not necessarily mean changes in the influence of individual lineages at the level of city politics (though it sometimes did; the heirs of the Cunimundinghi in 1200 were not among the dominant families of the Lucchesia, unlike their ancestors in 800 or 1000). But it certainly could change the nature of their *local* power. Lay rural patronage seems, indeed, rather less visible in twelfth-century texts than in the eleventh, in most villages in the Sei Miglia. If this is not entirely an optical illusion, due to changing structures of surviving documentation—and the documentary record does not seem to be so very different from one century to the next—then the contrast must testify to the even greater importance of city politics as a focus for élite families in the twelfth century than in the eleventh: village politics could more easily be left to villagers.

Our second Marliese example, Gerardino di Moretto or Morettino (documented 1147–93), shows some of the differences in the construction of local relationships that developed over the century after Moro's death, as a result of changes both in the socio-political and the economic environment. Gerardino is documented in nearly thirty texts, about half of them for Marlia: half the charters for the village in this period involve him.[50] His father was a local landowner and episcopal tenant, with a house in Lucca, who appears in a few texts in 1122–36; before this, the family cannot be traced (between Moro and Gerardino, and especially in the years 1075–1120, there are relatively few documents for the village). Gerardino was a substantial owner in Marlia. He had his father's house in Lucca, but also one in the village, and used both as rent-collection centres. This double loyalty, to city and country, was one we shall see elsewhere (pp. 140, 156); it did not, however, in Gerardino's case at least, signify the transformation of a local rural notable into an unambiguously city figure, for, although Gerardino was a citizen of some status, the family remained linked to both places across at least three generations

[50] Documents for Gerardino in Marlia: AAL ++R80 (*a.*1147), *D35 (*a.*1148), ++R34 (*a.*1151), AL 68 (*a.*1164), ++R20 (*a.*1167), +89 (*a.*1171), ++R45 (*a.*1176), +K54, +F57 (*a.*1178), ++R30, ++R1 (*a.*1179), +O15 (*a.*1182), ASL S. Ponziano 4 lugl. 1162, 27 mar. 1173, Arch. di stato 13 apr. 1185. Outside Marlia: C. Imperiale di Sant'Angelo, *Codice diplomatico della Repubblica di Genova*, ii (Rome, 1938), n. 14 (1166; Gerardino is *de Marcha* here, an obvious copyist's or editor's error. The text is an oath of alliance between Lucca and Genoa, sworn by leading citizens); and the texts listed in n. 53. Gerardino is the first of several small or medium proprietors in the 12th-cent. Lucchese countryside whose land transactions will be discussed in detail in this book. For contemporary parallels from Milan, see M. L. Corsi, 'Garbagnate', in *Contributi dell'Istituto di storia medioevale*, ii (Milan, 1972), 687–724; E. Occhipinti, 'Garbagnate Marcido', ibid. 727–44; ead., 'Trezzano', ibid. 747–78; H. Keller, *Adelsherrschaft* (Tübingen, 1979), 83–123.

—Gerardino's son Deodato, like his father and grandfather, was described as 'de Marlia' in documents up to and beyond his death in 1218.[51]

Gerardino, like Moro, is best known for his land deals, though these were more varied than Moro's were. In Marlia, four texts document his purchase of land between 1148 and 1179, always single fields or groups of fields; he sold land twice, in 1176 and 1185, on the latter occasion to the bishop; he leased land four times, again always single fields, in the years 1167–78, once back to its vendor. Gerardino also appears in three court cases from 1178–82 in which he took tenants to court for the non-payment of rent or for disagreements over the boundaries of the land leased. The two tenants he disputed with both caused him some trouble, and it is certain in one case and probable in the other that they were local landowners leasing extra land from him:[52] Gerardino was clearly prepared to enter into economic relationships with neighbours desirous of extra land, but there is little sign that this brought with it any firm relationship of friendship or social obligation.

The above-named transactions are pretty small scale, and are no guide at all to Gerardino's real economic position. That he was more than a small landowner is indicated by references to his land in boundary clauses for properties in Marlia otherwise unassociated with him; like Moro before him, he owned land in nearly every corner of a sizeable village territory. But he also, unlike Moro, held land elsewhere as well. His house and social position in Lucca has already been mentioned; and boundary clauses show that his family also held land in Guindolfo (modern S. Alessio) west of the city, and in Massa Macinaia to the south, though we do not have documents for either. We do have texts, however, for a Gerardino di Morettino owning land in Segromigno and Guamo; these may be for a different man, but Segromigno is next door to Marlia and Guamo is close to Massa Macinaia, so the identification is quite plausible. Our

[51] Moretto di Uberto, Gerardino's probable father: AAL ++N97 (*a.*1122), ++I23 (*a.*1128), *L4 (*a.*1136); for his house in Lucca, ASL ii. 534 (*a.*1142, the *cantone quondam Morectini de Marlia*). Gerardino is a city notable in the 1166 oath cited in n. 50; his city house is documented in AAL ++R20 (*a.*1167), +89 (*a.*1171), +F57 (*a.*1178); his Marlia house in ++R1 (*a.*1179). Deodato, his brothers, and his cousin as city-dwellers and also 'de Marlia': AAL ++R67 (*a.*1204), *A62 (*a.*1213), ASL Arch. de' Notari 4 sett. 1210, S. Agostino 7 mar. 1218. Gerardo di Moreccio, the city judge and notary of the 1170s and 1180s, and *consul treuguanus* in 1181 (AAL +E63, *RCL* 1446, 1451), must be a different man. Parallels for city immigration: see Ch. 5 n. 21, Ch. 6 n. 34.

[52] Court cases: +K54 (*a.*1178), ++R30 (*a.*1179), +O15 (*a.*1182). Bessignano di Rubertino, his opponent in the first and last, is an owner in ++R67 (*a.*1196); Rolanduccio di Guittone, the 1179 litigant, was probably related to the landowner Rolanduccio di Rolando di Guittone of ++R80, *D35 (*a.*1147–8), who sold (different) property to Gerardino.

Gerardino anyway seems to have been prominent well beyond Marlia; we find him witnessing for the Canonica in court cases for its lands in and around Massa Macinaia, and an 1185 text lists him among the creditors of the church of S. Pietro di Ponte S. Pietro near Guindolfo. He dealt with the bishop, too; he sold him land in 1185, which Bishop Guilielmo wanted enough for him to sell off other land in a city suburb to buy, and Guilielmo pledged land in the same suburb to Gerardino in 1185 as security for a loan. It was this episcopal association that must have resulted in Gerardino's charters ending up in the cathedral archive, together with a gift or sale to the bishop (probably a small one, however, given the small scale of most of these deals).[53]

Gerardino thus had a certain economic and social position all across the Sei Miglia, as well as in the city. None the less, the centre of his possessions remained Marlia, from where by far the largest proportion of references to him come, and which gave him his standard ascription, 'de Marlia'. Here, Gerardino must have had much the same status as Moro before him, as a prosperous and influential medium landowner. But even in Marlia, the way Gerardino's status was expressed was different from Moro's. Gerardino had no known associations with lay aristocrats at all, although we know that the Avvocati, for example, had land in the area at the time. And, although he was linked to locally influential churches— such as the cathedral, the bishop now being a major owner in Marlia (with even some local signorial rights)—these links were much more distanced than in the case of Moro's links with the Porcaresi.[54] Gerardino

[53] Gerardino outside Marlia: ASL SMCO 4 nov. 1175 for Guindolfo, *RCL* 1532 (*a*.1185) for Ponte S. Pietro; *RCL* 1337, 1400, 1405 (*a*.1174–9) for Massa Macinaia and Verciano— in these texts he is 'de Marlia'. In Segromigno and Guamo: AAL AI15 (*a*.1164), ++Q92 (*a*.1173), ++Q88 (*a*.1178), ++V33 (*a*.1184), AI94, AL34 (*a*.1187); the same man guaranteed a transaction by the pievano of Vorno, near Guamo, in ASL S. Nicolao 24 magg. 1181. Gerardino's brother Pietro (cf. AAL *D35, *a*.1148, ++R67, *a*.1204) may be the Compito owner documented in ASL S. Ponziano 25 lugl. 1165, 13 giug. 1181. These references would have been impossible to compile without the help of Arnold Esch's card index (see Ch. 1, n. 10). Gerardino deals with the bishop in ASL Arch. di Stato 13 apr. 1185, AAL ++R30 (*a*.1179), *Q45 (*a*.1187); the 1179 reference is a later endorsement that shows the bishop controlling, in the next generation, land that had been Gerardino's, though we do not know how or when he got it. [AAL Bibl. MSS n. 34, 200, shows Gerardino alive in 1193.]

[54] Avvocati land: AAL +F45 (*a*.1152), +K46 (*a*.1155)—they also held the castle of Coldipozzo with a small signorial territory in the hills above (below, Ch. 3 n. 3); a podestarial text from 1203 (AAL +O19, ed. in Tommasi, *Storia di Lucca*, app. pp. 7–8) and a diploma of Frederick II (ASF Strozziane Uguccioni dic. 1220) regard Marlia as one of their landowning centres, and recognize their signorial rights there. Signorial rights of the bishop over the *curtis* of Marlia: *MGH, Friderici I Dipl.*, n. 430 (*a*.1164). What these rights meant is hard to discern; they never appear except in formal charters of confirmation. But the bishop, at least, had *manentes* in Marlia: AAL AE90 (*a*.1193).

transacted with the bishop, but did not witness episcopal charters; similarly, he attended the Canonica's court cases as a local owner in the southern plain, but did not have direct dealings with that church. The truth
is that, for Gerardino, unlike Moro, we cannot build up a picture of any
sort of social network out of his land deals at all, either with the powerful or with his local neighbours. The patterns of recurring families that
were visible in Moro's charters are not visible at all in Gerardino's. This
contrast is not, as far as I can see, a chance feature of the documentation
for Gerardino; we will see it again in Moriano and in S. Margherita and
Tassignano, where evidence of groups of linked landowners in documents
predating 1150 or so gives way to much more fragmented references at
the end of the twelfth century, with few common associations.[55] This is
a pity, certainly, for it means that some of the main elements of social
development in the late twelfth century cannot be grasped at all; but it
indicates that something has changed.

One thing that had changed we have already seen: the expansion
of the commercial environment allowed land transactions to be made
according to purely marginalist calculations of profit and loss. Arnold
Esch has indeed discussed the personal archives of three mid- to late
twelfth-century plains landowners, Foliarello di Giovanni in Compito in
the 1180s–90s, Dolce the notary in Lunata in the 1140s–80s, and Ciofforo
di Rustico in the eastern plain in the years 1139–83, in precisely this
light.[56] If Gerardino, a person of similar status, cannot be analysed in a
similar way, it is only because the documents we have for him do not
give sufficiently continuous figures for prices and rents. But, as we have
also seen, the existence of these new commercial possibilities did not in
themselves undermine social relationships; if Gerardino did not express
social links through land transactions, then the social environment had
altered as well. In particular, personal dependence on the powerful, medi-
ated through land, was not the only way to status and wealth, unlike in
the eleventh century in Lucca, and unlike most of the rest of Europe
in Gerardino's time. In the traditional terms of the politics of land,

---

[55] See below, pp. 127, 148, for other villages, where late 12th-cent. social fragmentation
is closely associated with the sharp increase in city property-owning. In Marlia, however,
this increase cannot be seen; in the period 1180–1225, when the protagonists' villages of
origin come back into the formularies for documents, landowners are predominantly
still local—i.e. they all tend to be called 'de Marlia' or from other nearby villages. For
examples see, *RCL* 1619, AAL ++R67 (*a.*1196), ++R67 (*a.*1204), ASL SMFP 18 apr.
1194, S. Giovanni 24 genn. 1197, S. Ponziano 31 genn. 1207, 6 mar. 1224.
[56] Esch, 'Lucca', ch. 2.

Gerardino was living in a political vacuum in Marlia; it seems that political influence through vertical links of patronage, as Moro had, was simply
not useful, or accessible, to him, whether because it was not personally
worth while to a commercially minded entrepreneur, or because major
landowners themselves were less involved in the countryside. Certainly
the most important powers in Marlia in the late twelfth century, the bishop,
the Avvocati, or perhaps the monastery of S. Ponziano outside Lucca
(which was probably not a large property owner, but did hold patronage
rights over the church of S. Giusto),[57] do not appear as actors in very
many of our documents; local landowners in general, and not just
Gerardino, seem far less linked to them than Moro had been, and tended
to transact above all with each other. But this has a social, and not just
an economic implication; the lessening of outside, vertically organized
relationships is likely to have helped the development of local, more
horizontally organized relationships in their place. Such a diminishing of
external links allowed both for people like Gerardino to be economically
active on their own account, indeed all across the Sei Miglia, but also,
and not by any means in contradiction, for local social links to develop
in their place. And this gives us one context for the appearance of the
rural commune in the late twelfth century in the Lucchesia.

We do not, it is true, know much about the early rural commune in
Marlia—less, in fact, than for many smaller and worse-documented villages. Rural communes in the Lucca plain tended to crystallize around
churches, of which Marlia, a large area as we have seen, had eight by
1200; in the fourteenth century there were seven separate communes in
the old village territory. Two of these have some fragmentary documentation before 1225, the area around the pieve (the *vicinia plebis Marlie*),
recorded as a territory from 1191 (although not yet documented with
communal structures), and the community of S. Giusto, whose *vicinia*
had consuls in 1207, and a stable set of communally run lands established
to fund the local church. All these patterns, as we shall see in the next
chapters, are strictly normal in the plain, as is also the rarity of reference
to them, which in general seems to indicate their relative social unimportance at this stage. But we also have a text from 1193, a court case
about tenant status, which casually refers to a moment when 'datum fuit
inpositum a consulibus liberis homis de Marlia': the consuls for the free

---

[57] S. Ponziano as patron: ASL S. Ponziano 1218, a papal confirmation—but S. Giusto's
other documents never refer to the relationship.

men of the village were collectively responsible for the collection of a city levy, the *datum*.[58] This fragmentary, chance reference indicates a wider collectivity than the church *viciniae*, and one organized enough to be raising money at a very early stage (no Lucca city taxation is documented before 1182); in this case, it may show that Marlia had quite an influential collective structure, however generally invisible in our documentation. Not many Lucchese villages had particularly strong rural communes before 1200, as we will discover in later chapters; if Marlia did so, it was probably because of the continuing strength of its stratum of local owners, well into the thirteenth century, a stratum which was already weak in many plains villages by 1200.[59]

It is clear that we cannot say much about the commune in Marlia in the period we are looking at; the contrast between Moro and Gerardino, itself inevitably partial and impressionistic as a guide to the different 'feel' of the late twelfth century as against the eleventh, does not supply us with a convenient trajectory that leads to a clearly documented collective village identity. Nevertheless, for precisely this reason, I will use Marlia as a hypothetical example, to set out some of the contexts in which rural collective relationships *could have* formed in the late twelfth century, which will then be explored in later chapters in other villages with more empirical detail.

Moro di Petruccia was a major figure in Marlia in the mid-eleventh century. He was a very local landowner, but he prospered through extra-local links, notably with the diocesan aristocracy. Had there been a rural commune in Marlia in 1050 (which there was not) he would perhaps have sought to dominate it, as a further exemplification of his local influence; but he did not need it to be influential—his aristocratic connections were probably all he needed for that. And, in the eleventh-century social environment, these vertical bonds of patronage, expressed largely through leases of land (which would slowly, in the late eleventh century and later, be

[58] AAL ++R67 (*a*.1191)—a *vicinia* does not show a commune yet in place, but one would soon appear, AE90 (*a*.1193), ASL S. Ponziano 31 genn. 1207. See below, Ch. 3 n. 18.

[59] For local owners, see n. 55; compare pp. 127–31 below for Moriano, and contrast pp. 148–52 for Tassignano and Paganico. For Lucchese taxation, see Fiumi, 'Rapporti economici', 28, for 1182 (although earlier examples may yet be found in the unpublished documents for the city). Marlia's long-lasting identity as a large area may be the result of a tradition of local owners such as Moro and Gerardino owning all the way across its territory: the latter would have as a result remained a unit with a social identity. Marliese common land, on the other hand, was fragmentary: Barsocchini 1801 (*a*.1073), AAL ++B74 (*a*.1075), ++A40 (*a*.1196), *RCL* 1579 (*a*.1188) are the only possible examples in our texts, in each case apparently single fields.

renamed 'fiefs'), were the most common way of constructing influence; if there were no pre-existing links of economic co-operation between villagers, common lands for example, structured local collective relationships may have seemed relatively unimportant.

Gerardino di Morettino, a man of similar status a century later, may not have needed the rural commune either, with his personal economic activities and his city position; if it as yet existed in his lifetime (which it probably did), it did not appear in any of his land transactions, either as an actor, as an interested party, or as a guarantor or arbitrator in case of trouble. But Gerardino's world, one where land-based clienteles were less obviously visible, while it represented opportunity for him, represented danger for people more at risk from a more commercial economic environment; if notables were less available as protectors, villagers would have to protect themselves. Instead of participating in urban aristocratic clienteles, the Marliesi faced the city as a body, developing their own structures of local co-operation in imitation of the city commune: the city was a danger, but also a model. Cities, after all, formed their collective associations in the years around 1100 at least in part as defensive reactions to the failure of traditional royal (or, in Tuscany, marchesal) governmental hierarchies. In the countryside, across the following century, such defensive reactions were equally reasonable. Indeed, the twelfth century was not just the low point for aristocratic involvement in the local politics of the Lucca plain; it was the low point, throughout north-central Italy, for the effectiveness of the traditional structures of public power themselves. In this environment, urban models of collective action were the most potent ones available to fill the power vacuum; it is not surprising that rural communes spread across the century into every village in the Lucca plain, as indeed elsewhere. Horizontally organized forms of co-operation could become, for a time, at least as potent as vertical forms; Gerardino's neighbours could combine together to assist each other in at least some aspects of their lives, and indeed, shortly after his death in (probably) the late 1180s, were already collecting taxation locally. Vertical relationships of course continued to exist—no city in the consular period, as later, was short of factions, which were all structured by clienteles of kin-groups, and such relations had also always existed in villages (so also, of course, did *ad hoc* oppression, if individuals could get away with it). But structured co-operative relationships were also coming to be important, for the first time, and this gave a major encouragement to the growth of communal activity, in the countryside as in the city, as an option that people, and most crucially village élites, could adopt if they felt they needed it.

This briefly is the model for the development of the Lucchese rural commune that will be developed and fleshed out in the chapters to follow. If I have said nothing about widely accepted features of the basis for the development of communes, such as signorial power, class struggle, and the organization of common economic rights, this is because, despite their importance elsewhere, they happen to be relatively unimportant in the specific case of the plain of Lucca. I will argue, on the other hand, that variants of the patterns I have just outlined are generally applicable in Italy, and indeed elsewhere, in the twelfth century, even where other factors also existed.

One of the most important issues for the understanding of how rural communes formed is what geographical framework they formed inside. The first prerequisite for an effective village-based communal structure, the existence of a clearly bounded village as a territory with a social meaning for its inhabitants, might seem too obvious to mention. But one part of the specificity of the Lucchese Sei Miglia in the eleventh and twelfth centuries was precisely that such village territories barely existed at the beginning of the period. The slow crystallization of village territories out of the very informal social circles that preceded them is a crucial element in the formation of rural communes themselves in the Lucchesia, and had a decisive effect on the precise ways in which communes themselves developed locally. The next chapter will explore this rural geography, before we come on to some more specific examples of communes.

3

Rural Settlement, Village Identity, and the Parish in the Lucca Plain

The basic patterns of settlement and land use in the lands around Lucca have changed relatively little in more than a millennium, at least until the industrialization of the post-war period. Ever since AD 700, when the Lucchese documents begin, the Lucca plain and its surrounding hills have been a heavily exploited agricultural area, with grain production centred in the plain and tree crops in the hills, structured by the urban market (cf. above, pp. 17–20), and supporting a relatively high population in a dense network of highly dispersed settlements. There have been changes, of course; olive production seems to have begun to expand considerably around 1100, the first indication of Lucca's hegemony over the market for quality oil, which it still maintains; between the fifteenth and the nineteenth century this was matched by the development of mulberry trees for silk, though these have by now almost entirely disappeared.[1] But agricultural wealth, a dense population, and dispersed settlement are a continuous feature of the Lucca plain, then as now.

The settlements themselves have changed more, however: above all in how they were characterized and organized. Eighth-century charters for the Lucchesia show us a network of villages (called *vici* or *loci*) that often no longer survive with their old names and territories. Only in the tenth century do the settlements (now called *loci et fines*) named in the documents have names that are in most cases recognizable today, and only in the late twelfth century do the *confines* and *viciniae*, the village territories of the new rural communes, begin to represent the modern territorial structures of the plain, as we will see in more detail in what follows. Changes in

---

[1] Oil and silk: see Ch. 2 nn. 19, 20. For the rise of olive cultivation in the hills, see for example the sharp increase in references to *oliveti* (olive groves) and oil rents in Moriano and its environs: ASL i. 62 (*a.* 1025), 77 (*a.* 1032), ii. 77 (*a.* 1093), *RCL* 548 (*a.* 1097), AAL +S56 (*a.* 1111), AG11 (*a.* 1119), ++P34 (*a.* 1121), ++G50 (*a.* 1123), +G99 (*a.* 1141), etc. Note, too, *RCL* 1148, 1150–1, 1155–7, 1159, 1208–9 (*a.* 1156–63), a set of charters in which the monastery of Pozzeveri bought back the tenures of its estate at Palmata above Marlia, tenant by tenant, and systematically replaced mixed rentals, including signorial obligations, with fixed rents in oil.

terminology and in village names have been frequently studied in Italy in recent years, for they are often very precise guides to changes in settlement patterns, above all in the context of the tenth- to twelfth-century process of *incastellamento*, which created a network of new concentrated and fortified settlements across much of Italy between Siena and Naples, and in parts of the rest of the country as well.[2] In the Lucchesia, however, and still more in the Sei Miglia, this happened very rarely. Settlement patterns barely changed at all on the plain; castelli in the Sei Miglia were few, and mostly small and/or short-lived.[3] But the shape and social role of village territories, and with them the structures of sociability, changed substantially. It is this that we have to confront; for these territories, and this sociability, formed the basis of the twelfth-century rural commune. They will be the focus of this chapter. But, before we look at them, we must set them in a geographical context that will make them comprehensible.

i. Human geography

Lucca is ringed by a small plain, only fifteen or so kilometres across, perhaps 300 km.[2] in all (see Map 3). The river Serchio runs straight through it on its way from the mountains of the Garfagnana to the sea near Pisa. In the medieval period, the Serchio formed two main arms, the Auser and the Auserclo (only the second of which still survives); and several other linked streams wandered across the Lucca plain beside and between them, some running directly to the sea or to the Arno at Pisa, and some draining off into the lago di Bientina (or Sesto), the great marshy lake that, until the nineteenth-century drainage began, blocked easy access to the plain from the south-east. Like many Italian plains, then, large or small, that around Lucca is watery. But it has not been waterlogged in

---

[2] See, for refs., Ch. 1 n. 8.

[3] See, for 11th-cent. castelli, the refs. in C. J. Wickham, 'Economia e società rurale', in A. Spicciani and C. Violante (eds.), *Sant'Anselmo vescovo di Lucca* (Rome, 1992), 391–422, n. 16. The fortifications first documented after 1080, none of them, except Aquilea, obviously significant population centres, are Castagnori north-west of the city, destroyed by the Lucchesi in 1100 (*Tholomei Lucensis Annales*, ed. B. Schmeidler, *MGH, SRS*, NS 8 (Berlin, 1955), *s.a.*); Vorno to the south, destroyed by the Lucchesi in 1150 (ibid., *s.a.*; Bernardo Maragone, *Gli annales pisani*, ed. M. Lupo Gentile, in *Rerum italicarum scriptores*, 2nd edn., vi. 2 (Bologna of Moriano, see below, n. 39); the Avvocati castello of Coldipozzo, oddly situated high in the wooded hills above Marlia (*RCL* 1259, 1284, *a.*1167–71; AAL ++G18, *a.*1175, etc.; and Ch. 2 n. 54); and the late fortification of Maggiano in the west of the Sei Miglia, incastellated in 1189 (see Ch. 7 n. 13). For more on Moriano, Mammoli, and Marlia, see below, pp. 62–5.

historic times, or at least most of it has not. It can flood, certainly; but it is on a steady slope, and most water runs off easily enough, towards the sea or the lake. Marshland north of the lago di Bientina is rarely mentioned in the thousands of documents for the early medieval plain, and was probably relatively restricted in size; Map 3 shows its most likely extent. By 900 or so the Auser was a relatively unimportant stream, and was certainly not too unsafe to have allowed settlement beside it already in the eighth century. In the eleventh century, even the Auserclo, by now the major and thus more violent arm, begins to have its banks mentioned in the texts; trees were beginning to be planted along the river, probably to stabilize it.[4] And, as a result both of the control of the water and the dense settlement in the plain, there is little mention of waste and woodland in the documents; when they are cited, their scale is normally very small.[5] Land-clearance was correspondingly of little importance in this period, although we have evidence of two systematic projects organized by bishops in the Moriano area, in Bolognana above Sesto on the part of Giovanni II in 1029, and in the Vallebuia, further south and towards Lucca, on the part of Anselmo I (Pope Alexander II) in 1068–72, which may have cleared some of the few low-lying unsettled areas left.[6] The

---

[4] For general background, see D. Barsocchini, 'Sul/'antico corso del Serchio' *Atti dell'Accademia lucchese di scienze, lettere ed arti*, 14 (1853), 393–487; E. Paderi, 'Variazioni fisiografiche', *Memorie della reale società geografica italiana*, 17 (1932), 89–118 (with valuable maps); for trees on the Serchio, *RCL* 320 (*a.*1065). For later medieval river control, which remained vital, D. J. Osheim, *An Italian Lordship* (Berkeley, 1977), 100; S. Bongi, *Inventario* (Lucca, 1872), i. 284–95. River devastation of crops appears as a danger in, for example, *RCL* 649 (*a.*1105) for Guindolfo, AAL +K54 (*a.*1178) for Marlia (probably the Auser), and ASL S. Ponziano 28 ago. 1196 for Moriano. See now, for a new study of the water and marshes of the early medieval Lucchesia, P. Squatriti, 'Water, Nature and Culture in Early Medieval Lucca', *Early Medieval History*, 4 (1995), 21–40.

[5] Examples of waste and woodland on the plain include ASL ii. 545, *RCL* 988, 1054, ASL Arch. de' Notari 11 ott. 1172 for wood and marsh in Tassignano; AAL ++N17 (*a.*1071, Gemignani 270), AH75 (*a.*1092) for marsh at Massa Macinaia. AAL A47 (*a.*1179) describes the clearance of a small river island by Moriano; see also AL32 (*a.*1188) for the river apparently moving in the area. Common land is fairly rare too: see Ch. 2 n. 59 for Marlia; below, n. 16, for the eastern plain; Ch. 4 n. 28 for Moriano; AAL +O90 (*a.*1073, Barsocchini 1801) for Segromigno. The eastern plain, it should be noted, was certainly damp; it was normal to cite the *fossae* (ditches) between land-parcels (e.g., out of very many, *RCL* 988, 1047, 1284, 1571–2), presumably for drainage, and around 1200 the Tassignano consuls dug a new drainage ditch (below, p. 142); this dampness shows no sign of having menaced settlement or agriculture, however.

[6] Bolognana: see C. J. Wickham, *The Mountains and the City* (Oxford, 1988), 30–1, where it is wrongly located at Bolognana in the Garfagnana; against this, AAL *M93 (*a.*1029, Marchini 70) and *M94 (*a.*1031, AAL iii. 4) for Bolognana are for the same tenants as +R49, +Q21 (*a.*1034, AAL iii. 28–9) for Dardagna by Moriano; and +F97 (*a.*1066, Gemignani 163), A99 (*a.*1112–18), *RCL* 615, 646 (*a.*1101–4) trace a clearly Morianese

lowland around Lucca could thus sustain extensive settlement through-out the early Middle Ages, and as far as we can see consistently did so; indeed, this continuity is probably very old, for it respects, at least in the eastern plain, the main lines of Roman centuriation.[7] This is equally true for the south-facing hill slopes to its north, the hills of Moriano, Marlia, and Segromigno, at least up to the 200–300 m. level, the modern limit of agricultural exploitation; only on the Monte Pisano, south of Lucca, do woods begin on the edge of the plain. Plain and hills form an economic unit, which has for centuries been politically and socially homogeneous as well; for precisely this economic unit constitutes the territory of the Sei Miglia, which, as we have seen, was recognized to exist from at least 1081.

Inside this territory, of course, there are geographical differences, and some of these, especially in the areas I will focus on, Moriano and the eastern plain, need more detailed description. Climb up the fifteenth-century Torre dei Guinigi in the heart of the city of Lucca, stand under the trees that sit improbably on its top, and look north, on a clear day in spring. You will see a set of overlapping hill slopes, each side of the Serchio. On the right are the hills that rise above Saltocchio and Marlia, with the steep slopes of the settlements of Brancoli behind (these are the furthest villages up the river to have a plains economy, for they are a trap for the sun, and specialize in vines and olives), and, at the back of them all, the wooded mountains above the Serchio gorge leading up to the Garfagnana and the snowy ridge of the Appennine watershed. On the left of the Serchio, before the high land above the gorge begins, there is a hill, low enough at 180 m., but in control of all the access routes to the mountains: the hill of Moriano. Here, Bishop Pietro II in the years leading up to 915 built his major strategic centre to protect his holdings in the plain, the castello of Moriano, and this remained the centre for the episcopal signoria or *iura* of Moriano in the land to the west of the Serchio right up to the eighteenth century.[8] This area, the Morianese, lies both north and south of the castello, and is more or less divided into two by its hill (see Map 4). To the south was the major settlement area, rich vine- and olive-bearing slopes, overlooking a network of churches, S. Cassiano, S. Lorenzo, S. Michele, and S. Quirico di Moriano, and isolated houses

family from a Bolognana clearance-lease to land in Sesto Moriano. Valle Buia: the best survey is now C. Angeli, 'Anselmo I da Baggio vescovo di Lucca', *tesi di laurea*, University of Pisa, 1985–6, 49–95. Smaller-scale clearance elsewhere: e.g. AAL A47 (*a.*1179), ASL S. Ponziano 22 nov. 1211.

[7] See F. Castagnoli, 'La centurazione di Lucca', *Studi etruschi*, 20 (1948–9), 285–90.

[8] Osheim, *Italian Lordship*, for the *iura*; see further below, Chs. 4, 5.

scattered between them, all around a small marshy plain, beside the river; this area was called Vico Moriano in the eleventh and twelfth centuries (except for S. Quirico at the southern end, which was the centre of a slightly separate area called Licciano), probably in opposition to Castro Moriano on the hill above. South of S. Quirico is a long low ridge, called Pastinaticcio in the Middle Ages, which separates the Morianese from the Valle Buia, cleared in 1068–72, and, at the top of that valley, Arsina. The latter, another wine and oil centre (though there is more woodland here), lies just under the hill of Monte Catino, whose castello has recently been excavated.[9] One of its churches, S. Concordio, was in the pieval territory of Moriano (indeed, it is called S. Concordio di Moriano today), but socially it was separate from the world of the Morianese, and belonged more with the villages of the Val Freddana to the west, like Torre and Pieve S. Stefano.

The castello of Moriano and the ridge running westwards from it to the lay castello of Mammoli, isolated as a curious small mound, mark the northern edge of this fertile region. The river valley behind them, that of the Mulerna, runs through woodland; in the uplands to its north lie the settlements of Mastiano, Orzala, and Aquileia, in rolling vine and oil country, with woods again above them on Monte Catino to the west (Monte Giovis in this period) and Monte Castellaccio to the north, the western and northern boundaries of the *iura*[10]—the whole area is, I must add, one of the most beautiful I have ever seen, even in Tuscany. These villages, unlike the scattered houses of Vico Moriano, are and were clearly distinguishable settlements, although Orzala is more of an area than a defined centre, and Aquilea, the largest, is three linked centres, Piazza, Curcheta, and Collecchio. These latter were part of the village of Dardagna up to the twelfth century, another sprawling settlement area, stretching down the Bolognana stream to the Mulerna at the bottom; as a settlement, in fact, it was the second in the Morianese after Vico Moriano, and so was Aquilea when it replaced Dardagna after 1100. Below these upper centres, beside the river Serchio some 2 km. north of the castello, is Sesto Moriano. This was the pieve for the whole Morianese, and the major settlement documented there before 900, but by 1000 it was rather cut off from the thriving area south of the castello. Between Sesto and the castello, the bishop built a bridge across the river early in

---

[9] G. Ciampoltrini and P. Notini, 'Montecatino', *Archeologia medievale*, 14 (1987), 255–66.

[10] Boundaries: *MGH, Friderici I Dipl.*, ed. H. Appelt (Hanover, 1975–90), n. 430; but see further below, pp. 66, 87–9.

the twelfth century (it is first documented in 1113), and a hospital beside it by 1105; these became the foci of the *burgus* of Ponte a Moriano, which developed fast in the half-century after 1150, to become one of the principal settlements of the entire plain. This rebalanced the Morianese, bringing prosperity and political centrality back to the north, but contributed further to making Sesto something of a backwater, which indeed it still is.[11] Upstream from Sesto, you are in the Serchio gorge, overlooked by Brancoli; turn the corner, and you are already in the mountains; but you will have to travel rather further to find landscape to match the Mulerna valley, what with the blasting in a vast limestone quarry just on the other side of the hill, and the hydroelectric schemes on the river.

Ponte a Moriano was not only one of the major settlements on the plain; it was perhaps the only one to be a genuinely nucleated settlement, outside the few populated *castelli* (like Moriano itself, and Porcari, which had its own *burgus* on the Via Francigena[12]). Whether on the plain or the hills, other villages consisted in the eleventh and twelfth centuries (as earlier and later) of larger or smaller scatters of housing, over a few hectares for the smallest centres, or, in the case of the largest settlements like Marlia, over several square kilometres. In general, however, there was at least one clear geographical division: hill settlements, like Maschiano or Orzala, tended to be relatively small discrete scatters of houses, whereas plains villages, like Vico Moriano, were larger and more dispersed, and tended to run into each other. On the other side of the Serchio from Moriano, Saltocchio and Marlia were just such plains villages, not only large and internally divided around their several local churches (see below, p. 61), but difficult to distinguish from each other; above them, in the hills, Palmata, Ciciana, Matraia, and S. Pancrazio, were and remained sharply separable, consisting of areas of cultivated land cut off from each other by chestnut and oak woods. (The cultivated land was, once again, largely vines and olives, for these were not silvo-pastoral centres in any sense; they looked, that is to say, down towards the plain rather than up into the mountains. But even in the mountains of the Garfagnana and above the Valdinievole, more obvious silvo-pastoral country, such a specialization

[11] Twelfth-century references to the hospital and the bridge: AAL ++O55 (a.1105), AC67 (a.1110), ++P32 (a.1113), +F25 (a.1116), ++P34 (a.1121), *C84 (a.1132), ++P27 (a.1153), the first reference to the hospital's standard later dedication, S. Ansano), +L37 (a.1156), ++P28 (a.1161), ++P29 (a.1165), +E8 (a.1169), ++P26 (a.1192, the first reference to the *burgus* of Ponte a Moriano), etc.; ASL Spedale 20 ott. 1224 is the first citation of a two-storeyed house by the bridge, a sign of growing population density.
[12] *RCL* 498, 870, 907, 1040, 1431, 1456.

seems to have been a new development of the twelfth century, much as olive cultivation was in the Morianese and elsewhere.)[13]

If one moves south from the hills, a greater homogeneity becomes very apparent. Today, most of the plains villages resemble each other very closely, with a centre consisting of an ill-defined but relatively dense group of houses around a Romanesque church and campanile, and then a wider ring of farms and light industry intercutting with the houses, towards the edge of the village, and merging insensibly into the next. One can move south from Marlia, Lammari, and Lunata to Capannori, Paganico, Tassignano, and S. Margherita, the eastern group of villages that we will focus on, without ever being quite certain where one village ends and the next begins. The churches and their towers are about the only certain architectural markers for each settlement, now as in the twelfth century. Even Capannori, today the main rural centre of the eastern plain, with its semi-urbanized nucleus and futuristic communal offices, has a ragged scatter of houses running roughly along the centuriation to touch its neighbours in all directions; Tassignano and S. Margherita, their churches less than a kilometre apart, can only be distinguished at all because the house numbering changes along the road. Only Paganico, out of our four villages in the eastern plain, is a relatively discrete concentration of houses. These patterns, too, as we shall see, are old.

The Tassignano-Capannori area is now very visibly prosperous; it has its own railway station, motorway exit, and even airfield, and is full of small industrial plants. In our period it was slightly more cut off: to the west by the Auser, which ran between it and the city, to the south and south-east by marsh, to the east by the streams running down to the lago di Bientina, which separated it from the hill of Porcari on the eastern edge of the plain. The via Francigena, indeed, made a great loop northwards to avoid the area because of the river crossings and the general dampness of the area.[14] But it was certainly not poor; in the papal tax estimates of 1302, the local pieve, Pieve S. Paolo, and its constituent churches were among the most heavily assessed in the Lucchesia, and one of them, S. Stefano di Tassignano, paid the seventh largest sum out of the 519 churches of the *pivieri* of the entire diocese. In our period, it

---

[13] For silvo-pastoral references, see Wickham, *Mountains*, 25, 137. The evidence for silvo-pastoral specialization in the Garfagnana after 1150 shows a diocesan economy that was unusually tightly integrated for Tuscany in this period. There were other local specializations, too, such as the gardens which appear frequently at Saltocchio: e.g. *RCL* 873, 906, 1212, AAL *H91 (*a.*1133).

[14] A. Esch, 'Lucca im 12. Jahrhundert', Habilitationsschrift, University of Göttingen, 1974, ch. 4 for the Francigena. For dampness, see above, n. 5.

was at least of average wealth: land prices kept pace with those elsewhere in the twelfth-century plain, with the exception of the quasi-urban settlements closest in to the city.[15] The wheat and millet that dominate twelfth-century rentals were a basic source of supply for the city, which is, indeed, only four to six kilometres away. Although, as we have seen, local cultivators had their own tree crops as well, grain must have been the principal crop cultivated in the area—a dull but safe resource for its peasants. And, as an analogue to this, as in Marlia, there was relatively little sign of any common land, or even meadows and pasture land, in the eastern Lucca plain. Paganico, a little lower than the other villages and a little closer to the lake, may have had more meadows than the others, but this certainly gave no pastoral flavour to the area—there is no sign that any of its inhabitants kept more than plough oxen, a couple of pigs, and some hens.[16] These villages were simply grain-growing settlements on the flat land, with the highly individualistic agriculture typical of Mediterranean dry farming.

ii. Settlement patterns and village identities

I have stressed how difficult it is to distinguish between the settlements on the Lucca plain; the whole area shows an index of dispersal of habitat that is remarkably high even by Tuscan standards. How does one distinguish between them, then, and how has this changed?

Looking at the modern maps for Lucca and Capannori, the two large comuni that make up the Sei Miglia,[17] one is struck by the number of settlements there that are named after their church. The Vico Moriano villages all are; Castro Moriano is now the tiny centre of S. Stefano di Moriano. So are those of Brancoli, or most of them. Arsina is not, but one of its two medieval churches is now the separate *località* of S. Concordio di Moriano; Saltocchio is not, but one of its two medieval churches is now the separate *località* of S. Gemignano. S. Margherita, too, was once

---

[15] *Rationes decimarum*, nn. 4033–40, for the pieve; 4040 for S. Stefano. Esch, 'Lucca', ch. 1, pp. 4–18, for land prices.

[16] Commons: AAL +I30 (*a*.1156), Arch. de' Notari 11 ott. 1172. Paganico meadows: Barsocchini 627, 799, 1347 (*a*.845–952), ASL ii. 266 (*a*.1116), AAL +E65 (*a*.1172), +82 (*a*.1180), ++D47 (*a*.1185).

[17] I have used the Istituto Geografico Militare maps at 1:25000, fos. 105 IV SO, NE, NO, SE, III NO, NE; the modern catastal maps in the Ufficio Erariale at Lucca; and the copies of the Catasto Vecchio in the communal offices of Capannori. Some further place-names can be identified in the communal boundaries listed in the 14th-cent. Estimi, notably ASL Estimo 63 for Moriano. As an administrative guide, I have used ISTAT, *11° Censim. generale* (Rome, 1974), iii. 9, *Toscana*.

the second church of neighbouring Tassignano. Marlia is now a single sprawling village, much as it was in 1100, but this is only because in 1368, after the Black Death, the city *extimatores* united its seven constituent communes, focused on and named after eight churches, into one, since the seven were 'adio dispersa et diminuita, quia unumquodquem per se responderet non posset solitis et supervenientibus oneribus et expensis'— the seven must have been very small, occupying as they did an area of only some 6 km.^{2}.[18] Smaller centres, largely on the hills, have mostly kept their names since before the eleventh century; but the scattered plains settlements have normally divided up around their constituent churches, and have often taken their names from the latter. This is even clearer when we look at the list of late medieval rural communes recorded in fourteenth- and fifteenth-century *estimi*: their territorial division was simply the secular version of the network of parishes created around the churches already in existence in the twelfth century. The temporal relationship between the two seems quite precise: the parish system is first documented in the years after 1100, at the beginning of the breakdown of the pattern of pievi with subordinate chapels that had existed for centuries; the rural communes named from them, and to some extent centred on them, developed a generation later in most cases, in the later twelfth century or the early thirteenth. Of course, the twelfth century is the moment when these two territorial systems first appear in our sources, not necessarily the period when they first developed; I will argue, however, that it was that too in the case of the commune, at least. Anyway, when they appeared, the institutional framework of the Sei Miglia was fixed, and has not changed very much since.

The process of change I have just briefly characterized will be developed across the rest of the chapter. It is the principal geographical underpinning of the pattern of social changes analysed in this book. Its basic details need to be clear in the reader's mind, so that one can see what sort of significant differences can be found from place to place as the commune developed in its different ways. I will first discuss the crystallization of the present village structure in the twelfth century, and then the processes that underlay it, signorial territorialization and the development of the parish. Tassignano is a particularly clear example of what

---

[18] ASL Estimo 39, unnumbered fo. after fo. xlvii; cf. Bongi, *Inventario*, i. 136 n. Significantly, only one of the Marlia churches still survives, the former pieve. For the seven Marlia communes before the Black Death, see ASL Estimo 12 bis, fos. 252 ff. (on which see F. Leverotti, 'La crisi demografica,' in S. Gensini (ed.), *La Toscana nel secolo XIV* (Pisa, 1988), 67–150); ASL Capitoli 52, 182–4, 205.

might be called the 'classic' pattern of village development; it is, therefore, as good a place as anywhere to start.

The eastern Lucca plain showed an extreme dispersal of habitat in the eighth and ninth centuries; so much so that in the best documented settlements of that period, Gurgite (now Pieve S. Paolo) and Toringo, both just west of Tassignano, authors and scribes of charters were capable of ascribing the same plot of land, or even the same church, to two separate villages in different documents—the two must have been physically impossible to distinguish on the ground.[19] Tassignano was never actually confused with anywhere else, but it certainly sat very closely together with a number of other settlements. In documents of the tenth and eleventh centuries, it was surrounded by, among others, the localities of Cafaggio, Valiano, Pomaio, and Trentola to its north and west, the first three of which are listed as separate *villae* in the lists of the settlements subject to the pieve of S. Paolo in Gurgite of 926, 988, and 1014; and all four of which are recorded in other documents as separate villages, *loci et fines*.[20] (See Map 5.) But these ascriptions were not universally consistent. In 899, land is described as 'in loco et finibus Pomario ubi dicitur Trintula', Trentola thus being regarded as part of Pomaio; but Trentola was a separate *locus et fines* in 983, and generally remains cited as such in documents for another two centuries, up to 1184. Pomaio, by contrast, though apparently independent in 1049, 1095, 1139, and 1146, was part of the *locus et fines* of Tassignano in 1101 and that of S. Margherita from 1167.[21] What in detail underlies the shifts of these small settlements from being in some sense dependent to being independent or vice versa is far from clear, especially before 1100, for we do not have sufficiently tight concentrations of evidence. We certainly do not need to conclude that the settlement hierarchy was really changing as quickly and arbitrarily as these contradictory references might imply. It does, indeed, seem that the title of *locus et fines*, which we could in general translate as 'village', does not

---

[19] See C. J. Wickham, 'Settlement Problems in Early Medieval Italy', *Archeologia medievale*, 5 (1978), 495–503. This section restates and develops some of the arguments of C. J. Wickham, 'Frontiere di villaggio in Toscana', in J. M. Poisson (ed.), *Castrum 4* (Paris, 1992), 239–51.

[20] *Villa* lists: Barsocchini 1210, 1636, 1780. (*Villa* in Lucchese documents is a term largely restricted to documents dealing with ecclesiastical rights.) Examples of *loci et fines* for the four: respectively, *RCL* 740, Barsocchini 1385, 1038, 1559. In the Tassignano area, for some reason, houses rarely appear in the documents, so the pattern of house location cannot be used to back up these land identifications.

[21] Trentola: Barsocchini 1038, 1559, *RCL* 150, 220, 249, 369, 476, 480 (a copy of 476, and a better text), 553, 948, 950, 979, 984, 987, 1007, 1044, 1360, 1620, 1712, 1722, AAL ++K29 (*a.*1184). Pomaio: ASL ii. 90–1, *RCL* 232–3, 613, 932–3, 1003, 1257, 1568, 1620.

appear to have had any clear institutional status; it seems to have been available as a term to describe any unit of habitat, however small or dispersed, that managed to maintain some sort of social separation from its neighbours. Individual people or families may even, indeed, have somehow been able to choose which geographical unit they belonged to. It seems, in other words, that no unambiguous points of reference yet existed for village identity, or any fixed boundaries for village territories. Indeed, maybe 'village' and 'territory' are misleading words; as I have suggested elsewhere, pre-twelfth-century Tuscan settlements seem to have been rather more social circles or networks, changeable geographical groupings, than stable villages. People recognized the concept of mutually exclusive territorial identifications, for such identifications, however inconsistent, are a normal part of our documentation; but it is difficult to see how the labile *loci et fines* of the Lucca plain could have been the bases for any co-ordinated and systematic action, whether political, economic, or religious.[22]

The relative size of these centres is totally unclear in pre-twelfth-century documents, though Tassignano was always the most frequently documented, and was doubtless effectively the biggest; Trentola must certainly have been smaller, for it is generally described as 'prope' Tassignano, or Pieve S. Paolo, or even Pomaio, as if people might otherwise not have been sure where it was, and other settlements such as Valiano are sometimes so described as well.[23] But the major structural difference between Tassignano and the others, which would come to matter after 1100, was that Tassignano had a church, and the others did not. In fact, Tassignano had two, S. Stefano (first documented in 1076, but almost certainly founded earlier) and S. Margherita (first documented in 899).[24] In the twelfth century, the area normally termed Tassignano, either as a *locus et fines* or, after the 1180s, as a *confines*, began to expand at the expense of its neighbours. Cafaggio and Valiano are last recorded as independent

---

[22] See Wickham, *Mountains*, 174–9; id., 'Frontiere di villaggio'; cf. 'Aspetti socio-economici della Valdinievole', in A. Spicciani and C. Violante (eds.), *Allucio da Pescia* (Rome, 1991), 228–9, for Pescia. See further below, pp. 70–2.
[23] Trentola and Valiano *prope* other places: *RCL* 150, 249, 369, 480, 553; Barsocchini 1385 and *RCL* 679.
[24] First references, see respectively, *RCL* 420 and Barsocchini 1038. In *RCL* 431–2, 444 (*a*.1077–8), S. Margherita was given by private owners to the hospital of the cathedral Canonica, which kept control of it thereafter; S. Stefano had lay patrons in the 12th cent. (see below, pp. 137–40). Exactly why Tassignano had two churches cannot now be determined; several village areas did have more than one, however. In some cases, it goes back to what appear to be competitive foundations of private churches as early as the 8th cent., as with Asulari's three churches, all founded in the 750s (L. Schiaparelli, *Codice diplomatico longobardo*, i, ii (Rome, 1929–33), nn. 138, 140, 186).

centres in 1114, Pomaio in 1146, Trentola in 1184; by the end of the
century they had all been absorbed into Tassignano's territory. That this
was a result of the location of the churches cannot be in doubt, for the
confines of Tassignano was also, from the late 1180s, known as the *confines*
(or *vicinia*) *capelle S. Stefani de Tassiniano*; the inhabitants of Valiano,
who must always (or mostly) have gone to S. Stefano as their nearest
church, found that this now meant that they were stably part of S. Stefano's
village. The territorialization of ecclesiastical identity brought with it the
territorialization of village identity itself, even though there is no sign
that the pattern of habitat changed at all. And the next step was a logical
consequence of this fact: as Tassignano had two churches, this enlarged territory split into two as well, the *capella S. Stefani de Tassiniano* set against
the *capella S. Margarite de Tassiniano*, or, increasingly, just S. Margherita
on its own. (S. Stefano di) Tassignano took with it the old settlements
of Cafaggio and Valiano; S. Margherita those of Pomaio and Trentola,
as well as others with less clear documentation. The fit is nearly perfect;
there can have been little difficulty of local identification by now. People
must have known very soon which *confines* they belonged to, and this time
there were no overlaps, even for people living next door to inhabitants/
parishioners of the next *confines*.[25] The two Tassignano *confines* took on
separate identities immediately, not just as parishes but as rural communes; both, indeed, are first recorded with collectivities of *vicini*, each

---

[25] The last refs. for Cafaggio, etc., as separate villages: *RCL* 740, 1003, AAL ++K29
(*a.*1184). Cafaggio and Valiano under S. Stefano: e.g. ASL Spedale 25 febb. 1198, AAL
++K77 (*a.*1191); Pomaio and Trentola under S. Margherita: e.g. *RCL* 1620, 1712. Inconsis-
tencies are few, though one should note Trentola, or part of it, ascribed to the *confines* of Pieve
S. Paolo in ASL Fiorentini 12 apr. 1188. S. Margherita tends to be called *de Tassiniano*
until the 1160s (e.g. *RCL* 1044, 1166, AAL *D8, *a.*1164), and then loses the ascription
(e.g. ASL Serviti 18 ott. 1173, or *RCL* 1620). One should note that these divisions between
parishes in the countryside, despite the vagueness of pre-existing settlement divisions, almost
never led to documented dispute, unlike in the city (L. Nanni, *La parrocchia* (Rome, 1948),
157–8). Nanni concluded that they were carried out with relatively little difficulty, and he
must be right, though his explanations are unsatisfactory—they presume a discreteness of
rural settlement that the documents do not uphold. This would indicate, arguably, that church-
going, at least, had already become territorially organized, at some time before 1100. (Cf.
below, pp. 75–81.) Capannori and Lunata disputed over tithes in 1236 (Nanni, *Parrocchia*,
155). Otherwise the only rural disputes about the boundaries of parishes in the Sei Miglia,
RCL 1250 (*a.*1166) and AAL ++A65 (early 13th cent.), relate to new settlements, one around
Ponte S. Pietro that was expanding across the river in the direction of Nave, and another
around a similarly located church beside the Serchio bridge just north of Lucca: just
the sort of change that could be predicted to cause trouble. (For the second of these, see
L. M. Guidi, 'Per la formazione delle circoscrizioni parrocchiali a Lucca', *Pisa e la Toscana
occidentale*, ii (Pisa, 1991), 181–202.) It must be said, none the less, that the absence of parallel disputes elsewhere, at the very least in new settlements like Ponte a Moriano, is still
surprising; but cf. the tension in the latter in 1205–7—see below, Ch. 4 n. 36.

focused on the activities of their respective churches, in the same year, 1148.[26] That most of the church of S. Margherita dates in its fabric to roughly 1100 is not a coincidence, either; this new identity coincided with the considerable financial outlay of church rebuilding, here as elsewhere in the Sei Miglia. How these separate phenomena match up, and what may actually have caused them, we will see in more detail later.

In the Tassignano area, then, we see a process by which five or more settlements were replaced by one in the twelfth century, which itself simultaneously split, amoeba-like, into two settlements, each focused on a church: and all this without any significant change in the dispersed patterns of rural habitat. In the villages immediately north and east of Tassignano, similar processes were also occurring. In the eighth to mid-eleventh centuries, three settlements are documented in that area, Quarto, Rocta, and Paganico. Paganico was the most separate of these, although it is occasionally linked in documents to Rocta; in the years 1050–1200, a large proportion of its houses are identified as 'prope ecclesie S. Marie', the village church, and the settlement may have been by Lucchese standards relatively concentrated.[27] Quarto and Rocta were, however, not very distinct at all. Their local church, S. Quirico, was, like the Gurgite/Toringo churches, variously ascribed to *loco Quarto ad Roctam* (in the first reference to it, from 786, shortly after its foundation), or either Rocta or Quarto on their own. The two were separate settlements, but evidently ran into each other in ways with which we have become familiar. S. Quirico was an important church; it was a monastery of sorts in the eighth century, and, although this status lapsed, and there is a reference to the church as ruinous in 940, between 970 and 993 it acquired a cemetery and burial rights, one of the first non-pieval churches outside the city and its suburbs to do so.[28] Two probably substantial, if interconnected, areas could

[26] ASL ii. 583, *RCL* 1044—both among the very earliest such references on the plain. For the dating of S. Margherita, see M. T. Filieri, *Architettura medioevale* (Lucca, 1990), 48–51.
[27] Houses near S. Maria: e.g. *RCL* 258, 708, 716, 1571, 1632, 1774, ACL Q106 (*a.*1210). The main alternative settlement centre was Aqualonga, just east of the church and further still from other villages: ASL ii. 342, S. Giovanni 27 nov. 1195, *RCL* 1774. S. Maria is itself first documented in 1055–65, when it is given piecemeal by private owners to the Canonica (*RCL* 258, 306, 322, 324). Early links to Rocta: Barsocchini 1368, 1440, 1578 (*a.*955–83), and, later, *RCL* 739.
[28] S. Quirico: Barsocchini 204, 271 (a cession of the church by its founding family to the episcopal church of S. Salvatore—the bishop kept control of it thereafter), 1071, 1270, 1414, 1687, 1755 (all episcopal leases of the church). In 1687 it had a cemetery for the first time: see below, n. 65. S. Quirico was not the only church in the area at first; S. Miniato was founded at Quarto early in the 8th cent. (Barsocchini 189), but it is never documented again.

thus look to it as their church; indeed, so did two others that are first documented as *loci et fines* in the later eleventh century, Capanne and Greppo.[29]

Of these, it was Capanne, or, to use its twelfth-century form, Capannori, that would have the most successful future. It was certainly in the same area as Quarto, Rocta, and Greppo, and was very close to S. Quirico. It may possibly have been a newly built-up area of land, defined by the huts (*capanne*) that were apparently its core; the steadily increasing population of the period may well have contributed to the recognition of new *loci et fines* in the area that was previously just divided between Quarto and Rocta. But in the twelfth century, when the territorialization of the church restructured this area, it was Capannori that became the name for the territory of S. Quirico, not any of the others. Quarto was slowly absorbed into Capannori between 1108 and 1180; Greppo followed suit, rather more sharply, in the 1150s. Rocta, on the other hand, despite its closeness to them, became absorbed by Paganico in the 1180s, although it must have been on the very edge of Paganico's territory, and was occasionally described as being both in Capannori and Tassignano.[30] By the end of the twelfth century, the two *confines* of Capannori and Paganico, related firmly to their churches of S. Quirico and S. Maria respectively, had absorbed all previous settlement identities, just as the *confines* of the two churches of Tassignano had done to their south-west. But, as with Tassignano, no major changes in settlement pattern need be posited. That Capanne/Capannori may have been a newly built area is not in itself significant; house-plots change location with some regularity in a network of dispersed settlement, and frequently become renamed. Houses certainly still existed in Quarto, Rocta, and Greppo, though they were now dependent on Capannori and Paganico, in the late twelfth and thirteenth centuries. As at Tassignano, what had changed was above all the boundaries

[29] Greppo: *RCL* 442–3, 463, 470, 499–503, etc. (*a*.1078 and later)—though the place-name already existed in the 8th cent. (Schiaparelli, *Cod. dip. long.*, nn. 102, 106). Capanne/Capannori: *RCL* 204, 231, AAL *H34 (*a*.1067, Gemignani 174, 'near the church of S. Quirico'), AL 83 (*a*.1104), ASL ii. 246, 299, 302, *RCL* 1045.

[30] Quarto is independent in *RCL* 680 (*a*.1108), AAL +Q74 (*a*.1130), ASL SMCO 11 mar. 1161; in *RCL* 682 (*a*.1108), 942 (*a*.1140), and from 1417 (*a*.1180) it is subject to Capannori. Greppo is independent until 1150 (ASL ii. 618), and subject to Capannori consistently from 1162 (*RCL* 1199), with one lapse in 1180 (*RCL* 1412). Rocta drifts into Paganico's orbit between 1177 (*RCL* 1369) and 1182 (AAL *A8); before that, it is subject to Paganico only in two documents, *A65, +I30 (*a*.1153–6); thereafter, by contrast, it is never independent; although see AAL ++M54 (*a*.1160), *RCL* 1431, 1528, 1587, 1689 for parts of it under Capannori and Tassignano. The churches of Capannori and Paganico were both rebuilt around the early 12th cent.: Filieri, *Architettura medioevale*, 53–4, 89–90.

of territorial identity, and what determined these boundaries was association with a church—at Capannori, as at Tassignano and S. Margherita, the first documented act of the consuls of the commune was to approve a sale of land by the church, in 1191.[31]

These processes could be pursued elsewhere in the Lucca plain in as much detail, without adding anything to our understanding of them. Only minor differences can be identified in most places. In Marlia and Saltocchio, for instance, at the northern end of the plain, the same movement towards church territories is extremely visible. Here, though, there were no sets of little *loci et fines* to be amalgamated into *confines capellae*, but instead two largish areas with several churches in them, Saltocchio with two by 1000 and Marlia with six before 1060 and another two documented in the next century. The twelfth and thirteenth centuries saw the steady fission of these two areas into nine *viciniae*; although, as we have seen, Marlia maintained some sort of overriding identity at the end of the twelfth century, in the end all the churches came to have their own communes. Here, once again, the major new development was the increasing definition and social importance of the territories of the churches. Settlement patterns remained dispersed, with houses scattered evenly across the whole of Marlia, at most sometimes showing a slight tendency to cluster around some of the churches.[32] (Marlia, alone of the villages on the flat land of the plain, actually had a castello, around the church of S. Terenzo, documented between 996 and 1055. But it was certainly never a major population centre, and the bishop pulled it down inside a year of getting hold of it in 1054–5. As a ruin, it was merely the site for three small houses in 1135, although by 1191 the bishop had built a *palatium* there.)[33] But it is precisely this dispersal that makes the pattern so clear. In the hills above Marlia, villages were more discrete, and each had one church; the *confines* or *capella* of, say, S. Bartolomeo di Ciciana in 1200 simply replicated the *locus et fines* of Ciciana in 1000, and it would be

[31] Local people still living in Quarto, etc.: e.g., respectively, *RCL* 942, 1621, 1800. Capannori consuls: 1626. (At Paganico, too, the first consular text, AAL ++H34, *a.*1190, concerned the church, though the relationship was more distant. See below, p. 152.)

[32] Marlia communes: see e.g. ASL Estimo 14 (*a.*1333), with above, n. 18. Settlement near churches (S. Maria—the pieve—and S. Venanzio): AAL +K26 (*a.*1029, Marchini 59), ++M43, +N10 (*a.*1034, AAL iii. 25–6), +E48 (*a.*1041, AAL iii. 80), +O15 (*a.*1182); for S. Terenzo, see next n. But between 1000 and 1225 settlement is associated with at least ten other microtoponyms, widely separated in the territory.

[33] Castello: see above, Ch. 2 n. 38; cf. G. Rossetti, 'Pisa, Volterra, Populonia', in *Atti del 5° Congresso internazionale* (Spoleto, 1973), 302–3. It was already a ruin in 1056 (AAL ++Q44, Gemignani 4). For S. Terenzo thereafter, AE 17, +G16 (*a.*1135), *A22 (*a.*1191), AE90 (*a.*1193), ++O32 (*a.*1194), ++P57 (*a.*1207).

impossible to say whether the settlement or the church was more important in establishing its identity.[34] By contrast in Marlia, as at Tassignano,
Capannori, and everywhere else on the plain, a landscape of sprawling and
sometimes confused settlement was simply cut up between its constituent
churches, with every known church becoming the centre of a *vicinia* and
a *capella*, both commune and parish, in a territorial pattern that was clear
and consistent for the first time in Lucchese history.

The area of Moriano is the only one I know of in the Sei Miglia to
show a different pattern of development to this, and here the differences,
although still not very great, are instructive, and need some discussion.
In our period, as I noted earlier, at least from 1050 onwards, the major
settlement in the centre of the Morianese—just south of the castello—
was called Vico Moriano, with Sesto, Orzala, and the Dardagna area to its
north. Vico Moriano had three churches by the 1070s, and another is documented from 1152, as well as the eighth-century church of S. Stefano
overlooking it on the hill above, by the castello; it remained, like Marlia,
an area of scattered settlement throughout the period 900–1200 and
indeed beyond.[35] (See Map 4.) But here, unlike elsewhere in the Sei Miglia,
incastellamento resulted in some settlement change.

In 915 appear our first references to the episcopal *castellum* of Moriano,
situated on the hill. It seems to have been deliberately founded from scratch,
on open land, by Bishop Pietro II; the only known building on the hill
before it, the church of S. Stefano, remained outside it. Pietro built
several castelli, the first in the Lucchesia, at strategic points to protect
his estates, and Moriano was, with S. Maria a Monte in the Valdarno,
the most important of them.[36] From the first, it was intended as a serious
settlement: between 915 and 991, the bishops, who owned most of the
hilltop, leased out empty or already-built house-plots in their castello to

[34] AAL +N34 (*a.*1055, Bertocchini 76), *RCL* 577 (*a.*1099), 667 (*a.*1106), 1481–2
(*a.*1182), ASL Arch. Sardini 12 febb. 1187, SMFP 25 magg. 1194, Dono Mazzarosa-Cittadella
3 mar. 1211.
[35] Churches for Moriano: Barsocchini 286 (*a.*800) for S. Stefano, then the centre of its
own *vico*, apparently in or near the *loco Murriano* (with its own church, S. Pietro, not attested
later); +K16 (*a.*1075–80) for all the others except S. Cassiano, first attested in 1152 (ACL
Fondo Martini 19 genn. 1152). 'Vico Moriano' only appears as a name in the mid-11th cent.
(e.g. AAL *D49, *a.*1058, Gemignani 29, +K75, *a.*1072, Gemignani 274), but then is the
normal appellation until the late 12th cent., when it is slowly replaced by 'Moriano' again.
Heavily dispersed settlement in Vico Moriano is shown by the appearance of *casae* between
1000 and 1225 in at least fourteen microtoponyms: they are approximately located on
Map 4.
[36] Pietro's building policies: H. M. Schwarzmaier, *Lucca* (Tübingen, 1972), 103. First
reference to the castello, and location of S. Stefano: Barsocchini 1161, 1722–3.

tenants. These tenants must have come from the surrounding area, for the leases do not include arable land, only the house; they were evidently small owners or tenants from the Morianese, enticed into the castello to live but maintaining their lands elsewhere. This indeed makes the castello of Moriano a still more interesting phenomenon, a conscious attempt to agglomerate at least part of a local population into a single fortified village: the phenomenon is common south of Siena, and intensively studied, but very rare in northern Tuscany. For a time, it was very successful; at least twenty houses are documented there. By 940 the houses were expanding outside the castello walls, including in the direction of the church, and in 977 some of these were described as *sala et solario*, a formula for two-storeyed houses more common in city documents.[37] In 1014, furthermore, we have the first reference to a second castello, the *castello de Morriano que dicitur novo*, which continued in use at least throughout the twelfth century, though this fortification can never have been large, and was certainly abandoned by the fourteenth century. As a military centre, Castro Moriano and its inhabitants had their high point in 1081–2, when, loyal to Bishop Anselmo II, they held off the troops of the city of Lucca and of Henry IV, who were besieging them, thanks to (miraculous) rain and flood: it was clearly an effective strategic centre, and was indeed, as far as we know, never taken.[38]

The castello of Moriano was evidently a substantial addition to the settlement patterns of the Morianese, therefore. When we consider that 10 km. to its west the Montemagno family held the castello of Mammoli from 1072 at the latest, that Montecatino overlooked them both from the west by 1082, and that in the early twelfth century Dardagna turned into the episcopal castello of Aquilea, halfway up the hill that Dardagna stretched down, altogether constituting nearly 40 per cent of the castelli known for the entire Sei Miglia, it might look as if the process of *incastellamento*

---

[37] Leases: Barsocchini 1159, 1161, 1245 (?), 1246, 1269 (a.940), 1290, 1327, 1336, 1429, 1482 (a.977), 1571, 1681, 1722–3. The papacy was the principal other owner on the hill: 1159, 1245, 1336, 1429. For conscious creations of settlements, see Ch. 1 n. 8, and, with reference to Moriano, C. J. Wickham, 'Documenti scritti', *Archeologia medievale*, 16 (1989), 91–5. *Sala/casa cum solario/solariata* in the city: I. Belli Barsali, 'La topografia di Lucca', in *Atti del 5° Congresso internazionale* (Spoleto, 1973), 517, 542–52.
[38] Second castello: AAL *M61 (a.1014), Barsocchini 1795 (a.1072–3), AAL ++I81 (a.1085), +L91 (a.1121), *MGH, Friderici I Dipl.*, n. 430 (a.1164), and, for the castelli and the 1081–2 siege, Rangerio, *Vita Anselmi*, ed. E. Sackur, G. Schwartz, and B. Schmeidler, in *MGH, Scriptores*, xxx. 2 (Leipzig, 1934), 1152–1307, ll. 4857–5010, 6443–4. In the 14th cent., +L91 was copied into the Libro della Croce in AAL, with 'castellis' replaced by 'castello' (pp. 70–1); by now the copyist evidently did not know there had been two. The *estimi* for 1389 refer to it as a 'casalinum destructum cum muris': ASL Estimo 63, fo. 130.

had a considerable effect on Moriano's settlement. But Mammoli was probably always small; there are at any rate very few references to inhabitants inside its walls. The same is probably true for Montecatino. As for Aquilea, it consisted of three or four linked settlements, of which probably only one, Piazza, was actually fortified; all of them predated the twelfth century by well over a hundred years. It is far from clear, indeed, how much of Dardagna's scattered settlement was ever absorbed into it; it is likely that *incastellamento* here only led to a minor shift of housing into a pre-existing central nucleus.[39] And even Castro Moriano did not obviously maintain its position as a major settlement centre. In the eleventh and twelfth centuries, there are no more leases, and indeed (apart from the possibly atypical period of the siege) very few references to people actually living in it at all, despite the nearly 200 documents for the Morianese as a whole; we only find consistent reference to the bishop's *curtis* and *curia dominicata* (after 1115, his *palatium*) there. The bishop may have given up his project of maintaining a settlement of armed tenants in favour of a more typical pattern for a north Tuscan castello: a strongpoint defended by retainers, with warehousing, and enough living quarters to allow its owner to live there when he chose.[40] Only in the 1180s does the castello become a centre for private habitation again in our documents, possibly as a spin-off from the new centre just below it to the north,

[39] Mammoli: AAL +K16 (*a.*1075–80), RCL 383 (*a.*1072), 654–5, with Rangerio, *Vita Anselmi*, ll. 4445–54, for the 11th cent.; later, ASL Serviti 18 ott. 1173, Arch. de' Notari 2 giug. 1189, SMFP 8 febb. 1209, 13 apr. 1213. A cryptic sentence in Rangerio and then the 1173 text are the first references to inhabitants. Montecatino: RCL 464, 622, 961–2, *a.*1082–1142 (and see n. 9). Aquilea: AAL +G20 (*a.*1118), ++G50 (*a.*1123), +G75 (*a.*1125) are the first citations. They are followed by the replacement of references to Dardagna by those to the new settlement: ASL ii. 404 (*a.*1132), AAL +I48 (*a.*1139), *A46 (*a.*1164) for Dardagna, and, for Aquilea, ASL ii. 460 (*a.*1137), RCL 1042 (*a.*1148), AAL ++B36 (*a.*1159), *A22 (*a.*1191), RCL 1795 (*a.*1198: inhabitants of Aquilea holding land in the *villa* of Dardagna—cf. the dorsal note to RCL 394, *a.*1072), ACL A11 (*a.*1201), N137 (*a.*1202), A+1 p. 19 (*a.*1220), ASL Arch. di Stato 21 ott. 1225. But the three modern *frazioni* of the settlement of Aquilea, Cerqueta, Collecchio, and Piazza were already *villae* in 988 (Barsocchini 1628).

[40] *Curia* and *palatium* of Moriano as a political centre or a centre for rents: Barsocchini 1591–2, 1717, 1721, and any number of 11th-cent. leases, such as those for Bolognana and Valle Buia cited above, n. 6, or AAL iii. 28–9 (*a.*1034), AAL *D49 (*a.*1058), +P16 (*a.*1059), Gemignani 46), AE100 (*a.*1080). In the 12th cent.: ASL ii. 273 (*a.*1117), AAL +F62 (*a.*1111), ++A20 (*a.*1115, *curia palatii*), +L91 (*a.*1121), *K85 (*a.*1141), AE80 (*a.*1145), ++S9 (*a.*1148), ++B36 (*a.*1159, the *cisterna de palatio*), ++A98 (c.1170), RCL 1014 (*a.*1146), ACL Fondo Martini 19 genn. 1152. In a number of these, the bishop is present in person. Pozzeveri and a city layman both had private warehousing there, presumably leased from the bishop: ACL F123, 132 (*a.*1206), RCL 1465 (*a.*1182). In AAL ++P78 (*a.*1217), the Moriano consuls judged a case in the castle *aringo*, presumably, as elsewhere, an open space used for ceremonial purposes.

Ponte a Moriano;[41] and in the end it was the latter that would represent the real movement towards nucleation in the Morianese, for commercial more than military-political reasons—the hilltop today has only a couple of houses on it. Until Ponte a Moriano developed to its full extent, in the later Middle Ages and after, the overwhelming majority of the documented inhabitants of the Morianese continued to live in scattered settlements, most notably in Vico Moriano; however large the castello may ever have been, it never significantly replaced this open settlement, and, at best, represented a temporary addition to it, constituting the community of S. Stefano as set against those of S. Lorenzo, S. Michele/S. Angelo, S. Cassiano, and S. Quirico in the plain.

Moriano was thus less atypical than appears at first sight in its settlement history. But the interest in military and signorial power that these castelli denote certainly made the area in some respects different from the rest of the Sei Miglia, and this is relevant to what happened to the local organization of its inhabitants. Territorially, 'Moriano' was three phenomena, which did not entirely coincide. It was the territory of the pieve of Sesto, which covered the entire area from Dardagna to Licciano, with the addition of S. Concordio di Arsina (now di Moriano) to the west, S. Genesio di Mammoli to the north-west, and, east of the Serchio, S. Gemignano di Saltocchio and S. Angelo di Tramonte, though these settlements remained in social terms entirely separate from the Morianese.[42] It was also a settlement unit, the *locus* (*et fines*) of Moriano of the eighth to eleventh centuries, the *locus et fines Vico Moriani* of the century and a half after 1050; this area only covered the southern half of the Morianese, leaving out Sesto, Dardagna, and the other settlements on the hills north of the river Mulerna.

The third territory in the area was that of the episcopal signoria, the *districtus* or *iura* of Moriano. This I will discuss in the next chapter, but at this stage it must at least be noted that it is first documented in the 1070s, and was then described as including the *loci et villae* of S. Stefano, S. Lorenzo, S. Angelo (di Villorbana), and S. Quirico (di 'Nicciano', read Licciano): Vico and Castro Moriano. It was in this territory that the rural

---

[41] *RCL* 1440 (*a.*1181), ASL S. Ponziano 22 nov. 1211, AAL ++A84 (*a.*1212, a reference to a *casa solariata* there for the first time since before 1000), ++P78 (*a.*1217), *Q56 (*a.*1221). It remained inhabited in the 14th cent., as the *estimi* show: ASL Estimo 63, fos. 63–130 for 1389.

[42] So, for instance, *Rationes decimarum*, nn. 3987–98; see further below, n. 64. The churches beyond the river were the remnant of a former Sesto responsibility for the entire Brancoli area, which got its own pieve only in the 10th or maybe 11th cents.: Nanni, *Parrocchia*, 60–1.

commune of Moriano appeared in 1121; the 293 men who swore allegiance to the bishop in the communal oath of that year all came from Vico Moriano and the hill above it, but not from beyond the Mulerna, even from Sesto. In the twelfth century, the *iura* was larger, possibly covering Sesto in a text of 1115, and certainly extending to include the Dardagna/ Aquilea and Orzala hill country in an imperial diploma of 1164: the boundary of the *iura* for the next six centuries stretched stably from Licciano to Aquilea. The structures of the commune extended along with it; Sesto, at least, was subject to the Moriano commune in the later twelfth century and until it was formally separated in 1223; Aquilea was a separate commune from at least 1159, but it, too, had and maintained a close association with Moriano, and its institutions seem to have been modelled on Moriano's.[43] It is clear that the boundaries of the communes of Moriano and Aquilea were associated with—in effect determined by—those of the local episcopal signoria, and not, as elsewhere in the Sei Miglia, by the boundaries of ecclesiastical identity. The commune of Moriano, the first in the Lucchese countryside to be called such, was not in fact associated with any church in particular, and indeed included within it at least four at the outset. Nor was the pieve associated with it, even though the final boundary of the *iura* nearly coincided with that of the *piviere*. Moriano, here, in the formation of its communes, would seem to be the exception that proved the rule for the Lucchese Sei Miglia: the only substantial area in the plain to constitute a private signorial lordship, it was also the only substantial area where rural communes followed signorial rather than ecclesiastical boundaries.

Even in the Morianese, however, the crystallization of sociability around *capellae* can be followed in the sources. Leaving aside the references to the Moriano commune itself, the changes in settlement identity that we have seen in Tassignano, Capannori, and Marlia appear in our documentation across exactly the same period. As elsewhere, the *locus et fines* or *confines* of Moriano began to be replaced by more precise ascriptions: the *confines S. Laurentii de Villorbana ubi dicitur Stabbianum* (S. Lorenzo di Stabbiano di Moriano) in 1194, the *vicinia* or *capella* of S. Michele di Villorbana in 1207 and 1223, each with its own inhabitants;

---

[43] AAL +K16 (*a.*1075–80—see Wickham, *Mountains*, 73 n. for Nicciano), ++A20 (*a.*1115), +L91 (*a.*1121), *MGH Friderici I Dipl.*, n. 430 (*a.*1164). For the communes, see below, pp. 98–106. The internal divisions of the *iura* are well put in a diploma of Frederick I from 1185 (*MGH, Friderici I Dipl.*, n. 910), which confirms his *defensio* of the *castrum Morianum* and its *districtus*, together with the *capellae* of Mammoli, Aquilea, Maschiano, and S. Concordio: all these last except S. Concordio were already inside the bounds of the *iura*.

S. Quirico is a *capella* by the 1220s, too.[44] These *capellae* are not yet
described as communes, but they are clearly units of settlement whose
identity focused on the churches of the old Vico Moriano, as well as being
the parishes of these communities. Their relationship with the commune
of Moriano was probably analogous to the relationship between city
parishes/neighbourhoods and the city commune (cf. below, p. 77). And
it continued to be so, at some levels. Moriano's rights and privileges as
part of the bishop's *iura* maintained its single identity *vis-à-vis* the city
administration at least until 1350. But the parishes slowly gained their
own rights and identities. Sesto's formal separation from Moriano in 1223
was the establishment of the autonomy of a *vicinia corporis plebis*, of the
local parish of the pieval church itself, very much along the lines of developments elsewhere in the Sei Miglia. And by the late fourteenth century,
when the *estimi* list every rural commune of the Republic of Lucca, Moriano
appears for the purposes of city taxation as divided into its constituent
churches: from the viewpoint of the city, there was no difference between
Moriano and the rest of the Sei Miglia. The city had long contested the
independence of the *iura*, however, and its omission of the commune of
Moriano was probably not by chance. The true picture may rather have
been that outlined by local witnesses in a 1276 court case about the *iura*'s
independence; they described a situation in which the communes of the
parishes and that of the *iura* existed together, in a clearly defined hierarchy, in which the bishops and the consuls of Moriano together chose
the consuls of subordinate parishes. This pattern probably took shape in
the early thirteenth century, and probably lasted a long time.[45]

By 1200, the process of the formation of rural communes in the Lucchese
Sei Miglia was more or less complete everywhere except in Moriano, and
maybe Marlia. The pattern is already quite explicit in an arbitration of
1199 concerning common lands on Monte Pisano, on the border between
Lucca and Pisa, in which the villages on the Lucchese side agreed on the
establishment of a neutral zone between their commons and those of the

[44] ASL S. Giovanni 12 lugl. 1194, Spedale 28 mar. 1207, Serviti 28 genn. 1209, S. Ponziano
22 nov. 1211, Spedale 2 apr. 1221, Spedale 20 ott. 1224, ACL F119 (*a.*1223), AAL ++S6
(*a.*1223), AD49 (*a.*1231). They were certainly all distinct by 1256: AAL ++A93 (P. Guidi
and E. Pellegrinetti (eds.), *Inventari* (Rome, 1921), 49–52). Sesto, unsurprisingly, developed
even earlier: AAL +T99 (*a.*1187), AB50 (*a.*1223), and below, pp. 103–5.
[45] For the city's point of view, ASL Estimo 26.2 (*a.*1343), 63 (*a.*1389); for the real situation, Osheim, *Italian Lordship*, 80–5, and Estimo 12 bis, from 1331–2, which excludes the
iura from the detailed list of taxpayers, listed commune by commune (fos. 204–18), and
records it only as paying a lump sum (fo. 474 v). For the 1276 case, see AAL Libro della
Croce, pp. 31–8.

nearest Pisan villages. The issue was clearly of great political sensitivity, and the compromise was managed by the *podestà* of both Lucca and Pisa. But it was also agreed to by the consuls of every rural commune with claims on the mountain: those of the *corpus plebis* of Massa Pisana and that of Vicopelago, and those of the *capelle* of S. Maria del Giudice, Meati, S. Cristoforo di Vaccoli, S. Lorenzo di Vaccoli, S. Salvatore di Vaccoli, S. Giovanni di Escheto, S. Ambrogio, S. Bartolomeo di Gello, S. Michele di Escheto, Pozzuolo, and Gattaiola for the Lucchesi, as well as the *plebs* of Rigoli and the *villa* of Quosa for the Pisans. The Lucchese villages could virtually be read off directly from the *Rationes decimarum* of a century later; nearly every church listed by the papal tax collectors of 1302 in the pievi of Massa Pisana and Vicopelago is already a rural commune in 1199.[46] The pattern we first saw in Tassignano can be carried all the way across the Sei Miglia. And it would last; much of it is still in place.

iii. Signoria, parish, and commune

What does all this mean? Does this territorialization tell us more about parishes or about rural communes? What do the changes in documentary formulae really imply for the structures of rural sociability and identity? A full answer cannot be given without detailed analysis of what people were doing in each village, which is the theme of most of the rest of this book. But some points can already be made about the significance of boundaries, to give a framework to what follows. The first is to stress that the *capellae* and *viciniae* of the late twelfth-century Lucchesi, and the rural communes that corresponded to them, were developments of a different type from the vague village structures of previous centuries; the second is to look at the relationship between signorial and parish territories and the developing structures of the commune.

There is no general consensus about how villages functioned in the early Middle Ages anywhere in Europe. There can have been little homogeneity in village identity across Europe, of course, but it is instructive that the same arguments tend to recur in each country, between people who maintain that village collectivities were extremely weak or non-existent before the year 1000 or so, and people who see community action as immemorial. So, for example, Jean Chapelot and Robert Fossier believe that villages in Europe as a whole developed only in the tenth century or so, and that previously they were perhaps no more than clusters of houses; by contrast, Gianpiero Bognetti, in one of the most seriously

[46] ASL Tarpea 27 giug. 1199; cf. *Rationes decimarum*, nn. 4016–25, 4106–8.

documented contributions to the continuitist side of the debate, argued that the common lands and the collective structures of Lombardy, and thus Italy as a whole, simply replicated pre-Roman patterns.[47] As generalizations about wide areas, these two are extremist. But there were undoubtedly places and times in the European past when village territorial identity *was* extremely weak, as for example in the Roman period in lowland Italy, where the predominant territorial structure was the fragmented patterns of landowning, and not settlement geography at all—a structure that in some areas, such as parts of Lazio, continued beyond 900; conversely, there were places where local collective action was strong well before the eleventh century, such as many mountain regions (including Bognetti's Lombard Alps, even if probably less than he thought), or, north of the Alps, in the areas that followed the precepts of *Lex Salica*. One must not take any model of local collective action for granted in the early Middle Ages; the degree of variation, even inside a single country such as Italy, was vast.[48] Nevertheless, one development of the years around 1100 that was general across Italy, and indeed elsewhere in Europe, as Susan Reynolds in particular has clearly shown, was a sharpening of the boundaries of such local action, and a greater degree of internal organization and collective consciousness for all communities, strong and weak alike.[49] I will return in the final chapter to what this may mean as a general trend; here, I will restrict myself to observations about Tuscany. But Tuscany clearly fits the model.

Tuscany in the early Middle Ages certainly had something that could be described as a village structure. Like the rest of Lombard Italy, a geographically organized network of territories, called variously *vici, loci et fundi, loci et fines, casalia,* and many other names, had replaced the estate-based frameworks of the Roman world. Sometimes the inhabitants of such territories can be seen acting together, as, for example, in the assembly at Musciano in the Lucchese Valdarno to elect a priest in 746, one of a number of well-known texts tracked down early in the century by legal

---

[47] J. Chapelot and R. Fossier, *Le Village et la maison au moyen âge* (Paris, 1980), 75, 133–4 (cf., for similar arguments, G. Duby, *La Société aux XIe and XIIe siècles dans la région mâconnaise* (2nd edn., Paris, 1971), 122–4); G. P. Bognetti, *Studi sulle origini del comune rurale* (Milan, 1978), esp. pp. 3–105.

[48] For weak villages see Wickham, 'Frontiere di villaggio', another version of this argument; a particularly good analysis is A. Castagnetti, *L'organizzazione del territorio rurale* (Turin, 1979), 169–204, which focuses on the Romagna. Strong villages: *Pactus legis salicae*, cap. 45; Bognetti, as in previous n. (but see Ch. 8 n. 5).

[49] S. Reynolds, *Kingdoms and Communities in Western Europe* (Oxford, 1984), 101–54; cf. R. Fossier, *Enfance de l'Europe* (Paris, 1982), 288–601.

historians desirous to discover (or fabricate) a juridical framework for village communities from the earliest times.[50] But when we look at the total documentation for an area, the nature and even the territorial presuppositions for such co-operation become much less clearly visible. The Lucca plain, as we have seen, is an example of this. It may have marked an extreme, with its dispersed and confused settlement and the unimportance of its common lands; the local dominance of the nearby city from the earliest times may well have further contributed to the apparent vagueness of village co-operation and even identity. But other areas, rather further from cities, show a similar uncertainty of local structure. The host of tiny *loci* or *casalia* documented in the early Amiata charters from the unurbanized hill country of the south of Tuscany, or in the charters from the uplands of the southern Chianti around the monastery of Coltibuono, seem an inadequate basis for village co-operation, for example. The Valdinievole, between Lucca and Pistoia, represents even more lability than the Lucca plain, with no reference to settlement geography at all in the documents for the water lands around Pescia until after 1100; here, a substantial populated area, with access to wide and potentially collectively organized lands in the marshes, did not visibly recognize any formal geographical divisions between the individual family house and the entire physical unit of the river valley. And the loose structure of the early medieval Lucchese villages was clearly replicated in the mountain valley of the Casentino, above Arezzo, in the eleventh century. There, a group of small and dispersed villages (*casalia*) were at least more clearly defined than in the Lucchesia, in the sense that there was little or no confusion between them, and that they did seem to recognize some *de facto* collective framework for their activities; but they could still appear and disappear with relative ease, depending, as far as one can see, on the preferences of their principal inhabitants—they were as informally organized as those of the Lucca plain. Here again, the villages were surrounded by uncultivated land, this time mountain woodland, but there is no sign at all that its exploitation was, before 1100, organized collectively or divided territorially; in Tuscany, unlike Lombardy or Abruzzo, there is no evidence that the control of uncultivated lands structured village activity before the expansion of systematic silvo-pastoral economies in the twelfth

[50] Schiaparelli, *Cod. dip. long.*, n. 86; see in general Castagnetti, *Territorio rurale*, 7–42, and below, pp. 186–8. The church did, it is true, see *pivieri* territorially (see n. 53), and by the 10th cent. in the Lucchesia listed them according to their constituent *villae* (lists in Nanni, *Parrocchia*, 66–75). But *villae* did not have any homogeneous status or legal responsibilities; the lists were often merely lists of local place-names.

century and onwards—and the twelfth century was anyway to show a rather different attitude to village identity.[51]

These are single instances, of course, and one must be careful not to fall into the same trap that caught so many historians at the beginning of the century, when they invented entire constitutions out of isolated examples. But they do come from socio-economic environments that vary greatly, from heavily settled agrarian economies around cities to isolated woodland communities. I would not wish to claim that there was nowhere in Tuscany with an effective village society before the eleventh century. Most notably, areas with more concentrated settlement patterns—which certainly existed in some parts of Tuscany, such as the Garfagnana, from the earliest times, and which became rather more common with the *incastellamento* process of 1000 and onwards—are very likely to have had more organized communities.[52] The same is true for villages subjected to a single landlord, whose pressures on the whole community would logically have produced at least occasional collective responses—although here, too, the general fragmentation of most landowning in Tuscany ensured that such villages were relatively rare. But the informality and lability of village structures elsewhere must at least indicate that there was no formal public role that was regularly devolved to the level of the village in early medieval Tuscany, whether in the organization of justice, or of common land, or of the church; the coherence of village activity was dependent on local needs and choices, and these do not seem in the best-documented parts of the region to have led to particularly strong communities.[53]

---

[51] For these local areas, see C. J. Wickham, 'Paesaggi sepolti', in M. Ascheri and W. Kurze (eds.), *L'Amiata nel medioevo* (Rome, 1989), 112–16; id., 'Documenti scritti'; id., 'Valdinievole', 288–9; E. Conti, *La formazione della struttura agraria del contado fiorentino* (Rome, 1965), i. 26–36; Wickham, *Mountains*, 174–9, cf. pp. 136–41.

[52] Wickham, *Mountains*, 31–9 for the Garfagnana; id., 'Documenti scritti', for a survey of the effect of *incastellamento* in Tuscany as a whole. As research stands at present, 10th- to 12th-cent. Tuscan *castelli* only significantly altered settlement patterns in certain well-defined areas of the region, notably along major roads and in the far south; but there is more to be done here.

[53] The territory of the pieve has sometimes been argued to have had a secular role in the early Middle Ages, not least because it is often, in 11th-cent. Tuscany, called a *iudicaria*. (See, for Lucca, Nanni, *Parrocchia*, 64; more generally, e.g. G. Santini, *I Comuni di pieve* (Milan, 1964)). There is no sign, in areas of eastern Tuscany where this term is most common, that it had any real secular institutional significance (C. Violante, 'Pievi e parrocchie', in *Atti della VI settimana internazionale* (Milan, 1977), 717–19; Wickham, *Mountains*, 171–3), although in the Casentino pievi certainly had social identities (ibid. 206–7). In the Lucchesia, the term *iudicaria* is also sometimes found for pieval territories, above all during the period 1050–1150, but it is largely restricted to three pievi, Pieve S. Stefano and S. Macario in the Val Freddana, in the hills north-west of the plain, and Segromigno

It is because of this informality that the appearance of signorie, parishes, and rural communes in the years around 1100 represented a real novelty; they meant that, for the first time in much of Tuscany, rural areas had come to be divided into territorial units with exclusive identities. Belonging to a village would henceforth be fixed by location, without the possibility of choice; as a result, local sociabilities could finally develop into a structured set of affective relationships, and, indeed, antagonisms. Such relationships and antagonisms must have preceded the communes; informal identities are capable of being pretty clear, and factions existed even in the tiny Casentino villages of the eleventh century, probably thereby giving coherence to the developing village unit itself. But parishes and communes would, slowly, develop formal organizational structures that were themselves worth fighting over by parties; this was a real difference. The older more inchoate patterns of sociability and opposition simply folded into them.

Signorie, parishes, and communes have long been recognized as linked. Indeed, it was very common for all three to have a single boundary, which of course contributed still more to the coherence of each village unit that they bounded. As a result, historians have argued for a long time as to which one was prior, and, by implication, which one 'caused' the others. Cinzio Violante has dismissed the issue as one of a 'pseudo-problem of precedences', and has emphasized the dialectical relationship between the three, independent, phenomena. But even he has stated categorically that 'The "territorial" signoria thus not only set out the framework, but was the stimulus that provoked, as a reaction, the formation of the rural commune', and he would extend the importance of this territorial framework to the development of the parish too. He states here, in particularly lapidary form, what has come to be a standard view, that early communes gained their coherence above all as reactions to signorial power, which itself developed independently in the post-Carolingian world, when all power was coming to be ever more privatized and ever more local, reaching an extreme

north-east of Marlia; the word is only occasionally used elsewhere. It is just possible that these three had some particular institutional role in the period that others did not really obtain, but, if so, we cannot tell of what it consisted. There is no reason to see the pievi of 1100 as in any sense the forerunners of the later (i.e. 14th-cent.) institution of the *pivieri* (below, n. 64). For refs., and further discussion, see V. Tirelli, 'Il vescovato di Lucca', in A. Spicciani and C. Violante (eds.), *Allucio da Pescia* (Rome, 1991), 122–46; he attributes more judicial significance to *iudicariae* than I do. One pieve, Villa Basilica, was actually granted its own low justice in 1104 by its Cadolingi lords (AAL ++L3), but the circumstances were exceptional—Villa Basilica was a small pieve in an isolated settlement area with an unusual relationship to its lords.

in the twelfth century.[54] It is in this framework that the Sei Miglia looks so decidedly odd. In this context, then, before we come back to what Lucchese territorial development was, it is as well to remind ourselves what it was not.

The process of territorialization associated with the signoria (and its military analogue, the castello) depended on the weight, coherence, and social importance of military and signorial relationships, of course, and these were very diverse. In some areas, the inhabitants of a given territory became subject to the almost unrestricted power of a lord, which even threatened their legal freedom, at least until the acquisition of protective communal agreements and rural statutes. In others the socio-political impact of a castello was sufficiently great that all or most of the inhabitants of its territory moved, or were moved, inside it, in an act that necessarily recognized the hegemony of the castello's lord. In both of these cases the effects of such developments were clearly sufficiently generalized for both parish and rural commune to be directly conditioned by them, and this indeed occurred: the effective community of any settlement subject to a domineering lord or fortified inside its castello was not the same as a rural commune, but it is easy enough to see how it could result in one. Indeed, any collective reaction to signorial power, including that of more independent groups of villagers such as the mixture of local notables, small proprietors, and tenants of various lords that was normal in the villages of most of Italy, would easily enough lead to local organizations of a communal type in the environment of the twelfth century. But even where, as in many areas of northern Tuscany—including much of the Lucchesia— signorial obligations were so light as to have little effect at all on the lives of local inhabitants, and were often anyway divided between several lords, the division of the land into signorial territories (mostly, even if not always, focused on castelli) was normal. It was these territories that provided the geographical framework inside which both parishes and rural communes appeared, whether these communes were the result of signorial interest,

[54] Violante, 'Pievi e parrocchie', 655, and id., 'La signoria "territoriale"', in W. Paravicini and K. F. Werner (eds.), *Histoire comparée de l'administration* (Munich, 1980), 342–3, for quotes; for basic bibliography, see G. Tabacco, *Egemonie sociali* (Turin, 1979), 250–7; A. Castagnetti, 'Il potere sui contadini', in B. Andreolli *et al.* (eds.), *Le campagne italiane* (Bologna, 1985), 219–61; F. Menant, *Campagnes lombardes* (Rome, 1993), 487–559. For a critique of this, see below, Ch. 8. For the origins of the signoria itself, Tabacco, *Egemonie sociali*, 236–50; H. Keller, *Adelsherrschaft* (Tübingen, 1979), 147–96; Wickham, *Mountains*, 105–8, for further bibliography; id., 'Economia e società rurale', for local development. For its relationship to the castello, J. Plesner, *L'emigrazione* (1934; Ital. edn., Florence, 1979), 57–79 (who was one of the first to stress the structural difference between signorial rights and landholding); A. A. Settia, *Castelli e villaggi* (Naples, 1984), 168–76.

of opposition to lords, or of processes entirely unrelated to signorial politics. Even in the last of these cases, the territorialization and privatization of local political relationships was a prerequisite for the commune itself to crystallize.[55] This is the precise point that Violante was concerned to argue, and, in general, he must be right. We will see several examples of the process in Chapter 8.

Inside the Sei Miglia Lucchese, however, these processes worked differently. The model certainly fits Moriano, where, despite the relative weakness of signorial power (see below, pp. 93–8), the commune developed entirely inside the signorial framework, and indeed is documented as early as 1121, as the first rural commune in the Sei Miglia (only the third known from the entire diocese), only two years after the first reference to the consuls of Lucca itself; a signorial territory could certainly speed up the process that led to the formation of a commune, in Lucca as elsewhere.[56] But the other villages of the plain do not fit the pattern at all; they were not subject to signorie, but developed communes nevertheless. In nearly every case, these communes were of the community of the local church; the first references to communal leaders show them in association with their church, which was itself simultaneously becoming their parish as well. If they had problems with local aristocratic or military landowners, as did, for example, the men of Tassignano in 1206 (see below, pp. 140–8), the local authority of such lords was based on their *ius patronatus* over the local church; the closest link to secular signorial rights in these villages was the occasional claim by these lords that they had powers over their quasi-servile tenants (*manentes*), powers that were never over all tenants, and never organized territorially (p. 109). The territories of

---

[55] Some Tuscan examples, in roughly ascending order of signorial influence: Wickham, 'Economia e società rurale'; G. Volpe, *Pisa* (2nd edn., Florence, 1970), 103–6; Wickham, *Mountains*, 307–35; Plesner, *Emigrazione*, 57–103; O. Redon, 'Seigneurs et communautés rurales,' *Mélanges de L'Ecole française de Rome*, 91 (1979), 619–57, and G. Salvemini, 'Un comune rurale', in id., *La dignità cavalleresca* (Milan, 1972), 274–97, for the southern Senese and the Amiata. [See further C. J. Wickham, 'La signoria rurale', in G. Dilcher and C. Violante (eds.), *Strutture e trasformazioni* (Bologna, 1996), 343–409.]

[56] The first two rural communes known in the Lucchesia are Villa Basilica from 1104 (AAL +L3) and S. Maria a Monte from 1120 (AAL ++C75: see below, Ch. 4 n. 30). Schneider showed that the Valdera communal charter of '1075' (AAL ++R79, ed. Barsocchini, *Memorie e documenti* (Lucca, 1837–44), v. 1, 325–7 n.) really dated from the 1140s or later. *Origini dei comuni rurali*, 226. Another signorial commune was the tiny Avvocati centre of Coldipozzo, which was apparently founded, and granted signorial rights by Frederick Barbarossa, only around 1160 (see refs. to Barbarossa in the 1203 and 1220 charters, cited in Ch. 2 n. 54; Barbarossa tended to grant cessions like this in the early 1160s, as in examples such as *MGH, Friderici I Dipl.*, nn. 456–8, 462–3), but was already a commune in 1167 (*RCL* 1259).

these communes were, furthermore, as we have seen, those of the church—
in Tassignano in 1206, the consuls acted for the village '*in quantum est
vicinia S. Stefani*'[57]—and not of any secular jurisdiction, public or private;
whatever social reality previous village geographies had, they were entirely
effaced by the new territories of what was coming to be the parish. In this
framework, the Violante model evidently does not fully work.

On one level, this observation is banal enough: it is not difficult, in the
multiplicity of different local realities in medieval Europe, to find an exception to every rule. But it presents a problem of causation. Parishes, like
communes, are developments in Italy of the twelfth century, for the most
part, and are similarly regarded as being influenced in their formation by
signorial territories; or, if not that, then by the communes themselves. In
the Lucchese Sei Miglia, signorial influence can be discounted; but the
parish developed at the same speed, and along the same lines, as anywhere else in Italy.[58] How far was it influenced by the structure of the
rural commune, and, if not, what was it influenced by?

As it happens, the origin of parishes in the diocese of Lucca is more
fully studied than for anywhere else in Italy, by Luigi Nanni in 1948.[59]
Nanni looked at all the documents for Lucca until well into the thirteenth
century, and is one of the very few people ever to have done so (Pietro
Guidi and probably Salvatore Bongi are the only others known to me);
his collections of examples, though not exhaustive, are for most purposes

[57] ASL Arch. de' Notari 14 nov. 1206.
[58] Basic for this section is Violante, 'Pievi e parrocchie', esp. pp. 730–50; C. Boyd, *Tithes
and Parishes in Medieval Italy* (Ithaca, NY, 1952), 87–195; and, for background, Violante,
'Le strutture organizzative', *Settimane di studio*, 28 (1980), 963–1162; A. A. Settia, 'Pievi e
cappelle', *Settimane di studio*, 28 (1980), 445–89. In a comparative perspective, see Reynolds,
Kingdoms and Communities, 81–90. The clearest analogue to the breakdown of the pieve in
Italy is the formation of parishes out of 'minster parishes' in England across the period 900
(at the latest) to 1200: see, most recently, R. Morris, *The Church in British Archaeology*
(London, 1983), 63–76; J. Blair (ed.), *Minsters and Parish Churches* (Oxford, 1988). In England,
however, parishes tended to follow the boundaries of landed property, which tended to be
concentrated in blocs, often covering whole villages, in a way that has little parallel in the
fragmented landholding of most of Italy; thus, both Morris (pp. 64, 75) and Blair (pp. 7–8)
stress the contribution of local lords to parish formation. In Italy the process must have
been more complex. It may also be noted that a common reason advanced for the formation of parishes in northern Europe, the separation of privately owned churches from the
'public' (i.e. episcopally controlled) church network—an argument already criticized by Blair,
Minsters and Parish Churches, 8—does not work in Italy either, where 'public' and 'private'
churches were, for the most part, equally subordinate to the ecclesiastical hierarchy of
cathedral and pieve in their financial burdens (though see A. Castagnetti, *La pieve rurale*
(Rome, 1976), 140, for monastic exceptions). I benefited in this section from the helpful
advice of Julia Barrow and Steven Bassett.
[59] Nanni, *Parrocchia*, 107–90.

complete. Nanni proceeded along positivist principles, so that for him
the appearance of the parish began quite simply with the first references
to the word *parochia*, in the first decades of the twelfth century. Before
that time, he argued, the only defined ecclesiastical territories were those
of the pievi, whose territories covered several settlements, often a dozen
or more; village churches, whether episcopal or private, may have been
the *de facto* religious centres of a growing number of settlements, from
as early as the eighth century, but had no formal ecclesiastical status except
as subordinate chapels to the pievi. This would change in the twelfth
century, as parish territories formed; from the 1120s we find the first disputes between parishes and their mother churches over their rights, and
between rival parishes over their boundaries. These disputes show what
sorts of rights were beginning to be decentralized to the village churches.
The major financial perquisites that devolved to the parish were dues
for burial in the local cemetery (*sepultura*), and it was this that parishes
principally fought over, going so far, in the cities, as to divide streets up
house by house, as we can see in the run of Lucchese city court cases on
the subject dating from the century after 1135 (especially in the years
1170–95). Where one would be buried in fact seems to have become the
major indicator for which parish one belonged to, more even than attendance at church services; Mauro Ronzani, whose work on Pisa provides
us with the most nuanced account of the slow appearance of city parishes,
stresses that *sepultura* was the most 'probative' of parish rights, and notes
that in some Pisan texts it even came to be a synonym for the word *parochia*
itself.[60] (Of the other major financial resources of the church, baptismal
dues tended to remain with pievi until the late Middle Ages; the tithe,
the most important of all, tended to be divided between parish and pieve.)[61]
With the appearance of cemeteries and burial dues in village churches,
the villagers became more and more involved in their upkeep; the twelfth
century saw an ever greater financial commitment to local churches,
culminating in the more or less systematic rebuilding of all the village
churches of the Lucca plain, as in many other parts of Italy, in the twelfth
and early thirteenth centuries. Villagers contributed to these rebuildings, and

---

[60] Ibid. 145–58; Violante, 'Pievi e parrocchie', 740–6; M. Ronzani, 'L'organizzazione
della cura d'anime', in C. Wickham *et al.*, *Istituzioni ecclesiastiche* (Galatina, 1980), e.g. 49–61;
id., 'Parrocchie cittadine', in *Pievi e parrocchie in Italia* (Rome, 1984), 337–49, for a
general survey; and see P. Sambin, *L'ordinamento parrocchiale di Padova* (Padua, 1941),
for a good parallel. For the specific weakness of Lucchese pievi, see the comments in
D. J. Osheim, *S. Michele of Guamo* (Rome, 1989), 32–4.
[61] Nanni, *Parrocchia*, 182–9 (who notes that pievi kept a part of *sepultura* dues as well,
p. 188); Violante, 'Pievi e parrocchie', 745–8.

often organized them through their own communal officials (*operarii*); they often claimed the right to choose parish priests as a result, and sometimes got it, too, against contemporary canonical tradition.[62] Nanni saw these developments simply as the result of the rural communal movement, for, with the strengthening of village solidarity, people became more disinclined to go to the pieve for the major elements of their religious lives, in particular for regular services and for burial. This must be too simple; the relationship was a much more dialectical one. Rural communal identity doubtless aided the commitment to rebuild churches, just as the cost of the latter doubtless reinforced the developing financial organizations that represented one aspect of rural communal activity. But, although it cannot be shown for any village in the Sei Miglia that the structures of the parish *predated* those of the commune (indeed, it is usually the same document that gives the first reference to both), the way *viciniae* crystallized around churches in the twelfth century seems to indicate that village identity in the Lucca plain followed the territorialization of the church, and not vice versa. And the argument that parish structures followed secular developments, whether the signoria or the commune, does not work at all in cities. Cities were communes themselves; they would not easily permit rival bodies to develop in city neighbourhoods. But neighbourhood loyalties did develop in every city nevertheless, around the local parishes of the city churches. These did not correspond to any clear previous identities—it is indeed in part precisely because of this that they were more likely to dispute over their boundaries than were rural parishes. But they were identical in structure to rural parishes, and developed across exactly the same time-span in the twelfth century. They were called *viciniae*, just like in the countryside, and had their own consuls; cities often eventually used them as a basis for their own secular neighbourhoods. It is almost impossible, at least in the Lucchesia, to draw any sort of structural distinction between urban *viciniae* and early rural communes, except to note that the former were somewhat richer.[63] Urban *viciniae* transparently derived from the slow

---

[62] Nanni, *Parrocchia*, 158–71; Violante, 'Pievi e parrocchie', 754–65; in general, D. Kurze, *Pfarrerwahlen* (Cologne, 1966), 96–140. *Operarii* in Lucca: see below, Ch. 7 n. 10. For the reconstruction of Lucchese churches, see Filieri, *Architettura medioevale*; the height of such rebuilding seems to have been the early 12th cent. The best-studied parallel in Tuscany is the territory of Florence, where patterns were very similar to those in the Lucchesia: for this, see I. Moretti, 'Pievi romaniche', *Ricerche storiche*, 13 (1983), 50–69.

[63] Nanni, *Parrocchia*, 111–13, for the rural commune; see refs. in n. 60 for the city, together with Kurze, *Pfarrerwahlen*, 102–7; A. I. Pini, *Le ripartizioni territoriali di Bologna* (Bologna, 1977), 19–23; R. Davidsohn, *Storia di Firenze* (1896; Florence, 1956), i. 484–91.

crystallization of parish identity and the devolution of ecclesiastical rights to city quarters, not the other way round. Parish territorialization had its own autonomous roots, then, both in the city and the countryside, and this needs more explanation than it has hitherto been given.

The development of the parish is, in fact, something that has been described more often than it has been explained; and, when it is explained, it is normally in terms of something else, such as the signoria-rural commune nexus itself (Violante), or the rural commune on its own (Nanni), or, in the case of cities, demographic and especially extra-urban expansion which undermined previous ecclesiastical structures (Ronzani, by implication). These explanations work as far as they go, but do not explain all the cases; and nor do they explain why lay piety, which is what underlay at least part of the development of the parish structure, automatically favoured the parish rather than the traditional pieve, even where pievi remained important socio-economic and political centres. Reynolds, who has pointed out many of these problems, had to content herself with commenting that 'the whole process . . . looks both more complex and more mysterious than has always been recognised'.[64]

It may be that we cannot yet get farther than this. But it is worth looking further at one aspect of the development of parishes, the localization

Lucchese city parishes seem to begin to crystallize by the 1130s, a few decades earlier than in Pisa or Padua. Examples of city *viciniae* in Lucca: see Ch. 7 nn. 1, 10—their wealth can be inferred from the number of their *operarii* and other officials, which could be large. Secular neighbourhoods in Lucca (*contrade*), however, were not always based on *viciniae*: Osheim, *S. Michele of Guamo*, 26–7.

[64] Reynolds, *Kingdoms and Communities*, pp. 88–90 (p. 90 for quote). For the solutions of English scholars, see above, n. 58; they get no further in explaining the dates, although they show at least that the process of localization was long and complex. Other reasons for the breakdown of the pieval structure can be adduced on a more local level, such as Toubert's discussions of settlement change, which certainly work for Lazio (*Les Structures du Latium médiéval* (Rome, 1973), 855–67). Pieve territories could, on rare occasions, survive as foci for rural communes—see refs. in Violante, 'Pievi e parrocchie', 651, and, for Villa Basilica, above, n. 53. They often, of course, had an important role as administrative divisions (*pivieri*) for late medieval *contadi*, as well. In the Lucchesia, in fact, the boundaries of these latter were exactly those of the ecclesiastical territories of the pievi, as the *estimi* make clear. Most strikingly, the *piviere* of Sesto Moriano in 1331–2 only consisted of the four, geographically unconnected communities of S. Concordio, Maschiano, Mammoli, and S. Gemignano, i.e. those parishes of the pieve of Sesto remaining to the city when the *iura* of Moriano was excluded (cf. above, p. 66): ASL Estimo 12 bis, fos. 204–18. The importance of the mental template of the ecclesiastical pieval territory is here very evident. These *pivieri* were more than administrative divisions; they had their own consuls and social identity. (I thank Franca Leverotti for helpful discussion of this issue; see now her ' "Crisi" del Trecento', in *Pisa e la Toscana occidentale*, ii (Pisa, 1991), 204.) But I can see little sign of such an identity in the 12th-cent. Sei Miglia, and there seems to be no continuity with the hypothetical institution of the *iudicaria plebis* of the 11th cent. (above, n. 53).

of *sepultura* (burial rights) and its dues, for this was less sudden than the
flurry of references to *parochiae* in the early twelfth century might indicate. Burial dues in fact depended not only on devolved rights, but also
on the existence of village cemeteries; and some of these in the Lucchesia
were not new in the twelfth century. Two non-pieval churches, both
suburban, seem to have had cemeteries and rights to burial dues already
in the ninth century; three rural churches, including S. Quirico di Rocta,
are referred to as in possession of them in leases from the 990s. (S. Quirico
in 993 had burial rights 'sicut consuetudo retro tempus fui' [*sic*]; but the
immediately previous lease for the church, from 970, makes no reference
to them.) The number climbs steadily upwards throughout the eleventh
century, reaching at least twelve known in Lucchese documents by 1100.[65]
This slow increase in the number of rural churches with their own cemeteries was a European-wide phenomenon; it began with the association
of cemeteries with the church itself, which was not, outside cities and
their suburbs, necessarily normal before the Carolingian period (previously, cemeteries were generally isolated in the countryside, as in the case
of any number of 'Germanic' cemeteries excavated by archaeologists), but
which thereafter gradually extended to every church with a following of
the faithful. It was, that is to say, an organic development across several
centuries, and probably derived more from changes in local concepts of
the community of the dead and the rituals of passing than from ecclesiastical administration or canonist theory.[66] It would come into the arena

---

[65] Nanni, *Parrocchia*, 58, for a list, although he misses at least two, Barsocchini 1685 and
1725 (Ciciana and Nicciano). S. Quirico: Barsocchini 1414, 1687.

[66] This characterization is a simplification of a very complex and heterogeneous process.
'Germanic'/'pagan' cemeteries (whatever their real ethnic or religious connotations) could
be themselves the bases of Christian cemeteries and indeed church buildings, as at Castel
Trosino in the Marche in the 7th cent. (R. Mengarelli, 'Castel Trosino', *Monumenti antichi*,
12 (1902), cols. 173, 243–7; L. Jørgensen, 'Castel Trosino and Nocera Umbra', *Acta archaeologica*, 62 (1991), 42–4), or in the Anglo-Saxon instances cited by Morris (*Church in British
Archaeology*, 49–62), or with the extramural cemeteries of many Roman *municipia*. In Italy,
the local variation is best discussed by Settia, 'Pievi e cappelle', 453–60. In other cases in
England and Francia, local churches were at first the burial-places for the élite, and only
later did lesser people come from external cemeteries into the churchyard (Morris, *Church
in British Archaeology*, 54, 58; H. Steuer, 'Archaeology and History', in K. Randsborg (ed.),
The Birth of Europe (Rome, 1989), 113–16; D. A. Bullough, 'Burial, Community and Belief,'
in C. P. Wormald (ed.), *Ideal and Reality in Frankish and Anglo-Saxon Society* (Oxford, 1983),
177–201; cf, in Italy, for episcopal church burials as one starting-point, J.-C. Picard, *Le
souvenir des evêques* (Rome, 1988), e.g. 387–92). By the mid-11th cent., it was normal for
local churches in England to have cemeteries (Morris, *Church in British Archaeology*, 49),
and this must have been true of much of Europe. The subject badly needs Europe-wide
comparative study, however. For changes in ritual, see, for a stimulating parallel from
Zimbabwe, T. Ranger, 'Taking Hold of the Land', *Past and Present*, 117 (1987), 158–94.

of ecclesiastical administration and politics, however, when local churches began to charge for burial, or, at least, when these charges became a substantial part of church revenues; a church (a pieve, say) with a monopoly over the burials of the faithful of several other churches could well want to prevent the latter from gaining their own cemeteries, or at the very least from gaining the burial dues normally attached to them, and would certainly lose wealth and power when it failed to do so.[67]

I have used the conditional tense here deliberately; the fact is that we know very little about the early history of *sepultura* rights and dues. It is indeed not at all impossible that they were growing in importance between the tenth and the twelfth centuries, along with the steady elaboration of local church rituals and pastoral care in general. But, if an important church such as S. Quirico di Rocta was already burying its dead and charging for it in 993, then the only development needed to turn it into what would be a parish in everything but name would be the right to church attendance and to burials from a specific *area*. We cannot know whether it had a territorially defined community of the faithful before the crystallization of church *confines* in the mid-twelfth century, although, as I have argued, it is likely enough (see above, pp. 59–60, and n. 25). Still less can we guess at the exact procedures by which churches could establish mutually exclusive communities of this kind, in a world of fragmented landowning and dispersed settlement.[68] But these processes were undoubtedly occurring nevertheless, before their results emerge in the

---

[67] For the importance of *sepultura*, at least in the late Middle Ages, see L. Génicot, *Une source mal connue de révenus paroissaux* (Louvain, 1980). Note that in this respect one cannot use English parallels for the localization of pieval rights, for in England tithes were devolved from minsters to parishes first, before burial dues. This difference was probably caused by the relatively late (by Carolingian standards) development of the tithe in England (it was not stably organized until *c*.960); from its first documentation it was partially devolved to estate churches. Minsters, on the other hand, controlled village cemeteries for centuries before they had to cede devolved burial *dues* to the new parishes of the churches of those cemeteries. But the clear archaeological evidence for local church cemeteries in England for a long time before the development of local control of *sepultura* dues makes one wonder how long rural cemeteries had been quietly attached to churches in Italy, too (as with Castel Trosino, above, n. 66); S. Quirico di Rocta may have long had a cemetery, and then in *c*.990 simply gained the rights to the dues for burial there. For the English material, see Blair, *Minsters and Parish Churches*, esp. Blair, 'Introduction', 8–13, Kemp, 'Leominster', 84–9.

[68] One way territorialization might develop inside the pieve might be through the devolution of the collection of the tithe from the pieve to the individual *villae* that made it up. There are some hints of this in our first tithe and *sepultura* dispute for Lucca, *RCL* 841 (*a*.1127) between the pieve of S. Macario and the chapel of Vecoli, though the same text shows that burial rights in that chapel had not yet become fully territorially determined in 1127.

documentation in the years after 1100, in order to be ratified by bishops and popes. Parish rights were gradually taking shape, forming around local churches, like signorial rights around a castle or aristocratic *curtis*, well before the stabilization of parish (or, for that matter, signorial) boundaries in the early twelfth century. However this occurred in detail, its importance for us is that it gives us an indication that religious identity at the parish level could be developing around churches for reasons quite separate from the parallel territorializations of signoria and village/commune. They each had their own independent genealogy, although, of course, all three processes, where they were simultaneous, were mutually reinforcing: they were not inextricably bound together, that is to say, but they could act as preconditions for each other.

What parishes may have been beginning to offer in the Lucchese Sei Miglia in the early twelfth century was, then, analogous to the role of the weak signorie of other parts of northern Tuscany (see below, pp. 220–9): a territorial boundary, involving a certain amount of financial obligation, which could act as a framework and a focus for local collective action. Parishes did not cause communes in the Sei Miglia, any more than signorial oppression did elsewhere; but they could, and did, guide their geographical crystallization and supply some of their early political objectives, much as Caggese pointed out in opposition to Sorbelli in 1911.[69] This explains why in the Sei Miglia the boundaries of Lucchese communes so exactly replicate those of the parish, which is the phenomenon we have been exploring across this whole chapter. It was the novel tightness of such boundaries which enabled communes to develop fully. But what in detail caused the origin of individual communes, and how and why they differed from each other, can only be seen by the tracing of specific examples. In the chapters to follow we will look at what the developing commune meant for its inhabitants, at what the commune was for, what use it served, what needs it met: for only these will show what the internal reality of such a collectivity actually consisted of.

---

[69] R. Caggese, 'Chiese parrocchiali', *Studi storici*, 20 (1911–12) e.g. 143, responding to A. Sorbelli, *La parrocchia dell'Appennino emiliano* (Bologna, 1910) of the previous year. Volpe had made the same point earlier in his own critique of 1908 (*Medio evo italiano*, 166–71) of Caggese's 1907 parish arguments (*Classi e comuni rurali* (Florence, 1907–8), i. 195–228); Caggese was probably picking up on this, but distinctly did not admit it ('Chiese parrocchiali', 150–1).

4

Signoria and Commune in Moriano in the Twelfth Century: Institutions

Moriano is first documented in 1121 as a rural commune, the first in the Sei Miglia. It was part of, and territorially defined by, the episcopal signoria from the first; most of the early references to its existence derive from the signorial involvement of the bishop in its affairs.[1] Such patterns, although common features of rural communes elsewhere in Italy, combine, as I have already argued (pp. 62–7), to make Moriano in these respects atypical of the Lucca plain. Not in other respects, however; as we shall see, the exceptional documentation for twelfth-century Moriano brings into relief social structures and developments that have close analogues in the non-signorial villages of the Sei Miglia. In this chapter, I will discuss Moriano's signorial and communal institutions, which are what makes it unrepresentative, and set them into the framework of similar patterns elsewhere; in the next, I will set this against what we know of the people of the Morianese, for their activities are rather more similar to those of the inhabitants of the rest of the Sei Miglia, and are illuminating for wider discussions. It is neither easy nor legitimate to separate institutions too sharply from the personnel who make them up, least of all in a period like the twelfth century, when it can be argued that the very concept of local institutions had not yet properly developed. The only way of justifying it is to argue that it helps to make the arguments clearer; I hope it does.

i. The signoria

The bishop of Lucca was far and away the most substantial owner in the Morianese, that is to say Vico and Castro Moriano, in the twelfth century, and had been for a long time. How much he owned cannot be calculated exactly; but, by adding up references to episcopal properties on the boundaries of lands documented in charters, we can arrive at some

---

[1] For a general survey of the episcopal signoria or *iura*, see D. J. Osheim, *An Italian Lordship* (Berkeley, 1977), 51–85; and V. Tirelli, 'Il vescovato di Lucca', in A. Spicciani and C. Violante (eds.), *Allucio da Pescia* (Rome, 1991).

figures. In the first half of the twelfth century, some 30 per cent of the properties referred to in the charters are the bishop's; in the later twelfth century, the percentage falls to 20 per cent, and, in the first quarter of the thirteenth, to 16 per cent. These are very rough figures, and must be assessed bearing in mind the fact that two-thirds of the charters for 1101–50 are from the bishop's own archive, but less than a third of these for 1201–25; episcopal land is thus likely to be overstated in the first period, and understated in the last. Very approximately, we might conclude that the bishop consistently held something in the order of a fifth of the land area of the Morianese, in a network of properties that was visibly scattered all over its area, as well as outside it, in Sesto and Dardagna.[2] This percentage is not overwhelming, but it is high. No other owner, lay or ecclesiastical, came anywhere near it. Even put together, the dozen and more churches whose properties we know of in the territory never owned more than the bishop.[3] And substantial lay owners were still less in evidence. The richest local owners only had a few tenant houses apiece, as we shall see, and the diocesan aristocracy is almost entirely invisible in the texts; the Montemagno, whose centre in Mammoli adjoined and indeed threatened the Morianese, are the only exceptions, and they are not extensively attested either.

This episcopal hegemony cannot have been chance. Elsewhere in the diocese, bishops leased a high percentage of their estates and their tithes to lay lords in the tenth and eleventh centuries. But they never leased Moriano; nor is the fact surprising, given the importance of the castello there. This was codified as a policy in 1072–3, when Bishop Anselmo I issued a bull listing the (now relatively few) estates and pievi the bishops still possessed—which henceforth they should never lease away, save to direct cultivators—with Moriano prominent on the list; and the policy was maintained, for, while later episcopal lessees in the area did not by any means always cultivate their tenures, they did at least remain resolutely non-aristocratic.[4] The resultant relative absence of large-scale lay

---

[2] These percentages are derived from the complete run of Moriano documents, excluding Sesto and Dardagna. Lands of the episcopal hospital at Ponte a Moriano are counted as the bishop's. The sample size for boundary percentages varies between 100 and 210.

[3] The principal churches owning land in the area were, apart from the cathedral; the cathedral Canonica, S. Ponziano, S. Giustina, Pozzeveri, and S. Pietro in Vaticano. (For S. Pietro, see above, Ch. 3 n. 37, with AAL *M58, *a.*1021, *RCL* 446, *a.*1078, and *Le Liber Censuum*, ed. P. Fabre, L. Duchesne, and G. Mollat (Paris, 1910), ii. 92–3, *a.*1070/1.)

[4] The Montemagno and their Fralminghi cousins are documented in Moriano in Barsocchini 1584, ASL i. 62 (*a.*1025), AAL +P79 (*a.*1062), +K75 (*a.*1072, Gemignani 274), +K16 (*a.*1075–80), *RCL* 409, 446 (*a.*1075–8), AAL ++B59 (*a.*1225). See C. J. Wickham, 'Economia e società rurale', in A. Spicciani and C. Violante (eds.), *Sant'Anselmo* (Rome, 1992), 391–422. Other isolated examples of substantial owners include AAL *M7 and AE5

landholding is in sharp contrast to nearby villages like Marlia, and is, for that matter, lower than in Dardagna in the north of the pieve of Moriano.[5] The bishop thus had no rivals as local landholders at all, until city owners began to acquire land in the area from the 1180s.

Most of the land in Moriano was owned by local medium and small owners, in fact. They were not necessarily beholden to the bishop, but many of them were. It is a common pattern, in the fragmented landowning environments of Tuscany, for landowners at all levels to hold much of their property in lease from others, sometimes in units as small as a single field. If the bishop held a fifth of the Morianese, he could certainly have had as tenants, either directly or indirectly, well over a fifth of its inhabitants. And it can be shown that he did. We have two particularly important texts from the early twelfth century, a list of 57 episcopal fiefs (the word *feudum* here being probably just a recent term for what in the eleventh century had been called long-term leases, *libelli*) and their holders in Moriano dating from 1112–18; and a list of the 293 oath-swearers of the commune of Moriano, dating from 1121, which is likely to be a nearly complete list of the adult males of the locality. Both will recur as essential points of reference, both in this chapter and the next. As sources, they back each other up; and, as a pair, they shed a good deal of light on episcopal landowning.

The 57 fief-holders do not all appear in the oath, but a minimum of 20 certainly do, and others, less securely identifiable, must do as well. They were, that is to say, largely living in Moriano itself, and they do not appear anywhere else in the diocese. They all held fiefs in the form of rents, i.e. the right to receive quantities of produce due from cultivators of the bishop's lands in Moriano, in 104 units. These units did not all correspond to a tenant holding; indeed, few of them did. Where we know the names of the cultivators, they sometimes appear in more than one fief, and sometimes themselves as holders of other rents in fief (occasionally, most remarkably, of their own rent); the interconnection and complexity of local landholding is already extremely visible, even in this one text. If we take account of people appearing more than once, and

(*a.*1080); see below, Ch. 5 n. 20, for owners after 1190. Anselmo I's bull on episcopal lands is Barsocchini 1795; the northern part of the pieve of Moriano (i.e. north of the castle) had however been leased out in 988 (Barsocchini 1628), and was not reclaimed by the bishops until 1119 (AAL +H31).

[5] For Marlia, see above, Ch. 2 nn. 39, 40; for Dardagna and Sesto landowning, Barsocchini 1628, *RCL* 156 (*a.*1035: the Porcaresi in Sesto), AAL +H31 (*a.*1119), +E83, A40, G75, ++B30 (all 1125), *RCL* 1042 (*a.*1148).

exclude people from outside the strict area of Vico and Castro Moriano, then, adding together fief-holders and cultivators, we come to a figure of about 100 families, well over a third of the total number in the Morianese (see below, p. 110). And this is from only a proportion of the bishop's land in the area, for it is not to be supposed that he gave all his property away in these small local fiefs: the gross totals of rents in the fief list might make one guess that he had enfeoffed between a sixth and a third of it.[6] The rest of it was presumably still leased away directly, rather than through the ambiguous mediation of the fief; we have, indeed, some of the leases.[7] The lessees will often have been the same people who appear as fief-holders or cultivators, but presumably not always; even if we are cautious, and only assume that we could add on half as many names again, the end result of these speculations would be that a good half of the population of the Morianese might have been in some way the bishop's dependants, and the proportion could well be somewhat higher.

The breadth of the relationship between the bishop and the Morianesi —and it was certainly very broad, no matter how we calculate it—is important, and will underpin much of what follows. It must have been a deliberate choice by the bishops, and, to some extent, by the Morianesi too. I conclude that the bishops pursued this policy deliberately, because there were certainly more financially advantageous ways of exploiting property than by enfeoffing a substantial section of it for what were certainly low and sometimes probably recognitive rents; but, conversely, if the aim was to gain a political advantage from such enfeoffments, it is striking that the bishops here chose local medium landowners and even cultivators as their dependants, and not the aristocrats and city notables normal in such cessions elsewhere in the diocese. What this means we shall

---

[6] Fief list: AAL A99. Oath: see below, n. 15. The date of A99 is established by references in the main text to fiefs granted by Bishop Rodolfo (ruled 1112–18), and by a reference to changes made by his successor Benedetto in a later addition to the text (see below, n. 17). It covered fiefs from Valle Buia, Dardagna, and Sesto, not just Vico and Castro Moriano; my estimate, based on the names in the oath and other contemporary texts, is that a third of the people and lands cited were outside Moriano as narrowly defined. The total renders from cultivators listed in the fief list come to 80 *solidi*, 228$^{1}/_{2}$ *stai* of grain, 637 *stai* of new wine, 4 *stai* of chestnuts, and a few assorted renders. I estimate that this represents the equivalent of the rentals of between 10 and 20 tenant holdings. If the bishop's lands were a fifth of the Morianese, this latter would represent 50 or so full holdings on my estimates for the total population of the area (below, p. 110); 10–20 holdings is between a fifth and a third of this. These figures are of course totally speculative—quite apart from being spuriously exact, for land was far too fragmented to have been really held in this way.

[7] The only leases roughly contemporary with the fief list, AAL *M49 (*a.*1105), ++A20 (*a.*1115), the first to cultivators, the second not, are not on the list, even though the tenants are in the 1121 oath. For later leases, see next n. For fiefs, see below, pp. 118–19.

see later (below, p. 119). This choice of local social relationships over economic advantage went together, in the Morianese at least, with an extremely unadventurous tradition of episcopal estate management; the bishop was late into oil cash cropping, in particular, and less systematic about it in our period than either lay landowners or other churches (Pozzeveri and S. Ponziano were particularly obviously entrepreneurial).[8] But the bishop still owned a fifth of the land, and his gross rent was considerable. His castle and its warehouses were the agrarian focus of the Morianese, and indeed beyond, as far as Diecimo, and his *castaldiones* and *villicarii* important men.[9] This land was both the social and the economic basis for a firm territorial signoria, at least in principle.

The signorial territory of the bishop of Lucca in Moriano is first documented in a well-known text from the years 1075–80. In it, Bishop

[8] Episcopal rents, 1115–1225: AAL *H46 (*a.*1131), *C84 (*a.*1132), AE80 (*a.*1145), ++D24 (*a.*1149), *F30 with *K85 (*a.*1149), +L37 (*a.*1156), ++P29 (*a.*1165), *E71 (*a.*1175), ++B44 (*a.*1179, oil rent), ++P30 (*a.*1182), ++R26 (*a.*1187), AD46 (*a.*1189, oil rent), ++P26 (*a.*1192, oil rent), ++D34 (*a.*1195), ++Q3 (*a.*1214), *M29 (*a.*1216), A98 (*a.*1217), ++S6 (*a.*1223), ++R81 (*a.*1224), *N81 (*a.*1225, oil rent), ++B59 (*a.*1225). Given the total number of episcopal documents, these texts—not all anyway leases to cultivators—are not in reality so very numerous, which in itself argues for a relatively stable episcopal estate management. Only three of the texts—those for 1149, 1179, and 1214—are the buying of increases or conversions (from money to kind) of rents in leases. In the Valle Buia area, which the bishop had actually had cleared in 1068–72 (above, p. 49), rents had begun in money, and were still in money in 1195 (++D34). In the 13th cent., these new features did become more common on the episcopal estates in the diocese (Osheim, *Italian Lordship*, 103–5; see also the oil in a 1256 episcopal rent list from Moriano, AAL ++A93, in P. Guidi and E. Pellegrinetti (eds.), *Inventari* (Rome, 1921), 49–52), but nothing like on the level of landlords elsewhere in the Lucchesia or, by now, even bishops elsewhere (G. W. Dameron, *Episcopal Power and Florentine Society, 1100–1320* (Cambridge, Mass., 1991), 93–140). But Lucchese rents were already mostly in kind, even on the episcopal estates, unlike in most of Tuscany (above, pp. 19–20; A. Esch, 'Lucca im 12. Jahrhundert', Habilitationsschrift, University of Göttingen, 1974, ch. 1). Other church leases are: *RCL* 646 (*a.*1104), 654, 936, 1440, 1492, 1541, ACL M184 (*a.*1201), F123 and F132 (*a.*1206), F140 (*a.*1208), mostly Pozzeveri leases, and from the first mostly involving rents in oil; ASL ii. 167 (*a.*1105), 460, 579, S. Ponziano 6 febb. 1188, SMFP 13 ott. 1189, S. Giustina 23 febb. 1190, S. Giovanni 5 nov. 1193, S. Ponziano 28 ago. 1196, 6 apr. 1202, SMFP 8 febb. 1209, S. Ponziano 22 nov. 1211, SMFP 13 apr. 1213, 15 mar. 1215, 25 mar. 1223, again privileging oil (and wine). For lay leases, see Ch. 5 n. 22; here, oil rents tended to be on land owned by city-dwellers.

[9] *Castaldi(ones)*—also, variously, *missi, villicarii, massarii, vicecomites*: Inghizo di Marco in 1014 (AAL *M61), Angelo in 1121 (+L91—very low down on the list, so he may not have been a *castaldo* for the bishop), Rodolfino and Martinello in 1146 (++D50), Rolandino in 1179 (++B44), Riccardo di Ubertello in 1187–9 (++R26, ++T99, AD49), Paganello di Malazano in 1216–18 (*M29, ++I22, +E96, in the second of which he is enfeoffed with the role for life), Moricone di Ubertello in 1225 (+B59). In 1141 the *castaldio* had common rights in Moriano in fief from the bishop: ACL Fondo Martini 40 (22 mar. 1141, Guidoni 60). See, in general, Osheim, *Italian Lordship*, 39–41.

Anselmo II established the boundaries of the 'districtus et iudicaria de castello et curte de Moriano' against the claims of Itta, widow of Ildebrando di Guido of the Montemagno family, who controlled the *districtus et iudicaria* of nearby Mammoli. The Mammoli signoria must have been small, and probably recent; nor is its jurisdiction explicitly referred to again in the next century and a half. But this may have been simply the result of Anselmo's political success: in an apparently informal tribunal, but nevertheless in the presence of at least fifteen men, mostly important city laymen and ecclesiastics, Anselmo had three elderly locals witness in his favour: they testified that his castello controlled the *districtus* of the four *villae* of S. Stefano, S. Lorenzo, S. Angelo, and S. Quirico, i.e. the area of Castro and Vico Moriano, and that only the *manentes* (quasi-servile tenants: see below, p. 109) of the Montemagno in these villages were under the jurisdiction of the latter. This text contains the first references in the Lucchesia to any form of private judicial rights over a whole territory, and appears in the first decade in which signorial jurisdiction is at all common in Tuscany.[10] Anselmo's old men none the less claimed that episcopal judicial rights had been recognized by all the inhabitants of the four villages 'ab antiquis temporibus': that in living memory (or, at least, for the legal limit of thirty years) not only episcopal tenants but everyone else in the Morianese owed justice to the bishop.

Anselmo's claim cannot have been entirely true. Only fifteen or so years before, in 1059, Marquis Godfrey had heard a plea in the public tribunal in Lucca by the monastery of S. Giustina against a lay family for two tenant-houses and other land in Moriano, without any reference to the bishop. The castello of Moriano had been built by 915 (see above, p. 62), and was the only castello the bishops built in the Sei Miglia, but the marquises of Tuscany had never given much political space to the bishops of Lucca, and would certainly never have given them territorial rights over such a strongpoint; indeed, they did not for a long time make such cessions of private judicial powers to anyone in Tuscany, and only when marchesal politics began to weaken, from the 1070s onwards, did even counts begin to claim them for themselves. It is thus unlikely that the

---

[10] AAL +K16; the edition in Bertini, *Appendice* 84, is incomplete, and makes the text needlessly incoherent. The text is undated, but it must predate Anselmo's expulsion from Lucca in 1080, and postdate 1075, for Ildebrando di Guido was alive in that year (*RCL* 409). The Mammoli signoria was certainly recent, and may have been restricted to the lands of the Montemagno—i.e. not fully established as a territory. For refs., see Ch. 3 n. 39; it had its own measures in 1105 (*RCL* 654)—cf. below, n. 14. For the relationship between +K16, local politics, and the development of signorial rights, see Wickham, 'Economia e società rurale'.

bishops got a formal grant of Moriano from the marquises; and, anyway, Anselmo cited no document ceding these rights, which he certainly would have done had it existed.[11] The most probable alternative is that his claim for a territorial signoria in Moriano was a *de facto* development, and almost certainly a very recent one, for, as already stated, it is the first reference to territorial signorial rights anywhere in the diocese. It was probably no more firmly based than the claims of the Montemagno, except in that it was built on a far more extensive landed base, some 20 per cent of the total territory of the signoria.

Exactly how the networks of long-standing proprietorial jurisdiction over landed estates meshed with the disintegrating structures of public justice to create individual signorial territories cannot be easily followed anywhere in Italy; how it happened here is equally invisible.[12] But a recent date for such an informal development is important, for it shows that episcopal power was accepted very fast, and largely without difficulty, well beyond the tenants of the bishop's lands. The Morianesi may have feared the Montemagno in Mammoli more than they did the bishop, while recognizing that in the new political situation they were likely to end up with one or the other. Hence, or otherwise, they were soon to be aligned politically with the bishop, too, for Moriano supported Anselmo II in the civil wars of the 1080s; the *Morianenses* (or *castrenses*) held an imperial and Lucchese army back from taking the castello in 1081-2, and the clerics of Sesto were prepared to go to prison on Anselmo's behalf. It must have been largely because of this support, as well as through the maintenance of the castello in episcopal hands, that the signorial territory survived at all in the face of city hostility, summed up by Henry IV's diploma to Lucca in 1081 abolishing all castles and private jurisdictions in the Sei Miglia. The return of a 'legitimate', i.e. papally approved, bishop, which was delayed until Rangerio's arrival in 1097, may well have been accompanied with negotiations that recognized Moriano's anomalous signorial status; something of the kind should at any rate be assumed, for the

---

[11] R. Volpini, 'Placiti', in P. Zerbi (ed.), *Contributi dell'Istituto di storia medioevale*, iii (Milan, 1975), n. 39 for 1059. General contexts for marchesal politics: H. M. Schwarzmaier, *Lucca* (Tübingen, 1972), 253-60, 322-34; M. Nobili, 'Dominazioni marchionali', in *Atti della VIII settimana di studio* (Milan, 1980), 235-58; C. J. Wickham, *The Mountains and the City* (Oxford, 1988), 110-12. Even the bishops of Arezzo, very independent political figures, were only counts from the 1050s, although they ran courts from *c.*1010: J.-P. Delumeau, 'L'Exercice de la justice', *Mélanges de L'Ecole française de Rome*, 90 (1978), 578-85. Osheim, *Italian Lordship*, 53 ff., does not distinguish sufficiently between land and judicial rights in his account of the origins of the episcopal *iura* over Moriano and elsewhere.

[12] For bibliography, see Wickham, *Mountains*, 105-8; see further below, n. 24.

territory was for the most part recognized by the city thereafter.[13] The Moriano siege was thus a decisive event in the history of the *iura*: it was the basis for the survival of the signoria, as well as the moment of the crystallization of local political identity, behind the bishop and against the city, that would underlie the early appearance of the commune. But how much power the bishops really held in Moriano as local *signori* in the next 150 years or so is another matter. We have the bishop's documents, which ought to refer to such power if any texts do; but they are at best infrequent as attestations of episcopal control. The bishops were certainly prominent in the area; they had a *palatium* in the castle and could often be found holding court there, with local Morianese followers in attendance. The area of their signoria even expanded, to include Sesto and Aquilea, at some time between 1121 and 1155, possibly as an imperial cession (Frederick Barbarossa certainly ratified it, in 1164). The content of their power, as revealed in the documents, can be characterized under three headings: political loyalty, justice, and powers over common rights. Let us look at each in turn, to see how strong, and onerous, they actually were.[14]

Loyalty to the bishop was expressed, at its most formal level, through collective oaths. We have the texts of two for Moriano, from 1121 and 1159 (the latter including Aquilea as well), but there were evidently,

---

[13] Rangerio, *Vita Anselmi lucensis*, ed. E. Sackur, G. Schwartz, and B. Schmeidler, in *MGH, Scriptores*, xxx. 2 (Leipzig, 1934) ll. 4857–5010, 5177–5253; *MGH, Heinrici IV Dipl.*, ed. D. von Gladiss (Weimar, 1952–3), n. 334.

[14] For the *palatium* and the bishop, see Ch. 3 n. 40. The 1121 oath, AAL +L91, only contained men from Vico and Castro Moriano, since fief-holders from Sesto listed in A99, the 1112–18 fief-list, do not appear in it. (++A20, *a.*1115, seems however to show episcopal rights over the river-bank up to Sesto.) The *iura* boundary included both Sesto and Aquilea in 1164 (*MGH, Friderici I Dipl.*, ed. H. Appelt (Hanover, 1975–90), n. 430; see also above, Ch. 3 n. 43); that Aquilea was already part of the episcopal signoria in 1155 is implied by a text for Marlia (+K46), presumably dealing with Aquilea landowners, which has a penal clause linking 'pena episcopi . . . et consules de Aquilegia'—cf. below, n. 22, for Moriano—and when the men of Aquilea swore oaths to the bishop in 1159 they were exactly parallel to these of the Morianesi (++B36). Another aspect of the episcopal signoria was local weights and measures, which, though not an infallible sign of a signorial territory, were most commonly to be found in them. Already in 955 (Barsocchini 1365) there was a Moriano *staio* for grain; in the early 12th cent. the local *staio* for grain and wine, together with the *libbra* for oil, appear with the first systematic rents in kind in Moriano (ASL ii. 167, *a.*1105; RCL 702, *a.*1111; AAL ++A20, *a.*1115), and are frequently referred to thereafter. This is unusual for the Sei Miglia; although local measures did exist elsewhere in the plain, they were much less common in documents, and Lucchese measures were normal. In Moriano there was, however, a sharp shift in the 1180s: RCL 1492 (*a.*1183) is the last reference in the century to local measures, and those for the city are henceforth almost the only ones cited; Moriano measures, when they appear, as in AAL *K85 (*a.*1232), are isolated.

from casual references, many more; they probably occurred collectively at every episcopal succession, and were individually sworn (as it appears from the 1159 text) at the age of majority of every male inhabitant. The 1121 text includes the already mentioned list of the 293 free adult laymen living in Moriano. This may be the first that was exacted, for such formal and collective re-enactments of private relationships are not a prominent part of eleventh-century politics. It certainly had a specific political context, for it is part of a series of oaths that Bishop Benedetto (1118–28) exacted from various centres of his *districtus* in the Lucchesia, along with Villa Basilica (1121), Vallico (1122), S. Maria a Monte (1123), and others, apparently as a response to the rapid development of the city commune, which is first documented, as we have seen, in 1119–20: Benedetto needed as ceremonial a recognition of his signorial rights as he could manage in a time of city affirmation, not least in Moriano, his largest territory in the Sei Miglia, and successive bishops maintained the tradition.[15] Benedetto, in fact, perhaps more than any other twelfth-century bishop, was responsible for re-establishing a certain political centrality for his office. His episcopate saw a sharp increase in gifts to the bishop, notably by aristocrats, which reached the highest level since the time of Anselmo I fifty years before; and he had close political links with the commune, for city consuls appeared at his court as early as 1119, and were present at Moriano in 1121 as well.[16]

Inside Moriano, Benedetto probably increased his influence, too, as we can infer from the fief list. This document, originally compiled under

---

[15] Moriano oaths: AAL +L91 (a.1121; copies in +C23, and Libro della Croce, pp. 70–1; partial edn., Bertini, *Appendice* 99); ++B36 (a.1159). The text of +L91 states that the oath was void if Benedetto's successors did not exact it; by 1223 (AB50) it was regarded as normal that it should be sworn at each episcopal succession. It is clear that the bishop swore a set of counter-obligations to his subjects; those for Diecimo in the Val di Serchio in 1146 (+R9) and for Aquilea in 1191 (*A22) show that they consisted principally of promises not to alienate the signoria or subject its inhabitants to anyone else. For other oaths in the 1120s, see the 14th-cent. copies in the Libro della Croce, pp. 70–2; judging by the texts of the Moriano oath, they are fairly accurate. For Vallico, see ++D40 (a.1122) and Wickham, *Mountains*, 118–20. The oaths do not seem to have been hidden oaths to the city commune; they were from episcopal castles. They may have been intended to buttress the bishop *vis-à-vis* not only the city commune, but also local aristocratic families and indeed, not least, Marquis Conrad, with whom the bishop was disputing the large Cadolingi inheritance in the diocese (see R. Pescaglini Monti, 'Le vicende politiche,' in C. Violante and A. Spicciani (eds.), *Pescia e la Valdinievole* (Pisa, 1995), 57–87).

[16] AAL ++P99 (a.1119, ed. T. Blomquist and D. Osheim, 'The First Consuls at Lucca', *Actum luce*, 7 (1978), 31–8), +L91 (a.1121) for the city consuls; Osheim, *Italian Lordship*, 131–5, for the gifts, which were beginning under Rodolfo, and which were boosted dramatically by the Cadolingi inheritance, which came into the bishops' hands in the years following 1113.

Bishop Rodolfo (1112–18) as a simple and apparently uncontroversial list of the bishop's feudatories, was corrected and updated by a writer who claimed that they had all held their fiefs 'iniuste et violenter', until, under Benedetto, they began to fulfil their obligations to the cathedral; the new bishop evidently interpreted these obligations more strictly than in Rodolfo's time, and managed to exact them as well.[17] Benedetto was none the less close to the Morianesi, or some of them, for several of its notables were his immediate dependants; it is, furthermore, significant that his reaffirmation of power was not at all at the expense of the collective organization of the locality, for the 1121 oath explicitly recognizes the status of the commune as well (see below, pp. 98–9). The commune of Moriano in no way derived from any environment of hostility to, or defiance of, the bishop, that is to say; it would be fairer to argue that one context for its appearance was the support (or acquiescence) by the Morianesi for an expansion in episcopal authority, both locally and regionally.

The loyalty oaths for Moriano, and indeed elsewhere, have similar texts. Their participants had each to swear not to plot against the bishop's rights and properties (particularly his castles), or his person or those of his representatives, or aid anyone who so plotted and so on; and also to respect the bishop's justice. These oaths were not exclusive of all other loyalties. There is no doubt that rights of the city in Moriano, as part of the Sei Miglia, existed, for in 1159 the oath for Moriano and Aquilea explicitly excepted the city commune from the obligation of the inhabitants to go to war for the bishop against everyone. (The bishop of Lucca did get them out to fight, on occasion, for we know that in 1218 the men of Aquilea fought against Castiglione di Garfagnana for him—and, by extension, for the city; the bishop had to pay their expenses.) But conversely, oaths to the city commune, which were certainly exacted by the 1180s, excepted the rights of the bishop, as one can see from a court case of 1229; and these exceptions were by no means empty. Indeed, from perhaps 1160–1, as imperial confirmations of 1185 and 1209 show, the men of Moriano, as the bishop's dependants, were formally exempt from most direct city taxes and public services, and, when civic obligations steadily increased into the thirteenth century, these privileges would have been ever more

---

[17] AAL A99; see n. 6 for the date. The document has two hands. One gives the basic text, entitled *Breve recordationis de curte de Moriano*, and ends the list 'Qui ssti homines sup°[. . .] habent [. . .] de corte de Morriano', without further comment. The second goes through the main text correcting the Latin, and then adds four names and the comments about Benedetto at the bottom. Neither writer lists what people actually owed for their fiefs: see below, pp. 118–19. Rodolfo, incidentally, bought back fiefs as well, as in Barsocchini 1811 (*a.*1117) for Dardagna, a fief not mentioned in the list.

valuable to the Morianesi.[18] The Morianesi seem to have valued them, too; they certainly seldom contested them. We only see them reacting differently in one text, a dispute from 1192, in which the commune of Moriano appealed an unpaid debt from the bishop to the city courts; the latter, doubtless with some glee, sequestered all episcopal rights in Moriano until the bishop paid up. But the incident left no lasting effect, either in city communal influence in the territory or in the relationship between the rural commune and the bishop. The *status quo* between the city, the bishop, and the Morianesi remained stable until the late thirteenth century. Both the bishop and the city wanted recognition from the other of their authority in the area, and both got it; the city, which certainly had the strength to override episcopal privileges, as yet rarely chose to do so. Only in the 1270s did the Lucchesi begin to exact city taxation in Moriano, which was followed in 1287 by the bishop's recognition that communal regulations for the feeding of the city could apply to the area; on the legal level, too, the city commune formally contested the existence of the *iura* at Moriano in a series of disputes between 1276 and 1309. But the bishop won these disputes, both in the city courts and in front of the pope; the Morianesi ended up paying some city taxes, but not all of them, and this position was, although not without trouble, maintained in the years that followed.[19]

These tax privileges give a certain concreteness to the issue of loyalty. However hostile the Morianesi may on occasion have been to the highhandedness of the bishop in the exercise of his signorial rights, they were never tempted to try to escape the signoria altogether, for the city would

[18] Castiglione war: AAL +E96 (*a.*1218): cf. *F20 (*a.*1227), a curious text that details the coercive measures the city commune tried to use to get the men from the *iura* to settle Castiglione, as well as the bishop's probably successful defence of his own dependants. The context was the city wars in the Garfagnana: see *Tholomei Lucensis Annales*, ed. B. Schmeidler, *MGH, SRG*, NS 8 (Berlin, 1955), 98, 104, 112, and C. de Stefani, 'Storia dei comuni di Garfagnana', *Atti e memorie*, 7 ser. 2 (1925), 13–66. Rights of city and bishop: K. F. Stumpf, *Acta imperii* (Innsbruck, 1865–81), 168 (*a.*1185, ed. from AAL Libro della Croce, p. 31: it says the exemptions are valid for all exactions already in existence for 25 years), 178 (*a.*1186, ed. from Libro della Croce, p. 14); E. Winkelmann, *Acta imperii inedita* (Innsbruck, 1880–5), i, n. 30 (*a.*1209, Libro della Croce, p. 15); AAL *O21 (*a.*1229). For increasing civic direct taxation, see E. Fiumi, 'Sui rapporti economici', *Archivio storico italiano*, 114 (1956), 25–38; id., 'L'imposta diretta', in *Studi in onore di Armando Sapori* (Milan, 1957), 329–55; A. I. Pini, *Città, comuni e corporazioni* (Bologna, 1986), 104–8, 113–16; D. Herlihy, 'Direct and Indirect Taxation', in *Finances et comptabilités urbaines* (Brussels, 1964), 385–97.
[19] AAL +B28 (*a.*1192: it is cancelled with a knife cross, indicating that the bishop paid up, probably pretty soon); for the contests after 1250 see Osheim, *Italian Lordship*, 73–83, who shows how stable the partially exempt status of Moriano really remained.

have been far more exacting. This would be a natural limit to their preparedness to play the bishop off against the city as in 1192, something most episcopal communes did when they could. The political situation in Moriano was evidently very different from that in the tense villages of the Fiorentino, where, as Dameron has shown, rural communes sometimes actually formed in the decades after 1200 to appeal (unsuccessfully) to the city of Florence against the signorial and proprietorial exactions of the bishop.[20] Loyalty to the bishop of Lucca was not much of a problem for the inhabitants of Moriano.

Episcopal justice was a more serious obligation, and indeed is the most explicitly documented in the texts, as it is in most signorie. This documentation is ambiguous, however. There are very few charters detailing the workings of the signorial courts of the bishop, and none before the 1170s. This is not that surprising, given the fact that few such texts survive from any signoria; indeed, for the first half of the twelfth century there are very few court cases even from city tribunals.[21] But one can at least say that in the spheres of justice for which court records survive in our period—mostly civil actions over property rights—the bishop by no means had a monopoly of jurisdiction in Moriano. The first references we have to episcopal powers over property jurisdiction are in the standard penal clauses at the end of charters, which begin to add to traditional money sanctions an unspecified *pena episcopi* from 1146 onwards; there are a dozen more such references to the bishop's *pena* in the next eighty years. Most of these also add the *pena* of the consuls of the city courts as well, however, and even that of the consuls of Moriano; and texts that only cite the city consuls certainly outnumber those that cite the bishop. Whatever these sanction clauses really meant in practice, they give no sign that the bishop had any monopoly over local fines in this field.[22]

The court cases for which there are records in Moriano in the half-century after 1175 confirm this pattern. In 1175 the bishop, in dispute with some lay owners over land in Moriano, put the matter to the arbitration

---

[20] See below, pp. 224–6.

[21] For signorial tribunals, see Wickham, 'Economia e società rurale', n. 40. The first consular case surviving from Lucca is ASL ii. 452 from 1136; there are another 9 before 1151, as opposed to nearly 180 from the second half of the century.

[22] *Pena episcopi*: RCL 1011, 1078, 1100, 1102, 1132–3 (*a.*1146, 1152–5); AAL ++K35 (*a.*1150), ++P27 (*a.*1153), ACL Fondo Martini 19 genn. 1152; RCL 1492 (*a.*1183), ASL Spedale 18 mar. 1192, ACL F140 (*a.*1208), AAL ++B59 (*a.*1225, a ref. to the *curia domini episcopi*). One should add to this two references to the *pena* of the local signoria, +G99 (*a.*1141), *in pena illius signoratichi qui terram de Moriano pro tempore distringit*, and AL32 (*a.*1188) for the *pena* of the local *potestas*.

of the Moriano consuls, who duly split the land between them, though not before taking the advice of two members of the Avvocati family, who were major urban aristocrats, city officials, and episcopal advocates. This arrangement was so *ad hoc* that it looks as if there were as yet no clearly recognized procedures for deciding on land disputes locally. They would appear: in 1216 and 1217 three Moriano consuls judged disputes, over debts and rents owed to the bishop, using procedures clearly borrowed from the city courts, 'pro eorum officio consolatus et ex auctoritate et iurisdictione quas habebant pro comuni de Moriano et a Lucano episcopo et episcopatu'; clearly episcopal justice was run directly by the rural commune here, though probably up to half its profits went back to the bishop, judging by other texts. But even then the pattern of local land disputing was imperfect: similar rent disputes of 1183, 1197, and 1217, with the bishop as a party in each case, were decided by the city courts, with no reference to episcopal or local communal jurisdiction at all: it looks indeed as if it was up to the parties to decide whom to go to.[23]

It must be remembered, of course, that most disputes were not over land. The great bulk of local regulations, which begin to appear in the twelfth century and increase geometrically in future centuries, are for crimes of violence. They are to be found in Moriano from the first communal oath of 1121, which demanded from oath-takers that they should not commit theft, robbery, arson, or wanton damage in the *curtis* or the two castelli of Moriano; subsequent oaths include such requirements too. This was probably the main meat of the bishop's *placitum* that is safeguarded in the formulae of many formal oaths and agreements; it went back a long way, to the immunitarian jurisdictions over landed property of the Carolingian period, out of which indeed, in Moriano, the *iura* probably largely developed.[24] But, at least after 1121, it is important that our main

---

[23] AAL *E35 (copy *E71, *a.*1175), *R20 (*a.*1183), *K85 (*a.*1196 *recte* 1197), *M29 (*a.*1216), ++P78 (*a.*1217), A98 (*a.*1217). For the division of fines, see AB50 (*a.*1223); cf. D. Corsi, 'Il "breve" dei consoli', *Atti dell'Accademia lucchese*, NS 10 (1959), 171, for S. Maria a Monte, and below, pp. 103, 175. It may be that the signoria only had full jurisdiction when inhabitants of Moriano were the parties, leaving city-dwellers to the city; these cases do not force that conclusion, but do not disprove it either. If this was so, however, it was a notable weakening of episcopal authority, and would have become more so as city landowning increased (below, p. 128). These are not the only cases from Moriano, but the bishop in cases against the local commune in 1141 and 1179 clearly preferred private arbitration to anyone's jurisdiction (ACL Fondo Martini 40, ed. Guidoni, 60; AAL A47); in other cases again, when the decision came up before the city court, the bishop's representatives simply did not turn up, which may well reflect arguments about jurisdiction (++P26, +B28, *a.*1192; +N81, *a.*1205).

[24] Bishop's *placitum* or legal rights safeguarded: AAL ++B36 (*a.*1159), ++A98 (*c.*1170), see below, pp. 247–8), *A22 (*a.*1191), +E96 (*a.*1218). The link with Carolingian proprietorial justice (for which see, classically, P. Vaccari, *La territorialità* (2nd edn., Milan, 1963),

source for the regulation of violent crime is not the bishop at all, but the rural commune. In *c.*1170 we have our first set of communal regulations for Moriano (or, indeed, anywhere in the Lucchesia); they barely mention the bishop, except in a formula at the end. In 1223 an episcopal document creating the commune of Sesto makes it clear that the consuls of Moriano (and, in future, Sesto) already dealt with all local disputes except homicide, bloodshed, perjury, adultery, and treason, and kept over half the proceeds; the bishop judged only these five major felonies, as well as acting as a court of appeal if any *vicinus* sought it.[25] The document is important, for it shows that the episcopal *iura* included high justice, which not every signoria did, especially so close to a city; but it also shows that the daily affairs of Moriano were run by its inhabitants, and not by the bishop at all. We shall come back to it in that context.

A standard image of the rights of rural communes over justice is that they were taken over from the local lord who previously controlled them, with greater or lesser difficulty. But in Moriano it is striking that all our information about justice beyond the most superficial shows the bishop as developing his signorial rights alongside and through the rural commune. The signoria seems to have gained an organized structure *at the same time as* the commune, the one developing in a dialectical relationship with the other; there is no sign that the commune's judicial rights were in opposition to those of the bishop, and it may be doubted if one could have existed without the other. Indeed, there is barely any sign of another rural commune in the Sei Miglia with the judicial authority the consuls of Moriano had (for one exception, see below, p. 169); the consuls needed the special situation of the signoria, as the bishop needed the consuls. The main sticking-point will have undoubtedly been how to share out the fines and other profits of justice, but that seems to have been largely sorted out by 1223. This close association between commune

6–14, 45–64) is at least terminological: in 1075–80 (AAL +K16) the Morianesi had to 'legem et iustitiam facere' to the bishop, and this precise phrase is normal in 9th-cent. leases as well: see e.g. Wickham, *Mountains*, 69 n. See further, now, Tirelli, 'Vescovato di Lucca', 92–6, 105–18, who gives an important and careful analysis of how the bishop's signorial rights could develop from Carolingian justice, buttressed by an immunity granted by Otto II to the bishop in 980. He gets no further on how these powers over properties developed into the territorial jurisdiction over Moriano, however. His specific discussions of Moriano, ibid. 101–5, 118–22, do not take into account all the documentation.

[25] For 1170, AAL ++A98 (see below, pp. 247–8); for 1223, AB50 (see below, pp. 103–4); proceeds of justice were also shared, without details, in +E96 (*a.*1218) for Aquilea. It may be that AB50 did not end all potential problems, for in it the bishop claimed bloodshed as an episcopal felony, although the commune of Moriano certainly regarded it as its province in 1170 (++A98).

and signoria is one that can be found elsewhere, too, as we will see. Lords, indeed, usually needed local figures to run their judicial business for them; bishops and aristocrats had better things to do, and even *castaldiones*, local signorial administrators, could not be everywhere at once. Where rural communes, or their leaders, were prepared to co-operate, they could be very useful to rural lords, and could well benefit thereby.[26]

Few communes, however, developed without discord with their lords, over many issues; and even in Moriano the relationship between bishop and local inhabitants was not always harmonious. Who chose the consuls, for example? In 1218 in Aquilea, apparently the bishop did, although in Sesto in 1223 the rights of election certainly lay with the villagers. Behind this could well lie a century of discord; it certainly did elsewhere.[27] The 1192 case mentioned above, when the commune successfully brought in the city, shows that conflict was entirely possible, although we do not know its origin. And we have disputes between bishop and commune about common rights, almost from the start; indeed, most of the references to the commons of the Morianese imply some dispute. In 1141, the commune of Moriano tried unsuccessfully to regain the sheep-pasture dues that it had formerly received from the men of Dardagna (presumably the latter brought their sheep down from the hills to the river marshes in winter), which Bishop Rangerio (1096–1112) had abolished. In 1179, the bishop successfully claimed dues for the woodland and land clearance of a small island in the Serchio, which his opponent said were more properly owed to the communes of Moriano and Saltocchio. Although the bishop won in these two cases, this sort of right seems to have been slowly passing from the bishop to the communes; for the bishop had riverbank rights uncontested in 1115 and perhaps even in 1192, but he certainly recognized that some of them pertained to Moriano and Sesto in 1223. On the other hand, the common rights documented in these texts relate almost entirely to the Serchio and its banks; although these included substantial river tolls at Ponte a Moriano, they were not the major source of wealth in one of the great wine and olive zones in the diocese.[28] The texts at

---

[26] See, for a comparative analysis, below, Ch. 8.

[27] AAL +E96 (*a.*1218), AB50 (*a.*1223). Parallels are too numerous to list, but see below, pp. 140–3, for Tassignano.

[28] ACL Fondo Martini 40 (22 mar. 1141, Guidoni 60), AAL A47 (*a.*1179), ++A20 (*a.*1115), +B28 (*a.*1192), AB50 (*a.*1223). The last two refer to tolls at Ponte a Moriano, for wood and animals; the bishop controlled them in 1192, but in 1223 part at least of the dues went to the communes. The 1141 text does not say where exactly the Dardagna sheep fed, but since the latter area is full of uncultivated hill country it is unlikely that the hill areas of Moriano would have been useful to the men of Dardagna; the marshy lowlands by the river

least show that the bishop's archive kept records of disputes with communes; but they seem to have been over relatively marginal economic resources, not over the major elements of collective life. This is important. The relationship between commune and signoria in Moriano seems, as I have been stressing, to have been relatively easy; there was not much tension, at least over major issues, and one could even argue that the commune was an essential element in the structure of the signoria itself. This is very far from the conflictual model that is usually—and rightly—posited as a major feature of communal development. But in Moriano there was not much real signorial pressure to fight against. In the 170-odd Moriano charters from between 1100 and 1225, in charters of sale (including those of episcopal tenures), gift, lease, and dispute, as well as the oaths and agreements mentioned above, we find no mention of manual labour, guard duty, *albergaria*, cart service, *fodrum*, *datium*, *malus usus*, or any servile duty owed by any inhabitant of Moriano, to the bishop or anyone else. These were the standard dues of Italian signorie; in Moriano, however, if they were exacted—and some dues presumably were—they were not so notable as to be worth mentioning in the sources. That there were quasi-servile tenants (*manentes*) in Moriano at all we only know from the 1075/80 Montemagno agreement, and they were not the bishop's.[29] The profits of justice were the major fiscal preoccupation of the 1223 Sesto charter, and all the signs are that they were the cornerstone of signorial power in the *iura*. They were an important feature of any signoria, of course, but not to the exclusion of everything else; and here they were anyway split roughly evenly with the commune. Apart from this, the bishop claimed some common rights and river tolls (once again split with the communes), and exacted army service, which was presumably an infrequent obligation and would anyway

are the most likely location. (They were probably larger then; there is a whole low area south of S. Cassiano devoid of early microtoponyms. See Map 4.) The bishop's 1179 claims were probably legally correct; he had certainly taken *terraticum* from an *insula* in the 1110s (A99), and he also bought land on a river island off Pettori in the 1150s (below, p. 124).

[29] For terminology, see Vaccari, *Territorialità*, 100–5, 149–53; P. Cammarosano, *Le campagne nell'età comunale* (Turin, 1974), 17–24. For further discussions of signorial dues in the Lucchesia, see the appendix to this chapter, below, pp. 107–9. In Moriano, *manentes* appear in AAL +K16 (*a.*1075–80). The only sign that the bishop could have had similar dependants is AAL AE80 (*a.*1145), where a man renews a customary lease and also pays a substantial entry fine (*servitio*) of 40s.; this *servitio* in other areas can be the commutation of personal obligations (Osheim, *Italian Lordship*, 105–7). But the example is isolated in Moriano. (In Aquilea, there were a few *manentes*, on the other hand: ACL N137, *a.*1202; AAL ++C32, *a.*1248.) See further C. J. Wickham, 'Manentes e diritti signorili', in C. D. Fonseca (ed.), *Società, istituzioni, spiritualità* (Spoleto, 1994), 1067–80.

have been due, outside the *iura*, to the city. That was the sum total of signorial obligations in the documents; apart from these, virtually all the *districtus* of Moriano imposed on its inhabitants was the territorial identity involved in political subjection to episcopal authority and, as the city of Lucca increased its exactions, in the fiscal privileges deriving from it. This territorial identity structured the commune (later, communes) of the area, in whose creation and internal workings, indeed, the bishop and his *castaldio* had some say. But the slow development of communal identity would barely be—did not have to be—at the expense of episcopal power at all.

Two hypotheses follow from this. The first is that the real impact of the bishop on the society of Moriano was less as a signorial lord than as a landowner, owner of by far the largest estate in the area; and, following on from this, that the power of the bishop over his *fideles* in the Morianese was not so much as a ruler or lord, but rather as a rich neighbour and patron, in a traditional pattern of clientelism that goes back at least to the Carolingian period. The second is that the socio-political situation of the Morianese, even at an institutional level, was less atypical of the rest of the Sei Miglia than it looks at first sight; the commune of Moriano was not greatly determined in its formation, either positively or negatively, by the signorial power of the bishop, even though episcopal interest ensured it earlier and better documentation than any other commune in the Sei Miglia. The following chapter will, among other things, develop these hypotheses further.

ii. The commune

Our picture of the origins of the rural commune of Moriano derives mostly from the same documents as that of the signoria, and could almost be read off from my analysis of the latter's development. Not entirely, however: so let us go back to the start, and see how it appears from the other side.

Moriano's commune was not created in 1121; the episcopal oath that is its first documentation, far from constituting it, mentions it almost casually. But the reference is a very clear and significant one: it is to the *communis populus* of Moriano, and any conspiracy or association (*conpagnia*: see below, p. 102) to divide it was put on a par with conspiracy against the bishop. This is the first documented use of the adjective *communis* in this context in the Lucchese countryside, although this is certainly chance; we could scarcely deny the category 'commune' to Villa Basilica, whose pieve (which covered little more than a single village) controlled its own low justice already in 1104, or to S. Maria a Monte, whose inhabitants were acting collectively, with their own representatives, in violence and court action over the boundaries of its common rights in 1120. As with cities, in an environment where public powers were collapsing everywhere, rural communities with a pre-existing identity could easily move in these decades in the direction of a collective self-awareness and control over their own affairs. In these three early cases, we can also hypothesize what their basic structures might have been. Villa Basilica, an isolated centre with few outside landowners, probably owed its cohesion to the importance of its collective economy, for it had long been a major chestnut centre. S. Maria a Monte was already a large and ambitious castello, a strategic outpost of the Lucchesi overlooking major military and trade routes; Osheim has compared it, in the thirteenth century at least, with S. Gimignano, and it was certainly very similar to the military/commercial small towns (*borghi*) which were the first 'rural' communities in Lombardy to appear with communal structures.[30] Moriano, too, had its castello, which was politically important and had recently withstood the siege of 1081–2; indeed, for a decade or more, in defiance of the city, it may have been virtually self-governing, and its collective cohesion inside its signorial territory seems, as I have argued, to have been supported by the bishops. These sorts of patterns, though ill-documented, are not really very difficult to guess at; had they been typical of Lucchese villages, communal development in the area would have been fairly straightforward.

The initial step towards a commune, the recognition of a structured collective interest on the part of a community, is not, however, the only issue in its development that is worth studying; what purpose it actually served for its inhabitants, especially while its institutions and territorial identity slowly crystallized, is important as well. These processes are reasonably clear at Moriano. In 1121 the commune existed; but it is described simply as an indivisible entity. In the list of its members that accompanied the oath, the first names are certainly those of its most prominent men,

---

[30] AAL +L91 (*a*.1121) for Moriano; ++L3 (*a*.1104) for Villa Basilica; ++C75 (*a*.1121; *recte* 1120, for the charter is dated according to Pisan reckoning: see the incomplete edn. in F. Schneider, 'Nachlese in Toscana', *Quellen und Forschungen*, 22 (1930–1), 68) for S. Maria a Monte. For Villa Basilica see C. J. Wickham, 'Aspetti socioeconomici della Valdinievole', in A. Spicciani and C. Violante (eds.), *Allucio da Pescia* (Rome, 1991), 291–2; for S. Maria a Monte see Osheim, *Italian Lordship*, 60–9; cf., for Lombardy, below, pp. 214–15. The word *communis/e* is an adjective or adverb, rather than a noun, in early communal references; it only appears as a noun meaning 'commune' in the second third of the 12th cent. (see O. Banti, ' "Civitas" e "commune" ', now in G. Rossetti (ed.), *Forme di potere e struttura sociale in Italia* (Bologna, 1977), 217–32). If there is an early noun which we could translate as 'commune', it is, significantly, *compagnia/conpagnia*: see below, n. 34.

as we will see (pp. 111–15), who were doubtless in practice its leaders; but they are distinctly not referred to as its explicitly constituted representatives. This is the first development that we can see, for in 1141 the *communis populus* of Moriano did indeed have three representatives who could act for it, at least on an *ad hoc* basis; by 1150, these representatives had come to be called *consules*, a term that was by now spreading from cities to the countryside all over Italy. The *consules* first appear in penal clauses, which refer to the legal penalties due to the 'consules de Moriano que per tempore erit': they were probably already annual, again on the model of the city. It is worth noting that had Moriano not been in the episcopal signoria, which preserved a number of its more public records, these penal clauses would be the first references to the commune: still early by Sei Miglia standards, but not quite so precocious (S. Margherita, a small village, had consuls already in 1148: see below, p. 134). But actually, even more than in the case of the *pena episcopi*, the *pena consulum* is not a regular feature of Moriano documents, and is in fact only known from short periods: 1150–3 and 1179–82 are the most substantial (see below, p. 126).[31] Its appearance probably tells us not that such sanctions were already a right institutionally pertaining to the commune, but rather that the consuls were recognized, at least by some, as a possible choice as guarantors of transactions. None the less, consuls at least were henceforth a fixture, and we occasionally know some of their names, in 1165, *c.*1170, 1175, 1191 (for Aquilea), 1192, 1214, 1216–17, and 1229.[32]

The next documented moment in the development of communal institutions is 1159, when we have a text in which the men of Moriano swear to defend the *castrum* of Aquilea, which the bishop had in the meantime acquired and added to the signorial territory of Moriano; the men of Aquilea presumably swore similarly for Moriano in a parallel text. Here, the

[31] ACL Fondo Martini 40 (*a.*1141, Guidoni 60); AAL ++K35 (*a.*1150), ACL Fondo Martini 19 genn. 1152, *RCL* 1078 (*a.*1152), AAL ++P27, *RCL* 1100, *RCL* 1102 (all *a.*1153), AAL ++B44 (*a.*1179), *RCL* 1465, 1492 (*a.*1182), AAL AL32 (*a.*1188), ASL Spedale 18 mar. 1192; there are no later references than 1192 known to me.

[32] AAL ++P29 (*a.*1165), Brunetto di Dominico; ++A98 (*c.*1170), Rolandino, Ildebrandino, and Gualfredo; *E35, *E71 (*a.*1175), Rolandino di Gerardino and Guarcino di Pietro; *A22 (*a.*1191), Brunicardo di Coltello, Stefano di Piero, and Marco di Passamonte; +B28 (*a.*1192), Manno; ASL Compagnia della Croce 6 febb. 1214, Lamberto di Armanno of Arbusciana and Bonaccorso di Martino; *M29 (apr. 1216) and ++P78 (febb. 1217), Martino di Pandolfino, Albertino de Stabbiano di Rolandino de Rivo, Manno di Gualfredo—their term may have changed in March; *O21 (*a.*1229), Rodolfo di Iacopo. The title of the commune is variable in this period: it is a *comune* in 1159 (++B36) and a *populus* in 1170, but in 1165 Brunetto is consul in the *curtis* of Moriano, linking the commune very clearly to the signoria; in 1217 Martino *et al.* were consuls of the *comune et curia* of Moriano.

777298575466

...

commune is a little more explicit than in the 1121 oath, for Moriano and Aquilea are both called *comune* as a substantive; their inhabitants are, as in 1121, called on to avoid any *conpangia* (*sic*) except *comuniter*. What being a *comune* actually meant in this period is, however, by now clearer as well, for in a text from slightly later (it is an undated *breve*, but probably derives, judging from the names of its consuls, from around 1170) we have what amounts to our first set of communal regulations. This text is in the form of an oath, but this time not to the bishop; it is the oath of 'nos homines de toto districto de Moriano' (this time certainly not including Aquilea), in effect to themselves as a collectivity.[33] As it is the first such text for the diocese, it is edited below in an appendix (pp. 247–8), but it needs to be summarized here as well. The men of Moriano swore that no man from the *districtus* should wound or assault anyone inside the *castrum*, on penalty of life expulsion from the *districtus* by the *consules cum toto populo*. (Whether the *castrum* only means the walled centre here is unclear. Once in the text it certainly does, but elsewhere the word is also used as a metaphor for the *districtus* as a whole.) If any man put his hand on a weapon inside the *confines* of the *castrum*, the takers of the oath, with the consuls, should determine the truth and fine the malefactor 20*s*.: all the oath-takers were held to this unless they were attacked first. If a former inhabitant of Moriano returned to attack any oath-takers, they must aid each other, against a penalty of 100*s*. The consuls, 'cum consilio de quadraginta bonis hominibus', could amend this text, except the *sacramentum de castro*, the oath itself, which was perpetual. Treason to the *populus de Moriano* brought perpetual exile. The three consuls swore to this, and it was provided that future consuls should so swear to their predecessors; the safeguarding of the honour of the bishop was added at the end, almost as an afterthought. More of a real afterthought was, perhaps, the final addition, in the same hand but in a different ink, enacting that any other *compagnia* or oath was to be invalid.

This text tells us more than any other so far about what the Moriano commune was. Not in its provisions, which were common enough in their

---

[33] AAL ++B36 (*a*.1159)—cf. *MGH, Friderici I Dipl.*, n. 430 (*a*.1164) for the signorial boundary; ++A98 (*c*.1170). The latter is undated, and catalogued as 'sec. XII'; it is in a mid 12th-cent. hand. Of the three consuls listed in it, Rolandino, Ildebrandino, and Gualfredo, the first two are not particularly uncommon names, though the third is rather rarer. In 1175, the consular charter (*E35) also has a Rolandino as consul, and witnesses to it include the son of a late Gualfredo and an Ildebrandino di Domenico. The latter (as Aldebrandino, a synonym) also witnesses to the Moriano oath in 1159 (++B36), and must thus have been a person of some influence in the third quarter of the century. Circumstantially, these names tie up, and a date not too long before 1175 seems indicated, to give Gualfredo time to die; I have thus chosen *c*.1170.

tenor (though they were certainly severe: later communal legislation, like early medieval law codes, gives the impression that people wounded each other a lot, and were normally only fined). It is, rather, the sort of community the commune saw itself as being that is significant. It was defined, not by territorial identity, but by participation in an oath—even if it does seem that the oath-takers were expected to be the whole population. Over and over, mutual obligation depends on this oath. The concern with rival *compagniae*, in this text as in 1121 and 1159, is thus explicable: they would be associations of the same type as the commune, and their very existence would threaten it—*compagnia*, in fact, can itself be one of the earliest words for commune, as in Genoa from the 1090s. The episcopal signoria is recognized as sovereign, and its boundaries define the field of interest of the commune, but neither create the commune; only the oath does that. A document of this kind resembles nothing so much as early city communal texts like Bishop Daiberto's arbitration about the height of the towers of Pisa from around 1090, which also rested mutual responsibility entirely on the force of an oath, even if the oath was expected from all Pisans; it was these oaths, which sat at the core of most early city communes, that Volpe and (among others) Cassandro were talking about when they argued whether the commune was initially a private or a public association. We cannot enter into that debate here; nor would it be helpful, particularly in view of the more recent recognition in Italy that, in the world of the twelfth century, public and private are rather difficult to distinguish, and that 'public' power had a lot to do with oaths ever since the Lombard-Carolingian kingdom of Italy.[34] But it does force us to remember that the early city commune was a body of very uncertain legitimacy, even to its own members, and of still less certain institutions. The moral force of oaths, rather than any even nominally institutionalized rules of behaviour, was at the heart of most city governments in Italy until well into the mid-twelfth century; and even the definition of city 'offices' and 'responsibilities' was for long directly dependent on the personal power and interests of the people that filled and fulfilled them. It is this pattern that Moriano was reflecting in 1170, and we should probably not be surprised to see it.

[34] *Compagnia*: Caffaro, *Annali genovesi*, i, ed. L. Tommaso Belgrano (Genoa, 1890), 5–16. Daiberto: G. Rossetti, 'Il lodo del vescovo Daiberto', in *Pisa e la Toscana occidentale*, ii (Pisa, 1991), 25–47. See G. Volpe, 'Questioni fondamentali sull'origine e svolgimento dei comuni italiani', now in his *Medioevo italiano* (Florence, 1961), 87–118; G. Cassandro, 'Un bilancio storiografico', now in G. Rossetti (ed.), *Forme di potere e struttura sociale in Italia* (Bologna, 1977), 153–73. On the contradictory relationship of public and private, see e.g. G. Tabacco, *Egemonie sociali* (Turin, 1979).

Towards the end of the century, however, things would change. The consuls already in 1170 had the right to alter the detail of Moriano's regulations (though not the constituting oath), with advice from forty people—around a seventh of the adult male population; they could, that is to say, in effect legislate. When their position as representatives for the community became more permanent, as references from the 1190s seem to indicate, so the expectations placed upon them became more stable. And in 1216–17, as we have seen, the consuls of Moriano could judge: as bishop's representatives, certainly, but also as communal officials.[35] The office of consul by now involved not only headship of a community and recognition of local influence, but also a set of recognized and defined powers to represent, legislate, judge, and presumably, inside limits, coerce.

The process of institutionalization was complete in Moriano by the 1220s. This we can see clearly enough in the 1223 charter by which the bishop formally split Sesto off from Moriano as a separate commune. Sesto was always somewhat separate from Moriano; it was geographically distinct, and was initially not part of the *districtus* either (see above, p. 66). It was, furthermore, the ecclesiastical centre of the pieve of Moriano, and must have resented its secular marginality. Elsewhere in the Sei Miglia, a centre like Sesto in the late twelfth century would be becoming called a *vicinia* or the like, with its activities focused on its church. The commune of Moriano dominated the formal collective activities of its *districtus*; but in 1187 Sesto is referred to as a *vicinantia* with its own *confines*, making a collective agreement with the episcopal administrator (*villicarius*) to end a dispute, and in 1223 the body the bishop instituted as a commune was already called a *vicinia corporis plebis* (and, for that matter, a *comune et universitas*)—it was, in fact, a pre-existing body with its own representatives that was being granted independent communal status. Sesto was gaining coherence inside the umbrella of the Moriano commune, probably particularly quickly because of its geographical separation and pieval status; the Moriano chapels, as we have seen, crystallized rather more slowly (pp. 66–7). But in 1223 its success was marked by the gift of a set of clearly defined institutions, such as it did not previously possess. Sesto was already called *vicinia* and even *comune*; henceforth, however, it would be 'una vicinia per se et principaliter', judicially independent from Moriano. Its inhabitants were to have full authority to elect consuls, *consiliarii*, *guardiani*, *custodes*, *randaiolis*, and other officials. The consuls were to have

---

[35] AAL *A22 (*a*.1191), +B28 (*a*.1192), *M29 (*a*.1216), ++P78 (*a*.1217), +E96 (*a*.1218). For changeable *brevia* for communes, see below, p. 142, for Tassignano. Contrast the stability of judging in 1216–17 with the *ad hoc* arbitration of 1175 (*E35); see above, pp. 93–4.

full rights to judge any case put before them, take half the fines above 5s., and all those below 5s., except where the bishop claimed high justice and rights of appeal. The men of Sesto no longer needed to participate in the *consulatus* of Moriano, since they had their own; they did not need to do their duties to the bishopric through any other body. The representative of the bishop had to be invited to any consular or 'proconsular' election, but definitely not anyone from Moriano. The Sestesi would, too, have their separate part of the tolls due at Ponte a Moriano from wood coming down the river. All this was granted in exchange for an annual rent of 12 lb. of oil, apparently the produce of a specific tract of communal land.[36]

It is very evident in this text that the men of Sesto were establishing their independent identity, not at the expense of the bishop, but in opposition to Moriano. Their independence from the Morianesi is stressed over and over again; their subjection to the bishop is defined in rather vaguer terms (their principal obligations are to hand over judicial dues to him, and in general to do 'ea que facere debetis'). There can be no doubt that the bishop in creating the commune of Sesto was simply reacting to popular pressure directed against another commune rather than against him as lord. It follows that the institutions they gained were simply those that the Morianesi already had, and that the bishop readily recognized; the text thus tells us as much about the Moriano commune as about Sesto. Its institutions were by now complex; five distinct sets of officials were as much as any rural commune needed—indeed, they were probably too many for the smallish community of Sesto. Their principal role was doubtless judicial, and maybe increasingly financial, although collecting wood tolls and paying dues to the bishop are all that is mentioned in that area. But the existence of precise, defined, judicial powers and responsibilities for consuls in Moriano and Sesto is now clear; and a permanent income for the commune—and for the officials who controlled it—existed as well. The commune was a structured body, and no longer simply a community based on oaths. The regulations that it would produce would henceforth be enactments, not agreements of mutual obligation. We do not have such regulations for Moriano, but we do have

[36] AAL ++R26, ++T99 (a.1187), AB50 (a.1223). The latter, a long and complex text, is summarized with extracts in S. Andreucci, 'Sesto di Moriano', *Rivista archeologia storia costume*, 13. 1 (1985), 3–8. Sesto had a tense relationship to the bishop, too, at least at an ecclesiastical level, for the pievano tried to claim the hospital of Ponte a Moriano from the bishop in 1205 (+N81), and the bishop, presumably in response, tried to get rid of the pievano in 1207 (++P57). The collectivity of Sesto in 1223 is characterized by a great variety of words: *vicinia, comune, universitas, colegium, corpus, comunitas, cognoscentes*; only the word *consulatus* seems to characterize the novelty of the instituted commune.

an oath sworn by the consuls of S. Maria a Monte in the Valdarno, a substantial document that dates to around this time.[37] In it are listed what are in effect a set of communal statutes, mostly as usual about crimes of violence. The consuls simply swear to carry these laws out, with the occasional help of *consiliarii*; the sense of mutual responsibility found in the Moriano oath of 1170 is entirely gone, and has been replaced by the assumption by communal officials of the predetermined burdens of office.

The change that I am describing is essentially that between a community and an institution; between a group whose mutual relationships, although buttressed by an oath, depended on personal bonds and did not need to be spelled out, and a body with its own funding and defined rules and responsibilities for its leaders. (The difference between them is a sociological cliché: it corresponds roughly to Tönnies's venerable distinction between *Gemeinschaft* and *Gesellschaft*, as long as one excludes the cosy egalitarianism often implicit in the former term.) Moriano had first to develop a group identity as the collectivity of the inhabitants of a territory, something which it could do perhaps earlier and more easily than elsewhere in the Sei Miglia, thanks to the episcopal *districtus* and the 1081–2 siege; second, to accept that this collectivity could act politically, a step that was completed by 1121; third, to recognize community representatives, however informal their roles, a development first visible in 1141 and complete by 1170; but only after that, by 1216–17 and 1223, was the commune fully formed as an institution, with its internal structures and roles defined independently of its personnel. Institutions can be changed, and certainly twisted for private gain. They can be fought over, too, as rural communes were everywhere, between local figures who wished to use them as an instrument of autonomy and protection against interference and oppression, and, on the other side, ruling powers (in this case the bishop and increasingly the city), who saw them simply as convenient and preferably obedient instruments of local government. Rural communes were also, of course, the foci for internal faction-fighting as well, particularly if they were rich enough as a corporation to be worth controlling.[38] But the institutionalization of the commune marks a break with the past; for all these oppositions would, instead of being fought out directly, henceforth be channelled through the new collective institutions.

[37] Corsi, ' "Breve" dei consoli'. The names in the text, particularly the *filii Molesti*, fit S. Maria a Monte documents of the 1210s–20s: AAL ++E42, ++E43 (*a*.1215), ++E86 (*a*.1227), cf. ++E131 (*a*.1241).

[38] Examples of these later patterns: M. Berengo, *Nobili e mercanti* (Turin, 1965), 320–41; D. J. Osheim, 'Countrymen and the Law', *Speculum*, 64 (1989), 332–5.

The process by which this development occurred happened everywhere, in Italy and indeed in western Europe. Communes ended up very different from one another, nevertheless. Their different external constraints and local economic obligations were very often responsible for that, of course. But one variable in these local differences needs more exploration: the activities of communal élites. In the gradual crystallization of communal roles, the interests of their incumbents in the development of strong or of weak collective institutions was of considerable importance. And we cannot get any idea of what a commune was for unless we know who was in the community it served, and what interests they had: unless we move from the formal exterior of communal institutions to the content of social relationships. This is the subject of the next chapter.

Appendix
Signorial Obligations in the
Twelfth-Century Lucchesia

How typical were the comparatively light signorial obligations documented for Moriano by the standards of the diocese in general? Any reply will have to be impressionistic, for signorie are badly documented in charters for land transactions everywhere (Moriano has more documents than most, but its signoria is far less clearly defined than are the structures of its estates), as well as less well documented in the twelfth century than later, but even impressions can be helpful in an attempt to unravel material like this.

I noted above (p. 97) that there was an array of obligations that were owed for signori in various parts of Italy. (See, for guides, Vaccari and Cammarosano, as in Ch. 4 n. 29.) Were any of them owed elsewhere in the Lucchesia? In the Sei Miglia, which was of course in general subject to city jurisdiction, there is only one village showing as much signorial activity as Moriano, Massa Macinaia in the southern plain, which belonged to the lords of Vorno and the cathedral Canonica. Here, in 1160, most of the dependent tenants of Enrico di Sigifredo of Vorno owed him donkey service, gifts of hens, eggs, and linen, guard duty and military obligations (or their equivalent in hospitality, *commestio*), as well as judicial dues (*placitum*); the latter, too, were claimed by the Canonica there in 1184 and 1188. (*RCL* 1188, 1521, 1575, 1582; cf. 1382, *a.*1178 (*MGH, Friderici I Dipl.*, n. 727), a diploma of Frederick I which confirms signorial jurisdiction over Massa Macinaia to the Canonica.) The long list of tenants owing these obligations in 1160, together with an oath sworn by their descendants in 1188 to do the canons' *comandamenta*, convey a sense of subjection that we have not seen in Moriano. It was, however, as far as we can see restricted to tenants, although these were certainly a substantial proportion of the village population. Conversely, as Jones has shown ('An Italian Estate', *Economic History Review*, 2 ser. 7 (1954), 20), the canons' lands were not immune from *fodrum* and *datia*, unlike most of the territories of the bishop; in that respect their signoria was actually weaker than that in Moriano. No other signorial territory is significantly documented in the Sei Miglia; the lay lordships of Coldipozzo for the Avvocati and S. Gennaro for the Porcaresi, both postdating 1150, only appear in penal clauses: see Wickham, 'Economia e società rurale', nn. 28, 36, and below, Ch. 7 n. 15. In Coldipozzo, anyway, the few inhabitants may have all been direct military dependants of the Avvocati: see *RCL* 1259, 1284, ACL Fondo Martini 12 magg. 1243.

Outside the Sei Miglia, the diocese was, as elsewhere in Italy, divided between signorial territories, whose boundaries were relatively clear by the late twelfth century. Here, too, it is difficult in most cases to say much about what signorial dues actually consisted of; but in S. Maria a Monte, an important episcopal castello in the Valdarno, the Moriano pattern of relatively light obligations due from both landowners and tenants seems to recur (see Osheim, *Italian Lordship*, 63, 67–9), whereas in the Canonica's signoria of Massarosa in the Versilia we find again a somewhat heavier hand on the tenants of the estate, as at Massa Macinaia. At Massarosa, most of the inhabitants were tenants, however; and it is significant that this combination of collective tenure and substantial signorial exactions, which was very unusual in the Lucchesia but which had parallels in much of northern Italy (see e.g. A. Castagnetti, 'Il potere sui contadini', in B. Andreolli *et al.* (eds.), *Le campagne italiane* (Bologna, 1985), 219–51), produced the only known example in the diocese of a rural commune trying to establish itself against the opposition of its lords, in 1191–1227. (See, for Massarosa, G. Dinelli, 'Una signoria ecclesiastica', *Studi storici*, 23 (1915), 217–24, 231–42; Jones, 'Italian Estate'; *RCL* 1629, 1642; below, pp. 174–5.) Elsewhere in the Lucchesia, burdens could certainly be lighter: in Gragno in the Garfagnana in 1170 they seem trivial (*RCL* 1278; see Wickham, *Mountains*, 118–33 for the Garfagnana in general). Signorial justice is conspicuous by its absence from our court records, even when disputes are between two people in the same signoria (e.g. AAL *C48, *a.*1121, Fucecchio; *F46, *a.*1157, Montopoli; ASL ii. 535, *a.*1143, Dicimo)—though by the end of the century the bishops had a tribunal at S. Maria a Monte, similar to that at Moriano (ASL Altopascio 8 mar. 1199). In some of the lake villages dependent on S. Salvatore di Sesto the weight of the signoria was visibly as heavy as in the episcopal and canonical lands, until local communities bought much of it off in the late thirteenth century (A. M. Onori, *S. Salvatore di Sesto* (Florence, 1984), 81–6, 95–108). For some other signorially subject villages, see Ch. 7 n. 26.

Broadly, signorial obligations seem to have been of four types in the Lucchesia. First, territorial signorie with relatively light obligations, which however were due both from local landowners and tenants, such as Moriano and S. Maria a Monte, and probably the other militarized castelli of the Valdarno (see, for example, G. Volpe, *Pisa* (2nd edn., Florence, 1970), 24–33, 65–75). Second, signorie with rather heavier obligations, which were apparently restricted to tenants; there were probably rather fewer of these, but they included Massa Macinaia, Massarosa and Sesto, probably Maggiano (see below, Ch. 7 n. 13), and maybe other places in the Versilia (Dinelli, 'Signoria ecclesiastica', 217–24). Third, signorie 'fondiarie', which involved generalized rights of justice (but maybe not much else) over scattered landholdings, such as those recognized by the emperors to the bishop at Marlia, or to the Porcaresi and the Montemagno throughout the Sei Miglia (see Ch. 2 nn. 9, 54). The fourth type was that due from *manentes*. I discuss this category of tenant in more detail elsewhere ('Manentes e diritti signorili'), but they need some introduction here.

Manentes were subject tenants. I have described them in the text as 'quasi-servile', for, although they were legally free and able to make contracts, they were very dependent on lords, and people emerging from the status of *manentia* were often said to be becoming *liberi homines* (e.g. *RCL* 1318, 1329, 1472, etc.). Rights over *manentes* were very burdensome on individuals, but also very scattered indeed in space, for they were restricted to the lands cultivated by the particular *manens* in question, and not always to all of them, for *manentes* could also hold land in free tenure. The specific burdens on *manentes* are sometimes described in their leases (which were in the *tenimentum* form standard in the twelfth century: cf. e.g. Ch. 2 n. 21): they were tied to the land, subject to the *placitum et districtum* of their lord (even in the Sei Miglia), and they often owed *albergaria* and other 'signorial' dues to their lords as well. They were denied citizenship of the city, and on occasion (as in Marlia in 1193, AAL AE90) by the rural commune as well; their presence in other communes (as in Tassignano in 1206, below, p. 144) was a prima-facie argument against that commune having certain forms of autonomy. *Manentes* thus fit very clearly into that vague category called by some historians 'servi della gleba'. They could, however, be tenants of any landowner; they were not restricted to those with wider signorial rights, and these latter were anyway very rarely as burdensome as individual *manentia*.

I would argue that *manentia* was not the lineal descendant of Carolingian serfdom, but, rather, a relatively new form of dependence, which came to form part of the array of rights available to landlords at the same time as private signorial rights of other kinds crystallized (which in the Lucchesia was in the late eleventh century), and for much the same reasons. (See E. Conti, *La formazione della struttura agraria* (Rome, 1965), i. 179–92, 216–17; F. Panero, *Terre in concessione* (Bologna, 1984), 207–76.) It added considerably to the capacity of lords to coerce the lowest rung of free peasants in the countryside. But it is significant that *manentes* are not really very extensively documented in the Lucchesia, and they were not as subject as their analogues elsewhere: I know of no case, for example, in which *manentes* are bought and sold in Lucchese documents, unlike the *coloni* of the Fiorentino. Their relative absence and relative independence (see, for example, AAL AE90, *a.*1193: above, p. 27) seem to me to be an analogue to the relative weakness of signorial rights in the diocese in general, even outside the Sei Miglia.

To conclude: there were indeed more burdensome signorial obligations in the Lucchesia than those at Moriano; but probably not so very many. Along with the Pisano (above, Ch. 2 n. 8), the diocese as a whole was one of the least signorially orientated areas in Italy. [For comparisons with other parts of Tuscany, see C. J. Wickham, 'La signoria rurale in Toscana', in G. Dilcher and C. Violante (eds.), *Strutture e trasformazioni della signoria rurale* (Bologna, 1996), 343–409.]

5

Signoria and Commune in Moriano in the Twelfth Century: People

It is not normally easy to obtain any sort of total picture of the inhabitants of a medieval village, at least before the tax registers of the fourteenth century; even the richest charter collection is not likely to produce either a balanced or a complete representation of its inhabitants. In Moriano, however, we are luckier than in most places, for, as we have seen, the document that first attests to the commune, the oath of 1121, lists 293 adult males as oath-takers, representing perhaps 220–50 separate nuclear families. Are these the entire male population of Moriano? None of them can be identified from the documents as being based elsewhere; the one or two who are listed with place-names from outside the area, such as *Widucius* (Guiduccio) *de Matraia*, could well be immigrants. Conversely, no one who is documented elsewhere as living in Vico or Castro Moriano seems to have been excluded; the only categories of people who we can be sure were not part of the *communis populus* were the *manentes* of nearby Mammoli (see above, p. 87) and the clerics of the local churches, neither of them very numerous in all probability. Indeed, there were so many oath-swearers in 1121 that there is unlikely to have been a substantial group excluded from the oath: up to 250 families, maybe 1,000 people, is well over the maximum number that could have comfortably lived in the 6 km.^{2} of the district of Moriano in 1121. Some had property elsewhere as well, as we shall see, but the poor of the district must already have had lands that were too small to live off; they presumably survived by gathering in the woodland of Monte Catino above them, and quite possibly, by now, on grain bought in exchange for the wine and oil surplus of the Morianese. There is no reason, in fact, to doubt that the list of oath-takers is a good guide to the population of the district; combined with some fifty documents for the half-century 1100–50, and the register of fief-holders of the bishop of Moriano and their tenants of 1112–18, we can begin to say something about at least some of the Morianesi with a fair degree of confidence, in and around the moment when the commune of Moriano began.[1]

Not every one of the 293 Morianesi is documented elsewhere, by any means: only about fifty can be more or less certainly identified even once outside the oath (although there were seventeen Gerardi in the oath, thirteen Martini, eleven Ceci, and so on, mostly without further identification; many of these must appear elsewhere as witnesses and owners on land boundaries). Fifty is not a bad haul, but the fact that the other 250-odd, five-sixths of the adult male inhabitants of the village, cannot be identified with security even in what is a good set of texts by twelfth-century standards is a sobering thought. On the other hand, it is certainly significant that four of the best documented figures in the period are listed among the first six names in the oath.

The first two oath-takers of 1121, like too many others in truth, are only identified by their given names, *Rodufus* (i.e. Rodolfo) and *Gottifredo*. There are, however, only three Rodolfi(ni) in the oath and two Gottifredi, the names thus not being so very common in Moriano; it seems certain that we can identify them with two well-documented figures of the early twelfth century, Rodolfo di Andrea and his son Gottifredo. Rodolfo was a local landowner and episcopal tenant. In 1105 he gave land with his brother Ildebrando to the bishop's new foundation, the hospital at Ponte a Moriano,

[1] AAL +L91 is the oath; Bertini, *Appendice* 99, which edits the text of the oath, omits the names of the oath-takers. 293 is the most likely number of swearers, but there are one or two ambiguities in the list; it could be a couple more or less. A99, the fief list, contains a few obvious locals who are not in the oath (as well as men from Sesto and Dardagna, outside Moriano in 1121—see above, Ch. 4 n. 14; below, n. 9), but they could have died in the meantime—no adult demonstrably from Moriano is documented from both before and after 1121 and not in the oath itself, save Uberto di Rodolfo (see n. 2). I guess that clerics were excluded, solely because no one is given a clerical title in the oath, although there were a certain number of trades (three oath-takers were called *mantaio*, glove-maker, two *fretiano* or *froitano*, embroiderer; there were two cowherds, one vine-dresser (*ceppeturo*), one lawyer (*avogaro*), and one man was perhaps a smith (*ferruci*)). The calculation of 1,000 people or 220–50 families is based on standard multipliers. At most, these families will have averaged $2\frac{1}{2}$ ha. of land each, half—or less than half—of the hectarage that has been argued to be the minimum for rent-paying families based on grain lands alone (see M. Montanari, *L'Alimentazione contadina* (Naples, 1979), 197–211; C. J. Wickham, *Studi sulla società degli Appennini* (Bologna, 1982), 39–40; cf. E. Conti, *La formazione della struttura agraria del contado fiorentina* (Rome, 1965), i. 120–4 for overpopulation). How the economies of their survival worked exactly is unclear. Many or most will have had to pay at least some rent, but mostly to other Morianesi; the only major external outgoing was to the bishop. It must finally be noted that the fact that the 293 oath-takers were all male symbolizes the male orientation of all our documentary material, and represents the overwhelming male dominance of the society under study: women almost never appear as independent actors, and, given the evidence, cannot easily be discussed as a social group separate from men.

and in 1113 he sold land and pledged two tenant houses to it along with his four sons Gottifredo, Romano, Enrico, and Uberto—the two transactions being the earliest texts we have for the hospital. In 1119 he sold off an inherited episcopal fief of a field, and at another date he sold another fief (or lease) as well, as a text of 1141 reveals. It thus seems reasonable to identify him further with Rodolfo the *sescalco* or seneschal in the episcopal fief list from the 1110s, who received a fief directly from Bishop Rodolfo of rents in Sesto and Dardagna amounting to 48 *stai* of wine and 12*d.*, one of the larger fiefs in the list. His brother Ildebrando appears in other transactions, pledging and then selling off and leasing back portions of two tenant houses in Moriano and five fields in S. Gemignano across the river, where the only properties of the family outside Moriano lay (Gottifredo held land there too, in 1133). Gottifredo appears without his father or brothers in 1115, holding one or more mills below Ponte a Moriano with two partners, again from the bishop: this transaction was important, for the bishop was prepared to lease them the exclusive rights over mill-building for half a kilometre of river bank—enough for several mills, as the text itself implies. Rodolfo was dead by 1123, but Gottifredo and Uberto witnessed an episcopal transaction concerning one of their father's old holdings in 1141; after that, the family is lost sight of.[2]

All Rodolfo's family except Uberto have names that correspond to names in the oath; Romano was listed tenth. (Uberto, who was 19 in 1121 and the youngest of the four brothers, might possibly have been considered too young, although he was certainly legally adult.) Nearly all the people they transacted with were in the oath too; their context was clearly local. Indeed, one can place Rodolfo's family in geographical terms more exactly still: most of their transactions were on the northern edge of Moriano, along the Mulerna river and beside the bridge over the Serchio, with more land

---

[2] For the family as a whole, see AAL ++D21 (*a.*1102), ++O55 (*a.*1105), +S56 (*a.*1111, with *RCL* 702), ++P74 (*a.*1111), ++P32 (*a.*1113/1119), A99 (*a.*1112–18), ++A20 (*a.*1115), +F25 (*a.*1116), +G20 (*a.*1118), ++A80 (*a.*1119), ++G50 (*a.*1123), *H91 (*a.*1133), *K85 (*a.*1141), ++P28 (*a.*1161—this text, which I could not find in original in AAL, may be misdated on the *scheda* in the archive. It refers to Gottifredo owing on a boundary in Moriano). Uberto's age is explicit in ++P32; he must have been born in July or Aug. 1101. Neither of the two other Rodolfi in the oath can be Rodolfo di Andrea, it should be added, for they have other patronymics; and there are almost no other Rodolfi in the documents. The only exception is an episcopal tenant who gave land to the hospital in 1132 (*C84); he is not attested elsewhere. (This procedure of elimination is too *ad hoc* for comfort, but it is the only one available. Fortunately, outside the oath, patronymics are normal in our texts.) Exactly how many of the men listed at the head of the oath were there because they were leaders, as opposed to people who happened to be at the front of the queue to swear, is anyone's guess; any number, I suppose, between three and ten.

in S. Gemignano over the bridge, fiefs in Sesto and Dardagna to the north, and only two references to land over the hill, south of the castello of Moriano. They seem to have been medium landowners, owning some land and houses, and holding others in lease or fief from the bishop. They were clearly in some real sense part of the episcopal entourage, if Rodolfo was, as seems likely, the seneschal of his namesake the bishop in the 1110s; but their village involvement must have remained great if they thought it worth while to run the mills of the northern Morianese too. It was these men, then, who were first, second, and tenth at the oath in 1121.

Sixth was Gerardo di Daniele, who is equally well documented in the decade leading up to the oath, thanks largely to his wife Biacca di Alberto, who sold her *morgincap* (her marriage-portion from her husband), which she itemized, to the bishop at Gerardo's death in 1123. Gerardo, *abitator in loco et finibus Moriano*, had married her in 1111, and given her, as normal, a quarter of his properties; putting this document together with Biacca's sale, we can calculate Gerardo's property at death as approximately eight tenant houses and twelve other fields, scattered from Moriano up to Aquilea. The rest of his property, as an 1121 text states, went to his daughter Conciura, whose heir, if she died without children, would be the bishop; the fact that we have this document too indicates that she was indeed childless. Gerardo had no fiefs in the great fief list, but he was none the less also part of the episcopal entourage, for he acted as Bishop Rodolfo's representative when the latter bought back a fief in Aquilea in 1117; from 1118 he held a large lease from the bishop in nearby Carpineto as well, on a temporary basis. Gerardo was, then, a prosperous medium landowner in the same area of Moriano as Rodolfo di Andrea, and also associated with the bishop; not surprisingly, Gerardo and Rodolfo witnessed each other's charters. He had closer links, and more land, outside Moriano than Rodolfo had, however, including a brother-in-law, Adanolfo di Rustico, who probably lived nearer to Aquilea, and was not in the oath.[3]

[3] AAL ++P74 (*a*.1111), ++A20 (*a*.1115), *F81 (*a*.1117, partially ed. Barsocchini 1811), +G20 (*a*.1118), +H31, AG11, +B67 (*a*.1119), +40 (*a*.1121), ++G50, ++G84 (*a*.1123). +G20 is a large-scale lease of episcopal property on a low rent as a pledge against a loan to the bishop of 650s.; Gerardo was not short of money. It is cancelled by a cross, so the loan was repaid. That Adanolfo was Gerardo's brother-in-law is clear from ++L81 (*a*.1136), in which Gerardo's sister and nephews sell land to the hospital. For Adanolfo's documents see A99 (the fief list), A93 (*a*.1115), +F25 (*a*.1116), ++A80 (*a*.1119), *C84 (*a*.1132). Adanolfo was another episcopal tenant, and also closely linked to Rodolfo di Andrea and to the hospital in these texts; he must have lived close to them, most likely just on the other side of the Mulerna, i.e. just beyond Moriano's 1121 boundaries.

The third man listed in the oath, just after Rodolfo and Gottifredo, was Gerardo *de Petture*, who appears in other charters as Gerardo di Teuzo of Pettori, Pettori being a kilometre down the Serchio from the bridge, just to the south of the castle hill. We do not have any of his transactions, but he held fiefs from the bishop in the 1110s of renders and tithes from five cultivators, largely in the south of Moriano, worth roughly the same as Rodolfo's fief. He was an active charter witness, witnessing for Rodolfo di Andrea and his sons, Gerardo di Daniele, the hospital at Ponte a Moriano, and the bishop, across the years 1105–41. His position in Moriano continued to be prominent, for he was one of the three formal representatives of the commune in 1141. Unlike the two families just discussed, Gerardo di Teuzo's descendants can be traced; they are numerous and well documented until well into the thirteenth century, when many of them still lived at Pettori. We shall see more of them later; it is clear, however, from these later texts that the family was once again one of medium owners and episcopal leaseholders. Gerardo di Teuzo had much the same economic position as Rodolfo di Andrea and Gerardo di Daniele, and, though he lived slightly further away, he was closely associated with them too.[4]

Prima facie the best documented leaders of the commune in 1121 were prosperous but not rich local men, who were also episcopal fief-holders. Whether local prosperity or episcopal association was the more important reason for their appearance at the head of the oath list would be hard to tell from these three examples. In other cases, however, links with the bishop seem rather more significant. The fourth name on the list, Mencucio of Arbusciana, was also an episcopal fief-holder in the 1110s, but much of his fief he cultivated himself; his son and grandchildren were no richer, for in 1188 they were reduced to ceding land to the city monastery of S. Ponziano, and getting it back as a *tenimentum* with a heavy rent obligation. Mencucio's family was probably one of small owners and tenant cultivators, that is, and not obviously natural leaders of the commune; but they were linked to the bishop, who may have had his own reasons for having Mencucio as one of the first to swear.[5] Whether rich or poor,

---

[4] AAL ++O55 (*a*.1105), ++P74 (*a*.1111), A99 (*a*.1112–18), ++P32 (*a*.1113/19), +F25 (*a*.1116), +40 (*a*.1121), *C84 (*a*.1132), +F14 (*a*.1140), *K85 (*a*.1141), ACL Fondo Martini 40 (*a*.1141, Guidoni 60). Pettori appears on the modern catastal map; it was described in the 12th cent. as touching the river (see ++A20, *a*.1115, and texts cited below, n. 16). Gerardo di Teuzo was much younger than Rodolfo di Andrea and Gerardo di Daniele; his children were most active in the 1150s.

[5] AAL A99 (*a*.1112–18); ASL S. Ponziano 6 febb. 1188. (For Ildebrandino, see also AAL ++B44, *a*.1179, and below, n. 23. Ildebrandino did have a public role as an arbiter for

then, five of the first six men to swear in 1121 were episcopal vassals and associates. And the pattern of episcopal patronage continues if we bring in the three communal representatives of 1141 as well, for two of them, Gerardo di Teuzo and Rodolfo di Paganolfo, were certainly in the bishop's entourage. Gerardo has already been mentioned; Rodolfo was another fief-holder in the northern Morianese in the 1110s, a witness for the bishop, and quite probably the episcopal *castaldus* in Moriano in 1146.[6] These episcopal links are even more striking when we recall that the 1141 document is actually a dispute between commune and bishop, with Gerardo and Rodolfo leading the commune. There is no sign that the 1121 and 1141 leaders were representing the bishop rather than the commune; that a fair number of them seem to have been in the bishop's clientele as well is, then, highly significant for our understanding of the context in which the commune of Moriano originated.

How typical were these men of the rest of the Morianesi in 1121? The first point to stress is that no one richer than Rodolfo and the two Gerardi is documented as living in Moriano, or indeed living elsewhere and owning property in Moriano. The only other family which matches them is that of Ghisolfo di Fantino and his son Binello (the latter certainly in the oath; the former probably). Ghisolfo held an episcopal fief in Aquilea with his son, and, with two associates, the tithes of Aquilea and Carpineto, both of which he sold back to the bishop in 1117–19: control over tithes tends to indicate not a little wealth and social status. But about Ghisolfo's other holdings we can say nothing; he does not even appear in the fief list.[7] This in itself highlights a problem, which we have already encountered with Gerardo di Teuzo: men who did not transact with the bishop, or with his hospital at Ponte a Moriano, do not in general appear in the records before the late twelfth century, except as witnesses and owners on land boundaries; the documents, that is to say, only tell us

S. Ponziano, which indicates a certain local status: ASL S. Ponziano 10 mar. 1191, 31 mag. 1193.) Arbusciana cannot be placed certainly, but was in Vico Moriano, south of the castello, and perhaps in Villorbana. Of the first ten oath-takers, four are not documented elsewhere, Mencallo, Antoniello, Mataracio, and Bachianus, respectively fifth, seventh, eighth, and ninth; one would have recognized them from the rarity of their names had they been.

[6] The 1141 case is ACL Fondo Martini 40 (Guidoni 60). Rodolfo di Pagano(-lfo): AAL A99 (*a.*1112–18), +L91 (*a.*1121), *K85 (*a.*1141), AE80 (*a.*1145), ++D50 (*a.*1146— the *castaldus* reference: here, Rodolfo is not given a patronymic, but, as we have seen, the name is not so common in the period. The third representative, Rolando di Rolando, is not in any other text except the 1121 oath.

[7] AAL *F81 (*a.*1117, partially ed. Barsocchini 1811), +H31 (*a.*1119). The only other known owners of a substantial property in Moriano in the first half of the 12th cent. are mentioned in *RCL* 700 (*a.*1110).

about the section of Moriano the bishop was interested in. At least Ghisolfo and Gerardo were episcopal vassals; but some of the other hundreds of oath-takers could in principle have been rich or influential people who stayed entirely outside the bishop's orbit. The only check we have on this comes from later in the century, when documents survive from other archives; these do not show any new rich owners suddenly illuminated by an unaccustomed light, but only families of small and medium proprietors, just as in the 1110s. It is for this reason relatively unlikely that there was anyone in Moriano in 1121 who was richer than a Rodolfo di Andrea or a Gerardo di Daniele. Beneath the stratum of medium landowners like these two, the bulk of the Morianesi must have been cultivators, for themselves or for others, or for a myriad of combinations of the two. But we still cannot tell precisely how far Rodolfo and the Gerardi were representative either of their stratum or of their poorer neighbours in their attachment to the bishop; we cannot tell which, if any, of the Morianesi were ill documented because of opposition or indifference to the bishop and his party, either in 1121 or at any other time, rather than just because they were too socially insignificant, as owner-cultivators and tenants, to get into the network of episcopal documentation.[8]

One can at least say one thing: there were other social networks around in the Morianese that did not look to the bishop. They included the three sons of Homiccio Lupo, who figure fleetingly in documents of the period. Homiccio Lupo had been a tenant cultivator of the bishop in Bolognana in the Mulerna valley in 1066, and his three sons and one grandson, based in Sesto, were cultivators in the fief list, owing in total 12*d.* and 60 *stai* of wine, a tenant-holding's worth perhaps, to four separate fief-holders. They also owned land, however: the brothers gave two fields in Sesto to the monastery of Pozzeveri in 1104. And their association with Pozzeveri was tight enough for Porcello di Homiccio to witness a monastic act in Palmata across the river in 1101, and to act as the local monastic representative when two owners from Mammoli granted rents there to the monastery in 1105. (Pozzeveri's link to Mammoli, the local base for the aristocratic Montemagno family, had previously appeared in the sources when owners attached to Mammoli gave land to the monastery in 1097.) Pozzeveri seems to have extended their field of actions further afield, too, for Porcello's brother Rustico probably had a Pozzeveri tenure in

---

[8] Cf. the discussion of factions and their documentation in C. J. Wickham, *The Mountains and the City* (Oxford, 1988), 256–68.

Capannori in 1120; they are not found outside the Sesto area except in Pozzeveri contexts, however. We can build up a simple picture from those details of the *filii Homiccii* as a reasonably prosperous family of owner-cultivators with much land in lease (including from the bishop, by far the largest local owner), who chose to associate themselves not with the bishop but with Pozzeveri, a monastery that was in this area most closely connected to the Montemagno, certainly the bishop's rivals.[9] There may well have been others in Moriano and its environs, either at the level of the *filii Homiccii* or higher, who looked to Mammoli and the Montemagno rather than to Castro Moriano and the bishop. It is, indeed, hardly imaginable that there were not; in a large and over-populated territory, the bishop (and, perhaps more immediately, Rodolfo and the two Gerardi) must have had enemies. All that we can say is that, first, if there were, their affiliation did not result in much spin-off to Pozzeveri, for the above references exhaust the local documents for the monastery before 1138; and, second, that rivalry to the bishop did not result in leadership of the rural commune: here, doubtless thanks to the far greater potential of episcopal landed patronage, the bishop's associates dominated.

Let us come back to the episcopal clientele, then, for, however far it stretched exactly, there is at least no doubt that it was extensive; and it is certainly documented, unlike its possible rivals, most notably in the fief list of 1112–18. We have already looked at this text from the standpoint of the bishop (see above, pp. 84–5); let us look at it from the standpoint of the Morianesi. Some 10 per cent of the oath-takers of 1121 held fiefs of the bishop in the 1110s, if not more. These fiefs, which were (to recapitulate) mostly of rents of grain, wine, and money from cultivators, were not homogeneous. If we use known early twelfth-century prices of grain and wine to establish rough money values for them, it is clear that they fell into two well-marked groups: a third of the fifty-seven fief-holders on the list were receiving the equivalent of 24*s.* and upwards, up to 50*s.*; the great bulk of the others had fiefs of 12*s.* and less, down to as

---

[9] AAL +F97 (*a.*1066; Gemignani 163), A99 (*a.*1112–18, where they are called 'de Sexto'; they are not in the 1121 oath), *RCL* 548 (*a.*1097), 615 (*a.*1101), 654–5 (*a.*1105), ASL ii. 299 (*a.*1120; Rustico's Capannori land was certainly a tenure held from another—unnamed—landowner, and Pozzeveri was the largest owner in that village—see below, p. 159). The only other cessions to Pozzeveri from the Moriano area before the 1160s are *RCL* 920 (*a.*1138) and 936 (*a.*1139). Pozzeveri, it should be noted, was a foundation and protectorate of the Porcaresi, rivals of the Montemagno (*RCL* 261: see H. M. Schwarzmaier, *Lucca* (Tübingen, 1972), 381–3); evidently this opposition was less important in the Moriano area than elsewhere.

low as 1s.[10] This represented a clear gradation of tenure, at least on the surface, with some people more generously supported than others. Nine of the second, lesser group held their own rents in fief, which may indicate that they were direct cultivators; only one of the first group was in this category, Martino di Petricino, whose fief consisted of rent due from his father. The first group included, on the other hand, some of the best documented people in Moriano, such as Rodolfo di Andrea and Gerardo di Teuzo. Broadly, and with some exceptions, the bishop probably enfeoffed larger quantities of rents to local notables; smaller quantities to local cultivators. But he was prepared to seek out, or accept, clients from all levels of Morianese society, and to use between a sixth and a third of his local land to do so.

What did having a fief from the bishop really mean? *Feuda* in the twelfth-century Lucchesia were, in essence, the successors to the written *libelli* of the tenth and eleventh centuries, mostly granted to non-cultivators, only now renewed verbally instead of in writing, and with an oath of fidelity and service added or made explicit. They generally consisted of land; that they were in this case rents is probably an early example of the twelfth-century tendency to separate rents from the land they were due from (see above, pp. 23–4). They usually, as far as we can see, themselves involved the payment of rent by the fief-holder; not a very high one, necessarily, but not always an entirely nominal one either. Two episcopal reacquisitions of fiefs in Moriano from 1225 and 1232 show, respectively, a field rendering 8 pounds of oil to the fief-holder, of which the latter paid a full half in rent to the bishop; and five fields and other properties rendering 14 *stai* of grain, 12 *stai* of wine, 2 *stai* of chestnuts, 7*d.* and other rents, of which the bishop got only 2 *stai* of wine. This range of rents for fiefs is as great as for any type of written lease; it is evident that the bishop could exploit his lands more or less effectively through fiefs as well as through leases, if he wanted. But the reason why *libelli* had begun to be called *feuda* in the first place was because *libelli* already involved the establishment of personal/political as well as economic links between lord and tenant; the symbolism of the feudo-vassalic relationship only continued this, and was not lessened by the payment of rent.

[10] For all this, see AAL A99. For wine and grain prices, see, respectively, *RCL* 702, 704 (*a.*1111)—only isolated texts, but at least contemporary. The figure of 10% of the Morianesi as fief-holders is only indicative: in fact 20 fief-holders certainly swore the 1121 oath, which is 7% of 293 people (above, n. 1), but, as usual, there are many less easily identifiable people, who may well appear in both. Note that these fief-holders are never called vassals in Moriano texts; I have therefore tried to avoid the word, since it is often regarded as a technical term, but I do not doubt that they were just *like* vassals elsewhere.

Fiefs in the Morianese certainly did represent personal links to the bishop, and are so generalized among the local population that they may have been the product of a specific political event: most likely the military-political readiness that accompanied the siege of 1081–2. Exactly how tight the link was must have varied; we have seen (p. 91) that Bishop Benedetto considered the dues or obligations given by the fief-holders to his predecessor Rodolfo so low, or so laxly collected, as to indicate that they were held 'iniuste et violenter'. But Benedetto evidently re-established them, and we find casual reference to episcopal fiefs, however intermittently, through the next century and beyond.[11] Moriano's fiefs did not make it a strikingly militarized area, none the less. Its *castaldiones* do not appear as military figures, and there are no references to personal military burdens (or privileges) for a local élite. Military obligations seem, indeed, to have been expected from the population as a whole, as from Aquilea in 1218, much as they were from the citizen armies of contemporary cities. And the fief network ran through the district from top to bottom, structuring every level of society in a direct relationship to the bishop.

This is important. Consider, once again, what the standard picture is for a lord who has a signoria over a village, overlooked by his castle, in twelfth-century Europe. His local power will be legally defined by his signorial rights and by the rents he takes from his peasantry; these may be administered by local inhabitants, the only people who know the land well enough to be able to deliver judgement and assess rentals, but they will be essentially based on the power of his armed men—for this is, of course, the world of ideal-type military feudalism. Signorie were very clearly based in Italy and elsewhere on the exactions of military élites, dues called *mali usi* and the like, from the eleventh century onwards. It is in fact only in the eleventh century, or shortly before, that the aristocracy began to define itself as an exclusive military stratum at all, but from then onwards the imagery of military activity and the personal obligations associated with it spread ever further down the social spectrum

---

[11] For *libelli* and fiefs, see C. Violante, 'Pievi e parrocchie', in *Atti della VI settimana internazionale di studio* (Milan, 1977), 664–6; Wickham, *Mountains*, 97–8, 311 ff. Fief documents are very rare, which gives us a prima-facie argument in favour of the idea that the relationship was generally unwritten; the presupposition is explicit in one Florentine document I have seen, A. M. Enriquez, *Badia* (Rome, 1990), ii, n. 255. (I thank Luciana Mosiici for showing me A. M. Enriquez's then-unpublished edition of this text.) Rodolfo di Andrea had a fief from his *antiqui parentes* (AAL ++A80, *a.*1119) that was presumably two or three generations old: it is the earliest that we know of for Moriano. Later references include AAL Fondo Martini 40 (*a.*1141, Guidoni 60), *N81 (*a.*1225), *K85 (*a.*1232).

—the term *lambardus*, which in Tuscany tended to mean a small diocesan-level aristocrat in 1050, came to mean a member of a militarized village élite in many places by 1150. This steady militarization of social relationships among the (relatively) privileged separated them off—and was intended to separate them off—from those who did not participate in, or were excluded from, the army; society became clearly divided between the two groups, *milites* as against *cives* or *rustici*. These developments can be seen in Lucca as much as elsewhere, with the exactions of the lords of Montemagno around their main stronghold in 1099, or the local dominance of the *lambardi* of the strategic centre of S. Maria a Monte in the later twelfth and thirteenth centuries, or indeed with the *curia militum* the bishop had around him by 1150 or so, even if its construction was not always organized along orthodox 'feudal' lines.[12]

Moriano was, however, not like this. There were no families of local *lambardi*; no élite military obligations. The village was, of course, socially stratified. The leaders of the commune were from the outset, as we have seen, its richest members and close to the bishop; the Morianesi who were tenant cultivators for all or most of their land were mostly by no means episcopal feudatories, and probably had relatively little say in village life. In general in peasant societies, if there are independent landowners living in the village they are going to dominate their neighbours who are someone's tenants, and the only circumstance in which tenants gain village leadership is if everyone is a tenant; there is no sign that Moriano was an exception to this. But none the less Morianese society was not *divided*, in the sense that there was no structural division between a landowning and militarized élite and the mass of cultivators. Episcopal vassals came from all levels of society; and, although this certainly in general meant that the status of most individuals was not radically affected by episcopal association, a few relatively poor people, such as Mencucio of Arbusciana, could gain as a result a relatively high standing by local criteria. For the bishop to maintain his position as the focus of Morianese society, he had to be not just landlord and signorial lord, but patron; and he had to patronize not just a few people, but an array of clients from

---

[12] G. Volpe, 'Lambardi e Romani', *Studi storici*, 13 (1904), 53–81, 167–82, 241–315, 369–416, is the classic, with H. Keller, *Adelsherrschaft* (Tübingen, 1979), 342–79; for military élites in villages, Wickham, *Mountains*, 325–9. For Lucca, *RCL* 561–4 (*a.*1099) for Montemagno; D. J. Osheim, *An Italian Lordship* (Berkeley, 1977), 67–8, for S. Maria a Monte; for the episcopal *curia militum* see AAL +S11, AD10 (*a.*1168), *G76 (*a.*1171); and *M12 (*a.*1188), AE24 (*a.*1200) for some of its odder features.

all levels of society.[13] The Morianesi co-operated; the territory remained loyal to him. And they maintained their relative lack of division inside the commune: in 1121 it was considered necessary for every inhabitant, not just a minority, to take the oath to the bishop, and worthwhile for every one to be listed in the corroborative document. The mutual oaths of the mid-twelfth century were also given by everybody, and not by a restricted group of leaders. In all these respects, Moriano looks much less like the standard picture of a castello with a local military élite, and much more like many cities of the early communal period, at least in the sense that the whole population, though in practice excluded from power, was invoked in the collective rhetoric of the *civitas*, and was on occasion expected to fight for it. Indeed, Moriano, like the other communes of the Sei Miglia, may have been directly influenced by the city in this; the communal identity of the village after all, as we have seen, followed hard on the heels of that of the city. But the underpinning that allowed such imitation to take place was the fact that the collectivity of the village/signoria was not undermined by a social break between a military élite and the rest. Rodolfo di Andrea was richer than his neighbours, and more influential; but he was not sufficiently different from them to be able to ignore them.

I have argued that the principal moment at which the territory of Moriano gained a sense of collective identity as a *communis populus* was probably the siege of 1081–2 (see above, pp. 63, 99). But, now we know more about the social structure of Moriano in that period, we can also make some guesses about the importance of the commune for the leaders of 1121. Rodolfo di Andrea or the two Gerardi did not need to be communal leaders to be active and influential in the bishop's clientele. Eighty years earlier, Moro di Petruccia in Marlia (pp. 29–34) had happily prospered by being in the clientele of some of the dominant landowners in his own village, without needing an institution that could embody his influence locally; had a military stratum existed in Marlia, Moro is the classic type of man who would have aspired to it, and did aspire to it elsewhere. Rodolfo, too, was active in some of the same ways as Moro, getting land from his patron and also endowing, and thus associating himself with, the bishop's new local hospital: these were direct ways of increasing his local status and influence. But participation (and for a few, even prosperity) in the bishop's clientele was not restricted to men like Rodolfo; local social

[13] See Wickham, *Mountains*, 283–92, for a similar Aretine instance of episcopal dependence as one of a number of structural features that blurred the line between military aristocrats and others, even in a more militarized society than that of Lucca.

structures in Moriano in the early twelfth century did not allow the local rich to be dominant through privileged access to their lord and patron, simply because this access was not privileged. Precisely because of the integration of Morianese society, Rodolfo, like the bishop himself, in order to confirm his local status, had to establish a relationship with the rest of the village as well: it was increasingly necessary to be a leader of the local village collectivity in order to establish one's local supremacy. The relationship probably worked dialectically: Moriano as a community, starting from the events of the 1080s, was gaining enough social coherence to be a body worth leading; but it needed the group around Rodolfo and the two Gerardi, who formed a tight cluster of episcopal clients with a similar economic position, knowing one another well and witnessing each other's charters, to provide a core of leadership for the early commune—it may indeed have been this group who established the mutual oath, which in itself created a collectivity that was sufficiently structured to lead.

The purpose of the commune of Moriano in and around 1121 was, then, twofold. To the Morianesi as a whole it was an affirmation of political identity, quite possibly in the context of collective loyalty to the bishop as signore—something that was more advantageous than disadvantageous (see above, pp. 91–2), and certainly something that gave form to their local territory earlier than elsewhere in the Sei Miglia. To their leaders, it was the beginning of the slow institutionalization of their local dominance, a dominance that in the territorial framework of the twelfth century mattered increasingly, and that in the relatively undivided hierarchy of Moriano required a format that linked leadership to the consent of the whole population, rather than to a dependence on an outside aristocracy. The new collective politics was, however, not yet necessarily formal or fully institutionalized; that would be a development of the half-century after 1175, which, as we will see, was rather different for the Morianesi than the years around 1120.

The society of Moriano in 1121, thanks to the oath, is clearer than that of any other village; but it is also clearer than it would be for a long time. We can trace the participants in the oath piecemeal into the 1120s, 1130s, and 1140s, but already after the 1120s the patterns of the early decades of the century are less explicit; more of the oath-takers must have died; their children are less clearly identifiable. We can pick up the next generation most easily in the 1150s; all that can be said before that is that, for the moment, the society of Moriano does not seem to have been changing particularly fast. The land transactions of the whole period up to

1175 or so that survive in the archives show fairly stable relationships inside the village, and between it and outsiders. About half the sixty or so documents surviving for the half-century after the oath are cessions to churches (either gifts or sales), to nine different institutions in all, all of them urban except the bishop's hospital at Ponte a Moriano and the Porcaresi monastery of Pozzeveri. The great bulk were to the bishop or his hospital, which shows in itself the stability of the long-dominant episcopal patronage network. The bishop and his hospital were not the recipients of many gifts, however; the hospital was buying land rather than receiving it in pious donation, and the bishop was buying back the leases and fiefs ceded by his predecessors.[14] If one restricts oneself to gifts, then the other city churches seem rather more privileged than the bishop; indeed, the Morianesi gave land to most of the main churches in the city in the twelfth century. I have argued that the Pozzeveri gifts may be the tip of an iceberg of factional rivalry in Moriano, and so, for all we know, may some of the others. Taken as a group, however, they show, rather, a recognition of the drawing-power of the whole urban ecclesiastical establishment, even in the heartland of episcopal authority; the power of the intercutting patronage networks of the city, that structured and united the whole Sei Miglia, made themselves felt even here. None the less, as yet the impact of the city was of minor importance; we are talking about two dozen texts in fifty years, and all for small properties. Moriano maintained its links with the bishop as privileged; its inhabitants still, as far as we can see, transacted with few lay owners outside Moriano—very few from the rest of the plain, apart from nearby Aquilea and S. Gemignano, and not many from the city either, except for one exceptional set I will come on to. The strong local identity that the documents around the 1121 oath attest to seems to have remained essentially unaltered until the 1170s.

---

[14] Hospital: AAL ++O55 (a.1105), ++P32 (a.1113/19), A93 (a.1115), +F25 (a.1116), ++P34 (a.1121), *C84 (a.1132), ++L81 (a.1136), ++S9 (a.1148), +E8 (a.1169), etc. Pozzeveri: see n. 9, with *RCL* 1234, 1541, 1793, 1795. Canonica: *RCL* 700. S. Reparata: ASL ii. 288, 390. The hospital of S. Michele in Foro: AAL Frat. Cap. 5 (a.1130). S. Ponziano: ASL ii. 460, 579, ASL S. Ponziano 6 febb. 1188, 28 ago. 1196, 7 febb. 1202. S. Prospero di Tempagnano, a rural church: AAL +45, +C95, ++P66 (a.1152). S. Frediano: ASL S. Frediano 20 genn. 1208. S. Maria Forisportam: ASL SMFP 8 febb. 1209, 13 apr. 1213, 15 mar. 1215. I have included some later references to show how such cessions built up at the end of the century. For sales to the bishop, see AAL ++G50 (a.1123), and below, n. 16; for the bishop buying in leases and fiefs, see e.g. *F81 (a.1117), ++H31 (a.1119), *L85 (a.1149). But the bishop had never really received gifts from the Morianesi; at this social level, links to the bishop had tended to be expressed through him, rather than his clients, ceding land—cf. Wickham, *Mountains*, 284–5. For parallels to the early sales to the hospital, ibid. 192–3; D. J. Osheim, *S. Michele of Guamo* (Rome, 1989), 59–61.

The exceptional set does, however, represent the beginnings of change. In the period 1146–82, a city dealer called Malafronte (or Fronte) di Gerardo acquired land in Vico Moriano across quite a substantial number of transactions; and, although his own sudden appearance in the record is the chance result of his personal documents ending up in the archive of the cathedral Canonica, he sits at the beginning of a new trend, the steady increase in the influence of the city and its inhabitants in Moriano in the closing decades of the century. We have already seen one entrepreneur of the mid-twelfth century in action, Gerardino di Morettino of Marlia and Lucca in the 1140s–80s (pp. 39–42). Malafronte was a very similar figure. He certainly lived in Lucca, where he and his family had status and official position; he had, unlike Gerardino, no visible rural base. He had wine-vats (*butte*) in the castello of Moriano, but they were doubtless rented from the bishop—Pozzeveri had a warehouse there too.[15] He dealt in land in Vorno, Vaccoli, and Tempagnano as well as in Moriano; the detachment and geographical breadth of men like Malafronte and Gerardino contributed markedly to the increasing economic integration of the Sei Miglia in general. But, unlike those of Gerardino in Marlia, Malafronte's local links with the Morianesi cannot be understood simply through the idea of the 'land market'; they are more complex than that, and shed some light on Morianese society too.

Malafronte's deals with the Morianesi are themselves very consistent in type; they are all sales or pledges by locals to Malafronte, for prices or loans in money, of single fields in Vico Moriano. They are almost all from one small area, the half-kilometre of hill and plain running from Pettori down to S. Cassiano; and nearly every one is leased back to the alienator, for rents in grain, wine, or oil. In 1146 he acquired land from Ugo di Pietro and Guidolino di Moretto, in 1152 from Guarcione di Berto and Sizo di Moretto Guidolino's brother, in 1153 from Marchiese di Bonizo, Sizo again and Bonomoro di Uberto, and in 1155 from Vitale di Gerardo, son of Gerardo di Teuzo of Pettori, the village leader of 1121–41. These men all form a group, and indeed are further linked together in a second set of transactions from 1155, in which Guidolino and his niece Isabella di Sizo, Vitale and his brother Guidotto and their three nephews, and Guidotto's relatives by marriage Lamberto and Uberto di Homodeo, all sold land by the river, in Pettori, to the bishop. These people were

---

[15] Warehousing: see above, Ch. 3 n. 40. Malafronte and his family in Lucca and elsewhere: C. Imperiale di Sant'Angelo (ed.), *Codice diplomatico della Repubblica di Genova*, ii (Rome, 1938), n. 14, ASL ii. 658, ASL Certosa 31 dic. 1189, AAL ++R43 (*a.*1190), *G64 (*a.*1192), *RCL* 1001, 1055, 1078, 1122, 1273, 1299, 1300, 1374, 1394.

Malafronte's major associates in Moriano; he only ever, in the documents we have, dealt with other people twice, in 1172 and 1182.[16]

This set of transactions is coherent in several ways. They all transfer land to the same people, Malafronte and (to a lesser extent) the bishop, and are all for the same area, as I have said. But it is also notable how closely the participants are linked together. They witness each other's charters; they own land on each other's boundaries. They are linked by marriage: Guidotto and one of his nephews were kin to Marchiese's wife Caricciola (perhaps Guidotto was her uncle), and Guidotto's own wife Beldia was kin to the sons of Homodeo, as well as to another frequent witness of the period, Martino di Carbone, who was, though certainly Morianese, a prominent and active member of the episcopal entourage. These are close and organic links, that cross and intercross, and include nearly every actor in the 1146–55 Malafronte charters.[17] The men and women thus outlined must have dominated this corner of Moriano, which, indeed, until the end of the century, only appears in the context of them or their heirs; they ran it in effect as a collective group. It is in this context that their transactions with Malafronte cannot entirely be the chance results of the currents in land investment, but, rather, a deliberate choice (perhaps through the mediation of Guidolino di Moretto, who witnessed every one of Malafronte's local transactions) of a specific man to whom to sell and pledge land. Malafronte was the group's city money-lender. For Malafronte they may have been just part of the market (and not an important one either: all the 1146–55 transactions only cost him 162s.), but from the Moriano end Malafronte was the choice of a social, not an economic, grouping, and sheds light above all on that.

The transactions we are looking at were, then, in themselves relatively trivial; they are interesting above all because they throw a chance shaft

---

[16] *RCL* 1011, 1014, 1078, 1100, 1102, 1132–3, ACL Fondo Martini 19 genn. 1152 for Malafronte; AAL AD48, +P32, A45, A46 (all 1155) for the bishop. (See also *D23, an episcopal property list referring to the latter sales, ed. P. Guidi and E. Pellegrinetti, in *Inventari* (Rome, 1921), 30–1.) The group also appear in ++K35 (*a.*1150), a marriage transaction, and Gerardino di Vitale is documented in Pontetetto in ASL S. Giovanni 9 sett. 1161; but they are not known otherwise outside Pettori or Col di Fiocco (which was just north of S. Cassiano, as is clear from the boundary cited in ASL Estimo 63, fo. 63, *a.*1389). Malafronte's other Moriano deals are *RCL* 1298, 1465. His children continued to own land locally: ASL SMFP 13 ott. 1189, ACL F109 (*a.*1209).

[17] Martino di Carbone, outside the charters in n. 16: AAL *C95 (*a.*1126), ++P40 (*a.*1140), *K85, +M2 (*a.*1141), AE80 (*a.*1145), ++D24 (*a.*1149), AD30, AE36, +E84 (*a.*1150), all episcopal texts—in AD30 and +E84 he acts for the bishop; and ++B36 (*a.*1159), where he seems to be acting for the commune of Moriano. A simplified genealogy of the group can be seen in the Appendix at the end of this chapter (p. 132).

of light on a coherent social group, of small and medium landowners, who maintained episcopal links, while also transacting with a city dealer. But they are also interesting for a second reason: they constitute nearly every example before the late 1170s of the charters which have penal clauses recognizing the bishop and/or the consuls of Moriano as guarantors of the act (see above, pp. 93, 100). These clauses can be found in all the Malafronte charters and others for the inhabitants of Pettori (although not, curiously, those to the bishop); they only appear in one other text, a gift to the local hospital, which is very formal and has many witnesses.[18] What the rural commune meant to these people in particular can only be speculation. There were men in the group who can be linked to its development in some way: Guidotto and Vitale were, as we have seen, sons of one of its early leaders; and Martino di Carbone, who witnesses in so many local charters that he may have been a *bonus homo*, a man of some public status, as well as an episcopal vassal, was one of the fourteen witnesses to the 1159 consular oath, one of only two, indeed, who can be identified elsewhere (a sure sign that the society of the 1150s in Moriano as a whole is closed to us). It is possible that these sorts of links created, among some landowners in a part of Moriano around 1150, an ideological identification with the commune and its developing institutions. Many of them may have been consuls at some time, perhaps. But it is still striking that this identification is so localized; in ordinary private documents, there are no other references to the commune in this period. By 1170 (see above, p. 101), the commune was still based on mutual oaths, and still had a fairly informal structure, but it did have a certain presence: its rules were strict and its penalties heavy (and thus potentially profitable). But, two decades earlier, the role of the commune was, perhaps, as yet occasional, restricted to moments of confrontation, and to a small section of the population. One could, that is to say, argue that Moriano's commune, however early, scarcely imposed itself at all in daily life (outside Pettori?) before the last third of the century, when other communes in the plain were appearing too.

This group from the early 1150s is the last substantial, internally coherent group of documents that we have for Moriano, despite the

---

[18] See n. 16 for the Malafronte/Pettori charters, with *RCL* 1465, and ++K35 (*a*.1150), both connected to either Malafronte or Pettori. AAL A32 (*a*.1188), which has a consular *pena*, is a Pettori charter too; the other later citations of such *penae* are not (see Ch. 4 n. 31). The only other consular *pena* in the 1150s is AAL ++P27 (*a*.1153). The notaries for these texts, usually either Rainerio or Romano, wrote others which did not have such clauses.

hundred-odd texts surviving from between 1155 and 1225. The fact is itself striking; it reflects both the size of Moriano's population and the increasing heterogeneity of its documentation, with texts no longer principally from the episcopal archive, but from that of the Canonica and ten other urban churches as well. None of the Morianesi in these texts was more than a medium landowner with a few tenants, and most had rather less land than that. As we have seen, Moriano consisted of a very substantial number of landowners, and by the late twelfth century they were sitting on land whose tenurial fragmentation was an extreme; when they chose to direct their interests away from the bishop, they could operate in a number of highly distinct social circles, some as clearly structured as that of Pettori, but others potentially much looser and more incoherent. This is indeed what seems to have happened. And the breakdown of previous social cohesions, the growing diffuseness of the society of Moriano as a whole, would have been strengthened by the clearest development of the period, the appearance for the first time of substantial urban landowning in the Morianese.

Some ways this could occur are illustrated by a small group of texts concerning the next generation of the family of Gerardo of Pettori.[19] They show a social profile markedly different from that of the locally based consular élite of the 1110s–20s or the 1150s. In 1191 and 1194 Ranuccino di Malcanetto (who, with his uncle Guidotto di Gerardo, had sold land to the bishop in the 1150s) sold four pieces of land in Moriano to his cousin Guido di Guidotto, receiving them back in lease. It was not uncommon for kin to sell land to each other to help each other out, and indeed Guido had himself sold other land to Ranuccino and another cousin in 1188 to repay a debt. It was rarer, however, to find kin leasing land back, an indicator of a more permanent relationship of dependence, whether economic or social; one of the sales has a very small rent attached to it, perhaps indicating that Guido was helping Ranuccino out, but the rent of the other seems high enough. Ranuccino's family may have improved its position later, for in 1202 his son bought back a lease made, probably on the same terms, with an apparently unrelated neighbour Paganello di Ruberto; but he never bought back the land from Guido, or from the latter's brother-in-law Sinibaldo, who acquired the 1191 land from Guido in 1201 (for nearly twice as much as Guido had paid his cousin, too, though admittedly in a time of inflation). Ranuccino's son,

---

[19] AAL AL32 (*a.*1188), ++K6 (*a.*1191), ++L76 (*a.*1194), ++K6 (*a.*1201 and later), *L100 (*a.*1202), *Q56 (*a.*1221); for Guido as a witness see also ASL SMFP 19 giug. 1199. I have not found references to them elsewhere in the Lucchesia.

or grandson, was still tenant for Sinibaldo's heirs there in 1254; the im-
balance between the two branches of the family had become permanent.
And it is in that context that the major difference between the two is
particularly striking: Ranuccino was still an agriculturalist and based in
Moriano, but Guido was a saddler (*sellarius*), and, like Sinibaldo (a dyer,
tintor), lived in Lucca.

Being an artisan had not used to impose urban living on people; the
Moriano oath of 1121 had included both glovemakers and embroiderers
(see above, p. 111). None the less, Guido, and others like him who were
not necessarily artisans, were by now moving into the city, and Guido
became prosperous enough to buy out his kin back home of at least some
of their land. And other city-dwellers, without local links, were following their lead; for the first time, major urban landowners, such as the
Antelminelli, can be seen holding and buying land in Moriano around
1200, and less prominent citizens were doing the same.[20] By the first decade
of the thirteenth century, when (after a break of four centuries) people
in charters came again to be commonly identified by place of residence,
half the lay landowners in Morianese charters are described as being from
Lucca. When we add the city churches, the percentage of urban owners
increases still further; if we include the bishop, who had, of course, always
held a substantial proportion of the land there, then perhaps 75 per cent
of the territory of Moriano would seem on these figures to have been
controlled from the city in the first quarter of the thirteenth century. The
figures must be exaggerated, for, as usual, they exclude local owners who
did not alienate any land; Moriano owners are clearly attested in documents from the late thirteenth century. Still, they indicate a trend; the
society of local medium and small landowners is best documented during decades in which it was becoming considerably weaker.

None of these processes is in itself particularly unusual. That citizens
bought land in the countryside, especially immediately around cities,
and that rural landowners moved into the city at the same time, are

---

[20] Sales and pledges to city laymen, often with leases back: ASL S. Croce 7 lugl. 1202,
Spedale 28 mar. 1207, AAL *Q56 (*a.*1221), ASL Spedale 9 genn. 1225. For city churches,
see above, n. 14. Antelminelli: see the texts associated with Ugolino Scaffa and his son
Gottifredo (cf. Ch. 6 n. 8) for Moriano and Aquilea, ASL S. Giovanni 12 lugl. 1194,
21 ott. 1194, ACL A11 (*a.*1201), N137 (*a.*1202), ASL Spedale 26 apr. 1208; the last of
these shows Guinigi links as well (cf. ASL S. Giustina 20 nov. 1189, Spedale apr. 1221).
Other Lucchese aristocratic owners included the Ronzini (ACL F119, *a.*1223) and the
Montemagno (AAL ++B59, *a.*1225). For rural artisans moving into a similar city, before
and after 1200, see D. Herlihy, *Pisa* (New Haven, 1958), 136, 153–9; it should be noted,
however, that in the Lucchesia silk-weaving was put out to rural artisans for a long time
yet: Osheim, *S. Michele of Guamo*, 20–1.

commonplaces in the historiography of Italy from the tenth to the fifteenth centuries. But the impact these developments had on villages varied substantially depending on when they occurred (in Milan, sometimes as early as the tenth century; in Florence, perhaps only in the thirteenth, or, often, later still). In much of the rest of the Lucca plain, as we shall see for Tassignano and the villages around it, city landowning was already important and expanding in the early twelfth century.[21] In Moriano, the appearance of city landowners was later but also much more abrupt than elsewhere in the Sei Miglia, for it only began with Malafronte in the 1140s, and only became important in the 1190s; the city dominance of the thirteenth century was a very recent phenomenon. The interest of the Lucchesi in Moriano may have been largely for the sale value of its crops—they can be seen exploiting rents in oil, in particular; they were, perhaps, less interested in political patronage over its inhabitants, though some clientele relationships can be made out in the sources.[22] But the impact of their appearance on Morianese society was inevitably great, whatever their intentions. In particular, as already noted, the tightness of the society of Moriano around 1120 must have been markedly reduced in the years around and after 1200.

Yet it was precisely the years around 1200 that saw the final crystallization and institutionalization of the rural commune. We saw in the last chapter how in or around 1170 the commune was still constituted relatively informally, although it could already exact fines and control the rents of a few common lands; only in the 1210s, and, above all, by 1223, was it fully developed as an institution with defined powers and responsibilities for itself and its officials. What sort of people controlled it emerges fitfully from the sources. We saw that in 1121 and 1141, and probably in the 1150s, communal leaders tended to be medium landowners and episcopal vassals or dependants. This pattern continued. Rolandino di Gerardino, consul in 1175 (and perhaps in *c.*1170) was, like Rodolfino in

---

[21] C. Violante, *La società milanese* (Bari, 1953), 121–7; for Florence, see Ch. 6 n. 34. In the Vercellese, peasant allods sharply decreased around 1200: F. Panero, *Terre in concessione* (Bologna, 1984), 99–102. For Tassignano, see below, Ch. 6.

[22] Oil rents to lay Lucchesi: *RCL* 1100, ACL F109 (*a.*1209), AAL ++K6 (*a.*1191), *Q56 (*a.*1221), ++R81 (*a.*1224), ASL S. Giovanni 21 ott. 1194, S. Ponziano 7 febb. 1202, S. Croce 7 lugl. 1202, Spedale 28 mar. 1207, Serviti 28 genn. 1209. To city churches: see Ch. 4 n. 8. To Morianesi, *RCL* 1795, AAL *N81 (*a.*1225, an episcopal fief). Citizens clearly did most to exploit oil crops: oil rentals form 40% of lay leases after 1160. Political clienteles: observe how Giunta and Andrea di Guiscardo of Moriano, vendors to and tenants of Rolanduccio di Ugolino of Lucca (ASL S. Ponziano 1 dic. 1188, 7 febb. 1202) sell their own land to S. Ponziano (leasing it back again) only two months after Rolanduccio does (ASL S. Ponziano 7 febb. 1202, 6 apr. 1202).

the 1140s, probably episcopal *castaldio* of Moriano. He and his colleague Gualfredo could well have been the fathers of the two consuls of 1216–17, Albertino di Rolandino and Manno di Gualfredo. The consul of 1229, Rodolfo di Iacopo, was the holder of fiefs from the bishop in a text of 1224, one of the few local charters from the thirteenth century that mention fiefs. The consul of 1214, Lamberto di Armanno of Arbusciana, is not associated with the bishop (indeed, his brother Spectalo sided with the pievano of Sesto in a dispute with the bishop in 1205–7), but he was certainly part of a family of prosperous local landowners, and his father had owned land with a rent in oil (in Aquilea), probably indicating an interest in the produce market. This fragmentary and sometimes speculative information (all except the last from the episcopal archive) gives us some sort of social environment for six of the eight consuls we know of for the years 1170–1230. It looks as if, at the beginning of the thirteenth century as at the beginning of the twelfth, local medium landownership and/or episcopal associations were the major correlates with communal leadership.[23]

What had changed, however, was the context. In 1121, there were many prosperous local landowners, and the bishop was the only important patron from outside Moriano. A century later, by the 1220s, the bishop had many rivals, and the amount of land owned in Moriano by the Morianesi themselves had decreased considerably. One should not exaggerate this change. There were still many landowning Morianesi, more indeed than in many parts of the Sei Miglia, as we shall see in the next chapter; and tenants of citizens could be prosperous locals who did not cultivate their lands and had their own clients, just as tenants of the bishop often were. Local élites continued to exist, that is to say, and would continue to do so for the next century and more. But notables like Gerardo di Teuzo and Rodolfo di Andrea are significantly less clearly documented by the end of the century, and may have been fewer in number—Gerardo di Teuzo's family, indeed, certainly lost its former role, with some of them becoming tenants for at least part of their land and others moving to the city. Against the pressure of the city, the bishop may have seemed the clearest bulwark for the remaining landowning Morianesi (and maybe vice versa as well): against, that is, not only the political dominance and fiscal

---

[23] Consuls are listed in Ch. 4 n. 32. Back-up references: AAL ++B44 (*a*.1179) for Rolandino, *RCL* 1795 (*a*.1198) and AAL ++P57 (*a*.1207, cf. +N81, *a*.1205) for the Arbusciana family, *G100 (*a*.1224) for Rodolfo. Lamberto of Arbusciana cannot be shown to be related to Mencucio of the 1121 oath, but the latter's grandson Ugolino di Aldebrandino (cf. ASL S. Ponziano 6 febb. 1188, and above, n. 5) witnesses Lamberto's 1198 act. A later example of an episcopal dependant as consul is cited by Osheim (*Italian Lordship*, 65) for Sesto in 1243.

exactions of the city as a body, but also the rapid and abrupt increase in the local influence of citizens as individuals.

This is guesswork, for episcopal documentation had by now decreased substantially; the construction of the bishop's clientele is far less visible in 1220 than in 1120. But such a pattern would help to explain not only why the commune developed in such close association with the episcopal signoria—as we have seen (pp. 91–3), they maintained their joint institutional autonomy from city government—but also why the commune was *strong*, with its organized courts and precociously articulated legislation: for it was in the interest of the remaining Moriano élite to establish the commune as a real political focus, as an alternative to city patronage, and, with the bishop's help, it was possible. The visibility and organization of the Moriano commune after 1200 fits, that is to say, with a surviving stratum of influential local landowners who felt themselves under threat. The structures of the signoria fit this as well: both the institutions of the commune and the privileges and political backing of the episcopal signoria may have been necessary for the local élite to maintain their previous social position in the locality. We cannot prove these to be causal relationships, but the commune and signoria together were certainly felt in later generations to constitute the autonomy of Moriano as something special: this is clear in the support given to the bishop by Morianese witnesses in the former's dispute with the city in 1276–7.[24]

Moriano's special status as a signoria inside the Sei Miglia did not in itself make it socially dissimilar to many other Lucchese communes, except in the level of its documentation, for the signoria was too weak. But the possibility of a certain autonomy for the city that the signoria provided, together with the political backing of the bishop, still the largest local landowner, helped to make it in the interests of the local élite that the commune should be strong and active. The city was not a support for communal independence, but, rather, a threat; and, indeed, this was a general feature of the Lucchese Sei Miglia. Local élites controlled other communes as they did Moriano, and used them, too, as vehicles for their own self-assertion, sometimes, as we will see, in opposition to the dominance of citizens. But the local political situations in other communes were different from that in Moriano, and by no means all communes were as active. How this was so we shall see in the next chapter; we will then be in a better position to generalize about how communes appeared and how they developed.

[24] AAL Libro della Croce, pp. 31–8, *G31 (*a.*1277).

Appendix
Genealogy of the Families of Pettori

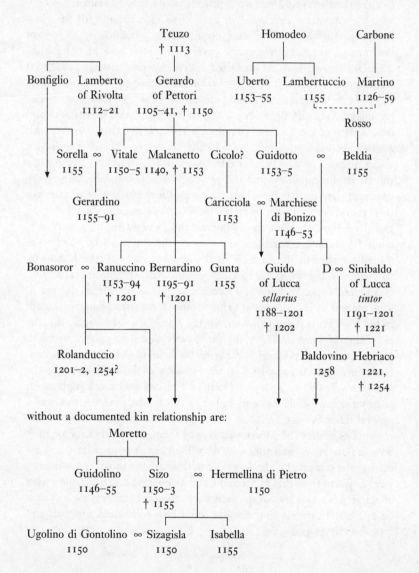

without a documented kin relationship are:

6

Rural Landowners and Rural Communes on the Eastern Plain

As soon as we move away from the privileged, essentially signorial documentation from Moriano, the evidence for rural communes rapidly declines. Although, as I have said (p. 67), we can safely assume that the Sei Miglia was routinely divided among its constituent communes/parishes by 1200, not by any means every village is yet explicitly documented with a commune, and in most cases the documentation only consists of one or two casual references. We cannot conclude from this fact on its own that communes were either incoherent or unimportant in 1200, though they often were; Tassignano and probably Marlia are counter-examples. But it does mean that the commune as an object of study recedes somewhat: in this chapter, inevitably, more attention will be paid to the tenurial environment of villages than to their local institutions. I will discuss three of the villages of the eastern plain, S. Margherita, Tassignano, and Paganico, particularly the last two, as examples of some of the differences in tenurial environment that geographically similar villages on the plain could have in the twelfth century, and I will relate these differences to perceptible contrasts in the evidence for the communes in each village. These are all places whose communal documentation is very restricted—the communes of Paganico and S. Margherita each only have a single reference in the documents before 1225, and that of Tassignano only three (although one is remarkable)—but we can in each case say something about their context. These contrasts will in turn provide a basis for comparison with the communal documents of other Lucchese villages in the next chapter.

The three villages in this chapter have already been described (pp. 53–4): they were grain villages, with rents in wheat and millet, in the flat plain between the via Francigena and the waterlands draining into the lago di Bientina. Their boundaries as distinct villages were derived from the parish boundaries of their churches, and did not significantly predate the twelfth century; as settlements, they ran into each other, and, in the case of S. Margherita and Tassignano, were closely linked historically and virtually indistinguishable as settlement areas. Nevertheless, all three had sharply distinct structures of property-owning by the early twelfth century, with very few landowners or tenants from one village holding significant amounts of land in the next; even the outside (mostly urban) landowners who owned much of the land of each were different.

S. Margherita is the least well documented of these three villages (forty-odd charters for the years 1100–1225), but it has the earliest evidence for a local commune. In 1148, Carbone, priest of the church of S. Margherita, sold a field to the monastery of Pozzeveri, in order to buy another, slightly nearer the church. He did so 'cum consilio et assensu consules communiter vicinorum predicte ecclesie et aliorum vicinorum', and the phrase 'cum consilio vicinorum' reappears elsewhere in the text; two consuls, furthermore, Cimbardo di Mencorello and Ubertello di Bichico, confirmed the sale in the witness list. This is our first reference to the office of consul anywhere in the countryside of the Sei Miglia, as it happens—it even predates those for Moriano; although, as we have seen in the case of the latter, communes can pre-exist the formalization of their representatives into consuls, a reference to a consul of a village can be taken by the mid-twelfth century as indicating that a local commune existed in some sense, even if (as here) they did not use the noun or adjective *communis*. In 1148 S. Margherita's *vicini* were organized enough to consider that how their church disposed of its lands was of importance to them as a collectivity; and they were organized enough as a collectivity to have two representatives at ecclesiastical transactions. This structure must have been pretty new, and may have appeared in the last fifteen years, for in 1133 the church had engaged in a transaction (less important, admittedly) without such advice. We know about the church's transactions because a group of its lay owners, connected to the family of the viscounts of Lucca, gave much or all of it to the hospital of the cathedral Canonica in 1077–8, but neither the hospital nor the ex-owners (who continued to own in the Tassignano area until at least 1115) are documented as having a direct say in church affairs; as we have seen, only the *vicini* consented in the 1148 document.[1]

What the significance of this sort of communal control over the church may mean we will see in the next chapter; S. Margherita's ecclesiastical affairs, which are barely documented after 1148, are not going to tell us much on their own. We can, however, say something about the group of laymen around the church in the 1140s. Of the two consuls of 1148,

---

[1] *RCL* 1044 for the consuls; 431–2, 444 (*a*.1077–8), 902, 948–50 for previous church transactions. For the lands of the 1077–8 owners, ASL i. 205, 300, ii. 261.

Ubertello is not otherwise known, but Cimbardo (fl. 1137–87) is. He belonged to a family of local landowners and tenants documented as holding land throughout the century in S. Margherita (they are only once found outside the village, as tenants of the Canonica in neighbouring Carraia). He had a family association with the church, for his uncle Beraldo was one of its priests in 1133; Cimbardo, on his own or with other family members, sold land in the village in 1137, bought land in 1144, and sold land to the monastery of Pozzeveri twice, each time leasing it back, in 1144 and 1146. Cimbardo and, later, his sons Cecio and Cimbardino are also recorded in the village on boundaries: as landowners in 1184, 1190, and 1194; and as tenants, of the urban Fralminghi family and of the Canonica, in 1144 and at the start of the thirteenth century. They were not a rich family; the lease they took from Pozzeveri on their ex-property in 1146 had a rent so high that they must have been cultivating it themselves, and the transaction must indicate that they were short of money. Certainly the scale of their transactions as we have them is entirely consistent with the proposition that they were owner–cultivators. But they remained owners, for at least part of their lands. Nor did they become wholly dependent on Pozzeveri; they contested the 1144 sale, despite the clear text of the charter, as late as 1194, and got a small pay-off from the monastery in return for peace. They had some local standing, for they witnessed local charters; Cimbardo had enough public status to be called on as a witness by a variety of owners in transactions across the plain. And in 1149, a year after Cimbardo is recorded as consul, he acted as an agreed arbitrator in a dispute between another local owner, Padule di Guido, and the Canonica over a tenure in the village that the latter was claiming from Padule (Cimbardo arbitrated that the Canonica buy Padule out, and then apparently succeeded him in the tenure). Cimbardo was a tenant of the Canonica, which was also patron of the local church, but he was also tenant of at least two other landowners, and his public position presumably made him independent enough to make him acceptable to the canons' opponent as well.[2]

---

[2] Cimbardo and his kin as actors: *RCL* 913, 979, 984–5, 1007, 1052 (the arbitration of 1149), 1722 (*a.*1194); on boundaries and in rent lists, AAL ++C50 (*a.*1184), *RCL* 1568, 1620, 1712–13, 699 (in a note to a 13th-cent. register copy); as witnesses, *RCL* 948, 956, 1002–3, 1044, 1091 (in Parezzana), ASL S. Ponziano 16 genn. 1157 (Nave), S. Giovanni 25 nov. 1162 (Sorbano del Giudice), Fregionaia 10 lug. 1170 (Carraia), Fregionaia 25 febb. 1191 (Carraia). Berardo as priest of the church: *RCL* 902—his co-priest Cigo had a brother who was a tenant of the Canonica in 1149 (*RCL* 1052). I draw the argument that rents of around one *staio* of grain for one *staio* of land are a prima-facie indicator that a tenant is a cultivator (that quantity being around the maximum surplus that could stably be got from

Padule di Guido and his brother Enrico were similar people, and were indeed linked to Cimbardo in other ways. Together or separately, the brothers bought land in S. Margherita from a city landowner in 1139, sold to the local church in 1140–1 (Cimbardo and his father witnessed the transactions), pledged and then eventually sold (to Pozzeveri) and leased back a garden in Lunata in 1144–6, sold to and leased back from Pozzeveri again, this time in S. Margherita, in 1146 (Cimbardo and his father were witnesses again), witnessed the 1148 consular charter, and were difficult tenants of the Canonica in 1149, as we have just seen. The rent Padule was due to pay for his S. Margherita lands was high enough to indicate that he too was a cultivator; Enrico, for his part, sold his lease of the garden back to Pozzeveri in 1152 in return for an agreement that the abbot of Pozzeveri should take him in and feed him if he ever wanted to follow the abbot's *comandamentum*, presumably as a servant or immediate dependant. The brothers were owner- and tenant cultivators, then, apparently poorer and less influential than Cimbardo's family, but associated with them; they were not particularly dependent on any landlord, either, as Padule's doings in 1149 further illustrate.[3]

The documents for S. Margherita from the 1130s–40s, which are much more numerous than for any other time in the century except, more briefly, the years 1180–95, are dominated by the two families we have just looked at; other local owners barely appear at all.[4] In the entire period under study here, no one more prosperous than Cimbardo and his circle, i.e. no one who was a non-cultivator, can be shown to have lived in S. Margherita. Apart from the lands of Pozzeveri, the environment of ownership that surrounded these families was dominated by the city; across the century, a good two-thirds of the land documented in the village was visibly controlled by outside, generally urban, owners. This could have overwhelmed a society of local owners as modest as those we have just looked at. But ecclesiastical and lay urban landowning was divided up between more than ten churches and at least as many major lay families;

---

land, over and above subsistence and seed), from A. Esch, 'Lucca im 12. Jahrhundert', Habilitationsschrift, University of Göttingen, 1974, ch. 1, 22–3, 41–4; in *RCL* 1007 Mencorello and Cimbardo contracted to give 36 *stai* per year for 35 *stai* of land. (A similar rental in a contemporary S. Margherita charter, *RCL* 997, *a*.1145, was due from tenants weak enough to need a clause in the charter to say they were not *manentes*: cf. pp. 107–9)

[3] *RCL* 932, 948–9, 956, 976, 1002, 1003 (*a*.1146: 24½ *stai* of land leased for 25 *stai* of grain *per annum*), 1044, 1052, 1087.

[4] The only other owner worth noting is Bonaldino di Alberto, a tenant who perhaps only briefly owned any land at all: he bought out the rental of his house in 1133, bought and sold for a few years, but sold his house again in 1145, taking it back in lease for a high rent. For the sequence, see *RCL* 902, ASL ii. 423, 451, *RCL* 919, 997.

despite their collective predominance, no single landowner or group of owners could claim local hegemony.[5] This fragmentation of local estates allowed a certain freedom of action for the group around Cimbardo and the local church. It is in this context, then, that S. Margherita's commune could crystallize in the 1140s. How it developed, on the other hand, cannot be seen, for the landowners of the 1140s cease to appear as actors in documents that survive from after that decade; in the 1180s new owners appear, who cannot be linked to them, and who may well have been urban. Only Cimbardo's family remain documented at all, and then mostly as witnesses and in boundary clauses—they had apparently ceased to transact with churches. After the 1190s, documents for the village decrease once more.

This relative independence of action for the small landowners of S. Margherita may seem fairly labile, and it may not have lasted to the end of the century. But the coherent organization of the local *vicini* in 1148 is very clear when set against another document of the same year for the church of S. Stefano di Tassignano, less than a kilometre away, a similar text but with a significant difference. It too is a land sale involving the church, but instead of being made with the consent of the *consules vicinorum*, it is 'cum consensu patronum et vicinum'.[6] S. Margherita's patrons kept out of their church's affairs, but not the patrons of S. Stefano. And their field of action included not just the church, but the commune too.

Who owned (or otherwise controlled) S. Stefano di Tassignano in the eleventh century we do not know, but probably they were not clerics, for the *ius patronatus* over the church that we have documented for the twelfth and early thirteenth centuries was certainly lay.[7] It was invested in some

---

[5] Churches, with first references, apart from the Canonica, S. Margherita itself, and Pozzeveri: S. Salvatore di Sesto (*RCL* 699), S. Michele in Foro (*RCL* 699), S. Giorgio (*RCL* 902), S. Bartolomeo in Silice (ASL ii. 439), S. Pietro Maggiore (*RCL* 913), S. Maria Forisportam (*RCL* 997), Altopascio (ASL S. Ponziano 7 mar. 1157), S. Ponziano (ASL S. Ponziano 27 genn. 1179), S. Reparata (AAL ++K29, *a.*1184). Lay families included the Avvocati (*RCL* 902), the Buthingi (ASL ii. 423), the Spiafami (*RCL* 932), the Fralminghi (*RCL* 979), the Soffredinghi (*RCL* 1003). Of these, only Pozzeveri, Sesto, Altopascio, and maybe the Soffredinghi were rural. The pattern of fragmented ownership described here still existed a century later: D. J. Osheim, 'Independent Farmers in Late Medieval Tuscany', in press.

[6] ASL ii. 583. Later church documents carry the consent of the patrons and no one else: *RCL* 1560 (*a.*1187), ASL Spedale 25 febb. 1198.

[7] *Ius patronatus* was the canonically acceptable successor to the church ownership of the pre-Gregorian period. Its terminology is universal in 12th-cent. Lucchese charters; the patronage rights it involved in practice were so similar to ownership rights as to make no real difference to its possessors. For the law, see P. Landau, *Jus patronatus* (Cologne, 1975), e.g. 3–9, 16 ff., 128 ff.

or all of a large and complex consorteria, consisting of at least three families, at least the first two of whom were probably linked by blood, for they occur together in boundary clauses very often, although we cannot show exactly how. One of them was the Lucchese family known as the Antelminelli (or, in the Italian of the late Middle Ages, Interminelli). This family was already among the most powerful in Lucca, with its leader Antelminello di Antelmino (fl. 1143–92) *consul maior* at least three times, in 1166, 1172, and 1188; they had a local dominance in a quarter of the city around their tower-house great enough to lead Antelminello to try to take over the patronage rights of two neighbouring churches in 1192, and they were landowners all over the Lucca plain as well. The Antelminelli were the least active locally of the three families of Tassignano patrons, presumably because they were so busy elswhere; they were classic examples of aristocrats more interested in urban than rural politics (see above, pp. 37–9). But Antelminello and his father Antelmino di Ugo owned widely in the village, judging by boundary clauses, and Lotterio di Antelminello consented to an act of S. Stefano in 1198. We could see them as acting as material backing for their kinsmen and associates who were more involved in Tassignano affairs.[8]

Perhaps more prominent locally were Rembo and Romeo di Gottifredo (fl. 1134–76 and 1144–88 respectively). They too were owners in many places in the plain, often alongside the Antelminelli, and in the city too, where Romeo was a cathedral canon. But they are above all attested in Tassignano, and their principal landed base was certainly there. It is documented in fifteen texts out of the seventy for Tassignano from the

---

[8] Antelminello as *consul maior*: C. Imperiale di Sant'Angelo (ed.), *Codice diplomatico della Repubblica di Genova*, ii (Rome, 1938), nn. 14, 71, 174; in the last of these he has a surname, *de Antelminellis*. As a city lord in his tower-house: *RCL* 1652. For the main location of the family's city land, see G. Matraia, *Lucca nel 1200* (1843; 2nd edn., Lucca, 1983), 33. His son Lotterio is S. Stefano's patron (together with the unidentified Gherardo *iudex* and Guido di Ildebrandino) in ASL Spedale 25 febb. 1198. Other family landowning and witnessing in Tassignano: *RCL* 905, 969, 1152, 1203, 1236, 1259, 1284, 1620, 1670, 1711, 1772, ASL ii. 487, AAL *H96 (*a.*1195), ASL Spedale 20 genn. 1199, 7 sett. 1202. Some of the large number of references to the family elsewhere are *RCL* 802, 806, 885, 921, 1146, 1197, 1206–7, 1229, 1247, 1268, 1345, 1420, 1423, 1471, 1479, 1505, 1576, 1627, 1722, ASL ii. 402, 418, 431, 449, 619, 677, AAL +92 (*a.*1123), *F82 (*a.*1146), +I35 (*a.*1162), +M80 (*a.*1173), AG10 (*a.*1177), ++C75 (*a.*1184), AH90 (*a.*1185), *M12 (*a.*1188), *A49 (*a.*1191), *Q53 (*a.*1191), ASL Fiorentini 2 sett. 1161, Certosa 31 dic. 1189, 23 dic. 1200, S. Giustina 20 nov. 1189, SMFP 19 apr. 1194; J. Ficker, *Forschungen* (Innsbruck, 1874), iv, n. 196A (Gonella as a *consul maior* in 1197), and above, Ch. 5 n. 20. These references, and those in nn. 9–11, could not have been compiled without Arnold Esch's name index. A genealogical table of the patronal families, much simplified, appears in the Appendix to this chapter (p. 160).

century after 1125, including those for Rembo's son and grandson and his cousins the *filii Matti*; it was substantial, and also tightly concentrated, for it did not extend to any neighbouring village, and seems indeed to have been mostly restricted to a couple of microtoponyms, Piano and Cafaggio, inside the village. The family probably did not actually live there; no charter says they did, and, by comparison with the extent of their landowning they are not as often recorded as they might have been as actors in local documents, though Romeo bought land in the village (leasing it back to the vendor) in 1174, and willed the same land to the Canonica in 1179 and 1187.[9] Given that Romeo was himself a canon, it is perhaps less likely that this relative absence of acts indicates a desire to stay out of the church orbit, and more likely that the family simply did not transact their land much. They did have dealings with S. Stefano, however. Romeo lent the church £9 in 1187 (against a pledge of a silver chalice and a gilded paten weighing 2lb.) to pay the *datum* and *fodrum* due to Henry VI, which its priest promised to repay with the agreement of his 'elector'; S. Stefano had problems repaying, however, and had to be bailed out by the Canonica after a court case in 1190. That S. Stefano looked to Romeo to help it out in paying its taxes (which were probably those for the whole village: see below, p. 143) indicates the family's local status. It does not in itself prove that Romeo was personally part of the consortium of 'electors', the patrons of the church, but his cousin Pandolfo di Matto certainly was—he ceded his portion of his *patronatus* in 1224 to the city church of S. Maria Forisportam.[10]

Less frequently attested was the third family in the consorteria, Soffreduccio di Ugolino (d. 1204) and his sons Albertino and Bandino.

---

[9] Rembo and Romeo as actors: *RCL* 1317, 1356, 1402, 1559; in boundaries and as witnesses: *RCL* 969, 975, 1029, 1064, 1184, 1203, 1222, 1229, 1282, 1581, 1620, 1670, ACL H92 (*a.*1208); ASL ii. 431, 490, 528, 619, ASL SMFP 30 ott. 1179, Fiorentini 3–4 ott. 1180, Spedale 7 sett. 1202, Arch. di Stato 24 genn. 1211; AAL ++P6 (*a.*1183), *H96 (*a.*1195), ++R44 (*a.*1205), mostly for Tassignano. Their father may be the Gottefredo di Savino of ASL ii. 198 (*a.*1109).

[10] *RCL* 1560, 1618 for the loan. For Pandolfo, ASL SMFP 12 febb. 1224; S. Maria used this gift as a basis for claiming the whole of S. Stefano in a court case eight years later (SMFP 9 mar. 1232), certainly improperly, and without final success—the Antelminelli still controlled the church in the 14th cent. (F. Leverotti, ' "Crisi" del Trecento', in *Pisa e la Toscana occidentale* ii (Pisa, 1991), 232). Pandolfo's family had come to be on bad terms with his co-patron Lotterio di Antelminello, as ASL Spedale 7 sett. 1202 makes clear; Pandolfo may have simply been leaving the consorteria in 1224. It may be observed that why the Canonica bailed S. Stefano out in 1190 (*RCL* 1618) is unclear; it certainly did not result in greater canonical influence over the church. But Romeo's loan to S. Stefano (1560) is written on the same document as a gift by him to the Canonica (1559); there must have been a hidden transaction here, but what it was is impossible to tell.

They also were urban aristocrats: they had a tower-house in Lucca near the church of S. Giulia in 1174, and their descendants were the magnate Tassignano family; Albertino was a *consul maior* in 1195 and an official city representative in 1198, and Bandino a *consul treuguanus*, a consular judge, in 1212. But they were not on Antelminello's level, and their ascription 'de Tassiniano' in many twelfth-century charters, although the origin of their later surname, was not one yet; they had not lost their local association, and indeed Soffreduccio's brother may have been prior of S. Stefano at the end of the century. Their landowning was mostly based in Tassignano, in fact; they may well have lived locally at least part of the time, as a half-urbanized family, like Gerardino di Morettino of Marlia, though somewhat more prominent. Even inside Tassignano, they may not have been quite as important as owners as the Antelminelli or Romeo and Rembo; they appear rather less often on boundary clauses, and not at all before the 1160s, though Soffeduccio's father Ugolino had a name that reappears in the other two families, and he may simply have been from a cadet branch of one of them. But they were certainly patrons of the church, for they appear dramatically as such in a court case of 1206, in opposition to the commune of Tassignano.[11] In this text, they are the only patrons that are named, though their actions are usually described as representative of those of other (unnamed) *consortes*, i.e. the other patrons. The *filii Soffreduccii* can best be seen as aristocrats with less strong a city position and involvement than the Antelminelli, and therefore more of a need to dominate their village directly as local ecclesiastical patrons than their associates, with their wider sphere of interests, had. How they did so can be seen through the 1206 text, which indeed tells us more about the status, organization, and purpose of rural communes in the Lucchesia, and their relationship to the local church, than any other single document from the period; although it is edited in full in an appendix, see below, pp. 248–53, we must look at it here in some detail.

In April 1206 Fiorentino, one of the consuls of the commune of Tassignano (called, in a mix of terminology that we have already seen in Sesto Moriano, 'consulatus et comunis. . . . et vicinia et universitas', and,

[11] The family in the city: ASL SMFP 9 ago. 1174, SMCO 10 dic. 1175, Spedale 13 febb. 1184, S. Ponziano 2 dic. 1168, 1 magg. 1169, 9 magg. 1191, 3 apr. 1212; *RCL* 1679; AAL +I45 (1213, *recte* 1212); G. Sercambi, *Le croniche*, i, ed. S. Bongi (Lucca, 1892), 11; E. Winkelmann, *Acta imperii inedita* (Innsbruck, 1880–5), i, n. 1 (*a.* 1195); P. Santini, *Documenti dell'antica costituzione del comune di Firenze* (Florence, 1895), 23–4 (*a.* 1198); cf. Matraia, *Lucca nel 1200*, 45. In Tassignano: *RCL* 1203, 1528, 1587, 1689–90, 1727 (for the prior), ACL H92 (*a.* 1208), H43 (*a.* 1224).

later, 'cappella' too), laid a plea against Albertino and Bandino as patrons of S. Stefano, before the Lucchese *consules foretanorum*, the judges of the court for the contado.[12] The dialogue form of the plea, which represents the case as an argument between the parties—a standard feature of Lucchese court documents of the period—allows the claims set out by each side to be understood; we can indeed at least in part work out what was really going on as well. Fiorentino's principal aim was to contest the power of the church patrons over the commune of Tassignano, especially in the matter of elections. He claimed that the commune had and should have the right to elect its own consuls, who would then be able to elect *guardiani* (roughly, local watchmen), with the agreement of a local board of *consiliarii*: excepting only the rights of the city, to which the commune was directly subject for civic taxation, and which recognized the consuls of Tassignano in turn. He stated that he and his associates were consuls of Tassignano 'in quantum est vicinia S. Stefani'; that there had been consuls in the *vicinia*, with *guardiani sive camparii* subject to them, for a hundred years; and that the *vicinia* had been subject to a *consulatus* for forty. These claims were opposed by Albertino, who said that his father (with other men) had organized the election of these consuls for forty years; that they had sworn the consular oath in his presence; and that at the beginning of this dispute (probably in 1205) it was he who had called in the city consuls—i.e. that the local commune was only attached to the city through the intermediacy of the church patrons. (Fiorentino contested this last point, saying that the city's intervention had been neutral as to the rights of the parties; later Albertino and Bandino conceded the point, and stated that the consuls and guardians had been there for fifty years, although as patronal, not communal, officials.) Albertino claimed further that in former times all the *rustici* of Tassignano had been *manentes seu servi* (subject tenants) of the patrons and the church, except one single household of incomers, and that now, by implication, most were, including the entire population of Ponzano. Fiorentino said the figure had never been more than half, and for the last forty years it had been

---

[12] The text is ASL Arch. de' Notari 14 nov. 1206; see below, pp. 248–53. For the *curia foretanorum*, see S. Bongi, *Inventario* (Lucca, 1872–6), ii. 298–9. Our text is earlier than the first one known to Bongi, and in fact the first references date back to the 1180s: the complete list for the 12th cent. is AAL +95 (*a*.1182, *recte* 1181), AL 35 (*a*.1186), ++N67 (*a*.1199), RCL 1729 (*a*.1195), 1826 (*a*.1200). For its later structure, see D. J. Osheim, 'Countrymen and the Law', *Speculum*, 64 (1989), 317–37. A version of my Tassignano discussion has already been published, as C. J. Wickham, 'Rural Communes and the City of Lucca', in T. A. Dean and C. J. Wickham (eds.), *City and Countryside in Late Medieval and Renaissance Italy* (London, 1990), 1–12.

only a sixth; in Ponzano they had been free for twenty years. Later he extended this, to claim that only five or ten families out of the eighty-three in the *vicinia* were now *manentes*; the latter were included in the commune, though.

The argument then shifted to who the consuls were and what they did. Bandino said that he himself had been one of the consuls one year with Ildebrandino and others, and that they had had the Island Ditch (*fovea de Ysola*) dug, had put up a toll-booth on the road, and had paid for a feast with the profits.[13] Fiorentino said that there were two sets of consuls, one or two for the patrons and three or four for the populus, and that Bandino had been consul for the patrons only (which the latter conceded); both sets had had the ditch dug. Albertino said that the consuls swore according to the text of the communal *breve* (which Fiorentino agreed), and that the *breve* contained an oath to the church and the patrons (which Fiorentino denied, except for the oath of the patrons' consul); the *breve* was in fact a new one, after the old one was formally destroyed (*scissum*) in a previous dispute. Fiorentino agreed that this last point was true, but said that the *breve* the consuls swore to was actually quite often changed, most recently in 1199, if the consuls and consiliarii agreed to do so—i.e. that the commune, not the patrons, had control of its content. (Albertino, predictably enough, denied this.)[14] Fiorentino further stated that on the occasion that Aldebrandino had been appointed consul by the patrons, a decade previously, the *vicini* had rejected him, and he had only served as patronal consul; once, as well, the patrons had appointed the guardians, but these too were boycotted by the *vicini*.

So ran the main lines of the dispute, as clear as I can make them (they are not all quite so clear in the text).[15] The city judges made the sort of 'compromise' that cities often made when faced with disputes of this

[13] Which road this is is not clear, but it must have been pretty minor: Tassignano was not really on the way to anywhere except its neighbouring communes, such as Paganico. They can hardly have been amused.

[14] The *breve*, presumably a text containing communal regulations, may have resembled that for Moriano in 1170, or perhaps, by now, the more structured text for S. Maria a Monte in the 1220s: above, Ch. 4 nn. 33, 36, 37. Why it was not produced as evidence is mysterious; but the formularies for cases in this period left little place for written evidence, and the judges may well in reality have had access to it. Fiorentino dated the latest change to after 'burgum S. Genesii fuit reedifficatum', which Tolomeo dates to 1199 (*Tholomei Lucensis Annales*, ed. B. Schmeidler, *MGH, SRG,* NS 8 (Berlin, 1955), 91, 300).

[15] In particular, the number of consuls on each side is not at all clear, and is confused by the fact that one of the issues most at odds between the parties was precisely which consuls belonged to which. There is also some action concerning a certain Paltonerio which is incomprehensible: it is likely that a claim about him by Albertino and Bandino was accidentally not recorded.

kind, conceding most of the case to the patrons: the latter were to have the right to choose the consuls, who were then to be 'elected' by their predecessors and would then swear in the presence of the patrons or their representative, and only if these did not turn up were the outgoing consuls to have the power to choose their successors; guardians, however, could be chosen by the commune. Evidently the city did not feel disturbed by the power that the patrons of S. Stefano might exert over the commune of Tassignano, presumably because the village was no political threat; the city could routinely include it in its jurisdiction (justice was certainly not one of the rights at issue in 1206), and the patrons were largely city based, as we have seen. We certainly need not conclude from the judgment, anyway, that the patrons were actually in the right—or even, for that matter, in the wrong. But some of the points at issue can be decided on from the texts for Tassignano that we have. There was certainly never a time in which all its inhabitants were *manentes* of the church and its patrons, for we have plenty of documents from independent landowners who were certainly local, while other inhabitants were tenants of other city owners; in this case the position of the commune is supported. Conversely, it is likely that taxes were paid through the village church, not directly by the commune, for the dues owed by S. Stefano in 1187 were certainly high enough to be for the whole village; this would support the claims of the church patrons that they were in some respects legal mediators for the commune.[16] Other unsupported arguments the parties made were perhaps not even meant to be credible, however; it was not uncommon to include claims for tactical purposes, to be conceded when compromise became possible, or for rhetorical purposes, to influence the judges forensically.[17] These arguments tell us at least what each side regarded as important for its case, none the less; and some points were, more or less explicitly, agreed to or assumed by both sides, and can be regarded as fairly firm.

---

[16] The exact weight of taxation in this period is impossible to estimate, but the imperial *fodrum*, the tax of 1187, was normally 26*d.* per hearth (C. R. Brühl, *Fodrum, Gistum* (Cologne, 1968), 707–10), which, multiplied by the 83 families Fiorentino stated lived in Tassignano, would come to exactly £9, the 1187 figure. Unfortunately, Fiorentino must have exaggerated here (see below, n. 19), and the dues are thus likely to have been unusually high; they may not have been for a single year or a single tax. (City taxes, it may be noted, could already be higher; in Pistoia in *c.*1180 they were already 3*s.* per hearth, nearly half as much again (E. Fiumi, 'Sui rapporti economici', *Archivio storico italiano*, 114 (1956), 25). This figure is more likely to have approached the sums owed at Tassignano in 1187.)

[17] I will discuss the issue in future work; for the methodological point see S. Humphreys, 'Social Relations on Stage', *History and Anthropology*, I: 2 (1985), 313–69.

Let us look at some of these latter points; for these, since they show how both sides regarded Tassignano, will enable us to see more clearly in what ways Tassignano was typical or atypical of its neighbours. One assumption shared by both sides was that the commune of the village was defined as that of the pre-existing *vicinia* of the church: in Tassignano, there is no doubt that the parish constituted the field of action of the developing commune. But, on the other hand, the church and its patrons were not always conceptually separated either; the same *manentes*, for example, were indifferently of one or the other. It is thus not surprising that the men of Tassignano never denied that the patrons of the church had some local authority *as* patrons, which extended to definitely secular activities such as participating in the digging of ditches. Elsewhere, however, it is much less evident that similar local potentates claimed such authority. We have seen that they did not have such a high profile in S. Margherita as in S. Stefano, and other churches tended to be more like the former than the latter; if patronal authority was so great in S. Stefano di Tassignano, then it is likely to be for reasons specific to that village.

Other points were more explicit. One concerned *manentes*: it was agreed by both sides that half the village (and more in the area called Ponzano) had once been *manentes*, and that fewer were now; there is no doubt, too, that the precise number was important, implying that a village with many *manentes* had less right to nominate its own consuls. Albertino and Bandino threw in the claim, not disputed by Fiorentino, that 'the men from the *tenuta*', by implication the *manentes* on their own estate, had contributed to the costs of the case; presumably they wished to argue that any participation by dependants in the commune devalued that commune's independence. A second point concerned the history of the consuls. Fiorentino claimed that there had been consuls in Tassignano for a century, but a *consulatus* only for forty years; he was presumably distinguishing between informal leaders of a *vicinia* and a more structured commune, which had developed more recently. We have seen in Chapter 4 just such a development in Moriano, and we have seen a formal moment of change (there too called the establishment of a *consulatus*) enacted at Sesto in 1223. These statements were not contested by Albertino and Bandino, who were more concerned to argue that the consuls that did exist, whatever their formal role, had always been chosen by the patrons. They did contest the date, however, claiming that consuls had existed only for forty years, though they later agreed to fifty. This latter figure is more likely than a hundred, for consuls did not appear among the undifferentiated *vicini* who consented to S. Stefano's sale of

1148—and anyway, a century before 1206 S. Stefano and S. Margherita had not yet divided into separate villages. But we cannot otherwise date the development of the commune; in particular, we cannot tell when Tassignano's *consulatus*, and its *brevia*, developed from the relatively informal oath-based community of the Moriano breve of *c*.1170 to the more fully institutionalized structure revealed in the 1223 Sesto document. By 1206, consuls in the village had clearly identifiable responsibilities, as the court case makes clear; but these need not have existed for very long, and political militancy could go with either pattern.

A further point of agreement was over the duties of consuls and other communal officials. They represented the commune publicly, organized the payment of city taxes (as Fiorentino stated and Albertino did not deny, although he presumably thought that the taxes should be paid through him), dug ditches, presumably for drainage (this feat was evidently important enough to be claimed by both sides), kept the peace (the only even quasi-judicial activity mentioned), and gave feasts on the proceeds of *ad hoc* toll-booths. These were decidedly political duties: they were not ecclesiastical, despite the functional link between commune and church (but perhaps the patrons dominated ecclesiastical life), and, apart from the ditch, they did not involve collective economic activity. The slight evidence for common land in the documents for the plain (see above, p. 49) fits with this absence; communally run property was, apparently, not sufficiently important to provide a firm economic structure for rural collective life. (This was certainly so in the sixteenth century, when Lucchese lowland communes had few common lands and relatively little organic economic responsibility.) This made them weaker than the silvo-pastoral communes of the mountains, but also, again, more politically orientated; such communes were as a result dependent for their autonomy on balances of power that were themselves political.[18]

What can we make of this? Tassignano was not in the territorial signoria of the church patrons; no other document gives any sign of it,

---

[18] See AAL +I30 (*a*.1156), ASL Archivio de' Notari 11 ott. 1172, for 12th-cent. references to common lands; only the latter, which refers to the *padule* of Tassignano, indicates that any of it was more than trivial in size. The commune of Tassignano by 1209 leased land (along with the commune of Capannori) from the Porcaresi, for either 8 or 80 *stai* of grain per year, in an unknown location (ACL Q84). This is not necessarily common land as we normally use the term; other communes held specific bits of property whose surplus was used to pay dues, to the church for example (ASL S. Ponziano 31 genn. 1207, AAL AB50, *a*.1223), and these two communes may have been doing the same. But it does at least show some local financial organization. For the 16th cent., see M. Berengo, *Nobili e mercanti* (Turin, 1965), 321.

and in the 1206 case, as I have said, judicial rights are not so much as mentioned. If one looks at the case from the standpoint of the Lucchesi, the patrons were not claiming to be anything more than intermediaries between the city and the village in certain public contexts. They had, presumably, judicial rights over their *manentes* on their lands, but this was not territorialized at all; the only formal relation that this power had to the question of the commune was a general recognition that the presence of many *manentes* in the commune weakened its claim to be wholly independent. Indeed, such rights do not seem to have been essential to the local power of the church patrons, for they evidently relaxed their control over many of their *manentes* in the late twelfth century, as both sides agreed; the patrons must have thought it sufficient to dominate the village by indirect means, through the church and the consulate. On the one hand, this might not seem surprising; there is no doubt that they could not have moved in the other direction and crystallized their local control into a territorial signoria over the village, as lords elsewhere would have tried to do, for the city was too close and too jealous of its authority. But it is notable that they did not feel they needed to maintain their residual legal powers either; it is in fact a truly striking testimony to the hegemony of urban and public jurisdiction that Albertino and Bandino's attempts to maintain political control over a village which they dominated as landowners was couched so largely in the terminology of informal patronage, the giving of feasts and the swearing of oaths, rather than according to the sharper lines of legal powers and privileges which were normal elsewhere. It is as if they were still in the Carolingian world, rather than the thirteenth century.

Tassignano in this respect contrasts notably with the signorial exception of Moriano, with its collective oaths and local courts. But the Moriano comparison brings out another, rather different, point as well. The rights that the commune of Tassignano was claiming against its patrons, the right to choose its own consuls, to co-organize local public works, to amend its own *breve*, were rights that the inhabitants of Moriano, though living inside the bishop's signoria and attending the bishop's churches, *already* had, with little episcopal opposition. We must conclude that the local proprietorial predominance of the patrons of the church of Tassignano, expecially but not only over *manentes*, was the major factor that allowed the subjection of the local commune; here, as in Moriano (see above, p. 98), the local wealth of the dominant landowning group was more important than its rights as patrons or territorial lords.

How strong the patrons actually were in Tassignano in tenurial terms is already indicated in the 1206 document. Albertino's claims were, as I have said, demonstrably exaggerated; but, even going by Fiorentino's figures, half of the families in the village had once been their *manentes*, and, although the percentage was by now only a sixth or perhaps even a sixteenth, Fiorentino did not claim that others (*liberi* or *franchi homines*) were not still the patrons' tenants. It is impossible here to distinguish between the tenants of the church and those of the three patronal families; there were differences between them, of course, but Albertino and Bandino evidently spoke for the whole group, and in terms of their local dominance they may have been in practice relatively homogeneous. If we look at the other documents for the village, to see how they fit with Fiorentino's statements, we will find that the rough figures for the landowning of the church and its patrons in Tassignano across the century 1125–1225 come to 21 per cent, less than half Fiorentino's calculation. This figure is, however, a minimum, given the fact that the documents we have come not from S. Stefano's archives but those of city churches and of Pozzeveri, and thus will overstress the landowning of the latter at the expense of the former; it is notable in particular that Ponzano, where the church and/or the *filii Soffreduccii* evidently had a substantial estate, rarely figures at all in the other documentation. We can thus accept that Fiorentino's already defensive claims do not exaggerate the extent of the land controlled by the patrons. But half a village was a huge property by twelfth-century Lucchese standards; the figure is over twice that for the bishop's property in Moriano and vastly more than anyone's lands in S. Margherita.[19] On the estate, maybe most tenants were *manentes* in 1150, although rather fewer in 1200; it must be admitted that there are rather few references

[19] For landowning percentages, compare the calculations for episcopal land in Moriano, above, p. 83. The only other references to Ponzano are *RCL* 1797–8 (*a*.1198), ACL H92 (*a*.1208), cf. ASL SMFP 26 ago. 1218, for a Ponzano-based family of landowners and tenant cultivators. Fiorentino's figures have another problem associated with them: they are based on a total population for Tassignano of 83 families. This is a convincingly precise number, and would be analogous, given the size of the village territory, to the very high figures for Moriano (see above, p. 110). But it is well in excess of the population documented in the *estimo* of 1331–2, a period when demographic levels are supposed to have been at their height: in that very detailed source, only 66 families (or, on a more restricted reading of the text, 58) are listed. See ASL *Estimo* 12 bis, fos. 391–4; and ASL Capitoli 52, p. 232, a contemporary oath, which is a good check on the *estimo*. (After the Black Death, the population dropped to under a third of that figure: pers. comm. Franca Leverotti; see now Leverotti, '"Crisi" del Trecento', 246, 261.) Until someone does detailed work on population trends in the 13th cent., a huge task, we must presume that Fiorentino exaggerated substantially.

in the other documents to *manentes*, but we have few local leases to cultivators of any kind, and none for S. Stefano and its patrons.[20]

The conclusion we can draw from this is clear: the subjection of a high percentage of the peasants of Tassignano to a single landowning group not only produced a formally subject commune, but also produced a commune that was prepared to fight for its independence. What we see in 1206 is a rare event in the Lucchese countryside of the period: explicit class struggle. The Tassignanesi did not have to fight a consolidated and domineering signoria, like the peasants in some of the well-known dramatic peasant conflicts of twelfth- and thirteenth-century Italy, on Monte Amiata or in the Veneto; but they had to struggle more than other Lucchese villages for a measure of independence, and they duly did so, with disputed elections, boycotts, and destructions of documents running on for at least a decade.[21]

If we want to compare Tassignano more fully with other villages, we must look at it from a wider perspective than that provided by just one document. We may not have other texts for the church or the commune, but we have plenty for the rest of the landowners and other inhabitants of the village, the 50 per cent who were not the patrons' tenants. Some of Tassignano's inhabitants were indeed, as elsewhere, landowners. Significantly, they included Fiorentino, who in 1194 got a tenant house as dower from his future son-in-law Amato di Ricciardo (surrounded, one may note, by the land of the church patrons); the scale of this transaction implies that both Amato and Fiorentino had enough tenants to allow them not to have to cultivate their own lands. Apart from them, we have a consistent set of smallish local landowners, men like Rolanduccio Penducoro di Federico (fl. 1140–75), in particular in the 1140s and the 1190s, appearing as a more coherent group in the 1140s than in the 1190s (a pattern we have seen before), but surviving up to 1200 and beyond, as casual references to individual owners 'de Tassiniano' indicate.[22] There

---

[20] Tassignano *manentes*: *RCL* 623 (*a*.1102), for the Canonica's land just beside S. Stefano; see above, pp. 107–9, and C. J. Wickham, 'Manentes e diritti signorili', in C. D. Fonseca (ed.), *Società, istituzioni, spiritualità* (Spoleto, 1994), 1067–80. Local leases: *RCL* 1236, 1670, 1689; ASL S. Giovanni 22 lugl. 1178, Spedale 8 ago. 1193 (= *RCL* 1692), SMFP 26 ago. 1218, Spedale 10 magg. 1225, 8 ott. 1225, none for the church and its patrons.
[21] See below, pp. 162, 164, 175, for the parallels.
[22] Fiorentino: AAL *H96 (*a*.1195); his son-in-law's father is a Pozzeveri tenant in ASL Spedale 8 ago. 1193 (= *RCL* 1692). Fiorentino's son Cristofano is a witness in Lucca for a Tassignano document in ASL Fiorentini 9 febb. 1226. For Rolanduccio Penducoro, who was a local owner in Pozzeveri's orbit, with a recurrent circle of associates, see ASL ii. 545, *RCL* 943, 969, 988, 1064, 1203, 1350; for some of the associates, *RCL* 1029, 1054. Owners from Tassiniano: AAL *H96 (*a*.1195), *RCL* 1797–8 (*a*.1198), ASL Spedale 20 genn. 1199, 12 lug. 1217.

is, unfortunately, not enough detail on any of them to make it worthwhile to pursue them individually. References to them survive, as usual, through the archives of the churches which got some of their land: Pozzeveri received most during the century, but other churches gained land locally too, particularly in the 1170s–80s. Pozzeveri was the closest rural monastery, but also the foundation of the nearest aristocratic family, the lords of Porcari, who also had substantial lands in Capannori, just to the north of Tassignano. Although the Porcaresi had little property in the latter village, they did lease land to the Tassignano commune in 1209; it would not be surprising if they were regarded as a possible ally against S. Stefano's patrons, and the predominance of gifts to Pozzeveri may perhaps be understood in that light.[23]

From the documents, if we looked at them in ignorance of the 1206 court case, we would derive a picture of local lay landowners, who might be slightly richer than the owner-cultivators of S. Margherita, and who were certainly more numerous after 1200—who lasted longer as landowners, that is. This pattern is set, however, against a slowly increasing documentation not only for churches, but also for lay citizens (excluding the church patrons, that is), who by the early thirteenth century were having their lands cultivated by Tassignano tenants, some of whom had sold out directly to them.[24] This picture is similar to that for S. Margherita, and has similarities to that for Moriano, except that city landowners in the latter hardly appear at all until late in the twelfth century. Although the inhabitants of Tassignano were less closely linked to Lucca than the church patrons were, its pull was felt by them too, as a result of the city's political dominance, and, still more, of the economic supremacy of its markets. Tassignano had already been fully integrated into the market structure by 1100, specializing in grain, as leases make clear (see above, p. 18); its inhabitants thus automatically looked to city buyers when they were short of money—as well as to city patrons when they needed social and political backing. And citizens, when they gained control over local land, brought the requirements of the market further

---

[23] The 1170s–80s date for the global increase in church land has been derived from a sudden increase in those decades in churches owning on charter boundaries. Cessions to Pozzeveri are *RCL* 679, 716, 740, 1054, 1203, 1587, 1711; to the Canonica, *RCL* 905, 1402, 1559 (the last two from Rembo's family); to S. Bartolomeo, ASL ii. 198, 305, 312; to Altopascio, AAL ++P6 (*a.*1183), ++K77 (*a.*1191); to S. Maria Forisportam, ASL Spedale 6 dic. 1177, SMFP 12 febb. 1224. The Porcaresi leasing to the Tassignano commune: above, n. 18; they own on boundaries in *RCL* 716, 740.

[24] *RCL* 1797–8 (*a.*1198), ACL H92 (*a.*1208), AAL ++R44 (*a.*1205), ASL S. Giovanni 26 apr. 1213, S. Nicolao 17 apr. 1222, Spedale 8 ott. 1225.

into village society, for they were certainly taking rents in produce to sell in the city.

These developments were by no means necessarily (or ever) to the advantage of the Tassignanesi, for city creditors were coercive and threatening. But they will have contrasted markedly with the much more static and traditional obligations of the *manentes* of the church patrons: we have seen tenants in various places in the Sei Miglia take advantage of the fragmentation and the multi-level leases characteristic of the commercial tenures of the late twelfth century (above, pp. 24–8), but the environment must have been much more closed on the patronal *tenuta* in Tassignano. It may well have been for these reasons that the 1206 document (unlike some of those for Moriano) shows no opposition at all to the city on anyone's part; indeed, Fiorentino at one point made a blatant play towards the judges, stating that 'it is of the greatest utility to have the consuls of the city and people of Lucca in Tassignano and other villages' (Albertino refused to reply, 'since he does not believe it is relevant to the case'). Fiorentino seriously sought city support, that is to say. If it seems clear to us that the commune was bound to lose, given the lack of interest in rural liberation generally shown by Lucca, and the important social position in the city of the church patrons themselves, which depended precisely on tenurial hegemonies such as this one, it may not have been so obvious to Fiorentino, who knew more about the detail of early thirteenth-century city politics than we do. He may, for example, have hoped for strictly factional support from the enemies of the Antelminelli; factional enmity was certainly high in this period, for there had been a brief civil war in and around Lucca in 1203.[25]

This city-orientated environment for half of Tassignano further emphasized the atypical feature of the village, the dominant bloc of land owned by S. Stefano and its patrons. The patronal *tenuta* and the subjection of its tenants gave political coherence and tension to the developing commune; its free neighbours, like Fiorentino, gave it leaders and an independent sphere of action; neighbouring villages (all of which were more autonomous than Tassignano) and all these close links to the city provided an awareness of alternative, and sometimes less totalizing, systems of subjection. This was a recipe for trouble, and trouble duly followed, uniting all the Tassignanesi against Albertino and Bandino. Nevertheless, given the degree of tension in the Italian countryside at large around 1200, the lack of response from the rest of the Sei Miglia

---

[25] *Tholomei Annales*, s.a.; Sercambi, *Croniche* i. 12–14.

is equally striking: from no other village do we have documents for any disputes between collectivities and lords, except over the control of churches. This is an important issue; we will come back to it in the next chapter.

Our third example, and a much less dramatic one, is Paganico, twenty minutes' walk eastwards from S. Stefano di Tassignano, in the direction of Porcari. Paganico's documents (around one hundred for the years 1100–1225) show the same sort of patterns we have seen for other villages, with churches, citizens, and local landowners jostling each other for possession inside the village territory. Here, the largest landowner was Pozzeveri, judging by the crude figures for landed property, based as usual on counting boundaries. Although it only owned 13 per cent of the land in the village, its local importance was undoubtedly increased by the local political influence of its patrons the Porcaresi, whose estates in Capannori and Porcari touched Paganico on two sides, and who had a little land in the village as well—there are occasional references to signorial rights in Paganico documents, too, which have Pozzeveri/Porcari links. S. Maria di Paganico, the parish church, which the cathedral canons controlled, also had substantial properties locally, second only to Pozzeveri; S. Bartolomeo in Silice on the eastern edge of the city comes third; and then we find the usual array of other churches (including nearby S. Stefano), with lesser portions of land. Of these, Pozzeveri's lands increased slowly over the twelfth century, whereas S. Bartolomeo gained property quite quickly from the 1170s onwards.[26] But the major movement of lands was, as elsewhere, lay: the proportion of city landowners climbed steadily after 1150, and they outnumbered local landowners by the early years of the thirteenth century. Examples of this development include known city-dwellers who bought up land in Paganico at various times in the twelfth century, notably Benefece and Landoino di Rospillo in the 1130s and, above all, Ciofforo

---

[26] Cessions to Pozzeveri: *RCL* 716, 739, 798, 1055, 1083, 1171, 1173, 1204, 1587, 1589, 1632, 1640, 1748, 1774 (cf. 1571–2, 1621), ACL Q43 (*a.*1214), Q176 (*a.*1220), Q112 (*a.*1224). To S. Maria di Paganico: ASL S. Giovanni 14 genn. 1195 (a lease); to S. Bartolomeo in Silice: ASL ii. 200 (*a.*1110), AAL +K35 (*a.*1166), +I45 (*a.*1183), +I3 (*a.*1185), +I31 (*a.*1187), *A49 (*a.*1191), +Q54 (*a.*1198), ++I98 (*a.*1222). S. Maria is seldom an actor in the documents; the others are *RCL* 258, 306, 322, 324 (*a.*1055–65), 908, AAL AL46 (*a.*1140), ++O51 (*a.*1168), ++H34 (*a.*1190). S. Stefano di Tassignano owning in Paganico: AAL +I31, *A8 (*a.*1182), ++D47 (*a.*1185), *RCL* 1528 (*a.*1185), ACL R49 (*a.*1224). For the Porcaresi, see *RCL* 1456, 1544 (signorial rights), 1701; for the Porcari estate touching Paganico, 870 (*a.*1130). Their signorial rights in Paganico, as in most other places, were doubtless restricted to their landed properties, as Henry VI conceded in 1186: A. N. Cianelli, 'Dissertazioni', in *Memorie e documenti* (Lucca, 1813), i. 198–200.

di Rustico in the years 1153–83. Ciofforo was an active dealer in the middle years of the century, living in the Borghicciolo on the eastern edge of the city, just outside the Roman walls. He bought land in Paganico and, to a lesser extent, Tassignano, Capannori, and Tempagnano—the villages on the roads leading out from his suburb—presumably to pick up grain to sell in the city (though he also leased land to city notables), before giving most of it on his deathbed in 1183 to the hospital of S. Bartolomeo, where he had been *lector* since at least 1178. (These gifts were the reason for the survival of his charters, of course, and also, in large part, for the sudden wealth of that church in Paganico; they were so complex, however, that S. Bartolomeo was still fighting court cases about them up to 1228.)[27]

As in S. Margherita, ownership by outside persons or bodies in Paganico was sufficiently widely distributed to stop any single owner, even Pozzeveri, from gaining the dominance that the patronal consorteria had in Tassignano. As in both S. Margherita and Tassignano, too, ownership by local men may have formed, at least by 1200, a relatively small percentage of the lands of the village. But the families that can be traced through the late twelfth and thirteenth centuries in Paganico included people rather more prosperous than their equivalents at S. Margherita, and, in some cases, somewhat better defined than their equivalents in Tassignano; a small but coherent group of local medium landowners still existed in Paganico in 1200, and appears in enough documents to allow them to be discussed. It is perhaps not surprising that they are also linked to what little we know of the early years of the local commune.

The commune of Paganico is documented only once before 1225, in a court case of 1190. In this text, the church of S. Maria claimed 3 *stai* of grain, and a future annual rent of one *staio*, from a certain Rustichello di Gilio, whose dead brother had promised it to the church; Rustichello said he would not give it, because the priest of the church had not fulfilled his side of the bargain, which was to pay for his brother's funeral expenses. They both put it to the consuls of Paganico, Guicciardo and Landuino, who gave judgment for the church. That is as close as the church got to the consuls in this period; we have a few earlier charters

---

[27] Benefece and Landoino: *RCL* 898, 903, 908, 1019, 1076, 1083, AAL AL46 (*a.*1140), +I30 (*a.*1156). Ciofforo: see, in general, Esch, 'Lucca', ch. 2; in Paganico, as an actor: AAL *A65 (*a.*1153), ++I30 (*a.*1156), +E21 (*a.*1164), ++V48 (*a.*1165), +K35 (*a.*1166), ++O51 (*a.*1168), +E65 (*a.*1172), +I43 (*a.*1176–7), *D80 (*a.*1180), +82 (*a.*1180), +I45, +I47 (*a.*1183). After his death, esp. +Q54 (*a.*1198), ++F38 (*a.*1199), *E99 ('XII–XIIIs.'), +I50 ('XIIIs.'), +I32 (*a.*1211), +I45 (*a.*1211–28), +82 (*a.*1214–28); see above, p. 27. *Lector* in S. Bartolomeo's hospital: ASL Spedale 23 febb. 1178.

in which it sold land to Lucchesi, but there is no sign of any *consilium* from any local bodies, whether patrons or villagers. Guicciardo and Landoino, however, we can trace. Guicciardo di Bottaccio was a landowner in Paganico; he sold land to S. Bartolomeo in 1186, and he and his father and brother are mentioned on land boundaries seven times in the second half of the century in Paganico and Capannori. He was also a charter witness, mostly in the same villages, acting for his colleague Landoino and for Cortafugga di Panfollia, another local landowner, among others. His father-in-law Rolandino di Benedetto was an associate of Ciofforo di Rustico and leased from him nearly 8 *cultra* of land (8 Lucchese *modii*, the size of a generous tenant holding) in the village in 1172. Rolandino is described as living in Lucca, but he must have had two residences, for his son Giovanni, the most troublesome tenant of S. Bartolomeo's land in the 1210s, was called 'de Paganico'; the family must have been reasonably well off. The other consul, Landoino, appears as a landowner too, in 1198, and also as a *tutor*, or legal guarantor, for child owners in the village who sold land in 1182 to pay off family debts.[28] Tutors, a standard feature of charters for orphaned children, were either kin, or else, as probably in this case, local men of some standing. Landoino's co-tutor was Cortafugga di Panfollia, who as we have just seen also had links with Guicciardo; he also lived in Paganico, and is the one out of all these men that we can say most about.

Cortafugga di Panfollia probably appears in more documents than anyone else mentioned in this book, excepting only a few bishops and the like. I have found fifty-one references between 1182 and 1215, and I may well have missed some, especially after 1200.[29] In few of the documents

---

[28] Commune: AAL ++H34 (*a.*1190). Guicciardo: +I3 (*a.*1186, the sale); owning on boundaries in *RCL* 324, 1204, 1571, AAL ++M54 (*a.*1160), +I43 (*a.*1177), ++D47 (*a.*1185), +Q54 (*a.*1198); witnessing in *RCL* 1502 (for Meati south of Lucca), 1768, AAL *A8, +I31 (*a.*1182). Rolandino and Giovanni: AAL +E65 (*a.*1172), +82 (*a.*1180, 1214–28), +L14 (*a.*1183), +I45 (*a.*1183, 1211–28). Landoino: *A8, +I31 (*a.*1182), +Q54 (*a.*1198). For the 8 *cultra*, see Esch, 'Lucca', ch. 1, 22, 42.

[29] Cortafugga transacts in land in AAL +I31 (*a.*1187), *RCL* 1597, 1682, 1684, 1819, ACL Q43 (*a.*1214), Q123 (*a.*1215). As an owner or tenant on boundaries: *RCL* 798, 1571, 1626, 1780, 1811, ASL Spedale 15 ott. 1188, 21 mar. 1192, AAL ++Q72 (*a.*1186), +I50 ('XIIIs.'), ACL T117 (*a.*1205), Q43 (*a.*1214); his *feudum* is in *RCL* 1830. As a *mensurator*: AAL ++D47 (*a.*1185, the only reference to him as 'de loco Capannore'), *RCL* 1571–2, 1583 (in Lunata), 1620–1, 1809 (in Pieve S. Paolo), AAL +I50 ('XIIIs.'), ACL T117, 127 (*a.*1205). As an arbiter: *RCL* 1768, 1801 (as *castaldio*; see further 1800), 1803, AAL ++F38 (*a.*1199). As a *tutor*: *RCL* +I31, *A8 (*a.*1182), *RCL* 1621. As a witness: ASL S. Ponziano 15 magg. 1184 (in S. Margherita), S. Frediano 5 nov. 1189, S. Giovanni 14 genn. 1195, AAL +I3 (*a.*1185), *RCL* 1632, 1640, 1712–13 (in S. Margherita), 1744, 1745, 1748, 1750, 1774, 1780, 1811, 1817, ACL S40 (*a.*1201), Q106 (*a.*1210), Q73 (*a.*1213). I am grateful, as elsewhere, to Arnold

is he transacting land for himself, and then only on a small scale: four
sales of fields, to S. Bartolomeo and Pozzeveri, in 1187, 1189, 1199, and
1214, one acquisition, in 1193, and a gift to Pozzeveri on his deathbed
complete the list. Cortafugga is, none the less, recorded in texts as holding land on the boundaries of other people's properties many times more,
in Paganico and in Capannori. (He probably lived near to the border between
the two, for his Paganico holdings tended to be on the Capannori side of
the village, and once he is described as from Capannori.) For most of
these properties he is described as a tenant, usually of Pozzeveri; in 1200
he had a *feudum* (for which he paid rent) from the cathedral Canonica,
too. He seems to have been a medium landowner; although holding much
of his land on lease, he was in possession of enough for him not to have
to cultivate. He was probably no more prosperous than that, even though
he appears more often as a landowner than anyone else, and must have
been the richest local inhabitant. His local prominence, however, was unusual in that it did not only derive from his lands: he was a *mensurator
terrarum*, a public land-measurer, and he measured land in Paganico
and Capannori, often along with a Capannori man called Godemanno di
Martinello, also a *mensurator*, for Pozzeveri and S. Bartolomeo throughout his active career.

What being a *mensurator* entailed in terms of expertise and training is
unclear. Cortafugga was not a measurer for the city, for his beat did not
extend much beyond the villages where he owned land; but probably his
local measuring authority was at least recognized by the city, for it had
a quasi-judicial element to it—he is often the author of the document
recording the measures, or else he and Godemanno are its sole witnesses.[30]
Doubtless this position was the reason why Cortafugga was also a witness in so many other documents, about twenty in all, including two-
thirds of those for Paganico from the last fifteen years of the twelfth century,
for lay owners as well as for every church with local interests. It certainly
must have been the reason why we also find him with local public responsibilities of greater weight: twice as *tutor* for children (one of which has

Esch for his card catalogue to 1200. Cortafugga seems to have been less active in later years,
but I may have missed some of the references to him after 1200, for the ACL *schede* are
extremely abbreviated and include no names. Cortafugga's father, interestingly, is only recorded
once, on a boundary, in AAL +I43 (*a.*1177); the family may have been newcomers to the
area, or else recently risen up the social scale.

[30] Godemanno is less prominent than Cortafugga, only being known outside the
mensurator charters (see previous n.) in *RCL* 1408, 1517, 1588, 1590, 1625–6, 1709, 1745,
almost always in Capannori, and always in Pozzeveri charters. There were also notaries
on the plain with extremely local remits, of only a few villages: Esch, 'Lucca', ch. 3.

already been mentioned), and four times, in 1196–9, as an agreed arbiter in local disputes, for Pozzeveri, the Canonica, and S. Bartolomeo. (The two Pozzeveri cases seem to have resulted in compromises; the Canonica won its case; but S. Bartolomeo lost its dispute in favour of some fairly obscure Paganico owner-cultivators.) There is no doubt that Cortafugga had acquired the local authority to determine disputes like these, even though they were informally agreed arbitrations between the parties (as over a fifth of documented Lucchese disputes still were), from his public standing; in three out of the four cases, he arbitrated on his own, an unusual position of trust. In the second Pozzeveri case, in 1198, he was also a *castaldio* of the monastery; but he was not exclusively a Pozzeveri client, for two years later he and two of his sons were sworn *fideles* of the Canonica for their fief. Pozzeveri in appointing him *castaldio* was simply taking into its employ a man already important locally.

Cortafugga evidently had a remarkable presence in Paganico, and to a lesser extent Capannori. It was mostly personal, but it had some effect on his family: his sons were sometimes witnesses, at least in his lifetime, and his brother Giunta was himself an arbiter in a dispute of 1220, after Cortafugga's death.[31] His land, his position as *mensurator*, and presumably after a while his recognized public experience, were the bases of this presence; it did not derive from his association with external lay or ecclesiastical powers. (He does appear in more documents for Pozzeveri than for any other landowner, but this is probably simply because that monastery kept the largest number of documents for the area; his position of monastic *castaldio* came latish in his career, and did not visibly bring wider responsibilities.) Cortafugga was in fact what would a century earlier have been called a local *bonus homo*, with a recognized public position related to landholding but going beyond it.[32] But he was not a consul, or at least he is never recorded as being one. He certainly was not one in the years he arbitrated disputes, for the texts would certainly have said so otherwise; so ought they to have when he witnessed documents, judging by parallels elsewhere, and he did that in surviving documents in every year between 1182 and 1202 bar four. This is important. One would have expected such an influential man, the most influential inhabitant of Paganico by far, with such local interests, to be the backbone of the local commune, the major thrust behind the affirmation of local

---

[31] Cortafugga's family up to 1220: *RCL* 1587, 1711, 1745, 1768, 1830, ACL Q123 (*a*.1214–15); AAL +I31 (*a*.1187), +B8 (*a*.1220, Giunta as arbiter).
[32] Cf. C. J. Wickham, *The Mountains and the City* (Oxford, 1988), 260–4.

identity of his home village. He certainly had links with the only two men who we can be sure did involve themselves in the commune. Yet he cannot be traced as being so at any stage.

There are two alternatives. Cortafugga may have been involved in the local commune, alongside his local associates; but if so, it left no sign in over fifty documents. Most Lucchese communes were not particularly well documented, as we are finding out, but the commune of Paganico would have been peculiarly shadowy if as well documented a man as this did not bother to acknowledge his major office in his own village. The other alternative is that he had some reason to avoid such involvement. In the context of this possibility, it is important to note that by the end of his life he had acquired a house in the city, in the Borghicciolo, where Ciofforo had lived before. In that house his son Ildebrando willed a *staio*'s rent to Pozzeveri from his sickbed in 1214; and, although it was still in his other house in Paganico that Cortafugga, himself sick, willed two more *stai* in July 1215, he had moved to his Lucca house by October to make an adjustment to Ildebrando's cession. Cortafugga evidently moved easily enough between his two dwellings, even though ill (of an illness from which he probably died: these are the last references to him). But the city house puts him into a new category, that of men like Gerardino di Morettino of Marlia or Guido di Guidotto of Moriano or even the *filii Soffreduccii* of Tassignano: men who were moving into the city, while still maintaining their local connections. Like Gerardino (though probably unlike Guido) he still regularly lived in his residence in the country, and identified with it—to the city, Cortafugga may well have still seemed a country-dweller. But he was beginning to make the break. His grandsons, who are documented between 1224 and 1270, kept on the house in Paganico, but are by now called not 'de Paganico', but 'de Porta S. Cervasii', the name for their city quarter that begins to be attested after the new walls of Lucca were built; they were tenants and landlords in Paganico, just like their grandfather, as well as being petty grain usurers, but their social link with the inhabitants of the village was now weak.[33]

Exactly how Cortafugga saw his social position and his relationship with the city is hypothetical, of course. But the slow movement of his family into the city is typical, and he can thus, even in this hypothetical form, serve as an example. To a man like Cortafugga, a prosperous

[33] Cortafugga in Lucca: ACL Q123 (*a*.1214–15). Grandsons: Q112 (*a*.1224), Q103 (*a*.1224), AAL *A58 (*a*.1254), ++V70 (*a*.1257), ++O43 (*a*.1260), *A77 (*a*.1265–70), *A7 (*a*.1268), all transactions of Forte di Parisio di Cortafugga, who is *de Porta S. Cervasii* in 1224 and 1260, and *Lucensis* in 1265; the house in Paganico appears in 1257 and 1260.

country-dweller with considerable personal status, the politics of the late twelfth century provided certain clearly defined possibilities. He could try to dominate his village from above, with the help of the most important local landowners (churches or aristocratic families like the Porcaresi or the Antelminelli), or through patronage over the local church, or both. He was certainly not rich enough to do that, but it was a solution adopted as close as Tassignano by people who were richer, and was thus at least available as an aspiration, although a less common one than a century or so earlier (see above, pp. 31–4). Alternatively, he could gain local hegemony by working through his neighbours, of the same social standing or less, to help set up or stabilize the rural commune; this was a common choice, and was made by people of a similar status to Cortafugga everywhere in the Lucchesia, whether together with external powers, like Rodolfo di Andrea in Moriano, or against them, like Fiorentino in Tassignano. It brought less direct power than the *filii Soffreduccii* had, but in practice quite as much local influence, and influence that was less liable to be challenged. Fiorentino's choice laid him open to quite a lot of challenge, of course, but being a leader of the Tassignanesi may have been preferable to being a client of the Antelminelli; in Paganico, anyway, with fewer dominant powers, gaining local authority would probably have been a much easier process, much as it seems to have been in S. Margherita. The third alternative was the city, less than two hours' walk from Paganico, and centre of a far greater range of chances of advancement than anyone could obtain in Paganico, although removing, at least at first, the satisfaction of local importance. We do not know if these possibilities were mutually exclusive. Cortafugga, like many others in the twelfth century (and every subsequent century up to the present) would have wanted to maintain his local residence and social influence while also exploring new possibilities in the city. He may not have seen his interests in Paganico and in the city as fundamentally in conflict. But in the end the conflict of interest was there, and the city would win. It seems to me, in fact, that Paganico's group of medium landowners would have been strong enough to act as the core of a fairly active local commune, at least as a political community (as perhaps was the early commune in Marlia, above, p. 44); but if its leader was moving to the city, and was not sufficiently interested in underpinning that political community, its strength would have been sucked out. The choice of men like Cortafugga resulted in the weakening of the local role of the commune at the precise moment of its institutional crystallization: hence a social profile for a commune like Paganico that was so low as to resemble the plain it sat in.

This emphasis on the political choices of local élites is not the only guide to the strength or weakness of a local commune, of course. How much collective economic or socio-political activity there was in any given settlement, that could be controlled or otherwise mobilized by its leaders, is crucial for understanding all communal developments. But in a village like Paganico, where such collective activity appears to have been largely absent, the status involved in local office may not have been enough to persuade people like Cortafugga to stay in village politics, if the attraction of the city was great enough. And Lucca was expanding fast, economically and demographically; people inside its walls could get rich. They bought land; other landowners were tempted into the city; either way, local landowners were diminished. Plesner stressed, as early as the 1930s, that the attraction of Florence had the strongest effect on rural élites, rather than the rural poor, with the effect in the countryside that the autonomous activity of rural communities was weakened *vis-à-vis* local lords. Exactly this process, which Plesner analysed for mid-thirteenth-century Passignano, on the very edge of the Florentine contado, was already in operation a century earlier in the villages around Lucca.[34] In these villages, social cohesion was demonstrably weaker in 1200 than in the early twelfth century; in all the settlements we have looked at, the relatively tight sets of local landowners of the 1120s–40s, who witness each other's charters and sell land to each other, do not have easily identifiable successors by the end of the century, though the number of charters does not diminish. Local landowners continued to exist, well into the late Middle Ages, but their internal relationships were diluted by city ownership. And, in the long run, the movement of village élites into the city meant that local society was going to be restricted to the poor, to owner-cultivators and tenants, in 'a compactly peasant society', as Berengo described the sixteenth-century Lucchesia. Communes continued, too, and indeed were ever more firmly institutionalized (not least by the city, which needed them to raise taxes and keep down crime), but they lost status. Their

---

[34] J. Plesner, *L'emigrazione* (1934; Ital. edn., Florence, 1979), 105–51. The process was, however, not uniform in the Fiorentino: at Impruneta, close to the city, it happened later (D. Herlihy, 'Impruneta', in N. Rubinstein (ed.), *Florentine Studies* (London, 1968), 256–72), and so did it in the hills behind Fiesole (P. Pirillo, 'I beni comuni', *Mélanges de L'Ecole française de Rome*, 99 (1987), 624 ff.). In outlying parts of the Lucchesia, such as the Garfagnana, the social attraction of the city was by now similarly weak: Wickham, *Mountains*, 134 ff. For a context, see G. Cherubini, 'La campagne italiane', in UTET, *Storia d'Italia*, iv (Turin, 1982), 344, and, more generally, 343–60. Although no one now accepts Plesner's claim that the rural poor emigrated into cities *less* than the rural rich, his analysis of the latter has not been undermined.

rulers were as often tenants as landowners; they often became simply
the local administration for the city rather than autonomous bodies, at
most acting to frustrate city policy as far as they could. Indeed, the major
enemy of *contadini* by 1300 was usually the city rather than any private
landowner.[35]

This was still in the future in Cortafugga's time, and is anyway an indication of a general trend, rather than an accurate description of every rural
commune on the Lucca plain. It does not fit Moriano or Tassignano,
at least in so far as we can tell from their histories up to the 1220s. But
the Paganico model was probably commoner than that of either of the
other two, or would become so; it certainly seems to fit neighbouring
Capannori, whose early commune is equally hard to characterize, despite
a relatively generous documentation for the village, and whose social context around 1200 is equally inconclusively evidenced.[36] It fits a number
of other settlements in the plain, too. At the moment of the institutionalization of the rural communes of the Sei Miglia, the point at which
they developed from informal bodies based on oaths to definable institutional structures, and thus emerged in the documentation, they became
denatured by the desertion of their principal supporters to the city. The
strong communal identity and institutions of Moriano and probably
Tassignano must be seen in the context of the weak polities of Paganico
and many other places. What we can conclude from this will be explored
in the next chapter, where the evidence for early rural communes in the
Sei Miglia as a whole will be set out and discussed. This will, I hope,
bring us closer to an understanding of the particularity of the territory
of Lucca.

[35] Berengo, *Nobili e mercanti*, 322; cf. F. Leverotti, 'Dalla famiglia stretta', *Studi storici*,
30 (1989), e.g. 199. For the opposition to the city, see Osheim, 'Countrymen and the Law',
332–5; more generally, A. I. Pini, *Città, comuni e corporazioni* (Bologna, 1986), 88–91, 102–5.
[36] Capannori has one rural communal charter before 1225, *RCL* 1626 (*a.*1191); as with
S. Margherita, it is a confirmation of a transaction of the church. Two of the four consuls
of 1191 are documented elsewhere as tenants of the canonica: *RCL* 1517, 1653, 1665; this
does not mean, of course, that they did not also own land. In Capannori, in fact, Pozzeveri
and its patrons, the Porcaresi, were by far the largest landowners in the village, with at least
20% of the land; but they did not control the local church, S. Quirico, and thus may have
been less domineering locally than the Tassignano patrons were. There were local owners
in the village into the 13th cent., as, e.g., ACL Q74 (*a.*1212).

Appendix
Genealogy of the Families of the Patrons of
S. Stefano di Tassignano

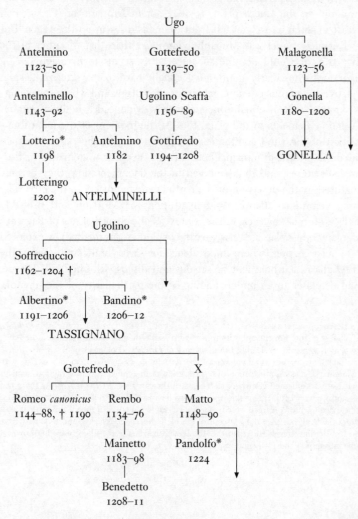

Ugo

Antelmino	Gottefredo	Malagonella
1123–50	1139–50	1123–56

Antelminello	Ugolino Scaffa	Gonella
1143–92	1156–89	1180–1200

Lotterio*   Antelmino Gottifredo   GONELLA
1198   1182   1194–1208

Lotteringo
1202   ANTELMINELLI

Ugolino

Soffreduccio
1162–1204 †

Albertino*   Bandino*
1191–1206   1206–12

        TASSIGNANO

Gottefredo   X

Romeo *canonicus*   Rembo   Matto
1144–88, † 1190   1134–76   1148–90

                    Mainetto   Pandolfo*
                    1183–98   1224

                    Benedetto
                    1208–11

* Explicitly cited as a patron.

7

Rural Communes in the Lucca Plain in the Twelfth Century

The three previous chapters have discussed four Lucchese rural communes, Moriano (including Aquilea and Sesto), S. Margherita, Tassignano, and Paganico. On the model of Moriano, the best documented of the four, backed up by the sketchier evidence for Tassignano, we may posit an institutional development for Lucchese communes that would roughly go like this: (i) around the start of the twelfth century, the beginnings of collective action by *vicini*, through informal representatives if necessary; (ii) the development, in the mid-century (though earlier or later according to circumstances), of an internal structure, with its own regulations, based on an oath—a structure which recognized stable representatives (consuls) and could be called a *consulatus*, but which was still informally organized; (iii) by 1200 or slightly later, the institutionalization of communal offices and powers, inside defined village/parish territories, often including the setting down of a *breve* (though *brevia* could go back, as with that of Moriano in *c*.1170, to the more informal period of consular government).

This pattern, based on the evidence from two communes, is not contradicted by the documents for any commune in the Lucchesia, whether in the Sei Miglia or outside it, although the dates may vary from place to place. Consuls certainly existed throughout the Sei Miglia by 1200 or so, as I have already argued (p. 67); in the rest of the diocese, we are less well informed, but all reasonably documented areas show some form of communal activity by then. By 1200, to have a consulate in one's village was normal in the Lucchesia. Indeed, by now every collective body had consuls—city neighbourhoods, artisanal associations, aristocratic consorterie; the twelfth-century passion for explicit power structures ensured it.[1] But it must be recognized that none of these developments in themselves ever appear to have been contentious in the diocese. We have no surviving examples anywhere, whether in the plain or outside it,

---

[1] City neighbourhoods: e.g. ASL S. Frediano 13 ott. 1164, S. Agostino 11 ago. 1165, S. Giovanni 22 genn. 1187, *RCL* 1654; associations: *RCL* 1296, 1726 (millers), 1532, 1656 (the corporation that ran Ponte S. Pietro); consorterie: *RCL* 1278, 1424.

of rural communes actually constituting themselves in the face of any-one's opposition. There was opposition between villages and lords, which was often expressed through communes and their consuls; but the exist-ence of the local commune, and its right to have officials, was challenged in no village known to me, with the sole (and in some respects peculiar) exception of Massarosa.[2] It is therefore reasonable to think that the devel-opment I have just characterized was a fairly common and stable one in the twelfth-century Lucchese environment.

What this process actually meant locally is, however, another matter. I have argued in general that the divergent interests of local leaders could contribute either to the strength and coherence of the developing commune or to its weakness. But the whole political context of each commune (as also its economic cohesion) varied from place to place. In Moriano's case, step (i) may have been accomplished by the social ag-gregation accompanying the siege of 1081–2; elsewhere in the Sei Miglia it is most likely to have come about in the context of the appearance of parishes with their own local identities and funds; in the rest of the diocese it can hardly have predated the growth of the signoria and its associated local military élites, themselves rarely appearing earlier than 1100. The further developments of each commune were even more diverse. In Moriano, the élite of 1121 may have been using the commune to estab-lish a local hegemony that was more widely and firmly based than would have been a simple attachment to the bishop, Moriano's lord; by 1200, however, their heirs and successors seem to have needed the structures of the commune/signoria merely to survive against an influx of city land-owners. In Sesto, the major political context of the early commune seems essentially to have been hostility to its neighbour Moriano. In Tassignano, city-based notables and church patrons were trying to control the com-mune from above, and the latter's principal political activity seems to have been resistance to this: here, a medium stratum of landowners, with the help of their tenant neighbours, was opposed to the notables around the church, a separation entirely absent in Moriano. In S. Margherita and

---

[2] Massarosa (in the relatively signorial Versilia) is atypical, for its right to have consuls was contested by its signorial lord, the cathedral Canonica, in 1227 (G. Dinelli, 'Una signoria ecclesiastica', *Studi storici*, 23 (1915) 276–8—see in general for Massarosa, ibid. 230–46). This looks like a standard Italian pattern, the dominating ecclesiastical lord unsuccessfully holding off the developing rural commune (see below, pp. 209–14); but in Massarosa's case the commune had been in operation for some time, and was publicly recognized by the city of Lucca, and even the canons, as it seems, in the 1190s (*RCL* 1642; ASF Strozziane-Uguccioni 23 lug. 1197)—it looks as if the Canonica was protesting retrospectively at an already established development.

Paganico, and probably Capannori and Marlia as well, the fragmentary evidence we have suggests communes uncontroversially headed by small- and medium-landowner élites focused on the church, and threatened not by any conscious danger from outside, but rather by two linked processes, the slow growth of city influence, and the consequent weakening of the stratum that in the twelfth century governed them. These processes affected villages in different ways: in S. Margherita the local leaders seem to have slowly lost their lands and become tenants; in Paganico some at least were drawn to the city and out of the local orbit altogether; in Marlia, however, strong local ownership may have lasted longer.

These villages each had very different local environments, even if some developments, like the expansion of city landowning, were common to all of them. They suggest, as is to be expected, that if there was any trouble involving the village as a whole (as at Moriano and Tassignano at different times) it would involve the commune. They also indicate, how- ever, that what we would call a commune would mean as many different things to villagers as there were different local social structures. There were any number of variables, in fact: the local importance of common land; the amount of external landowning, and whether it was balanced between many landowners or dominated by one; the identity of the local church patrons, and how much they involved themselves in local affairs; the local strength and coherence of any signorial rights; the number of local inhab- itants who were landowners, and of what standing, or who were tenants, and of whom; how involved in village affairs the local élite was, and how tempted by the city. We have already seen each of these variables in opera- tion in at least one village; if and when there was enough evidence to dis- cuss them further, they would in themselves provide much of the context of the local development of the rural commune in general. We cannot pursue them in detail for every village, however, even supposing we had the evidence for them and the space to describe them; the reader's patience would be excessively tried. But we can at least look relatively briefly at some more examples of Lucchese communes, taken from both inside and outside the Sei Miglia, to see if we can explore the problem further.

I will begin with a scene of violence, to show at least that Tassignano was not the only divided Lucchese village in this period. In 1157 the men of the *capella* of S. Concordio di Arsina (nowadays di Moriano) conceded in a court case, before the bishop and the pievano of Sesto Moriano (to whom S. Concordio was ecclesiastically subject), that they should no longer oppose the priests of the church. In this context, they listed a number of things they would no longer do, which implies that they had up until recently been doing them: lay hands on the clerics of the church, both inside and outside the cemetery; pillage church property; take the (church) keys by force; demand a feast on All Saints' Day or on the entry of any priest to the church; or require wine 'for the game which is vulgarly called *canterale*'. The men of S. Concordio seem a pretty boisterous lot, and not by any means always well disposed to their church, although fairly self-confident in their demands on it. It is therefore interesting to find that, of all the Lucchese rural churches, S. Concordio is one of the ones most clearly under the control of lay patrons. From the very first appearance of the church in 1134, up to the 1220s at least, a good half of the numerous texts concerning the church of S. Concordio explicitly involve the patronal families as participating, consenting, or witnessing.[3] The patrons were prominent citizens of the late twelfth century, who can be found holding consular offices in Lucca; but they clearly kept a tight control over S. Concordio's church. Only twice at most do the consuls of the local *vicinantia* visibly have a similar role of witnessing or consenting to church transactions, along with the patrons; significantly, the first occasion was in 1159, only two years after the court case.[4]

The similarities between these events and those at Tassignano fifty years later are pretty evident. But the local economic structure was different. The documents for S. Concordio (which seem to be the archive for the village church) show a large number of local owners in existence all through the century, alongside a large estate for the church, which was accumulating land and buying in tenements systematically; but, apart from the lands of the church patrons, very few city landowners or any other outsiders

---

[3] The dispute is ASL Archivio de' Notari 30 giug. 1157. Church acts involving the patrons: ASL ii. 425, ii. 478, Arch. de' Notari 1157, 9 mar. 1158, 11 ott. 1159, 20 apr. 1162, 30 magg. 1171, Arch. di Stato giug. 1184, Arch. de' Notari 10 ott. 1220, 18 apr. 1221 (cf. the 1171 text), AAL ++P20 (*a.*1224). Not visibly involving them: ASL ii. 635, Arch. de' Notari 8 sett. 1168, 12 febb. 1172, 1 dic. (*recte* 24 nov.) 1186, and then most of the texts from 1190 onwards (though we may not by now recognize the names of family members): 10 febb. 1191, 3 magg. 1196, 18 magg. 1197, 29 sett. 1200, 12 dic. 1213, 29 ott. 1214, 28 ago. 1215, 27 lug. 1217, etc. The most frequently attested family group among the patrons, the *filii Tadulini*, were plains landowners (e.g. *RCL* 1537, 1583, 1620, ASL Spedale 11 nov. 1199), and city notables (C. Imperiale di Sant'Angelo, *Codice diplomatico della Repubblica di Genova*, ii (Rome, 1938) n. 14; L. A. Muratori, *Antiquitates italicae*, ii (Milan, 1739), cols. 887–8 (*a.*1182); ASL Certosa 31 dic. 1189, and *RCL* 1512–13, 1521–2 for Uberto di Tadulino as *consul treuguanus* in 1184). The Canonica claimed control of the church in a number of late 12th-cent. papal confirmations, presumably falsely: *RCL* 1062, 1113, 1138, 1309, 1539.

[4] ASL Arch. de' Notari 11 ott. 1159, 30 magg. 1171. The latter shows Bellomo di Menco, one of the consuls of 1159, as a witness, this time possibly in a private capacity.

at all are documented.[5] As with neighbouring Moriano's relationship to the bishop in the early twelfth century, there was no intermediate group of outside powers to mediate between the local population and the church patrons; and since the patrons do not seem to have posed as local protectors (unlike the bishop in Moriano), the sort of trouble that would break out in Tassignano was already to be found, apparently in a more violent form, fifty years earlier. The church was the centre of local society; its neighbours were prepared to alienate land to it, or some of them were, and they were often the church's tenants—in this, they probably had little choice. When the tension broke out, too, the trouble was over the church itself; indeed, the details of the conflict that we have clearly focus on symbols of church patronage, keys and feasts.[6] The commune of S. Concordio seems to have aspired to a share in the control over the church alongside (or instead of) the patrons, and indeed probably succeeded for a time. But the church remains the only focus of their recorded interest; if the dispute involved more secular dimensions, the record of its resolution did not think to mention them.

Less violent disputes over the control of churches were commoner. They generally take the form of claims by a local community to the right to choose the priest, although the church patrons (if themselves ecclesiastical bodies) were recognized to have the right to invest him formally, and maybe veto his appointment. Such cases were very common all over Tuscany in this period, not least in cities, where they reflected the rising self-confidence of city neighbourhoods.[7] But, as we have seen (p. 77), city neighbourhoods were themselves very similar in structure to rural communes; it is not surprising that the latter would also try to exercise *de facto* powers of this kind as soon as they could. Nanni in his book on the Lucchese parish lists a dozen examples of local communes obtaining or trying to obtain such rights, usually in the context of dispute, in the

---

[5] There are some S. Concordio texts showing Montemagno/Mammoli connections, ASL Arch. de' Notari 30 magg. 1171, Serviti 18 ott. 1173, Arch. de' Notari 15 ago. 1188, 3 magg. 1196, but little else. The dominance of texts from a single archive, that of the local church, underlines the lack of involvement of other city powers in the village. For the transactions of the church, see above, n. 3; not all were for the village. Some of the patrons' dependants were *manentes*: AAL ++P20 (*a.*1224).

[6] For the symbolism of keys for patronage and signorial rights, see the remarks of O. Redon, *Uomini e comunità* (Siena, 1982), 33–42, which are valid well beyond the Senese, which she is discussing; for another example, below, n. 11.

[7] For Italy in general, D. Kurze, *Pfarrerwahlen* (Cologne, 1966), 111–40; for one classic case, ASF S. Maria Novella 29 apr. 1197, cf. R. Davidsohn, *Storia di Firenze* (1896; Ital. edn., Florence, 1956), i. 907–10; R. Caggese, *Classi e comuni rurali* (Florence, 1907–8), i. 215–18.

late twelfth and early thirteenth centuries (the first example he cites is for 1167). One of these can stand for all of them, as a typical instance: in 1182 the *vicini* of S. Bartolomeo di Ciciana, in the hills above Marlia, obtained through papally sponsored arbitrators the recognition of their right to agree with the Canonica, the local church patron, on who was to be their priest. Henceforth, the consuls of the *vicinia* (or the local notables, *meliores*, if there were no consuls there), were to begin this procedure, which, though hedged about with the usual rituals that reinforced the canons' patronage rights, gave most of the initiative to the community. Not every commune was as successful as Ciciana in gaining the capacity to choose its priest, but more and more communes would claim it.[8]

In other cases, the involvement between the commune and the church was less contentious still; these are instances where the commune or its consuls simply appeared alongside the priest, as advisers or guarantors for church transactions, as we saw for S. Margherita, or in court cases involving the church. Our only early references to the consuls of Vorno, Fiesso (modern Montuolo), S. Cassiano a Vico, Saltocchio, and, as we have also seen, Capannori, are of this type. Such communes are very shadowy indeed in the texts, although they may have been quite coherently organized. In S. Giusto di Marlia in 1207, for example, communal officials acting for the *vicinia* and the church bought up land to pay half of the 4 *stai* of grain that the commune/*vicinia* itself owed to the church annually; this sort of formal procedure presupposes a systematic communal structure, and one involving finance, too, even though the sums in this particular case were trivial.[9] It is further noteworthy that the commune's assumption of this financial responsibility to the church was indistinguishable from its association with ecclesiastical actions themselves.

---

[8] L. Nanni, *La parrocchia studiata nei documenti lucchesi* (Rome, 1948), 159–65, for references; p. 165 lists some unsuccessful attempts, and pp. 171 ff. analyse churches where *vicini* did not take over. He misses *RCL* 1694 (*a.*1193) for S. Vito and ASL S. Giovanni 23 ott. 1187, 22 ott. 1188, 26 genn. 1189 for Picciorano; and, among unsuccessful cases, ASL SMFP 30 sett. 1199 for Tramonte di Brancoli. For Ciciana, see *RCL* 1481–2 for the arbitration (comp. ACL A+1 p. 101, *a.*1220). There may have been relatively few active city landowners in Ciciana, for it is ill documented: for the years 1100–1225, I only know of nine other texts that mention it, *RCL* 667, 900, ACL Fondo Martini 25 (26 apr. 1118, Guidoni 42), 36 (7 febb. 1134, Guidoni 55), AAL AC67 (*a.*1110), ++N50 (*a.*1221), ASL Arch. Sardini 12 febb. 1187, SMFP 25 magg. 1194, Dono Mazzarosa-Cittadella 3 mar. 1211. Ciciana's social cohesion will have been strengthened both by this absence of external involvement and, possibly, by a woodland economy.

[9] Vorno: AAL + S10 (*a.*1151): Fiesso: *RCL* 1513 (*a.*1184); S. Cassiano: ASL S. Nicolao 3 magg. 1187; Saltocchio: ASL S. Giustina 25 nov. 1193, 31 magg. 1214 (though here there are two references to communal land too, AAL A47, *a.*1179, +95, *a.*1182); Capannori: above, Ch. 6 n. 36. S. Giusto: ASL S. Ponziano 31 genn. 1207.

The absence of frequent documentation for it may only mean that it was utterly routine. The linkage between stable communal organization, finance, and the church gives an additional context to the growing claim by communes that they should control church affairs and, indeed, choose priests. The linkage between all these features is given a further emphasis by another feature of the 1207 Marlia document: the communal officials named therein were not only consuls but also *operarii*. *Operarii* were the officials whose specific responsibility it was to organize (and sometimes underwrite) church building. They are best documented in the city neighbourhoods, which could certainly afford building programmes for local churches; indeed, outside the city I have only seen them referred to in texts for two other villages in this period, both near Marlia, Palmata in 1187 and Saltocchio in 1193 and 1214. But it was in the twelfth century that rural churches were built, all over the diocese, as we can still see today, including a clear majority of the parish churches of the plain (cf. above, p. 76); as Nanni already argued, the immense expense that this involved must have brought the village community into tight association with all aspects of the running of the church, and would have been one of the major justifications for the former's claims to be able to choose priests, notwithstanding the detail of canon law.[10] These new churches were the symbols of local prosperity and, one must assume, of the newly firm identities of the collectivity of the parish; it is not surprising that they therefore became foci for the developing commune.

We must note, however, that Nanni assumed, rather than demonstrated, that it was actually the village collectivity that put up the church. Indeed, in villages where patrons were strong, such as S. Concordio and Tassignano, it is most likely that they organized the rebuilding rather than any communal *operarii*; that subjected peasants eventually had to foot the bill does not affect the fact that it lay outside their control, though it may have added edge to their claims for church patronage in places like S. Concordio. The issue is explicit in a text of 1178 from S. Michele in Escheto in the southern plain, in which the *vicini* appear, unusually, as supporters of the lay patron in a dispute with the priests of S. Michele over the control of a second local church, S. Salvatore; but one of them declared that he 'and other *vicini* of S. Michele and Vincio [the patron] helped to restore the church [of S. Salvatore] . . . when it was

[10] *Operarii*: see J. F. Niermeyer, *Mediae latinitatis lexicon minus* (Leiden, 1976), 739. In the city: e.g. *RCL* 1394, 1654, ASL S. Agostino 7 mar. 1218. In the country: *RCL* 1565 for Palmata; see previous n. for Saltocchio. For church building, Nanni, *Parrocchia*, 160; and above, Ch. 3 n. 62.

menaced with ruin', as a justification for their claims for control.[11] Here, patron–community co-operation in church building had itself explicit wider political repercussions. Elsewhere, patrons organized building works without support, where they were powerful, or else, where they were weak, left it entirely to the *vicini* and their *operarii*; these differences presumably had political results as well. Church building thus did not so much emphasize communal identity, but, rather, gave to all existing local balances of power a further financial coherence; in this arena of local politics, there were resources to fight over.

All this means that it is not surprising that local communes, which were themselves, of course, communes of the parish (see above, pp. 56–62), should concern themselves so extensively with the church. But it emphasizes still further the fact that they are so seldom, in the Lucchese Sei Miglia, found doing anything else. Communes certainly had other roles, as the Tassignano case showed, and some of these do appear in a few texts. Water control was one: in 1209, the commune of S. Bartolomeo di Gello di Scheto in the southern plain deviated a stream, presumably for drainage, as the Tassignanesi did with their ditch. Common rights were another: the Monte Pisano text of 1199 that listed all the communes in the Vaccoli area (including Gello di Scheto) was, significantly, about common land on the mountain; rights to land clearance along the river were claimed by the communes of Moriano and Saltocchio in 1179. Where these issues were most important, as in the marshland communes on the lago di Bientina, or in the villages lying against the wooded hills north of the plain, from Brancoli eastwards to S. Gennaro, the commune will have gained more significance therefrom.[12] This must have been so, too, for the commune of Maggiano on the western edge of the Sei Miglia, when its consuls negotiated with the lords of the area to move part of the local settlement into its castello in 1189.[13] But in most of the plains

---

[11] *RCL* 1384–5. The case makes further use of key symbolism; cf. above, n. 6. This was not, technically, a rural communal dispute, for S. Salvatore, exceptionally, did not have its own parish, and therefore had no *populus* of its own.

[12] ASL Spedale 3 dic. 1209; ASL Tarpea 27 giug. 1199; see n. 9 for Saltocchio, and cf. above, p. 96, for Moriano; A. M. Onori, *S. Salvatore di Sesto* (Florence, 1984), 55–60, for the marshlands.

[13] ASL Certosa 31 dic. 1189. This little-known text is very remarkable, for it is one of only two *incastellamento* charters known for the diocese in this period, and is quite unlike others that exist elsewhere. (The other, for Montecalvoli in 1184, is in S. Bongi, 'Quattro documenti', *Atti della Reale Accademia lucchese*, 21 (1882), 231–4. For a contemporary example from the Aretino, see C. J. Wickham, *The Mountains and the City* (Oxford, 1988), 320.) It sets out the complex accords, backed up by a string of city notables, between the consuls of Maggiano and the *consules consortum podii* (who must have been local military

villages, as I have emphasized (p. 49), common lands and collective economic activities were relatively marginal for ecological reasons; although communes ran them, they were not enough to create a real political focus for the village. More directly political activities are also documented. In Marlia in 1193, consuls collected (probably city) taxes, as we saw earlier (p. 44). In Coldipozzo, the local commune was really quite active from the 1160s as a collective group, buying land, dealing systematically with its church, and, by 1243, organizing military service (with the financial help of the neighbouring communes of Matraia and Ciciana). Coldipozzo was a highly atypical settlement, consisting virtually of a military garrison for its lords the Avvocati, but Matraia and Ciciana were not; it is likely that military levies, or the money to pay for them, were indeed organized for the city by its constituent communes, at least by the thirteenth century— we have seen another example of it in Moriano (above, p. 91).[14] Finally, we have one example of a commune exercising some powers over justice, along the lines of some of our texts for Moriano, when in 1207 the consuls of S. Gennaro judged in favour of the monastery of Pozzeveri, using formulae and provisions for judicial penalties borrowed directly from city courts. This text is significant. Not because it might represent the tip of an iceberg of communal activities undocumented elsewhere, but, again, because S. Gennaro was like Moriano atypical: it was from the 1160s the focus of one of the only lay territorial signorie in the Sei Miglia, that of the lords of Porcari. Disputes, unlike references to taxation or military obligations, are common in documents from the late twelfth century onwards, and the S. Gennaro judgment points us to a significant pattern. We have dozens of disputes from around 1200 that were settled by local

aristocrats, including some from nearby Bozzano; they were not, however, the principal landowners in the village, which in fact mostly belonged to the cathedral canons. In these accords, for the 'utilitati commodi totius comunis populi de Maggiano, tam dominorum quam rusticorum', it is agreed that at least part of the village be moved up into the castello (cf. *RCL* 1729). The tenurial context is one of considerable local landowning by the canons (*RCL* 15, 1094, 1168, 1198, 1235, 1395, 1603, 1687, 1717, 1729), many of whose tenants were *manentes*, but the canons do not seem to have initiated the *incastellamento*. Maggiano was in the Sei Miglia (although on its edge), and this must explain why it has no visible signorial territory; although the whole atmosphere reminds one of the heavy signorial relationships of the nearby Versilia (see below, n. 22), the public contractual element, and probably the role of the city commune, are signs of the underlying power of Lucca. But why incastellate in the Sei Miglia in 1189? The whole business needs further exploration. See A. A. Settia, *Castelli e villaggi* (Naples, 1984), 329 ff., 441 ff.

[14] *RCL* 1259, 1284, AAL ++G18 (*a*.1175), ACL Fondo Martini 13 apr. 1243; see above, Ch. 4 n. 18.

arbiters: we have several for Cortafugga of Paganico, as we have seen, and one for the local consuls there (pp. 152–5); the consuls of Compito, too, arbitrated a dispute in 1168.[15] But the only two places where we know of formalized tribunals run by consuls are Moriano and S. Gennaro: two out of the tiny handful of villages controlled by a territorial signoria. In Paganico and elsewhere, the logical conclusion is that there was not such a tribunal: in the rest of the Sei Miglia, in fact, justice belonged to the city, and local arbitrations remained at the level of the informal.

This contrast between the formal judicial institutions of Moriano or S. Gennaro and the more informal ones of the rest of the Sei Miglia is one that can be generalized. The relatively scanty evidence I have just outlined is all that I have seen documented for the secular activities of Sei Miglia communes before the 1220s; the bulk of the evidence for them associates them with their churches. It may be replied that this is exactly what one would expect from ecclesiastical archives; the loyalty oaths and statutes from Moriano are only preserved because of the bishop's signorial interest in the commune, and other sorts of secular text, like Tassignano's *brevia*, may simply not have survived from other communes. But this is not an adequate response. Rural communes elsewhere in the diocese of Lucca appear doing many more things than just running their churches, as we shall see later in this chapter, even though their documentation is equally ecclesiastical, and so do those in other parts of Italy. Conversely, the consuls of Moriano (which in this respect is genuinely out of line with its non-signorial neighbours) are not found dealing with their local churches at all, which indeed were developing their own *viciniae* along the same lines as the rest of the Sei Miglia in what appears to be a process separate from the formation of the local commune (see above, pp. 66–7). Elsewhere, as I have just argued, consular court cases at least should have survived, if there were any. But the fact is that consular activities seem often to have been fairly *ad hoc*, the digging of this ditch, the establishment of that toll-booth, as we saw for Tassignano (p. 142). These would certainly not have got into the documents except through the highly unusual medium of a court case such as that of 1206; and that indeed is the point: they were not systematic enough to *be* documented. It is not that communes did not mobilize and act locally, but, rather, that most of their actions were informal, and indeed remained so

---

[15] ACL L33 (*a.*1207) for S. Gennaro. Consuls of S. Gennaro appear in occasional sanction clauses, too, like those of Moriano: e.g. *RCL* 1806, and cf. above, Ch. 4 n. 31. For the classic rural communal tribunal modelled on the city, see below, Ch. 8 n. 48, for Calci just south of Monte Pisano in 1165. Compito: ASL S. Ponziano 10 magg. 1168.

even after the consulates had themselves become institutionalized. It is because of this general informality that their association with their churches was the most important framework for communes, as well as being the best documented: it was the most formal aspect of their existence.

I argued in Chapter 3 that the territorialization of the parish gave to the communes of the Lucchese Sei Miglia a formal territorial framework that they would not have had otherwise, given the near-absence of signorie in the Lucca plain and the vagueness of earlier village boundaries. The parish was from its inception a territory with financial aspects, for it was defined by *sepultura* dues; these contributed further to the rapid sharpening of village/parish boundaries.[16] Such financial resources would have been a further incentive for the commune to associate itself with the parish, and, where it could, control the church and its funds. In an area without extensive common lands, these funds may indeed have been the first monies the consuls of the *vicinia* could try to control, perhaps from their first appearance; it is, at least, church land, dues to the church, and church rebuilding that we see them acting to control with most determination, when they emerge in the documents at the end of the century. The corollary seems to be that it took Lucchese communes that much longer to come to represent a really secular self-affirmation in any systematic way. The consular offices of each village doubtless developed along the lines mapped out for Moriano and Tassignano, resulting in the firm institutional existence that seems ensured for each by 1200 or soon after, but their most clearly defined functions remained not secular but ecclesiastical. This would only change with the intervention of the city, when at the end of the twelfth century it began to impose taxation. Even this it may have at least sometimes imposed through the church (see above, p. 139); but, as urban taxes steadily rose after 1200 or so, it would have suited the city better that they should be collected through properly constituted local representatives, i.e. the communal officials.[17] It may well be that it was sometimes the deliberate intervention of the city that moved communes on from being informal communities based on an oath to being public or quasi-public institutions—that is to say, from step (ii) to step (iii) as defined at the beginning of this chapter. It would certainly in future

---

[16] The pieve had of course for long been financially defined, by the tithe; but this does not seem to have had much political implication, possibly because pievi were too large. See bibliography in Wickham, *Mountains*, 93–5; cf. above, Ch. 3 n. 53.

[17] A. I. Pini, *Città, comuni e corporazioni* (Bologna, 1986), 104–5, 113–16; F. Menant, *Campagnes lombardes* (Rome, 1993), 544–57, the best specific analysis of the burden of the city on rural communes known to me.

years be city influence that led to communes copying their local statutes
from each other, as in the fourteenth century: by then, communal institutions could often virtually be bought off the peg. This sort of external
intervention was, however, not in the interests of villagers—indeed,
rather the reverse, since it involved taking more and more money from
them; there is therefore no reason to assume that it would lead automatically to a more formalized social arena for rural consular activity,
and there is no evidence that it did. The secular functions and powers
of consuls took a longer time to crystallize, and would do so according
to internal, rather than external, variables: the ecology, the social structure, and the political interests of the élites, of each commune.

Before we ask wider questions about these developments, the experience
of the Sei Miglia should be set, at least briefly, against the early development of communes elsewhere in the diocese. Osheim has summarized
this development in the areas under the episcopal signoria, notably with
respect to the Valdarno castelli of S. Maria a Monte and Montopoli;
Dinelli has discussed the villages controlled by the Canonica in Versilia,
in particular Massarosa and Fibbialla; I have elsewhere gone through the
relatively meagre evidence for the Garfagnana and the Valdinievole.[18] Given
the restriction of the documentation for the Lucchesia outside the Sei
Miglia to a relatively small number of areas, these studies have in fact
already covered the great bulk of well-documented communes before the
mid-thirteenth century. In synthesis, let us look at what these communes
were doing.

In terms of my models for the Lucca plain, the contado communes (as
it is convenient, though not accurate, to call them) tend to be much more
like Moriano than Tassignano or Paganico. This is not surprising; they
all formed inside signorial territories. Nowhere for which we have any
documentation in the rest of the diocese seems to have been untouched
by such territorialization by 1150 or so, even if the signorie concerned
were often weak. As a result, their secular power structures do not seem
to have experienced the problems of boundary definition that we can

---

[18] D. J. Osheim, *An Italian Lordship* (Berkeley, 1977), 58–69; Dinelli, 'Signoria ecclesiastica', esp. 225–65; Wickham, *Mountains*, 138–41; id., 'Aspetti socioeconomici della
Valdinievole', in A. Spicciani and C. Violante (eds.), *Allucio da Pescia* (Rome, 1991), 291–2.
[See now also R. Savigni, 'La signoria vescovile lucchese', *Aevum*, 66 (1993), 360–3.] These
are the basic references for what follows. Note that Fibbialla was geographically in the Sei
Miglia, but bordered on, and was fully part of, a compact group of villages that were in
the signoria of the Canonica, and thus outside the remit of city jurisdiction; I have therefore analysed it in the framework of that group.

sometimes see in the Lucca plain, though it is possible that some late-documented communes may have genuinely developed relatively late in time. (Dinelli has hypothesized this for, among others, Gualdo in the Versilia, undocumented as a commune before 1266—though by then possessor of a detailed statute, agreed between the commune and the canons its lords.) These communes often claimed to control the choice of their local priest, as they did on the plain: the exercise of this right, or disputes about it, are attested for Fibbialla in 1167, Fucecchio in 1202, S. Maria a Monte in 1230, Montopoli in 1232.[19] But a clearly demarcated secular politics is much more visible, paralleling that for Moriano and going well beyond it. Such a politics can be seen in disputes over communal boundaries, for example. Already in 1120 the men of S. Maria a Monte were disputing with their neighbours of Pozzo, under threat of 'guerras aut aliquas molestias', over a large neighbouring tract of woodland; Montopoli's consuls formally established their bounds in the direction of neighbouring Marti in 1156. These disputes could have a silvo-pastoral element to them, as is clear in 1120, and as can also be seen in a dispute between Massarosa and two neighbouring lordly families over wood rights in the coastal pine forests in 1197. In the 1156 Montopoli case, however, the agreed boundary ran through agricultural land, and is more likely to have delimited jurisdiction; and the later attempts of S. Maria a Monte to expand its territory at the expense of Montecalvoli were certainly signs of political rather than economic assertion. S. Maria a Monte was capable of acting like an autonomous political unit, in fact, and it was not the only commune to do so; Montecatini in the Valdinievole actually fought wars against its Pistoiese neighbours in the late twelfth century, with Lucchese backing. These two communes were large and prosperous *castelli* on or near major trade routes, and well away from direct city control, at least before 1200. Osheim has compared S. Maria a Monte with S. Gimignano, and the comparison is not unreasonable for Montecatini as well, even if S. Gimignano was so much bigger and more powerful. Indeed, the two Lucchese *castelli* could most usefully be regarded as urban, not rural, communities (see below, p. 214). The political affirmation that they represented was quite out of the reach of any Sei Miglia commune.[20]

---

[19] Dinelli, 'Signoria ecclesiastica', 252–65, for Gualdo and its neighbours; for the church disputes, *RCL* 1261–3, AAL AF40 (*a.*1202), Osheim, *Italian Lordship*, 60.

[20] AAL ++C75 (*a.*1121; see above, Ch. 4 n. 30), *F46 (*a.*1157, *recte* 1156), ASF Strozziane-Uguccioni 23 lug. 1197; cf., for S. Maria a Monte and Montecalvoli, Osheim, *Italian Lordship*, 61; ibid. 66–9 for the S. Gimignano comparison. Pescia established its

In terms of the relationship between communes and their lords, on the other hand, the contado communes such as Montecatini or S. Maria a Monte or Montopoli were less different from Moriano, for they all remained inside the bishop's signoria. They contested it, or parts of it: in 1180 Montopoli successfully laid claim to part of the local passage tolls through its territory, as did Diecimo, another episcopal castello in the mountains north of Moriano, in 1210; in the 1230s the *lambardi* of S. Maria a Monte claimed to control the bishop's mill. But the bishops managed to maintain recognition of their overall signorial hegemony, however little they could dominate the local politics of such independent centres. This sort of balance was characteristic of the stronger communes elsewhere in the contado as well. It is reflected in local collective oaths to lords, which continued; it can be seen, too, when the commune of S. Gervasio in the Valdarno consented (i.e. had the right to consent) to the sale of the *castrum* of S. Gervasio by the Gherardeschi counts to the bishop in *c*.1150: the consent of the inhabitants evidently mattered, although they in turn recognized the signoria.[21]

Other contado communes were less independent. This is very visible in the cathedral Canonica's signoria in the Versilia, where the canons kept a rather firmer hand on their villages. Massarosa, as I noted earlier (p. 162), though a coherent collectivity, made more coherent by much collectively run wood- and marshland, and by its common subjection to the canons as landlords as well as signorial lords, found after 1200 that the canons had withdrawn their at least *de facto* recognition of the local commune. Before papal arbitrators in 1227, the commune listed its demands: the right to elect consuls and other officials, the right of the consuls to decide court cases, the right of the commune not to pay more than agreed signorial dues, rights to cut wood, rights to be recognized by the emperor and to pay taxes directly to him, and the return of much property unjustly seized. It is clear that the canons were intent on subjecting the

rights in 1202 *vis-à-vis* neighbouring communes very carefully too, in statute form: ASF Com. di Pescia lug. 1202. [The text is now edited in L. Mosiici, 'Documenti di lega', in C. Violante and A. Spicciani (eds.), *Pescia* (Pisa, 1995), 122–6.] For Montecatini and the Pistoiese, Q. Santoli (ed.), *Liber censuum comunis Pistorii* (Pistoia, 1915), nn. 5, 6, with *Tholomei Lucensis Annales*, ed. B. Schmeidler, *MGH, SRG*, NS 8 (Berlin, 1955), 77.

[21] For the bishop's castelli, Osheim, *Italian Lordship*, 61–3, 67–8; the Diecimo text is AAL *H1 (*a*.1210). For collective oaths, see above, p. 90, and AAL ++D40 (*a*.1122), Libro della Croce, pp. 70–2, for the bishop in 1121–6; others include *RCL* 1278 (Gragno in the Garfagnana), 1642 (Massarosa), AAL ++D58 (*a*.1180, Casoli in the mountains of the Valdilima). S. Gervasio: AAL ++R79, redated by F. Schneider, *Le origini dei comuni rurali* (1924; Ital. edn., Florence, 1980), 226.

village by force, indeed on cancelling its collective judicial personality; none the less, the village was evidently already a complex communal organization, capable of running its own courts and finance. Violence was inevitable under these circumstances, in the world of the early thirteenth century; the canons did not recognize the commune again before the 1230s.

This hostility to communes as autonomous institutions must have been a particular weakness of the canons of Lucca; it reappears again in a 1204 dispute for Fibbialla, in which the canons demanded of the local consuls oaths of fidelity, military service, the recognition of the canons as judges, and the dissolution of all mutual oaths save those to the canons themselves, i.e. the constituting oaths of the commune. (The arbitrators gave judgment in favour of the canons, though they did not pronounce on the crucial issue of the dissolution of rival oaths.) But Fibbialla, like Massarosa, already had an organized commune, which indeed controlled the local church as early as 1167; the canons, however heavy-handed, in a way that recalls some of the most famous Tuscan communal disputes, such as those for S. Casciano Val di Pesa in the 1230s or Abbadia S. Salvatore in the middle of the century, were fighting a losing battle.[22]

The communes of the contado, or the best documented of them at any rate, thus seem to have had rather more active histories than most of those for the Sei Miglia. Unfortunately, few of them have many private documents to set these dramatic moments in local sociological perspective: the only exception here is the rich material for S. Maria a Monte, which would repay more detailed exploration by someone. We can already make certain generalizations, however, which seem to be valid even across the considerable local contrasts that separate the Versilia, the Valdarno, or the Garfagnana. The first is that the pattern of institutional development that we have seen in Moriano seems to have existed, with local differences, all the way across the diocese. So the men of S. Maria a Monte in 1120 are not characterized more concretely than 'hos de S. Maria a Monte'; their six representatives speak, very informally, for their 'sodales et seguaces'. This has analogies with the organization of Moriano in 1121, and can be described as step (i) of my Moriano model, the *vicini* as a barely differentiated community. The community of the oath (step (ii)) becomes more visible in later texts, such as the 1204 Fibbialla case just cited; indeed, late twelfth-century charters from all over the diocese show consuls stably representing a *populus* or a *comune*. Step (iii), the

[22] Dinelli, 'Signoria ecclesiastica', 230–52. For Fibbialla, ACL A1, A10 (*a.*1204); cf. *RCL* 1261–3. For the parallels, see below, pp. 224–8.

institutionalization of local responsibilities, is very clear in the S. Maria a Monte consular *breve* of the 1220s; but it is also visible in Massarosa in 1227, which was by now an organized body, even though the commune there was not recognized by its lords. In this respect, the Sei Miglia and the rest of the diocese had a concrete common development.[23]

A second common feature was the greater importance of political, rather than economic, activity. The contado communes had local élites that were not, as far as we know, yet attracted by the city, and thus were not menaced in their vigorous internal life. It should be observed that their political coherence was aided by a much greater nucleation of settlement in some parts of the diocese outside the Sei Miglia than inside it; in sharp contrast to the Lucca plain, nearly every contado commune so far cited was a castello, often with a considerable population residing in it. But they tended to privilege political, and indeed, military rather than narrowly economic objectives. The control of tolls had, of course, economic as well as political implications, and all forms of local affirmation, whether political or military, were aimed at making the victorious richer; many communes had considerable common lands as well. But only in the mountains, at Gragno in the Garfagnana or Villa Basilica in the Valdinievole, does the major focus of the twelfth-century commune seem to have been the control of collective economic resources.[24] This would, from the mid-twelfth century onwards, be a major distinguishing feature of mountain communes, dominating their local political structures too. But not in the plains: S. Maria a Monte's strength remained its armed men, not its woods or its tolls, and, in a rather more muted form, something similar can be said for the Sei Miglia communes too.

A third point is a contrast, between at least some of the contado communes and those of the Lucca plain. Moriano's élite was one of rich peasants, who maintained a working solidarity with their poorer neighbours. Not so that of Montopoli or S. Maria a Monte: these castelli had at their centre military groups, *milites* and *lambardi*, who made up the commune together with the *populus*. As communes, they had the internal social differentiation and internal class conflict of the great urban castelli of the Italian countryside, such as Prato or S. Gimignano or, in the North, Guastalla or Crema or Chieri. Their social structures thus had relatively little in common with the peasant communes of the Sei Miglia, and indeed many historians have classified them as 'comuni di castello' (or 'comuni

---

[23] See above, nn. 20, 22, 2 respectively; the breve is ed. D. Corsi, 'Il "breve" dei consoli', *Atti dell'Accademia lucchese*, NS 10 (1959), 153–72.

[24] Wickham, *Mountains*, 138–41; id., 'Valdinievole', 292.

curtensi', in Caggese's somewhat less satisfactory formulation), and not 'comuni rurali' at all.[25] The problems pertaining to their origin are similar, as are their institutional developments; but one must recognize that the lack of social separation between élites and the poor that we have seen in Moriano cannot be extended to every centre with a similar population—indeed, it is Moriano that may be atypical by the twelfth century, for far smaller places than it could have *milites* by now. How many of the contado communes were like S. Maria a Monte in this and how many like Moriano is less clear, however; not by any means every castello can have had a military élite set against a *populus* of *rustici* (Massarosa was probably one that did not), but exactly who lived in each is generally unknown to us.

The fourth and final point carries an implicit comparison with other parts of Italy: these communes all had signorial lordship, but they were all fairly forceful. It is difficult to see any Lucchese lord aiming at absolute control over a commune and its members, as many did elsewhere in the peninsula and in Europe. The hostility of the canons to Massarosa and Fibbialla was to already-constituted communes; in other parts of the diocese, communes had a widely recognized autonomy. It is difficult to be certain of this in all cases, and there may have been some subjected villages, Gualdo or Montisciano in Versilia, or Roggio in the Valdiserchio, or the villages around S. Salvatore a Sesto, where signorial control was relatively great.[26] But signorie were in general not so very heavy in the diocese (see above, pp. 107–9), and very few villages indeed were in the hands of one or even two landowners. The fragmentation of landowning that was an essential feature of the village societies of the Sei Miglia was equally present in the rest of the Lucchesia, with only very few exceptions; most villages were dominated by élites of landowning inhabitants, who could resist signorial power with relative ease. The weak Lucchese signorie, in S. Maria a Monte and Montecatini (and maybe even Massarosa) as in Moriano, served as territorial frameworks for independent development, rather than millstones that rising peasants had to struggle against and throw off; their internal factions were as important an element of their social structures as was their collective opposition to their lords.

[25] Osheim, *Italian Lordship*, 61, 64–9; cf., for the North, below, pp. 214–15. For 'comuni di castello', see e.g. G. Luzzatto, *Dai servi della gleba* (Bari, 1966), 354; for 'comuni curtensi', see Caggese, *Classi e comuni rurali*, i. 179–85.

[26] Gualdo and Montisciano: Dinelli, 'Signoria ecclesiastica', 252–65; Roggio: AAL ++Q84, AD1 (*a.*1166), where control over the very subject inhabitants of the village is contested between rival lords with almost no local participation at all; Onori, *S. Salvatore a Sesto*, 105–8.

Here, too, then, the Sei Miglia and the rest of the diocese of Lucca were merely at different points along a fairly tight spectrum. The implications of this we will see in the next chapter.

The Sei Miglia communes were sociologically analogous to those elsewhere in the diocese, but, as we have seen, they were also much weaker, much more informally orientated, and much less active. The first formal feature of most of them was their boundaries; and when, after several decades of communities based on oaths, consular institutions began to crystallize, the actual interventions that communal officials could make in local society were still pretty *ad hoc*. Even patronage was informal in most of the Sei Miglia; Albertino and Bandino in Tassignano were trying to establish a local hegemony, not in any sense a clientele defined by precise mutual obligations. Even when terms like *fidelitas*, *servitium*, and *dominus* were used, they tended (outside Moriano, as ever) to describe individual relationships of domination, over vassals or *manentes*, not those over or between collectivities, unlike elsewhere in Italy and even Tuscany. The informality of patronage fitted that of the communes; indeed, one could remark that the close association of the communes with the church fitted it as well, for, of all the institutions that structured the Italian countryside, the rural parish was probably the weakest, least coherent, and least suitable as a basis for effective social action.

One must ask, then, two related questions: why were the communes of the Sei Miglia so weak? And, why, given this weakness, did they none the less come to exist, and indeed develop in much the same way as elsewhere? One could start by stressing that they did not have to be weak. The Moriano commune, though for long informal, was very solidly constituted; and the troubles at S. Concordio and Tassignano seem to show that where there were local powers to oppose, local inhabitants could combine to oppose them. Moriano I will come back to in a moment; the other two, however, which are by far the most explicit examples of tension on the Lucca plain, do have something in common, for they are villages where we can show a social structure that was unusually highly divided by the standards of the Sei Miglia. I stressed in a previous book how hard it is to identify clear class oppositions in a village society, such as in the eleventh-century Casentino, in which nearly everyone is both landlord and tenant, exploiter and exploited, for different fragments of their land;[27] and the fragmentation of land and the complexity of levels of tenure were greater

---

[27] Wickham, *Mountains*, 265–6.

still in the twelfth-century Sei Miglia. Earlier in this book, I noted that this complexity could even make it difficult to coerce tenants for the non-payment of rent (pp. 25–8); this was not a propitious environment for clearly defined class struggle between tenants and lords, or even clients and patrons. Only in Tassignano and S. Concordio (at least from ammg the well-documented villages) was this network of mediations relatively absent, thanks to large percentages of land directly controlled by single landowners or groups of landowners, who also had their hands on the local church and the institutional powers deriving therefrom; only in Tassignano and S. Concordio do we find trouble. Where there were clear class oppositions, then, tension existed; but elsewhere the network was genuinely too strong, and it contributed not only to the smoothing over of class tension, but also to the smoothing over even of social differences between villages, thanks to the dispersal of the landowning of most of the larger Lucchese landowners right across the plain. This complexity of land-ownership was in my view a real and immediate cause of the relative calm of the Lucchese countryside.

A second cause was the strength of the city. The city market penetrated every corner of the Sei Miglia, which was not, after all, so very large; the whole network of agrarian credit, and even of local choices of crops, were determined by it. The larger landowners just mentioned, whether ecclesiastical or lay, were almost all city-dwelling, and their lands certainly furnished surpluses directed straight to the city markets. I have argued elsewhere that Lucca's socio-economic influence stretched up to the far end of the Garfagnana, in the mountains at the northern end of the diocese, and that even the silvo-pastoral orientation of the mountains owed much to urban commercial interest;[28] how much more must this influence have dominated the villages within sight of the towers and walls of Lucca. There were no local juridical autonomies to slow the impact of the city's political supremacy, either, apart from Moriano and one or two others; but the city was not, before the thirteenth century, sufficiently fiscally oppressive to be itself a body that might have to be fought (and it was too overwhelmingly powerful to be fought by then anyway). This hegemony, which was at once economic, political, and judicial, ensured that the local rural institutions of the Sei Miglia remained comparatively ill defined. And, as I have argued, city prosperity was in other ways too a reason for the weakness of the commune, in that it tempted away local leaders. The urbanization of the élites of villages such as Paganico was

[28] Ibid. 25, 168–70.

probably a cause of the relative marginality of the early commune there, just at the moment of its institutionalization; the commune of Paganico was, in effect, born weak, thanks to the choices of its élite. This was not a universal pattern; the survival of at least part of the local élite in Moriano led to the opposite development, the creation of a strong commune as a bulwark against the city—a process aided by the substantial solidarity of the Moriano area, and the political alignment between its inhabitants and their patron and lord the bishop. Elsewhere, particularly in the hills on the edge of the Sei Miglia, village landowners may well have survived longer, and probably created rather more coherent communal organisms; one example is probably Ciciana (see above, p. 166), though such villages, precisely because they were outside city interests, tend to be less well documented. But on the plain itself, Paganico was the dominant model: it was the classic city-dominated commune, as early as 1200.

It is in this city-orientated context that the choices of local élites were genuinely so important. It is important for Moriano that the local leaders were, although linked closely to the bishop, also not separated socially from their neighbours; they chose to back strong local institutions as a result. It is important for Tassignano that its élite found it most appropriate to oppose the local patrons, along with their poorer neighbours, rather than vice versa. It is important for Paganico that its richest local inhabitant moved to the city, thus rejecting the possibilities of local power. In the absence of firmly based collective economic activity, and in the face of the rising tide of city landowning, local élites were the principal foci that villages had, along with the local church; they could make or break local communal institutions, which indeed developed out of the individual practices of the early consuls of each village.

If communal development can be so clearly tied into élite interests, however, the rural commune cannot be used simply as a symbol of peasant resistance. It sometimes was, as in Tassignano, or still more, Massarosa; elsewhere, it evidently was not. Even if we use our definition of the commune (above, p. 6), it has to be seen, in mathematical terms, as a variable not a constant. None the less, once its value is determined, it acts as an organizing device for the historian, a guide to how the village run by that commune was really constructed and how it developed. How specific communes worked in practice for people, and what they were needed for, tells one more easily about the real interests of local inhabitants than many more generalized analyses, whether economic or political-constitutional. In fact, in most cases, the early communes of the Sei Miglia were not very useful to their inhabitants; they seem to have done little more than run the local church, mediate with the city, and maybe keep the peace on a small scale. But this in itself is a guide to what the villagers really needed: evidently, in these only recently defined villages, in the fragmented settlement and individualistic agriculture of the Lucca plain, strong local cohesion was not essential.

It is worth repeating at this point that the Lucchese Sei Miglia was a small area, as its name denotes, and exceptional even in the diocese, never mind in the rest of Italy. It was the richest area of the Lucchesia without doubt, and was thus locally important; it may, too, have analogues in some of the rings of villages closest to other Italian cities, some of which, as in Lucca, were subject to a special urban jurisdiction. But it was exceptional; rural communes were not normally this weak, or this independent of signorial pressure. My choice to study these communes gains force specifically from their exceptionality, for here, away from the more glamorous conflicts of other regions, some essential elements for the understanding of rural society can all the more easily be perceived: the complexity of social structure, the choices of élites, the varying political consequences of different sorts of land tenure, even the role of the local church. These elements are not a specific feature of the plain of Lucca, but they are not always fully recognized as factors in the development of rural communes. And there is one other element of analysis that makes their study in the Sei Miglia crucial: the fact that, despite the absence of collective economies, sharp rural conflict, or signorial oppression, the communes around Lucca nevertheless appeared in the twelfth century just as they did in most of north-central Italy, and developed institutions with a rhythm that certainly fits urban institutional development everywhere in the peninsula, and was probably pretty generalized in the countryside as well. To conclude, then, we will look at some reasons why this might have been so.

The world of the eleventh century in Tuscany was still dominated by the public institutions of the March. Private, local relationships existed, and were becoming stronger and more articulated, both in terms of personal relations of dependence and local territorial power; but these still existed inside the context of overarching frameworks of public power. In the twelfth century, especially after the death of Matilda in 1115, this power quickly weakened. It was replaced by local signorial territories, and by the cities, which quickly expanded their own jurisdictions—very quickly in the case of Lucca, which hegemonized not only the Sei Miglia but also the rural signorie by the late twelfth century. I have already alluded to these developments (p. 13), and they are anyway reasonably well known.[29] But the city, however aggressive, was not yet a fully coherent public power. Even Lucca did not yet have, or claim, the full legal sovereignty of an autonomous polity inside the Empire; its jurisdictions, however active, were uncertain and largely voluntary; its consuls, however influential, coincided with a considerable array of other powers (indeed its principal family, the Avvocati, many times consuls, owed their local status—which included the power to nominate all city judges—to the emperor and the bishop, not the commune, and continued to do so until the fourteenth century). Lucca was hegemonic locally, but, as an *institution*, the twelfth-century city was still not fully formed.[30] It is this institutional weakness of public power itself as an organizing principle, which, I would argue, was a particular feature of the twelfth century in Italy (see below, pp. 239–40), that facilitated the crystallization of relatively formal *local* territories, as the arenas for increasingly clearly defined local political activities, signorie, parishes and communes alike—just as, elsewhere in Europe, it led to the increasing formalization, even in law, of the traditional bonds of private dependence based on fiefs and vassal homage, which had hitherto often been so informal as not even to be registered in documents. One illustration of this general process is that signorie in the Lucchesia, far from being rural lordships set up as autonomous powers in defiance of cities, are often only attested after city conquest; they developed, often fairly slowly, in the framework of the weakness of public power as a concept, rather than of the weakness of Lucca's specific military and political system. And a further illustration of the same process is the development of the rural commune, even in areas where it remained weak, as an arena for at least some local political activity.

The twelfth-century economic and social environment in the Sei Miglia was also different, especially after 1150 or so. City landowning was increasing, and threatening the local landowning élites in the villages of the plain; clienteles based on land and its distribution are less visible in the documentation; in general, in fact, there was a sharp rise in the commercialization of many traditional social relationships, notably (and most obviously to us, given the documentation) those involving land. In this respect the city was a threat; but also, as I noted when discussing

[29] See, in general, e.g. G. Tabacco, *Egemonie sociali* (Turin, 1979), 229–77; for local formalization of personal relationships, see among others P. Brancoli Busdraghi, 'Patti di assistenza', in *Nobiltà e ceti dirigenti in Toscana* (Florence, 1982), 29–55.

[30] For Lucca as an institution, see V. Tirelli, 'Lucca nella seconda metà del s. XII', in *I ceti dirigenti* (Pisa, 1982), 157–231. I intend to discuss the issue further in future work.

Marlia (p. 45), a model: if old informal social relationships were in danger of dissolution, the example of the oaths at the basis of the city collectivity might serve to formalize and thus stabilize local relationships in the countryside as well. This rearguard move towards the explicit social rules of the *Gesellschaft* rather than the *Gemeinschaft* did not always work, but it worked in Moriano, and in Tassignano it even produced a local leadership capable of taking on a powerful consortium of landlords.

These widely based developments were not 'causes of the rural commune', however; rather, they provided an environment in which individual villages, and notably their local leaders, might feel that local political cohesion, oaths, elected representatives, and, finally, formal local institutions, might be advantageous, for the specific purposes of and in the specific environment of each village. It might have been that some fragmented Lucchese villages could have felt that an organized local community was entirely useless; it is just that in the twelfth-century Lucchesia, with such collectivities emerging everywhere, doubtless copying each other as well as the city, such a feeling was not very likely. Even such a possibility of choice was specific to the twelfth century; by the later thirteenth century, Lucca had imposed its own local governmental structures, based on local communes, everywhere in its territory. But it could not have come earlier than 1100, either; for local relationships were by and large far more informal in earlier centuries, and also differently constructed. Moro di Petruccia in Marlia around 1050 can be understood, before all else, in terms of his relations with aristocrats (see above, pp. 31–4). By contrast, when Rodolfo di Andrea and his friends in Moriano in and around 1121, local notables and clients of the bishop though they were, found it worthwhile to be the leaders of their neighbours rather than (or as well as) the local representatives of their lord, the collectivity that developed, structured by horizontal rather than vertical relationships, was genuinely new. There had been local communities before, in Italy and elsewhere, fused together by common economic interest or common economic or political subjection; but in the twelfth century, to some extent following the example of the city, community action became a norm even for the most factionally divided and independent-minded villages. Local élites now needed to deal with their neighbours; to lead them with their consent. This was an important basis for the future.

Lucca was in the twelfth century (and is still today) a society where structured class conflict, at least in the countryside, was relatively weak. All that I have written in the last few pages has been set down with that recognition in mind. But the patterns I have just delineated are not in all respects restricted to the Lucchese Sei Miglia; they are valid for much or most of Italy, and indeed much of Europe. It would not, perhaps, be interesting enough simply to reconstruct the local development of four to six villages in a highly atypical area of Italy in the twelfth century, without wider comparisons; and, indeed, if the analysis of local territorial crystallization and the activities of local élites, that is to say, the focus of this book, has any usefulness outside the Lucca plain, it ought to be instructive to see how it may be used. So the final chapter of the book will look at the general problem of the formation of rural communes in Italy and in western Europe as a whole.

8

Comparative Perspectives

i. Classic models

What theories have hitherto been used to analyse the origins of Italian rural communes? The two most substantial books written at the time of the classic debate on the rural commune in Italy, 1890–1930, those by Romolo Caggese in 1907 and Gianpiero Bognetti in 1926, may be seen as being at opposite extremes in their interpretations of the issue. If we want to approach the debate directly, they are as good places to start as any.

For Caggese, rural communes represented, quite simply, the class struggle of a dependent (and indeed servile) peasantry against their lords. Italian peasants had lost all their land by the tenth century, and were thus all tenants of lords; with the intensification of feudal and signorial oppression in the eleventh and twelfth centuries (the process which we would now call the development of the territorial signoria, the seigneurie banale of the French), peasants fought back. Eventually, with the help of (anti-feudal) cities, they won a measure of autonomy, with the emancipation of the serfs, with the recognition by lords of their communes, and, soon, with their local statutes, which gave their autonomy the institutional strength of law. 'One could almost say—by the strangest coincidence!—that the rural comune was the first experiment in direct action by workers' organizations, just like working-class trade unions in contemporary society, setting aside their political aims and their preconceptions about the means necessary to gain their ends.' This class resistance, based on informal relationships between neighbours (*viciniae*), was the prime mover in the development of the rural commune; collective aggregations around parishes had no role, because parishes did not represent class interests; common land and its management were unimportant as a basis for collective action. The victory of the rural communes was, however, only temporary; once cities had defeated signorial lords, bourgeois oppression replaced that of feudal lordship, and communes simply became the local administrative and (above all) tax-raising arms of the cities by 1300.[1]

---

[1] R. Caggese, *Classi e comuni rurali* (Florence, 1907–8), esp. i. 73–4, 200 (but cf. i. 374, ii. 254), i. 370 (quote), 195–228, 59–72.

Caggese's infuriatingly vast, sloppy, and rhetorical work is still worth reading, for the force of his argument and the acute insights that appear with regularity across its 600 pages. Not by any means all of the above is to be rejected, however schematic it is; the book is, even at its least coherent, the fullest statement of one of the major models for communal development, the rural commune opposed to the local power of lords, crystallizing around 1100 rather than earlier because it was only in the immediately preceding centuries that lords had been systematic in their oppression. It is worth stressing, incidentally, that Caggese's sloppiness and schematism were irritating then as well as now; Gioacchino Volpe cut up the first volume in 1908, in a 45-page review that is nowadays more often read than the book. Volpe accused Caggese of confusion and rhetorical sociologizing; of not reading the sources properly (particularly in the early Middle Ages); often of not reading them at all ('why do we not try to look a little at real life . . . ?'); of insisting rigidly on hierarchies of causes for communes, thus overstressing feudal relationships and understressing the local collective activities that had to pre-exist the affirmation of the commune, including the parish (Caggese accepted this in later work, in fact, though without admitting its origin); and of failing to recognize that small landowners as well as tenants were a basis of the early commune. But Volpe did not attack the basic thrust of Caggese's argument, that communes were essentially brought into being to resist lords, in the years around 1100, and that any local collectivities that pre-existed and underpinned them were extremely vaguely characterized, before the constituting oaths that founded communal identity.[2]

Bognetti twenty years later was very different. For the Milanese historian, the basis of the rural commune was collective land, and this went back a long way, indeed to pre-Roman Italy, making the rural commune 'the oldest and purest expression of the Fatherland'. Bognetti mingled accurate textual analysis with the widest possible generalizations, in the best traditions of the Economic-Juridical school, and his *comunalia*, *vicanalia* and *conceliba* (the common lands of medieval Lombardy, particularly in the Alps) were traced back with skill to the *communiones* and the *compascua* of the Appennines of the second century AD, and earlier still. He argued that it was the organization of common land that created village territoriality, long before 1100, and which created an economic focus for local collectivities. As soon as documents permit, in the early eleventh century, we can see such collectivities in operation; all that

² G. Volpe, *Medioevo italiano* (Florence, 1961), 143–88 (quote: 160).

happened in the twelfth century was that they became better documented. Signorial lordship (*dominatus loci*) was, by contrast, barely relevant to those developments, and indeed weak by European standards.[3] Forty years later, in a posthumous article of 1965, he had not substantially changed his mind, although he was by now prepared to attribute a greater role to the conceptions of common use brought in by the Lombards after their sixth-century conquest of Italy.[4]

Bognetti was a much tighter analyst than Caggese, but his argument convinces rather less. As early as 1929 Marc Bloch complained that Bognetti undervalued the signoria (though Bloch supposed that this was a defect in Italian scholarship rather than Bognetti's deliberate rejection of his predecessors, whom he relegated to the odd footnote), and the role of the signorial world in creating a territorial framework for local communal politics cannot, indeed, be dismissed as easily as Bognetti does. Bognetti's early eleventh-century groups of *vicini*, in fact, at Arogno or Velate on or nearby Lake Lugano, while certainly active in the defence of their village-based pasture rights, in a far more organized way than anywhere in the Lucchesia, had no obvious form of collective structure as yet; the latter only appears in mid-twelfth-century texts.[5] And Bognetti virtually ignored one fundamental characteristic of his material: that his best examples all related to the Alps, where one would tend to expect pasture to be rather more important than it was elsewhere. Indeed, he was not very interested in how much common land any village actually had, or how it was exploited, or how that exploitation changed (see below, pp. 215–16). None the less, it was he who did most in Italy to establish the importance of the economic basis of the village collectivity and, later, the commune, against the voluntarist readings of Caggese and his associates.

---

[3] G. P. Bognetti, *Sulle origini dei comuni rurali del medioevo* (1926), now in *Studi sulle origini del comune rurale* (Milan, 1978), 1–262; esp. 211 (quote), 87 ff., 174–211.

[4] 'I beni comunali e l'organizzazione del villaggio nell'Italia superiore fino al Mille', now in *Studi sulle origini*, 302–35. Bognetti was by now influenced by his own extensive researches on the Lombards, and also by the critical studies on the continuity of public lands in southern Italy by G. Cassandro, *Storia delle terre comuni* (Bari, 1943). Cassandro, however, did not believe that there were formal peasant groups in the early Middle Ages that exploited communal use-rights, or that rural communes were based on such commons: ibid. 100–4, 151–9.

[5] M. Bloch, 'Une nouvelle théorie', *Annales d'histoire économique et sociale*, 1 (1929), 587–9; for Arogno and Velate, see Bognetti, *Studi sulle origini*, 237–46. One may note, in general, that Bognetti's *comunalia* were largely fragmented and appurtenant to private properties: see examples ibid. 213–62. In the Abruzzo, too, common lands could provide the basis for coherent collective action in the early Middle Ages, without that action yet being particularly tightly structured: C. J. Wickham, *Studi sulla società degli Appennini* (Bologna, 1982), 18–28 and *passim*.

These two writers can stand for a host of other generalizing theories about the origins of the commune that flourished in the years around 1910. We need not spend much time on Pietro Sella, who held in 1908 that its origins lay in the *vicinia*, since, although in general historians would not dispute that some collective territorial sense often existed in the early Middle Ages, which could indeed be called a *vicinia* (it is, for example, a word occasionally used in the Lombard laws for village territory, and, as we have seen, crops up often in the twelfth century, both in the country and the city), Sella saw in the term a legally precise early medieval village institution which he himself had in reality almost entirely invented. Scarcely more interesting are the ideas of Arturo Palmieri and Alberto Sorbelli, who claimed the same thing of the parish, with a similar degree of schematism; or of Ferdinando Gabotto, who in 1903 derived the commune from the collective activities of local lords. All these writers, and others, supposed that it was possible to make claims about the legal situation of the whole of (at least north-central) Italy up to 1200 on the basis of a handful of early medieval texts, or, sometimes, late medieval ones. (One of their latest successors was Giovanni Santini, who in the 1960s 'discovered' the pre-Roman origins of the late medieval *comune di pieve* with equal detachment, although he at least was prepared to restrict it to mountain areas.)[6] More interesting were writers such as Salvemini or Checchini or Luzzatto who restricted themselves to more localized studies, for they often, whichever school they belonged to, produced model analyses of the origins of a specific commune, which one can still accept without difficulty.[7] Indeed, a large part of the lasting interest of Caggese and Bognetti was that they, too, were really producing local studies: Bognetti was explicitly restricting himself to Lombard examples, and even Caggese, as Volpe pointed out, was essentially generalizing from Florentine and Senese instances. But both these scholars, and most of their contemporaries, had a much wider remit in mind, and it is this, not their more specific analyses, that is the problem. What has bedevilled this

---

[6] P. Sella, *La vicinia* (Milan, 1908); A. Palmieri, 'Degli antichi comuni rurali', *Atti e memorie*, 3 ser. 16 (1898), 245–71; A. Sorbelli, *La parrocchia dell'Appennino emiliano* (Bologna, 1910), 17–48 (though Sorbelli published in the same year *Il comune rurale dell'Appennino emiliano*, a much more nuanced work, giving weight to a variety of different factors and to regional variation); F. Gabotto, 'Le origini "signorili" del "comune"', *Bollettino storico-bibliografico subalpino*, 8 (1903), 127–50 (on which see Volpe, *Medioevo italiano*, 121–40, and N. Irico, 'Comune di Biella', *Bollettino storico-bibliografico subalpino*, 69 (1971), 449–504); G. Santini, *I comuni di pieve* (Milan, 1964). The *vicinia* appears in Lombard law in *Edictus Rothari*, cap. 340.

[7] G. Salvemini, 'Un comune rurale', now in id., *La dignità cavalleresca* (Milan, 1972), 274–97; A. Checchini, 'Comuni rurali padovani', *Nuovo archivio veneto*, 18 (1909), 131–84; G. Luzzatto, *Dai servi della gleba* (Bari, 1966), 231–406.

subject from the start has been quite simply that authors have not hesitated to generalize about *the* rural commune, over the whole of Italy, from very localized and locally specific sets of empirical evidence, often without even realizing that they are doing so. It is in this respect that it is necessary to start again.

Of course, studies on rural communes did not stop with Bognetti. Simeoni and his successors in the Veneto, in particular, gave new life to more local analyses in a tradition which has lasted from the 1920s to the present day, as we will see later. And there have been in recent years some sophisticated historical syntheses, by Tabacco, Castagnetti, Pini, and others, that give great emphasis to the issue of the development of rural communes in ways that fit well into the most up-to-date historiography, which indeed each of them embodies. Broadly, these latter tend to fuse the two approaches set out above, that of Caggese (though the point of reference is now the more exact Simeoni) and that of Bognetti, in a now dominant historical interpretation that goes roughly as follows. Communes did indeed often crystallize around the organization and recognition of common rights and pre-existing village communities (often called *viciniae*), as bases for rural collective action, where these existed; but they were essentially established against the pressure of rural signorial power. It was territorially organized signorial obligations that unified peasants, whether landowners or tenants, into a common framework of collective subjection in the eleventh century, and which thereby made communes possible. (If local military duties, such as castle guard, were attributed to the community, it was even easier, though the commune sometimes then came to be in the hands of a local military élite.) Communes were, then, set up inside the framework of signorial territories, either against the arbitrary power of the lord (whose local judicial powers they often took over against the payment of a fixed due), or in order to facilitate the lord's organization of his own power, or both; either way, it was not possible for them to develop without the signoria. Indeed, although it was the failure of signorial control—often in the framework of the rising power of the city communes—that allowed for rural communal affirmation, it was also signorial recognition that legitimized and in some sense created the commune: most classically, around and after 1100, through early pacts, franchises, and eventually statutes, which fixed signorial obligations and peasant rights and duties.[8]

[8] L. Simeoni, arts. now in his *Studi su Verona*, iv. 89–250; G. Tabacco, *Egemonie sociali* (Turin, 1979), 250–7; A. Castagnetti, 'Il potere sui contadini', in B. Andreolli et al., *Le campagne italiane* (Bologna, 1985), 219–51; A. I. Pini, *Città, comuni e corporazioni* (Bologna,

There is nothing wrong with this model as a point of reference. It is, however, still partial. What Castagnetti or Pini are saying works very well in the general surveys they have written; but if the analysis stops there, then all it does is what Caggese did, though in a more sophisticated way: that is to say, to take regional analyses, largely of the Veneto (though also from other parts of the Po plain) and generalize them into an Italy-wide development. It is not very similar to my local model for Lucca; and, while I make no claims for the generalizability of my specific examples, one must ask how many other local realities with different sorts of histories existed as well. It therefore seems to me useful to set some of the main lines of development out again, but this time insisting on their regional specificities, in the light of the conclusions I have already drawn from the Lucchese material. Indeed, it seems to me useful to go even further afield in Europe, for the rural communal debate has by no means been restricted to Italians. There is no way of even trying to avoid the schematism in generalization of which I have complained, however, unless we stick resolutely to regional examples. We will briefly look, then, in turn, at Catalonia, Castile, southern and northern France (each of them, of course, also a congeries of different smaller regions), to see the ways in which the Italian evidence, and the Italian debate, is similar to and different from that in the rest of western Europe. (Other areas, such as Germany, England, or the Low Countries, could equally well have been included, but there is not space to cover them all; England, however, I will look at at least briefly: p. 205.) Then, returning to Italy, we will look at the Veneto and at Lombardy, and then come back to some of the different parts of Tuscany. We cannot generalize about the development of communes until we recognize the variety of local experiences that lay behind it.

This procedure, it should be conceded, is potentially dangerous. The different historians, and historical schools, who discussed these different areas have all had differing presuppositions: about how rural society worked in the Middle Ages, about how rural consciousness was structured, or about how general (or how desirable) class conflict has been at any time in the past; or else, reflecting the historiographies of each national community, about how the Middle Ages fitted into the genealogy of social

1986), 71–3; see further F. Menant, *Campagnes lombardes* (Rome, 1993), 425–506; H. Keller, *Adelsherrschaft* (Tübingen, 1979), 165–8; C. Violante, 'La signoria "territoriale"', in W. Paravicini and K. F. Werner (eds.), *Histoire comparée de l'administration* (Munich, 1980), 334–44; P. J. Jones, 'La storia economica', in Einaudi, *Storia d'Italia*, ii (Turin, 1974), 1677–8; G. Fasoli, 'Castelli e signorie', *Settimane di studio*, 13 (1965), 558–63.

development in any given country.[9] One must do one's best to avoid the trap of using them too uncritically, and, as a result, of ending up not comparing like with like. I have tried in each case to draw out the conclusions that seemed to me to follow from the evidence cited by each author, sometimes against the grain of his or her arguments, and I will on occasion point out lines of analysis that seem fruitful, but that have not so far been pursued in a given region. This relatively distanced approach is facilitated by the underlying aim of such a gallery of examples, which is to produce a set of parallels for the development of rural communes *in Italy*, rather than an overview of their origins in Europe as a whole. Such a gallery of examples is important, however; for it would be a great error to imagine that the reasons why rural communes appeared in any one country in the twelfth century were specific to that country alone, and only the presentation of parallel—although, often, crucially different —cases will make the point fully clear.

I hope that these examples will speak for themselves. But some of the diversity of rural communes (as defined in this book on p. 6) is worth signalling before we start. Rural communes can have a varied economic base, the organization of common land or road tolls, or simply the paying of signorial or royal dues. They can be set up by lords, or to oppose them. They can be the product of united or of divided communities, and these communities can be divided by status (e.g. *milites* vs. *populus*) or by faction. They can derive from strong or from weak pre-existing rural identity, and they can themselves be strong or weak, autonomous or dependent. There are, indeed, more differences yet. I will, none the less, be arguing that there are some continuities too. Rural communes tended to appear in the twelfth century over much of western Europe, and where they developed earlier, or later, we can usually see (or guess at) the reasons why. This general development can be seen in the context of a fairly widespread weakness or reorganization of public power; the twelfth century as a whole was an age in which all sorts of local groups —aristocratic lineages, local lordships, towns, villages—gained definition and cohesion as a result. And, inside villages, the newly coherent communities of the period needed leaders. We tend too easily to look at villages from the outside, as homogeneous groups facing their lords; the relationship between their élites and the rest of their neighbours is an equally

---

[9] See my remarks about a slightly earlier period in C. J. Wickham, 'Problems of Comparing Early Medieval Societies', *Transactions of the Royal Historical Society*, 6 ser. 2 (1992), 221–46. Susan Reynolds's criticisms were particularly useful for my argument here.

important issue to analyse. These points of reference, which of course are those I have already used when discussing the Lucchesia, will also serve to reframe the role of the signoria in the development of the commune. I hope to show that this role was less than, or at least different from, that often ascribed to it by the dominant historiography in Italy (and not only in Italy).

ii. European parallels

The history of village collectivities in Catalonia, as described above all in the work of Pierre Bonnassie, presents us with two important points straight off: it gives much firmer evidence than Bognetti did for the cohesion of at least some early medieval collectivities; and it puts at the centre of our analyses the crucial importance of regional geography. Pre-twelfth-century Catalonia was very largely a mountain land, and many of its best-documented zones before 1000 were in the high valleys of the Pyrenees. It was in some of these high valleys, notably in Urgell and Pallars, that, as early as the ninth century, collectivities of peasants were putting up local churches, which they often owned outright; by the late tenth century they can often be seen acting collectively in court cases, too, represented by *boni homines*, that all-purpose early medieval word for local notables. Most remarkably, we have, before 1000, a dozen franchises, ceded by counts to village communities, which include exemptions from fiscal dues and judicial immunities, and which in Cardona in 986 explicitly exclude the possibility that anyone from the locality might have any superiority over the others ('si quis vult inter vos maior fieri, sit sicut iunior'). If this were Italy, at least according to my definition (above, p. 6), and probably according to anyone else's, these would, beyond doubt, already be rural communes, despite their apparent lack of organized internal representation (which seems quite radical, at least at Cardona). This is the sort of evidence that Gianpiero Bognetti did not have for the pre-twelfth-century Alps; nor can it be seen at anything like such an early date in continental Italy's other major pastoral area, the high Abruzzese Appennines. The Pyrenees were evidently capable of generating clearly characterized communities rather earlier than in other southern European mountain areas, and well before the breakdown in government and the growth of signorial power that was a normal framework for them elsewhere. The reason for this was probably the frontier with Muslim Spain: these peasant communities were expected to fight. The areas with franchises tended to be those closest to the frontier, in fact. In the Iberian peninsula the frontier was already contributing to a quite unusual peasant autonomy by western European standards.[10] The situation did not last, however. The Cardona prohibition against *maiores* was probably somewhat defensive; the late tenth century was a period when local notables, the *boni homines* of the court cases, were beginning to gain property and authority in villages. In the mid-eleventh century, there was a crisis: successful notables and other aristocrats wrested local signorial powers from the counts by force. By 1100, few peasant communities were free from private lordship, and, indeed, dominant landlordship too. (One of the few was Andorra, in the remote Pyrenean fastnesses of Urgell, which fought lords off across the century, and maintained the *franceda* which lies at the root of its later independence.) While some liberties continued, at least in memory, and could be restored in later centuries, most villages had to start again. They did this in many cases by concentrating their settlement around local churches, making what use they could of the sanctuary (*sagrera*) offered by the Peace of God. In the late twelfth and thirteenth centuries, many subject villages got new franchises from lords, this time very often in the new frontier zone in the lowlands rather than in the mountains, in a process fairly similar to that found elsewhere in Europe, including in Italy: villages were freed from some of their signorial dues, or recognized as locally self-governing (though still subject) communities, or both.[11]

Analogous to this was the process in Old Castile and León. The Cantabrian mountains, the pre-tenth-century core of those kingdoms, evidently lent themselves to the same sort of local autonomies as in the

---

[10] P. Bonnassie, *La Catalogne* (Toulouse, 1975–6), 307–18; P. Bonnassie and P. Guichard, 'Les Communautés rurales en Catalogne', *Flaran*, 4 (1982), 79–85; J. M. Font Rius (ed.), *Cartas de población* (Barcelona, 1969), n. 9 for Cardona. A good general survey is J. M. Salrach, *El procés de feudalització* (Barcelona, 1987). For the Italian parallels, see above, n. 5.

[11] P. Bonnassie, 'Une famille de la campagne barcelonaise', *Annales du Midi*, 76 (1964), 261–303, for an example of a rising family of *boni homines*; Bonnassie, *Catalogne*, 810–12; Bonnassie and Guichard, 'Communautés rurales en Catalogne', 85–92; R. Martí, 'L'ensagrerament,' *Faventia*, 10 (1988), 153–82; id., 'Els inicis de l'organització feudal', Ph.D. thesis, Autonomous University of Barcelona, 1987, 95–111 (these two studies stress the role of lords in the development of *sagreres*). The best accounts of the oppressions suffered by villagers in the late 12th cent. and their protests are T. N. Bisson, 'The Crisis of the Catalonian Franchises', in J. Portella (ed.), *La formació i expansió del feudalisme català* (Girona, 1985–6), 153–72, and, more recently, P. Freedman, *The Origins of Peasant Servitude* (Cambridge, 1991), 56–118, which shows that the victory of lords was not complete before 1200. For later patterns, P. Freedman, 'La Condition des paysans', *Annales du Midi*, 94 (1982), 227–44; J.-P. Cuvillier, 'Les Communautés rurales', *Mélanges de la Casa de Velazquez*, 4 (1968), 73–105.

Pyrenees, which were then extended southwards to the river Duero in the tenth century, and southwards again with the conquest of the central Meseta from the Muslims at a later date. Here, where early evidence (pre-950) is less good than in Catalonia, there is more argument about the origins of peasant liberties; some ascribe them to frontier colonization, while others trace them back to pre-Roman traditions, as well as to the early medieval Basques, and, in some areas, the Berbers. They may simply derive, on the other hand, from a longer survival than elsewhere in Europe of the relatively independent peasantry of the post-Roman period, which was already on the defensive in Francia and Italy by 800. However this may be, the fact is that in the tenth-century villages in the high plains north of the Duero peasants tended to own their own land, and commonly belonged to local collective bodies called *concilia* (mod. Cast. *concejos*) which ran churches and collectively owned (generally pastoral) land, and which represented the villages in disputes; some frontier settlements had franchises, too, as in Catalonia. How active tenth-century *concilia* were is not clear; many documents, even for villages acting as collective groups (giving land to churches, for instance), just list the donors in family groups, without reference to an organized collectivity. But villages certainly operated as the principal units of social activity in many environments; there is as yet relatively little sign here of more organized vertical social links, such as the clienteles that linked small owners, through local notables, to the aristocracy and the church that can be seen in early medieval Italy.[12]

They would come, though. As in Catalonia, the Castilian and Leonese historiography of the eleventh-century property-owning peasantry is one emphasizing decline and subjection, and not without reason. In many documents of the tenth century villages already have *maiores* and *minores*, and, after 1000, *infanzones* (local hereditary *milites*) and *villani* (more subject

---

[12] For these discussions of Castile, basic surveys are R. Pastor, *Resistencias y luchas* (Madrid, 1980) and J. A. García de Cortázar, *La sociedad rural* (Madrid, 1988). For 10th- and 11th-cent. *concilia* and peasant society, see Pastor, *Resistencias y luchas*, 20–112; García de Cortázar, *Sociedad rural*, 24–46; M. C. Carlé, *Del concejo medieval* (Buenos Aires, 1968), 33–9; A. Barbero and M. Vigil, *La formación del feudalesimo* (Barcelona, 1979), 354–80; C. Estepa Díaz, *El nacimiento de León y Castilla* (Valladolid, 1985), 44–54; P. Martínez Sopena, *La Tierra de Campos* (Valladolid, 1985), 505–8; J. M. Monsalvo Antón, 'Transformaciones sociales', in R. Pastor (ed.), *Relaciones de poder* (Madrid, 1990), 107–11; J. M. Mínguez, 'Ruptura social', *Studia historica*, 3 (1985), 7–32, an important critique; I. Alvarez Borge, 'El proceso de transformación', *Studia historica*, 5 (1987), 145–60; C. Estepa Díaz, 'Poder y propiedad', in *Miscel.lania en homenatge al P. Agustí Altisent* (Tarragona, 1991); 301–4, and J. M. Monsalvo Antón, 'Concejos castellano-leoneses', *Studia historica*, 10 (1992), 203–43, an important synthesis of the debate, with bibliography.

peasants); village inequality—which, of course, had always existed—was increasing as the unlucky went into debt and the lucky increased their landowning. In the county of Castile, *infanzones* could sometimes be found representing—or maybe already controlling—villages, as in a court case of 1073 for Orbaneja in the uplands just east of Burgos. Village representatives are very rarely given titles, but in one of the few instances, a case of two *potestates* in 1012 in Nave de Albura (a small village further north-east, in the Rioja, on the Ebro), the families that furnished them were small local notables who were just becoming *infanzones*, and who in later generations would join the aristocracy of Burgos. Much is still unclear about village society in the eleventh century, not least about how it differed from area to area in northern Spain (as between, for example, the pastoral valleys to the north and east of the Meseta and the flat lands around Valladolid).[13] It is of course not surprising to find that villages are dominated by their local élites, whether or not in the context of commune-like structures like these *concilia*. But it looks as if village notables were only now beginning to be more ambitious; as military attributions came to be restricted to élites in the later eleventh century in this area (the frontier was moving south, away from the Duero), thus creating the basis for a defined military aristocracy, it was more advantageous for *infanzones* and the like to become, or attach themselves to, regional aristocrats, rather than simply to stay at home and dominate their village collectivities. Just such developments were going on elsewhere in eleventh-century Europe, not least in Italy; but in Castile, where villages were already so coherently organized, the growth of private bonds and signorial powers created a crisis for village autonomy. *Concilia* survived as the organizing structures for Castilian villages; indeed, they became more clearly structured in the eleventh century. But they often lost control of their pasture lands to local lords (the best documented, as usual, are churches), often by royal cession; and, increasingly, they became subject to territorial lordships.

There are certain differences in this pattern from that in Catalonia. The 'feudal crisis' of the eleventh century was less sudden and total; and, maybe as a result, village *concilia/concejos* maintained their cohesion even under the new signorial regime. Other differences will doubtless appear as more local analyses are published. But there are evident overall similarities, too; and these continue to be found after 1100. The twelfth

[13] Pastor, *Resistencias y luchas*, 41–3 and Carlé, *Concejo medieval*, 38–41, 63–5 (Nave de Albura); García de Cortázar, *Sociedad rural*, 26–7, 45–6, 94–5 (stressing regional difference).

century shows a steady crystallization of village community structures in the environment of the new signorial regime; boundaries become more explicitly defined; village officials appear more often in the sources. Towards 1200 and into the thirteenth century, village *concejos* north of the Duero often managed to gain *franquicias* and *fueros buenos* from their lords, which fixed dues, lifted signorial exactions (*fueros malos*), and established fiscal and market privileges and rights of justice. Villages gained similar structures elsewhere in Europe, of course; but in Castile, more clearly than anywhere else, such franchises did not create village communities and communal structures, for these had existed without a break for centuries. It would be useful to know more about why franchises began to be conceded only from the late twelfth century onwards. Historians tend to talk about peasant resistance, demographic growth, the expansion of production, and (of course) the frontier; García de Cortázar adds the territorialization of the parish, which he attributes to the twelfth century above all. I wonder whether one might guess that such cessions were often won by a newly forming bloc of village leaders, failed *infanzones* or new rising families, who were only now resigned to their exclusion from the aristocracy (to be part of a still open aristocracy, they would have to have moved south, closer to the frontier), and who needed a firmer local power-base: there are hints to this effect in the authors I am using, and it would certainly fit my Lucca models.[14] There is evidently still a lot more that can be said about these patterns, and people are still arguing about them. But the main lines of Castilian development seem reasonably clear.

These two Iberian examples are useful to us for two reasons. First, they show us what the evidence for early medieval village communities looks like when it exists: local collective activity like that documented in Catalonia and Castile up to 1000 has few if any parallels in Italy. It also, it should be further stressed, indicates that early medieval collectivities, even when they existed, were not normally very tightly characterized or frequently documented; and that is a rule to which I know of no exceptions in southern Europe. But they existed, and they could be active. On the other hand, the second point that needs stressing is that developments in the social structure of the aristocracy that are common to much

---

[14] Martinez Sopena, *Tierra de Campos*, 508–68; Monsalvo Antón, 'Transformaciones sociales'; Pastor, *Resistencias y luchas*, 230–44 and *passim*; García de Cortázar, *Sociedad rural*, 47–95 (90–5 for the parish), 172–4; I. Alfonso, 'Poder local', in R. Pastor (ed.), *Relaciones de poder* (Madrid, 1990), 203–23. It should be noted that south of the Duero, closer to the 12th-cent. frontier, the ways in which these patterns worked out were different again.

of Europe can be found south of the Pyrenees too, although with rather different results. By 1050 or so, aristocrats came to be defined by their military identity; ties of dependence inside the military strata took the *infanzones* and their Catalan equivalents out of village society and into a class more interested in signorial power over it. Like their Lucchese contemporary Moro di Petruccia of Marlia, they were more attracted by being clients of aristocrats than leaders of their neighbours. But in Lucca, village communities did not yet exist in 1050; in Castile and Catalonia, they did, and they had to be subjugated. A new generation of local leaders, probably lower in status, would be necessary in the twelfth century in order to gain what freedoms they could for their now dependent villages. The world of village franchises was international, but its roots were very different from place to place.

My third example is lowland Languedoc, a (relatively) small and coherent region like its Catalan neighbour, and with some similarities in social structure—as, for example, in the fragmentation of landed property—though without the determinant influence of the Pyrenees or the frontier. (Since the Languedoc is easily the best-studied region of southern France from this point of view, thanks largely to the work of Monique Bourin on Béziers, I shall restrict myself to it, and not look sideways to Toulouse or Provence for partial parallels.) Tenth-century Languedoc was not at all like Catalonia in the organization of its villages, and rather more like northern and central Italy; villages did not act consistently as coherent local communities, and local notables had an individual public position as *boni homines* in courts and comital entourages rather than specific village roles. Lowland Languedoc had a standard Mediterranean individualistic agriculture, and there was no need for any community involvement in it; pasture and other collective use-rights were of marginal importance as long as the population was low, and indeed do not greatly impinge on the sources even in the thirteenth century. Even when local settlement concentrated abruptly in the eleventh century, in an *incastellamento* process no less sharp than that in south-central Italy, agrarian practices did not become more collective. Here, in fact, communal institutions were largely political and administrative, even when they did appear, in the late twelfth century.[15]

[15] M. Bourin-Derruau, *Villages médiévaux en Bas-Languedoc* (Paris, 1987), i. 49–53, ii. 197–200; compare E. Magnou-Nortier, *La Société laïque et l'église* (Toulouse, 1974), 156–60, 211.

In Languedoc, as in other places, there was a crisis in post-Carolingian public power in the eleventh century, and the region came to be divided between private signorial territories. *Boni homines* (or, after 1100, *probi homines*) were now the clients of a local lord, running his estate, doing his justice locally, and organizing private arbitrations. They were solid local owners, generally the richer members of the community; they ran local villages, in effect. But, so far, they did so for lords rather than for their neighbours. In the territory of Béziers, it is only after 1190 that *probi homines* (mod. Fr. *prud'hommes*) appear as village representatives for the first time, as part of their slow separation from the lesser military aristocracy and from signorial clienteles, though many of them remained signorial administrators as well until past 1300. Why does such village representation begin to develop at the end of the twelfth century? Bourin would argue that villages themselves were only becoming coherent structures in that century, after the disruption of the *incastellamento* process, thanks to the development of local parish identity, which gave to each village a 'moral personality'; only then, in the absence of collective economic solidarity, was there anything in place to represent. She is distinctly less happy to stress the cohesion deriving from signorial oppression, for she sees little sign of systematic class confrontation at all. (Factions inside the dominant groups of each village were commoner than oppositions between peasants and lords.) Indeed, she argues that village representatives predated the full development of the village community, which is only documented, in the form of assemblies of the adult male population, in the thirteenth century.[16]

In the thirteenth century, village organization became more structured. All villages now had *sindici*, regular representatives, and a community with a definable identity. In addition, across the whole of the Languedoc and the Toulousain, a minority of villages gained a more formal administrative structure, a consulate, in the decades after 1250, although even these did not have the autonomy that they had in some other parts of Europe: consulates did not have any judicial role in the Béziers area, and, in areas where they did, lords generally chose the consuls. Signorial power remained strong in the Languedoc, and uncontested; there were relatively few franchises. But villages were left to be administered by their local (largely landowning) notables without any signorial opposition—lords may

[16] Bourin-Derruau, *Bas-Languedoc*, i. 311–26, ii. 145–202; cf. P. Bonnassie, 'Du Rhône à la Galice', in *Structures féodales et féodalisme* (Rome, 1980), 17–55. The most forceful argument against the relevance of legal personality in a juristic sense in our period is S. Reynolds, *Kingdoms and Communities* (Oxford, 1984), 59–64.

have found it convenient that they should do so, rather than dangerous. These notables, the *prud'homme* families, were quite a wide élite (up to a quarter of the population), and, Bourin argues, ruled consulates and other villages with a certain degree of public spirit. It was of course they who ruled, none the less; the development of a village community just meant the creation of a consensus for their local authority.[17]

The Languedoc (and especialy Béziers) pattern is at the opposite extreme from that in Spain, with unusually restricted and late communities, rather than unusually active and early ones. It is interesting that not even *incastellamento* and local signorial territorialization led particularly quickly to organized local communities in this area. The absence of collective economic activity is evidently one reason for this; the late organization of the parish may be another. There are thus some analogues here to what happened in the Lucchesia. It is, too, only in the late twelfth century that there came to be a sharp boundary between *milites* and nonmilitary notables, which probably pushed the latter, the *probi homines*, more firmly into village politics; *milites*, even those known to be living locally, were by contrast totally absent from twelfth- and thirteenth-century collective activity.[18] This pattern, which I guessed at for Castile, is here reasonably well documented, and is a good parallel for the behaviour of twelfth-century village élites elsewhere.

To counterpose northern France to these three regions is slightly more difficult, for here highly differentiated local studies are extremely common, each of them with its own particular political and economic logic. But one can none the less sketch an overall pattern in the North, against which specific areas had their own history; indeed, such sketches have been quite common in recent years. In northern France (including modern Belgium), the focus of historians has been on the franchises and other written custumals and statutes that unusually large numbers of settlements gained in the years between 1120 and 1270 (with a high point in 1190–1240): 20 per cent of the villages in the region have surviving charters according to Fossier, and that is of course a minimum. Historians recognize that these charters only legitimate and extend the rights of preexisting communities, but they tend to see what lies before 1100 in terms of 'origins', often somewhat schematically characterized: in part because

---

[17] Bourin-Derruau, *Bas-Languedoc*, ii. 145–202, 309–20.
[18] Ibid., ii. 188–94 (188–9 makes explicit the link between the development of communes and the boundary between military and non-military élites); M. Bourin-Derruau and R. Durand, *Vivre au village* (Paris, 1984), 150–2.

in this region rich local documentation is rare before the twelfth century; in part because many historians believe that there actually was no local collective identity before 1000, at least; in part because the simple volume of the franchises tends to focus attention on them. (We will see a similar pattern of attention in the parts of northern Italy with numerous franchises.) The franchises certainly are a rich source for the study of peasant society, but the exact relationship between their rules and the real patterns of forces in the individual villages they applied to is more questionable. This is particularly true in the areas dominated by the great model charters of rights, where dozens and sometimes hundreds of villages adopted the same texts for their franchises: the charter of Lorris near Orléans, a royal charter of 1155, or of Prisches in Hainaut, a cession from the lord of Avesnes of 1158, or of Beaumont-en-Argonne, from the archbishop of Reims in 1182. All the same, franchises do at least represent a clear point by which village communities had visibly developed into self-conscious organized bodies that Italians would call communes (though the French tend to restrict this term to a smaller group of effectively autonomous villages, and to towns): although the level of freedom and self-government of such communities was very various, village charters of franchise show that they were at least all structured and explicit collective associations, with some degree of local representation.[19]

Historians tend to stress three aspects of the development of village communities in this region, as elsewhere: economic, religious, and signorial relationships. Economic relationships include the organization of pastoral and woodland use-rights, which became more important as the population rose and the pressure on land built up; and, in many areas, the development of compulsory crop rotations, normally in large common fields which needed to be quite carefully regulated by the village. Religious relationships mean, in effect, the parish, which was becoming defined as the territory of a single village by the eleventh century at the latest; churches (and their cemeteries) were real social foci by 1100, as religious and secular meeting-places, and in the twelfth century were often rebuilt by villagers—they were centres of social aggregation for every local inhabitant. The territorial seigneurie, too, created, once again, an environment in which all villagers had a common experience as subjects, sometimes for the first time—for before that villagers had been split between owners and tenants, or free and unfree. In the twelfth century, these tendencies

---

[19] R. Fossier, 'Les Communautés villageoises,' *Flaran*, 4 (1982), 29–53, gives a good initial survey.

all met together; newly conscious village communities developed, and tried to gain all the advantages they could out of the divisions among the dominant class. Lords who needed to stabilize their local power, or who appreciated fixed dues in money, found it advantageous to cede franchises that granted what peasants wanted: the end of arbitrary services (and sometimes all corvées), the devolution of local justice, the local election of representatives, the regulation of use-rights, and the development of village-level land law.[20]

So far historians agree; but beyond this they argue as much as they do in Italy. How early did villages come together as communities? Duby argued (on the basis of the Mâconnais, a little further south in Burgundy), that they barely existed before 1000 as more than geographical units; only then did the seigneurie create the framework inside which they could develop an identity. Fossier even denies that they existed as geographical units before the tenth century or so, and has claimed that no community is possible without concentrated settlement (this, at least, no historian with any experience of dispersed settlement, from Norfolk to Tuscany, can accept). Reynolds, on the other hand, doubts very much that there was no social cohesion at the village level before the eleventh century, and sees the development of the community largely as an issue of rising documentation, though she does see economic development and the demands of government as producing after 1100 a need for tighter local organization. Génicot sees communities as fully coherent only in the twelfth century, almost at the time of the franchises, though he traces the origins of their separate elements way back, to the Carolingians and *Lex Salica*.[21]

Such differences, and others, depend largely on what one means by a 'community', which not all of these writers define very clearly or consistently. I will return to some of them, and to alternative explanations, in the Italian context. For now, however, it can be observed that in practice these authors do not all differ in their actual analyses so very much, even if they may stress different elements in the common matrix—Duby

[20] See, in general, ibid.; id., *Enfance de l'Europe* (Paris, 1982), 532–7, 549–60; id., *Chartes de coutume* (Paris, 1974), 25–123; id., *La Terre et les hommes* (Paris, 1968), 708–27; Bourin-Derruau and Durand, *Vivre au village*, 119–33, 205–19; L. Génicot, *Rural Communities in the Medieval West* (Baltimore, 1990); and the studies cited in the next n.

[21] G. Duby, *La Région mâconnaise* (2nd edn., Paris, 1971), 122–4, 227–33; Fossier, 'Communautés villageoises', 31, with J. Chapelot and R. Fossier, *Le Village et la maison* (Paris, 1980), e.g. 75; Reynolds, *Kingdoms and Communities*, 101–54; Génicot, *Rural Communities*, 12–31. (Reynolds and Génicot are, it must be stressed, syntheses for wider areas than just northern France, and indeed include Mediterranean examples, but their main empirical foci are northern European.)

tending to emphasize the seigneurie, for example, and Fossier economic growth. And all separate quite sharply the two issues of the (largely un-documented) development of organized communities, and the cession by lords of franchises to these communities, the latter being to an extent a cultural change, representing an increasingly explicit regulation of social relationships, rather than necessarily a real shift in these relationships. This distinction is one we can certainly accept, and it has parallels in both Spain and Italy.

There were important local differences of course, as well. Sivéry has argued categorically in a recent survey, extending his work on Hainault and the Terre de Guise, that the most autonomous communities tend to be in pastoral areas; the most subject to signorial power those in open cereal lands. Fossier has a micro-regional division in neighbouring Picardy, too, with the earliest and most autonomous village franchises around Amiens, and other areas, such as around Cambrai, rather later and weaker, though he ascribes this largely to the choices of individual lords, rather than to economic explanations. Chédeville has very weak communities around Chartres; he attributes this to the weakness both of seigneuries and com-mon lands, as well as to the local absence of urban franchises.[22] These more specific studies thus tend to stress more specific causes, which add to the range of explanations that people use. We cannot assess them further here; but it must be stressed, once again, that all the overviews I have just cited are also based on area analyses such as these: 'northern France' is nothing but Picardy, Guise, Hainaut, Coucy, Champagne, the Île de France, and, moving southward, Chartres, Berry, and Mâcon, rather than a homogeneous unit. Here, at least, the historians concerned are fully aware of the fact.

If we look at these studies of northern France from the standpoint of our Italian interests, we will find that, in some respects, they simply tell us what we already knew: that (much of) north-western Europe is different from (much of) the Mediterranean. We are here mostly in lands of collectively organized agriculture, which itself creates, from its appearance (whenever this was: the date varied from place to place, and is contested), a systematic village-based economic organization that is un-necessary in the South except for pasture, and for rare irrigated areas. In the North, too, there seems to be a far greater social divide between lords and peasants: villages were as usual run by their richest members, who

[22] G. Sivéry, *Terroirs et communautés rurales* (Lille, 1990); Fossier, *Chartes de coutume*, 109–21; A. Chédeville, *Chartres et ses campagnes* (Paris, 1973), 215–22.

may sometimes have held allods in the twelfth century, but these allods are hard if not impossible to document;[23] there seem to be few or no local notables, on the fringes of the military aristocracy, who have the intermediary role that is so common in the South, and indeed some northern villages were communities of serfs, who gained 'freedom' with their franchises in classic Caggese style. There is also no doubt that in the North of France written franchises were commoner than almost anywhere else in Europe; this, on the other hand, is a political rather than a structural contrast, for the variety of their terms shows that there is no direct correlation between the possession of a charter and the autonomy or degree of organization of a community. These franchises certainly mean that village norms are documented best in northern France; denser local documentation, however, ensures that, up to 1250 at least, village practice is better documented in the South.

On the other hand, even in such an un-Mediterranean ecological environment as open-field France—and one could say the same of pastoral Castile—there are some similarities of focus and explanation with the Italian experience. Everywhere, the seigneurie, the organization of common lands, and the parish appear as structural elements in the crystallization of village communities, in their 'prise de conscience' as the French often call it, just as in Italy. In Spain and France, too, as in Italy, the evidence for this development becomes abruptly clearer in the twelfth century. Indeed, something new seems to be happening to the society of most of rural Europe in that century, though in some areas it develops faster than others. The rules get tighter and more explicit, perhaps as the population grows and the economy becomes more complex; and perhaps as peasants and/or lords feel they have something to gain from written regulation. It becomes more necessary, in the newly defined 'cells' of this society, to develop an organized local leadership to decide on local matters on behalf of both lords and village communities.[24] These are western Europe-wide phenomena; in the light of them, explanation for Italian communes that depends too exclusively on Italian conditions risks parochialism.

In this context, then, what other specific insights can one take back to Italy from France and the Iberian peninsula to help us consider the Italian situation? First, the importance of ecology. It is obvious that there are

[23] On allods, see Fossier, *La Terre et les hommes*, 725–6.
[24] Fossier, *Enfance de l'Europe*, esp. 494–540; Reynolds, *Kingdoms and Communities*, 122–37; R. H. Hilton, *Bondmen Made Free* (London, 1973), 74–85.

huge differences in local organization between a high pastoral valley in Catalonia or Castile, a Picard village with a structured three-field system, and an Italian plains settlement with fragmented small fields and individualist agriculture; no one has doubted it, from Marc Bloch onwards.[25] But this is equally true inside Italy: an upland Alpine settlement in Bognetti's Lombardy and a scattered village in the Lucca plain have little in common, at least as economic units. We may all think we know this, but it is often forgotten in practice; it can hardly be too often restated.

A second point is the emphasis, stressed in particular by several historians of the North, that the local government and the regulation of villages is not necessarily to the disadvantage of lords, and does not necessarily mark the weakness of the seigneurie. Barthélemy, working on Coucy, actually inverts the Caggese model: franchises changed real social relationships so little that they were in effect just instruments of signorial power, which, through the institutionalization of local norms, penetrated more deeply into local society. This was certainly not always the case, for peasants often valued franchises enough to pay considerable sums of money for them, either as counter-gifts or rents. Fossier rephrases the simple class struggle model as a much more dialectical counterposition: 'The clash with the lords was a constant pressure and a muted aggression to snatch advantages where possible without disturbing society; for this was the essential objective: to maintain one's gains, and to risk nothing of the security one had obtained.' This seems to me a convincing formulation. The establishment of communes was not, for the most part, intended to destroy the seigneurie itself; the 'everyday forms of peasant resistance', to use James Scott's phrase, were aimed at what was possible, not at what was impossible.[26]

A third point relates to the role of local élites. Every historian, all over Europe, stresses that villages are run by their notables; and more than one emphasizes that this sort of authority is *de facto*, capillary, 'recognized by an unorganized and supple consensus', rather than based on access to specific institutions or roles—the same men (they are, in nearly every case, all men) are churchwardens for the parish, consuls or *scabini* (*échevins*) or *sindici* or *iurati* for the village, and *villici* for lords. Not much has been written in France or Spain about how the unorganized consensus was structured, although in the South of France some attention

[25] M. Bloch, *Les Caractères originaux* (2nd edn., Paris, 1955), 35–65.
[26] D. Barthélemy, *Les Deux Ages de la seigneurie* (Paris, 1984), 252–323, esp. 270, 274, 300–1, 322–3; Fossier, 'Communautés rurales', 43; J. C. Scott, *Weapons of the Weak* (New Haven, 1985).

has been paid to village factions, most classically in Emmanuel Le Roy Ladurie's Montaillou in the French Pyrenees, where village rivalries were visibly focused on clienteles supporting or opposing one dominant family (whose local dominance was represented, though not caused, by their possession of two offices, those of local priest and count's bailiff—two more official roles to add to the list). It is clear, anyway, that particular families were dominant in every village, very likely most of the local rich and some at least of the local middling peasants.[27] This point can be pushed further, thanks largely to Rodney Hilton's work on midland England.

In England, a region with few rural franchises and very little formalized village autonomy, many villages only get documentation as communities at all through the manorial court, the court of the local landowner and lord. But this court, whose powers could be wide (they commonly extended to the fixing and even the changing of local customs), was, in practice, run by villagers. They were the local élite, of course, and doubtless chosen and patronized by the lord, but they were peasants none the less; only local inhabitants actually had the knowledge to dominate and coerce their neighbours. Such richer peasants coerced their neighbours in more private ways, too, as local usurers, and indeed by force—they were often the most violent members of society. They were also, however, the leaders of the village in any confrontation with the lord.[28]

This short example allows us to formulate a further generalization. The fact is that, even in the most oppressive and violent periods of the Middle Ages, and even in the most inegalitarian local societies, with few people between tenant communities on the one hand and aristocrats on the other, lords could not control the detail of peasants' lives, either directly or through their armed men. Peasants have always been largely autonomous, both in their economic activities and their internal social relationships; lords can and do bring enormous pressure to bear on them, but only from outside. Lords can create the rules inside which peasants have to live; but the way they obey or fail to obey those rules can only be policed by other peasants. In the twelfth century and later, all over western Europe, the

---

[27] For notables, Bourin-Derruau and Durand, *Vivre au village*, 210 (quote); Génicot, *Rural Communities*, 51, 83, 104. Factions: E. Le Roy Ladurie, *Montaillou* (Paris, 1975), 88–107; Bourin-Derruau, *Bas-Languedoc*, ii. 181–3, 299–309, 338.

[28] R. H. Hilton, *A Medieval Society* (2nd edn., Cambridge, 1983), 149–66; id., 'Les Communautés villageoises en Angleterre', *Flaran*, 4 (1982), 117–28; C. C. Dyer, 'Power and Conflict in the Medieval English Village', in D. Hooke (ed.), *Medieval Villages* (Oxford, 1985), 27–32; id., 'Les Cours manoriales', *Etudes rurales*, 103: 4 (1986), 19–27; id., 'The English Medieval Village Community', *Journal of British Studies*, 33 (1994), 407–29; comp. Sivéry, *Terroirs et communautés*, 183.

explicitness of these rules increased substantially, as did the policing methods—sometimes to the advantage of lords, often to that of peasants, not seldom to that of both. But the basic pattern remained the same: villages in practice ran themselves, except for occasional armed signorial interventions, that, whatever their legal justifications, must often have seemed much like military raids. It follows that if we want to understand fully how peasant society worked and changed, we have to study not just how peasants related to lords, but how they related to each other; and even if we just want to understand how and why peasants obeyed lords, we also have to study how poorer peasants obeyed richer peasants, and in which circumstances richer peasants chose to further the interests of their superiors rather than undermine or (most occasionally of all) oppose them. A study of this kind, of what peasants do to each other rather than what lords do to the peasantry, could be summed up as the analysis of the complex systems of deference that Antonio Gramsci called 'hegemony'. Although, given the limits of most medieval documentation, it is in practice virtually impossible to carry out, it should be set out, none the less, as an ideal end-point of any research on peasant social structure, whether in the medieval period or at any other time.

Italy is part of Europe, and participates in a common European development; it is not surprising that these three points (which are anyway fairly generic sociological statements) can be carried straight into any Italian analysis, and indeed I have developed aspects of all three in the preceding chapters of this book. There are, none the less, certain features specific to at least northern and central Italy that transalpine comparisons throw into relief. One is the importance of peasant property-owning, what French historians call peasant allods. Fossier believes that his rich peasants have allods, but recognizes that these are very hard to find; Bonnassie for Catalonia, after the feudal crisis of the eleventh century, believes that his peasants do not; after 1200, of the regions I have cited, they seem to be well attested only in Languedoc.[29] But in Italy, without any doubt, peasant property-owning, according to the standard meaning that 'ownership' has in late Roman law, was wholly normal, in every century of the Middle Ages, and is extensively documented. Rare were the villages owned by a single landlord, at any time; even villages all of whose landowners lived somewhere else, leaving a local community restricted to tenants of different lords, were relatively uncommon before the growth

[29] Fossier, *La Terre et les hommes*, 726; Bonnassie, *Catalogne*, 816 (but Freedman, *Peasant Servitude*, sees some peasant allods survive until 1200); Bourin-Derruau, *Bas-Languedoc*, e.g. ii. 225–31.

of city landowning in the late Middle Ages. Peasant élites were normally groups of property-owners (although they could easily hold land on lease as well), perhaps headed by medium landowners rich enough not to have to cultivate, and with their eyes half on the bottom rungs of the ladder of the aristocracy. Élites of this kind, men of some influence, could greatly strengthen village collective identity and resistance, when they chose; they could also (as their equivalents did in Catalonia and Castile in the eleventh century) radically weaken it. The greater density of mediations between lords and dependent peasants in north-central Italy (as opposed to northern France, say, or England) continued, however, throughout the medieval period. Village society was far more complicated as a result, although, sometimes, more transparent to us.

A second difference in Italy is the power of the city. In the Iberian peninsula or in France (although not in England) it is generally accepted that the public power structures of the Carolingian world and its neighbours collapsed nearly everywhere around 1000–50 into the private signorial territories of the next two centuries; where towns fitted into this is debated, but they certainly were not in most places in any sense independent of the power (or at least of the buying power) of kings and aristocrats, whether these lived in town or country. In north-central Italy, the survival and development of the city as a dominant political and economic centre in itself created a different system. Italian cities were, as elsewhere, controlled by aristocrats and other landowners almost without exception, for successful merchants and artisans bought land too, if indeed they did not have it as the basis of their initial capital. But urban centres had to be run as more complex entities than did rural lordships. Italian city society moved from the public power structures of the Carolingian world to those of the thirteenth- and fourteenth-century city states with relatively little break; and the latter were, of course, from 1100 or so, also autonomous communes, whose institutions villages sought systematically to imitate. Cities moved to absorb the private lordships of the countryside, either by gaining their recognition of city domination or by their defeat and abolition. In Italy, then, almost uniquely in western Europe, there was in the period after 1100 an alternative to local signorial power for villages seeking to establish their own communes: it was possible to be autonomous of the local signoria, because it was possible to be directly subject to the city. Of course, the real liberties of such 'free communes' then depended on city policy, and cities could easily be as oppressive as private lordships; indeed, the real difference between public and private power is a problematic issue in itself. All the same, the political environment in which villages operated was different as a result: at the very least, they could under some circumstances hope to act to change their ruler, as cities for their own reasons supported rural communes against rural lords, and sometimes they managed it—a feat distinctly unusual in the rest of Europe.

A third difference was the greater professionalization of law in Italy. This partly derived from the hegemony of the cities, but not entirely; legal expertise predated the communes, and indeed stretched back in an unbroken line to the Roman empire. It was only partially relevant to the formation of rural communes, for, as we have seen in Lucca, rural communes (as also those in cities) derived from the world of the informal, the world of arbitration rather than that of tribunal-backed judgment, and only later crystallized into institutions with legally enforceable roles.[30] But cities were developing their own local law in the twelfth century, as rural communes soon would do. The twelfth century was a period of legal revival all over western Europe, from the Bologna schools to the court of Henry II of England; but in Italy the formalization of local law (as opposed to royal or canon law, or legal theory) developed rather faster than elsewhere. As a result, the greater explicitness and stability of village institutions was already a feature of the whole of north-central Italy by the early thirteenth century; it was an organic development, from inside village society, and did not necessarily have to be conceded from the top, in franchises, which were in fact not as common in much of Italy as in northern France.

A fourth and final difference is quite simply the extent of Italian documentary material. The structures of Italian village society can be traced back in some cases to the eighth century, without a break in the documentation: few if any other parts of Europe can claim as much. In the formative eleventh century, perhaps only Catalonia is more densely furnished with private charters. And, after 1200, when rural societies all over Europe began to gain generous quantities of their own evidence, Italy moved into the next phase, with the limitless riches of the notarial registers. Villages in northern France and in many other places in Europe north of, say, Dijon have for a long time to be seen from the outside, through the documents of lords, and thus from the latter's point of view; villagers tend to appear as relatively undifferentiated groups as a result. The survival in Italy of documents of the peasants themselves (however

---

[30] See, in general, W. Davies and P. Fouracre (eds.), *The Settlement of Disputes in Early Medieval Europe* (Cambridge, 1986), and Reynolds, *Kingdoms and Communities*, 12–66, for anti-institutional theories of early medieval law.

ambiguous the reasons for that survival) make it possible to investigate
at least some of their relationships with each other, sometimes from
the eighth century and very often from 1000, however hypothetical and
labile the results; it seems to me inexcusable not to try. The peasant land
market, local clienteles, factions: one can get away without studying them
in much of twelfth-century northern France, where they can only be a
matter of speculation, but not in twelfth-century Lucca.

iii. Italian parallels

All over Europe, we have the same problem, in this period as in others:
the opposition between the particular and the general. Each region, each
micro-region, each village, has its own particular social structure, its own
development for its own reasons, its own history; but they have common
features none the less.[31] Lucca and Picardy were very different, but each
developed what Italians call rural communes in the twelfth century; how,
and why? How can we construct a common western European (or indeed
Italian) history without doing violence to these particular experiences, that
is to say, without inventing a legal and institutional homogeneity rather
than recognizing the heterogenity of social history? And it scarcely needs
adding that the richer our understanding of these particular experiences,
the harder it is to compare them and generalize from them. As I have
indicated earlier (e.g. p. 191), one way is through the counterposition of
form and content: the 'rural commune' may have had a relatively standard social and—increasingly—institutional form across Italy in 1200 (and
not only Italy), but its real content varied dramatically from area to area,
and, inside them, from village to village. Seeing how these variations
could occur allows us to make distinctions between different local social
realities that can have resonance elsewhere; conversely, seeing how the
institutions of rural communes developed in the whole of a given region
or country allows us to see what sorts of overall developments affected that
region or country. These developments tend to come down to the same
factors, everywhere: the signoria, the parish, the exploitation of common
lands, the impact of the city, changes in landownership, the changing
structure of clienteles; but local analyses will throw up situations in which
some of these are more important than others, thus allowing us to see
which elements in the matrix affected developments in which way. From
this standpoint, then, let us come back to Italy, and look in turn at the
Veneto, Lombardy, and Tuscany, and at the individual local studies in

---

[31] See further C. J. Wickham, *The Mountains and the City* (Oxford, 1988), 1–8, 347–57.

each of these regions, before trying to reach some more general conclusions.[32] We will look at these studies in more detail than at our Iberian and French examples, but the same caveats as expressed at the end of section i above apply.

In the study of rural communes, the Veneto has long been the best-analysed region of Italy, thanks to Simeoni's early studies of the twelfth-century Verona franchises, more recently taken up again by Castagnetti, for such texts are more frequent in the Veronese than almost anywhere else in Italy before 1200. They begin with Bionde in the lower Veronese plain in 1091, a text that establishes the co-election between the lord and the local *vicini* of a *gastaldio* to run local justice, as well as the fixing of signorial dues: the context of the text is entirely signorial, and whether these *vicini* are small landowners or tenants is unclear. Similar limitations on signorial dues and/or jurisdiction are attested in documents for several other Veronese villages in the next fifty years. Are these ceded by lords by their own free will, as sometimes, supposedly, in northern France? Not necessarily, for in several cases they are preceded by refusals by villagers to pay dues and hospitality obligations, and sometimes, as at Zevio in 1180 and Bionde again in 1212, by violence: peasants were prepared to fight for the fixing of signorial dues, or their lightening, or even their abolition. (In Zevio their leaders seem to have been small local *milites*, though these are not documented at Bionde.) Sometimes, as at Marzana in the hills just north of Verona in 1121, the focus for community solidarity is a castello, which villagers defend for their lord (in this case the cathedral canons); this sort of commune, centred on defensive obligations, is also quite common further north in the Trentino (a classic case is Riva di Garda in 1124), and further east in the Trevigiano as well, and the castello tends to bring to the commune rights to control local justice too in most cases. Sometimes we may also guess at a local solidarity based on the organization of common lands: the men of Zevio, long before 1180, had pastures on the banks of the Adige, which were contested by a neighbouring village in 996. But here, unlike in the Bognetti model, even if we are on the edge of the Alps in the case of some of these villages at

[32] Not all Italian regions are very fully covered by studies of rural communes. For Piemonte, however, I could have used several, including H. Groneuer, *Caresana* (Stuttgart, 1970), Irico, 'Comune di Biella', P. Pezzano, 'Racconigi', *Bollettino storico-bibliografico subalpino*, 74 (1976), 619–91, and the important survey by F. Panero, *Servi e rustici* (Vercelli, 1990), 165–215; and the Marche has classic analyses by Luzzatto and others: see Luzzatto, *Dai servi della gleba*, 231–406, and the guide in J. C. Maire-Vigueur, 'Comuni e signorie in Umbria', UTET, *Storia d'Italia*, vii. 2 (Turin, 1987), 373–96.

least (Riva, Marzana), it would be hard to argue that organized communities significantly predated 1100.[33] The test case for this last statement is Lazise, on Lake Garda, where the plain meets the lowest Alpine ridges. This village, which was the centre of a royal estate (although also with some *nobiles*, probably local medium landowners), and which had its own castello by 983, was ceded some fiscal exemptions and local fishing rights in that year by Otto II, apparently to safeguard it from any private lordship. This immunity was renewed by Henry IV in 1073, together with generous woodland use-rights, and lasted until Lazise came under the control of Verona in 1193. Lazise was a fortification beside a major route to the Brenner pass, and depended substantially on common rights: maybe these diplomas could be seen as a rare Italian equivalent to the tenth-century frontier franchises for what were already, in effect, rural communes in Catalonia? But the Lazise texts refer only to 'quidam pauperes homines' as the local recipients of the grants, and even if we can presume that the twenty-odd names in each diploma were in some sense village representatives, we cannot easily deduce the existence of an organized collectivity, a commune by my definition (above, p. 6), before 1100.[34] The framework for such collectivities, when we find them in the Veronese, is in every case the territorial signoria and its local military-judicial exactions, and dates from the twelfth century. Even at Zevio, where we know of early common land, the commune of 1180 seems to be first documented opposing signorial rights, not defending its control over common land; even at Lazise, where there was no local lord, the framework of the eventual commune was what one could call the public lordship of Otto's immunity. Simeoni remarks that Veronese disputes were often begun by lords, not by communes: communes were in practice taking local rights into their own hands first, before lords resisted.[35] Whether communities were solider here, or more audacious in a climate of economic expansion, or lords more oppressive—or maybe indeed weaker—is not clear. But the context in which communes appeared was the territorial signoria, not common rights or disputes over land tenure.

[33] Simeoni's articles on communes are collected in *Studi su Verona*, iv. 89–250 (see esp. 91–4, 203–50); A. Castagnetti, 'Le comunità della regione gardense', in G. Borelli (ed.), *Un lago, una civiltà* (Verona, 1983), i. 48–87; id., *Valpolicella* (Verona, 1984); cf. his general survey, 'Il potere sui contadini', 221–33. For the Trevigiano, see S. Collodo, 'I "vicini"', in *Storia di Treviso*, ii (Venice, 1991), 271–97.
[34] See Simeoni, *Studi su Verona*, iv. 200–2, 214–15; G. Tabacco, *I liberi del re* (Spoleto, 1966), 151–7; Castagnetti, 'Comunità della regione gardense', 50.
[35] Simeoni, *Studi su Verona*, iv. 226–8.

The likelihood is that communal leaders were free landowners, and some-times (though not always) they were *milites*.

Similar patterns have been found on the low plains of the Padovano, by Checchini and Bortolami, and this time the documentation allows us to say more about the social composition of the communes. Checchini, who studied the Saccisica between Padua and the Venetian lagoon in 1909, could show that its inhabitants included both free tenants and small landowners; they were called, in a diploma of 1055, 'eremanni', the traditional word for free men subject only to the king. In that year they sought and gained royal protection from oppression by the bishop of Padua; they evidently owed judicial and public dues both to the king and the bishop, and the former wished to maintain his rights. Eventually, the king ceded these to the bishop, and the Saccensi thus had no more external aid; in 1080, however, they acted in concert to force the bishop's men off their pasture lands, apparently with success. Here, common lands were a basis for communal organization, inside the framework of the signoria. So far, the local community seems to have been a fairly inchoate collec-tivity; in 1118, however, collective representatives are documented in the villages of the Saccisica, and they ran local affairs in several texts sur-viving from the twelfth century, although here the bishop kept hold of most judicial rights.[36]

[36] Checchini, 'Comuni rurali padovani', 140–54; see further Tabacco, *Liberi del re*, 157–60; G. Rippe, 'Dans le Padouan', *Cahiers de civilisation médiévale*, 27 (1984), 144–7. Exactly when communes developed in the Saccisica is not clear, however (the authors cited disagree), precisely because a local collective consciousness developed relatively early, in opposition to the bishop. It must be stressed that collective peasant defences of rights against landowners long predated 1100 (there are some earlier ones listed in C. J. Wickham, *Early Medieval Italy* (London, 1981), 109–11; and they are related to pastoral communities in id., *Società degli Appennini*, 18–44), without them necessarily leading immediately to local structures of a communal type. It could be argued for the Saccisica that the twelve *castellenses* who led the Saccensi in a commercial treaty with Venice in 1005 were already in effect their representatives, in which case one might already call the whole area a commune; or else that their organized action in 1080 led to more stable village representation by 1118. I would prefer the second interpretation myself (and there are others still); but, either way, one finds one's interpretation depending less on varying readings of the texts than on the issue of how one conceives of the rural commune as an ideal type (see above, p. 6). One should add here that there is a whole historiography on the communities of the northern castelli in the tenth and eleventh centuries: major examples of it include A. A. Settia, *Castelli e villaggi* (Naples, 1984); G. Rossetti, 'Formazione e caratteri delle signorie di castello', *Aevum*, 49 (1975), 243–309. These, and others, allow us to understand the local social history of the period up to 1100, and sometimes beyond, very clearly. But their analyses rarely extend to the issue of the appearance of rural communities themselves. Although there are exceptions to this, such as H. Keller, *Adelsherrschaft* (Tübingen, 1979), 103–23, the fact remains that 12th-cent. society is rarely set against that of preceding centuries; the issue of communal origins has thus not often been greatly helped by analyses of earlier periods.

Bortolami pushed this analysis further, and with the fullest detail, when he studied Pernumia south of Padua in 1978. In this area, he was able to show not only that the fragmentation of tenure produced a complex network of small and medium landowners alongside tenants of various landlords, as (among many other places) in the Lucchesia; but also that this was accompanied by a similar fragmentation and superimposition of signorial rights, with a network of property-based signorial rights appertaining to local landowners (including local *domini*, small military aristocrats, and the cathedral Canonica), set against a territorial signoria over the whole of Pernumia controlled by a local aristocratic family, the da Carrara. Around 1200, local leaders found themselves able to play these lords off against each other, refusing at one point to pay the tithe (due to the Canonica), while at another succeeding in getting the da Carrara to lift some signorial dues and divide some judicial fines with the commune: the core of these troublemakers was a group of prosperous local proprietors, independent of all signorial obligations except to the da Carrara, and closely linked to the organization of the commune. Pernumia was not as precocious in its communal development as the Saccisica, which had a firm tradition of agitation inside the framework of late Carolingian public power at its back. Here, the origin of the commune lay in the twelfth century, with the tightening of the power of the signoria, and, probably, with economic advance (it was a period of considerable land clearance in the area, and of more systematic organization of common lands, with an eye to the market). References to the commune begin in the 1140s, but it took until 1225 for it to be documented as a fully developed institution, with several sets of officials, as the statutes of that year show. That was the high point for the commune, however; soon the city began to exercise more control over local common pastures, citizens bought up land in the area, and Pernumia notables emigrated into the city. By 1300 its autonomy had faded, and the commune became just an administrative circumscription for the city.[37]

Pernumia is a classic instance of a Veneto rural commune, explored in a model study. It has everything: the territorial framework of the signoria (and, indeed, the pieve, for the two were coterminous, and the latter an important node for local organization); a complex network of competing political powers; a fragmented tenurial pattern, and a set of local notables who dominated the commune; and some evidence, at least,

---

[37] S. Bortolami, *Pernumia* (Venice, 1978). See further, as a parallel, his 'Scodosia di Montagnana', *Mélanges de l'Ecole française de Rome*, 99 (1987), 555–84.

of a co-ordinating role for the organization of common land, though this may be new in the twelfth century. Signorial cessions to the rising commune follow, then the institutionalization of the commune, then a city take-over. The hypotheses of Simeoni and Checchini stand confirmed and nuanced by a wealth of archival documentation. We need more studies like that of Bortolami, both in Italy and in the rest of Europe. For now, however, it can serve to sum up the Veneto: a region in which communes formed, in all our documented studies, inside and against the signoria.

These Veronese and Paduan studies of the plains and hill margins exclude two important types of commune: those of the great rural *castelli*, and those of the Alps. Both existed in the Veneto, and have been well studied, for example by Fasoli for Bassano and Collodo for the Cadore;[38] but more attention has been paid to them in Lombardy, and it is Lombard examples I will use here, through the perspective of François Menant's recent book on the eastern half of the region.

Menant stresses an important point: that in his area, nearly all early examples of rural communes, in the late eleventh century and the first decades of the twelfth, are for large *castra* and *burgi*, like Piadena (1095), Soncino (1118), Crema, and, just south of the Po in Emilia, Guastalla (1102–16). These centres were often still under direct royal control, with consequent fiscal privileges; but, most importantly, they were already in 1100 major centres of exchange, and their leaders were small aristocrats and merchants—indeed, in Guastalla, peasants (*agricolae*) were excluded from many of the privileges. This is a category of commune that can be found all over Italy. Biandrate in the Novarese (1093) is another nearby early example; so are many of the communes in the Marche studied by Luzzatto, such as Fabriano and Matelica.[39] In Tuscany, instances include Montepulciano, Prato, and S. Gimignano. It must be remarked first that, if these centres had been placed in northern Europe, they would simply be regarded as towns and discussed in separate chapters from villages; only the restriction of most Italian urban historians' attention to cities, i.e. towns with bishops, lets them be seen as rural at all. They are almost never analysed across Italy as a whole, and they should be. But one can already generalize about them to an extent. Their immediate access to

[38] G. Fasoli, 'Bassano', *Archivio veneto*, 5 ser. 15 (1934), 1–44; S. Collodo, 'Il Cadore medievale', *Archivio storico italiano*, 145 (1987), 368–79.
[39] Menant, *Campagnes lombardes*, 489–94; for Guastalla, see also A. Castagnetti, *L'organizzazione del territorio rurale* (Turin, 1979), 57–62; for Biandrate, see id., 'Il potere sui contadini', 227–9; Panero, *Servi e rustici*, 165–75, the basic analysis; cf. Luzzatto, *Dai servi della gleba*, 231–406. For the general problem and the later history of these 'quasi-cities', see G. Chittolini, ' "Quasi-città" ', *Società e storia*, 13 (1990), 3–26.

money was a particularly easy reason for their ability to buy their independence from lords early. But the fact that they tended also to be headed by *milites*, small aristocrats or militarized notables, is another reason for their autonomy, which has closer parallels in smaller *castelli*, with rather less early commercial activity in them. Aristocratic leaders could more easily lead settlements out of full signorial control than could lesser notables. The other side of this was, however, that such communes ended up stably under the control of such *milites*, who were sometimes organized as a separate commune from that of the peasants, in effect as a sort of oligarchic signoria, which might itself be fought against by the peasantry.[40] In Tuscany, which was full of little *castra* with one or two military families in them, this pattern was quite common, and we will see it again shortly.

As to the Alps: Lombardy was, of course, the region studied by Bognetti, and several other authors have followed his lead, among them Schäfer, Toubert, Celli, and Keller. Recent work on the Lombard Alps has not, however, backed up Bognetti's theory of the immemorial commune (see above, p. 186). Rural communes in the Alps, as in the plains, tended to appear in the twelfth century, rather than earlier, and mostly did so in the context of the signoria, not the community that controlled local common lands. At Ardesio, in the Alps above Bergamo, which gained a charter in 1179 from its principal lord the bishop, dependants of other lords were excluded from the franchise; although fragmented, the signorial territory was the defining framework for the commune, rather than the village and its common lands. Indeed, in the Sottoceneri around Lugano, the rural commune did not normally control local pasture land at all; that was the responsibility of larger units, often the local pieval territories, whereas the communes concerned themselves with ex-signorial matters such as jurisdiction.[41] One can in fact argue, as I have for the Tuscan

---

[40] On *milites* and castelli, one of the best analyses is still Luzzatto, *Dai servi della gleba*; see further Settia, *Castelli e villaggi*, 155–76, with bibliography. A classic instance from further south of a semi-urban military commune, contested by its peasantry, is Assisi in 1198–1210: see Maire-Vigueur, 'Comuni e signorie', 386–90.

[41] P. Schäfer, *Il Sottoceneri* (1933; Ital. edn., Lugano, 1954), 207–18; R. Celli, *Longevità* (Udine, 1984), 68–100 (with a good bibliography); P. Toubert, 'Les Statuts communaux', *Mélanges d'archéologie et d'histoire*, 72 (1960), 412–16; H. Keller, 'Mehrheitsentscheidung', in H. Jäger et al. (eds.), *Civitatum Communitas* (Cologne, 1984), 2–41; compare, too, Collodo, 'Il Cadore medievale'. Legal historians tend still to maintain a more Bognettian position, as in O. Aureggi-Ariatta, 'Comunità rurali', *Recueils de la société Jean Bodin*, 43 (1984), 207–28. For Ardesio, see Menant, *Campagnes lombardes*, 495–8. At Chiavenna, however, a more independent commune in the mountains north of Lake Como, common lands were the first core of consular-run collective action, from 1097 at the latest: O. Aureggi, 'Chiavenna', *Bollettino della società storica valtellinese*, 12 (1958), 16–48; Keller, 'Mehrheitsentscheidung', 18–19; Bognetti, *Studi sulle origini*, 209, 256.

Appennines and elsewhere, that the need to organize silvo-pastoral activities in a systematic manner is not immemorial anyway; rather, it derives from periods of rising population (and thus pressure on resources) and increased exchange, which itself is the main cause of pastoral and woodland specialization—and these developments are rare before 1100. Common land, at least in the Alps, could well lie at the base of some early version of village co-operation, but even here it was rarely sufficiently organized before 1100 or so to act as the underpinning of the new collectivity, represented by the rural commune; the commune normally developed, here as elsewhere, in the framework of the signoria. Pastoral specializations did, on the other hand, lead to greater communal coherence, and even independence, once the commune had appeared: Bormio, at the head of the Adda valley, temporarily achieved an effectively total autonomy in the early fourteenth century, and this Swiss-style independence recalls another already cited pastoral autonomy, Andorra.[42]

In the plains, rural communal autonomies matched more closely those already analysed in the Veneto. Menant lists nearly twenty franchises before 1200 for the Cremonese, Bergamasco, and Bresciano: they are next door to Verona, and the patterns seem pretty analogous. Lords, weakened in the later twelfth century by the rising power of the city, were unable to resist the demands of their peasants for autonomy. Between 1175 and 1225, the movement reached its peak, with communes buying off signorial rights (notably powers over jurisdiction) and establishing local elections all across the plain; indeed, in the thirteenth century eastern Lombard signorie often broke up entirely. We do not have much documentation for communes before these franchises; they evidently existed, but exactly how they formed is as unclear as ever. We do have the documentation, at least sometimes, for who controlled the communes, and for what happened to leading families under the influence of the city; but we cannot as yet say much about these themes, for historians barely discuss them. One aspect of urban power in the countryside after the early years of the thirteenth century is, however, very clear: fiscal exactions forced communes as institutions into debt, usually to city creditors. After 1250, in fact, they tended to get

---

[42] For silvo-pastoral specialization, see Wickham, *Società degli Appennini*, 50–8; id., *Mountains*, 21–6, 161–70; id., 'Pastoralism and Underdevelopment', *Settimane di studio*, 31 (1985), 401–55; id., 'European Forests', *Settimane di studio*, 37 (1990), 522–45. Compare the role of iron-mining as part of early communal identity as early as the 11th cent. in the Val di Scalve in the Bergamasque Alps (J. Jarnut, *Bergamo* (Bergamo, 1980), 123–5; Menant, *Campagnes lombardes*, 493). For Bormio's independence, see Celli, *Longevità*, 103–6; cf. Sivéry, *Terroirs et communautés*, 107–42.

weaker again, and many plains communes had to sell off their common lands altogether to keep solvent in the last years of the Middle Ages.[43]

We cannot leave Lombardy without at least a glance at Rosario Romeo's classic work on Origgio, for this, although it does not discuss communal origins, is by far the clearest analysis of the relationship between signorial rights and landowning in the context of the development of local communal politics, and it thus makes some points that have not been greatly developed by more recent scholars. Origgio, just north-west of Milan, was in the signoria of the suburban monastery of S. Ambrogio. Its commune was already fully in existence by 1228, for there are statutes for that year; S. Ambrogio never contested it. But the commune contested the signorial rights of S. Ambrogio, in 1231; and in 1244 actually leased them from the monastery for a few years. Towards the end of the century, S. Ambrogio re-established its local jurisdiction, bucking the Lombard trend away from signorial rights: but in 1305–13 it was newly challenged, in an armed uprising that was only solved by compromise. Romeo could explain the timing of these confrontations: in the first decades of the thirteenth century the monastery was converting its rents from money into kind (see below, p. 224); and at the end of the century it was taking advantage of peasant indebtedness to increase its landholdings dramatically. It was, that is to say, because the peasants were tenurially under threat that they contested S. Ambrogio's local signorial powers. The former threat was to tenants, the latter to local proprietors; but, as usual, most proprietors held land in tenure as well and vice versa, so that the entire village could be involved in both. The argument is very plausible, and deserves further development elsewhere. We will see a Tuscan parallel to it, in S. Casciano Val di Pesa.[44]

I have set the foregoing analyses end on end, rather than presenting their common patterns synthetically. The justification for this has already been set out: they constitute regional and micro-regional examples, which must be discussed in their own terms, and compared, before any generalizations can be made. Not all these examples from Lombardy and the Veneto give us all the material we might like, either because the documentation

[43] Menant, *Campagnes lombardes*, 482–559. For the very start of the period, see also Jarnut, *Bergamo*, 123–7. For parallels further west, see C. D. Fonseca, *Arosio* (Genoa, 1974), 95–122; Groneuer, *Caresana*, 84–140; Keller, *Adelsherrschaft*, 103–6, 165–8.

[44] R. Romeo, 'Origgio', *Rivista storica italiana*, 69 (1957), 340–77, 473–507. Compare 13th-cent. Arosio in the account of E. Occhipinti, *Il contado milanese* (Bologna, 1982), 55–101, one of the few recent Lombard studies to make similar analyses.

is insufficient or because not all authors have the same interests as I have. In particular, the internal social structure of these communes (rather than just their relationship with the signoria) has been relatively infrequently discussed, outside Pernumia, Origgio, and Arosio. In every case where there is evidence, we can see at least that communes are, as usual, generally run by local élites (whether military or not); in nearly every case, too, we find the complex mixture of tenure that I have discussed for the Lucchesia. We also see, as a recurring pattern of interpretation, which has become overwhelming since the Second World War, the conclusion that the twelfth-century rural commune developed as a counterposition to the territorial signoria, fighting on the same ground and for the same rights (see above, p. 189). In the fusion between Caggese and Bognetti, Caggese's view (or at least, that view nuanced by Volpe and others, who showed that peasants were not all serfs, or even tenants) has become, in reality, the dominant one. Common rights were an important element in collective cohesion, but rarely acted as the basis for communal crystallization (instances probably included Arogno, Chiavenna, and maybe Lazise, but even then not before *c.*1100); indeed, when signorial rights were organized according to a different territorial pattern from common rights, communes followed the former not the latter. Communes were doubtless based on previous patterns of community identity, that is, which could be variously constructed and have greater or lesser force; but the *prise de conscience* necessary to move towards the commune was, it is argued, furnished by the territorialization of the signoria.[45] This model, however, based essentially on north Italian evidence, in my view overstates, or at least mislocates, the signoria as the prime cause of the communal movement. It is regarded as only one context out of several in France, for example, as we have seen. When we test it on Tuscan evidence, in the next section, the problems about it should become clearer.

It must be observed, finally, before we leave these studies, that even if we restrict ourselves to the theme of the signoria rather than that of rural society in general, there remain a number of questions unanswered. Historians have been prone to study their own individual areas, rather than compare them with their neighbours; even the major recent syntheses are generalizations of developments, rather than comparisons. Why does the commune appear in some areas early, in some late? Does the differing impact of different cities on their territories result in whole dioceses which have early communes, and whole dioceses where they are

---

[45] A particularly clear formulation of this is Tabacco, *Egemonie sociali*, 255–7.

generally later? Does an early commune relate to a strong signoria, which causes an early reaction through its oppression, or to a weak one that can easily be pushed back? (Some studies—Pernumia, eastern Lombardy— do indeed tend to associate communal development with signorial weakness; but is this in contradiction with an apparently opposite pattern at Origgio?) Finally, when, how far, and how fast did communal institutions eventually crystallize, both before and after the awarding of franchises by lords, and in the very many places—which seem, furthermore, to be relatively unstudied—where no franchises or other written concessions were granted at all? Were the latter, for example, villages with unusually restricted autonomies, as in England, as we have seen, or villages with lords so weak that they could be bypassed without any written permission, as in much of Tuscany, as we shall see? These questions have tended to be answered piecemeal, at best. I would imagine that many of them could be approached, with positive and interesting results, even if one restricted oneself entirely to already analysed material. Some of the answers could be guessed at with the help of my Tuscan parallels, or of my earlier discussions of French and Iberian examples. But there is quite a lot still to be done.

iv. Tuscany

Both the Veneto and Lombardy can easily be divided into two well-defined geographical regions, the plain and the Alps; there is of course diversity inside each, but each is a broad territory—there are in fact considerable local similarities between all the dry plains stretching from Turin to the Adriatic. Tuscany is not like this. Its northern plains are small, and divided by hills; south of them are a wide and variegated array of hill lands, which change dramatically in character as one moves further south from the rich terrain of the Valdelsa, out of the Tuscany of the cities, and into the empty tracts of the Maremma, which make up over a third of the region. Simply as a result of this geographical diversity, the examples that follow are more different, one from another, than some of those we have hitherto seen for Italy. But these differences can be counterposed to certain features common to the whole region as well, which set Tuscany up as distinct from the regions of northern Italy we have just looked at. I have referred already to the two that most concern us, and they need only be summarized here.

The first of these is the common political history of the March of Tuscany. *Tuscia* was an unusually coherent political unit around 1000 by the standards of the kingdom of Italy, with a strong, late Carolingian, public power centred on the marquis and extending over most of the region, which did not begin to break up and be replaced by signorial territories until the very end of the eleventh century. In many places (the Sei Miglia Lucchese, of course, being an extreme) city authority replaced that of the marquis with very little break, thus not allowing signorie to develop into units as coherent as they sometimes could be in the North; only in the south of Tuscany, in the Maremma, do they seem to have been powerful and oppressive over wide areas.[46] The second feature is the apparent weakness of village identity before the eleventh century (cf. above, pp. 55–71). On the plains, in the hills, and in the mountains alike, many parts of Tuscany show fragmented and unstable village territories which could only with difficulty have acted as a firm basis for collective action; even in areas where woods and pastures were held communally, the rules for sharing out use-rights do not seem to have been tight enough to require systematic village co-operation before the twelfth century.

These two particularities balance each other out. If in northern Italy signorial power is counterposed to collectivities based at least sometimes on common lands, it must be recognized that in Tuscany both sides of the equation were weaker. Communes appeared all the same, however, and across much the same time-span as in the North. I will come back to the problem of exactly why at the end of the chapter; but the pattern seems clear enough, and can be found all over the region. So, in the late eleventh century, signorial territories begin to be documented nearly everywhere in Tuscany, usually focused on *castelli* (with very varying populations, one should note, stretching from a handful of guards to several hundred inhabitants and more, small towns that is to say); the territorialization that this involved created newly clear identities not just for the signoria but also for the parish and the village, around 1100; and, in the twelfth century, rural communes begin to be documented, in the Pisano, the Volterrano, the Fiorentino, and the Senese just as in the Lucchesia. By 1200, *comune*, *universitas*, and similar terms denoted standard local units in the Lucchesia (see above, pp. 67–8); in the Pisano maybe as early as 1150; in 1208 a list of communities subject to Siena show that they existed in that area too.[47] Although not by any means every commune is documented by 1200, those that demonstrably do not

---

[46] For an overview, see Wickham, *Mountains*, pp. xxvii–xxxii [and, in more detail, id., 'La signoria rurale,' in G. Dilcher and C. Violante (eds.), *Strutture e trasformazioni della signoria rurale* (Bologna, 1996), 343–409].

[47] G. Volpe, *Pisa* (2nd edn., Florence, 1970), 59; P. Cammarosano, 'Le campagne senesi', in *Contadini e proprietari nella Toscana moderna* (Florence, 1979), i. 155.

develop before the thirteenth century can be thought of as late by regional standards. Thus far, Tuscany can be seen as a unit; but inside it local variation was huge. Take the Pisano, for example, studied in a magistral survey by Gioacchino Volpe in 1902, when he was still in his twenties. Volpe showed how communes appeared everywhere in the diocese in the twelfth century, thanks to the private association of small local aristocrats (*milites*, *lambardi*), who took over castelli and ruled them as collective groups— or, in smaller centres, thanks to similar but more small-scale groups of *boni homines*, usually local landowners, who were not necessarily aristocratic but had a similar leadership function. These communes were formed against local territorial lords, the archbishop of Pisa or one of the major diocesan aristocrats, but they were, as elsewhere, of course not egalitarian, and in the larger castelli the peasants were often forced to form their own communes against these military élites. Their internal structures were not particularly consistent. There were considerable differences: the major military centre of Bientina, on the eastern edge of the diocese, whose strategic importance to Pisa and to its lord the archbishop allowed a generous and uncontested recognition of its commune in 1179, which the inhabitants then built on, at the expense of the archbishop's signorial rights, across the next decades; Calci, nearer to the city and with no obvious lord at all, which already in 1165 had a fully autonomous commune with six consuls 'electi ad causas publicas vel privatas . . . diffiniendas' on the model of the city, and a public notary, that is to say a fully and legally constituted institution, appearing only a few years after the first Pisan statutes (which are themselves the earliest for any city in Italy); or Casciavola, a small village composed, it seems, entirely of peasants, first documented around 1100 with a set of local representatives who came to Pisa to lament the evildoing of their lords, and which in later years (the local power of their lords having disappeared) had consuls principally involved with the affairs of the local church, much like those in the Lucchesia. These local diversities, and others, make it impossible to generalize too simply about the rural commune, even inside the single diocese of Pisa.[48]

The point can be pursued further on the basis of some of the studies of the Florentine contado (consisting of the linked dioceses of Florence

---

[48] Volpe, *Pisa*, 24–123 (69–75 for Bientina, 84–6 for Calci); A. D'Amia, *Diritto e sentenze di Pisa* (Milan, 1962), 226–7, for the Calci document; see further G. Garzella, 'Cascina', in M. Pasquinucci, G. Garzella, and M. L. Ceccarelli Lemut, *Cascina*, ii (Pisa, 1986), 72–7, 81–3, 102–3; R. D'Amico, 'Note su alcuni rapporti', *Bollettino storico pisano*, 39 (1970), 15–29.

and Fiesole), which I will look at in more detail. Here, as at Lucca and Pisa, elements of communal identity, such as consuls or collective disputes, appear in the later twelfth century. At Cintoia in the hills of the central Chianti, a dispute over village boundaries with neighbouring Celle in the years leading up to 1073 already produced collective action involving what seem to have been *ad hoc boni homines*; but a revival of the same dispute a century later, in 1191, shows local powers that were much more tightly characterized, with a *consul et rector* for each village consenting to a neutral arbitration. Cintoia represents one clear Florentine pattern, the commune appearing in the framework of the signoria without any trace of an opposition between the two; the 1191 agreement was actually organized by local lords, with communal officials only consenting at the end. Similarly at Leccio in the hills below Vallombrosa, the local consuls first appear in 1172 witnessing for the lords of the local castello.[49] In the Valdarno superiore, the wide valley between these two localities, communes like Figline and Pianalberti (the modern S. Giovanni Valdarno) make their appearance equally quietly, in a framework of highly militarized signorial powers; the commune of Pianalberti was a developed institution by 1201–2, with a *podestà* and a register of communal acts (*quaterno comunis*), and could deal with local lords as an equal; but it had its own lord, too, who was fully active in local politics, and whom it did not visibly challenge. This is also true of Passignano, back in the Chianti, whose lord, the monastery of Passignano, was a controversial local power, certainly capable of throwing its weight around; the local commune, however, first documented in 1173 (its consuls appear in that year, 'a vice monasterii et populi de Pasignano', receiving lands for the monastery at the end of a court case), seems to have developed entirely peacefully without any dispute recorded in the huge Passignano archive, and had established by 1277 at the latest—if not, indeed, by a century earlier—an equal division between the abbot and the *populus* of the rights to choose the consuls.[50]

This common development, of communes forming unopposed inside signorial structures, once again hides considerable differences. Leccio was a small and highly subject centre; its commune could, at least in this century, merely be seen as a convenient means of control on the part of its

---

[49] R. Davidsohn, *Storia di Firenze* (1896; Ital. edn., Florence, 1956), i. 479–84. The three texts are ASF Badia di Ripoli 1072 (a text of problematic date: the indiction is six years out. Davidsohn, *Storia di Firenze*, i. 367 n. 4, assigns it to 1073), S. Vigilio di Siena 23 febb. 1191, Vallombrosa 4 mar. 1172.

[50] J. Plesner, *L'emigrazione* (1934; Ital. edn., Florence, 1979), 77–8, for Passignano, with ASF Passignano 12 ott. 1173, '12..n. 25'; for Pianalberti, 2 febb. 1201, 14 dic. 1203, '12..n. 26'.

lords.[51] Passignano was rather more independent, even though its lord
lived on the spot. It was a substantial castello, with a wide range of landowners as well as tenants living in it, including *milites*, some of whom
were closely dependent on the monastery, but others of whom were substantial local figures in their own right. One of the consuls of 1173 was
a monastic *castaldus*; but another, Borgnolino di Borgno, was a local notable,
who may sometimes have been in the monastic clientele but sometimes,
as in the mid-1190s, was an enemy of the monks, capable of causing
mayhem in the village. When he fought he did not do so in the name of
the commune; but any commune with someone like Borgnolino as a
consul was distinctly not under any lord's thumb.[52] Figline, finally, was
a mercantile centre of some local importance, like Guastalla and Bassano
in the north of Italy. Its consuls are first documented in *c*.1167, at a time
when the bishop of Fiesole (in whose diocese it lay) with papal agreement was actually trying to move the cathedral there from Fiesole;
and from that time onwards, although the move never happened (the
Florentines prevented it), the local society of Figline virtually took on
urban form, on a very small scale. In 1198 it had a *consulatus*, clearly
defined, with its own *podestà*; references to its consuls also appear in
sanction clauses from 1196, as at Moriano (see above, p. 100). Its leaders
were evidently at that time the petty military aristocracy; by 1248, however, and probably soon after 1200, its *podestà*, elected annually, came
from outside the commune, as in the case of cities. By now the *podestà*
ran local justice and military affairs with the help of a *generale consilium*;
the lords of Figline, though never systematically opposed, had in effect
vanished as a superior body, leaving the *populus* and its *podestà* (defined
in the 1250s as the *dominus terre*, a phrase traditionally used for territorial signori) in sole charge.[53]

These communes, then, though similar in institutional structure and
in the time-scale of their appearance, developed in very different sorts of
settlement, and had a very different content as a result. Not all Florentine

[51] Subject tenants (*coloni*) could certainly defy lords, however, as in a text of 1183 for
the Florentine cathedral chapter (P. Santini (ed.), *Documenti* (Florence, 1895), 224–5)—
and see the Amiata examples cited below, nn. 57–8.
[52] Plesner, *Emigrazione*, 77–8; see below, n. 64.
[53] Key Figline texts are P. F. Kehr, 'Die Minuten van Passignano', *Quellen und
Forschungen*, 7 (1904), 8–41, n. 1 (*c*.1167); Santini, *Documenti*, 41–6 (*a*.1198); id., *Documenti.
Appendice* (Florence, 1952), 314–19 (*a*.1253); ASF Passignano 1196, 19 magg. 1211. [See
now C. J. Wickham, 'Figline Valdarno in the Twelfth Century', *Mélanges de l'Ecole
française de Rome*, 108 (1996), 7–93.] Compare the Pianalberti texts cited in n. 50; and
ASF Passignano '12..n. 25', a text showing a semi-professional rural *podestà* seeking annual
positions in the early 13th-cent. Florentine countryside.

communes were so peaceful in their development, either. The clearest examples of this were those subject to the signoria of the bishop of Florence, as we can see in recent work by George Dameron. The bishop of Florence was a powerful landowner in his diocese, and controlled substantial signorial rights as well. From the late twelfth century he sought to exercise his signorial rights as systematically as possible; and in the thirteenth century (especially from the 1230s onwards), in the framework of the expanding urban market, he began to commute rents from money to kind, as S. Ambrogio did at Origgio at the same time, which both increased rents and deprived the peasants of their own access to urban markets. People resisted this, sometimes individually and sometimes, in stronger communities, collectively: by refusing to swear *fidelitas* to the bishop (thus refusing him recognition as local lord), or by refusing to pay signorial dues or the new rents in kind, or, in the case of collective resistances, by the rejection of signorial officials over the local commune. At Borgo S. Lorenzo and Castelfiorentino, two large castelli (about on the scale of Figline) respectively north and south-west of Florence, the local commune took over these disputes early, in 1207 and 1218 respectively, when communal officials of each were excommunicated for refusing to accept episcopal *podestà*. In each case, disputes continued until the 1230s, and were resolved by compromises: at Borgo, it was agreed that the bishop should choose the *podestà* one year in four, and the commune the other three; at Castelfiorentino, the commune gained full rights to elect the *podestà*, and controlled local justice as well. The bishop kept several other lucrative signorial rights, however, and stepped up the commutation of rents in kind on his estates: these estates certainly did not include more than a minority of the lands in each of the two territories, but, as elsewhere, probably affected a rather higher percentage of the inhabitants, given the prevalence of lease-holding even among landowners.[54]

It is not so surprising that the communes should have been involved in these particular disputes; like the large Lombard castelli, the two centres concerned had quasi-urban commercial elements in them, who were competing with the bishop for profit from the city markets, and doubtless chafed at the episcopal signoria—even though there is no reason to think that their communes were formed to oppose it. In some smaller villages, however, such as Valcava and Querceto, similar disputes over

[54] G. W. Dameron, *Episcopal Power and Florentine Society* (Cambridge, Mass., 1991), 93–110, 131–40; the Borgo events were already cited by Caggese, *Classi e comuni rurali*, i. 319–30.

signorial rights also came to involve the commune.[55] And in one well-documented case, S. Casciano Val di Pesa, opposing the bishop seems to have brought the commune directly into being. S. Casciano is just south of Florence, on the edge of the Chianti and on the road to Siena. It does not seem to have been an old centre; although on a hilltop, it was not fortified before the 1350s, and may still have been developing as a concentrated settlement in the twelfth and thirteenth centuries. It was not obviously an early signorial centre, either, and in the first decades of the thirteenth century was less active than neighbouring villages in opposing the bishop. But in 1230 the men of S. Casciano were taken to court in Florence by the bishop and condemned, perhaps for rejecting his authority; and they certainly rejected the episcopal *podestà* in 1236, a few months after the bishop began to commute money-rents into kind on a massive scale in the area. They refused to pay rents or to accept the *podestà* nearly continuously for seven years, despite contrary rulings and excommunications both from Florence and the pope. It was not, however, until 1241 that the judgments mention the commune (*universitas et communis*), which was now being fined £300 by the city. The Sancascianesi began to give up in that year, but the bishop issued statutes for the village; he did so 'ad conservationem iurisdictionis episcopatus', but they were statutes all the same, and presumably (they do not survive) contained recognition of the commune in them. S. Casciano revolted not, principally, against signorial dues but against episcopal rental policies. The difference at the time was probably minor, but it may well be that the bishop's signorial jurisdiction was less complete in the village than at Borgo or Castelfiorentino; interestingly, the early moves of the villagers were made with the support of the cathedral chapter, which presumably had rival signorial claims.[56] This lack of organization of any local signorial territory may further support the argument that S. Casciano was a new settlement; it may also help to explain why the commune appeared so late, for 1241 was decades after one would expect a commune to appear in a substantial village of the Florentine contado. One could even say that this power vacuum was necessary, in order to produce a situation in which S. Casciano's commune *could* appear late enough to be set up against the rental policies of the bishop. In this respect, however, S. Casciano was

[55] Dameron, *Episcopal Power*, 96, 103–5, for Valcava and Querceto. He tends to see the commune as a direct response to episcopal actions in these cases, as also in those discussed in the previous note (e.g. 137); the most likely example of this is Valcava.

[56] Ibid. 110–18, 127; id., 'San Casciano Val di Pesa', *Journal of Medieval History*, 12 (1986), 135–54; Caggese, *Classi e comuni rurali*, i. 324–7.

an exception that proved a rule: normally in the Fiorentino, communes appeared uncontentiously, inside signorial territories; structural oppositions between village and signorial interests, where they existed, certainly led them to fight their lords, but only once the communes were formed. S. Casciano Val di Pesa and Borgo S. Lorenzo were among Caggese's principal points of reference: emblematic examples of communes rising against signorial subjection. Another, moving out of the Fiorentino now, was Rocca di Tintinnano in the far south of Tuscany, subject of a famous article by Gaetano Salvemini in 1901. Rocca di Tintinnano (now Rocca d'Orcia) is on the lower slopes of Monte Amiata, at the southern edge of the modern Senese; the Senesi only fully established themselves on the mountain, against local lords and the city of Orvieto, after 1250, and even then their power was incomplete. This area is the classic zone of the strong signoria (it extends into Lazio), with aristocrats or churches often not only territorial lords with extensive rights over peasants who were so dependent they were barely free, but landowners owning all or most of the village territory as well. Under these circumstances, the village community could do no other than extract as many concessions from its lord as it could. At Rocca di Tintinnano the peasants—already organized into a commune—gained a franchise in 1207 by, as it appears from the text, threatening to leave the land altogether. The franchise's concessions were very basic, indicating the degree of subjection of the community: fixed rather than arbitrary rents and dues; the right to inherit; the right to elect one of the two consuls. The lords of the community, the Tignosi, sold out to Siena in 1250, but the condition of the Tintinnanesi did not improve under city jurisdiction; indeed, it worsened as city taxation increased, and even more after the city sold rights in the village to a local city family; by the end of the century they were worse off than at the beginning.[57]

This classic account still stands up to scrutiny; this is how peasants confronted lords in situations of unmediated signorial hegemony. And they could be luckier than in Rocca di Tintinnano, a small and weak village. At Abbadia S. Salvatore, a much larger settlement higher up the mountain, though once again wholly owned by its lord, the monastery of S. Salvatore al Monte Amiata, the inhabitants were more effective in their resistance. Abbadia was a new concentrated settlement around 1200, incastellated, as it seems, by the monastery during the previous half-century. It was also high enough on the mountain to have access to

---

[57] Salvemini, 'Un comune rurale'; O. Redon, 'Seigneurs et communautés rurales', *Mélanges de l'Ecole française de Rome*, 91 (1979), 157–64 for the text. For Lazio parallels, see S. Carocci, *Baroni di Roma* (Rome, 1993), 256–61, for a good recent survey.

extensive common lands, woodland for the most part, although how much this as yet added to its cohesion is uncertain. Already by 1212 the castello was forceful enough to get a franchise from the monastery which sanctioned its commune, commuted labour-services to money, and allowed not only full inheritance but the sale of tenures. It turned out that the monastery had ceded this unwillingly, at a time of weakness, and later in the century it set out to undermine it; but the commune was active, and it is clear by 1251, the date of a surviving case on signorial dues, that many of the latter had not been paid for a long time. Across the second half of the century, the men of Abbadia defied the monastery more and more, over the control of mills in particular; and, despite the regular excommunications they received, gained a wider franchise in 1299, the sign of their final victory.[58]

One could lengthen this list of fighting communes, whether victorious or defeated in the end. Anghiari, a castello in the Aretine Appennines, gained independence from the monastery of Camaldoli (this time with the help of local lords, scarcely disinterested, and also Rainaldo of Dassel, Frederick Barbarossa's Tuscan representative) during the years 1147–63, although it was newly subjected to lordship after Arezzo sacked it in 1179.[59] S. Gimignano, on a far larger, indeed urban, scale, gained its autonomy by force in the early thirteenth century from the bishop of Volterra, who had founded it as a castello and signorial centre.[60] One is tempted to go on; communes in open struggle against lords are, after all, far more interesting and attractive to study than those that quietly appear and cause no trouble. But it would not be helpful, for two reasons: they are too heterogeneous; and, despite their documentation (which is more extensive precisely because of the trouble they caused), they are not typical. There is almost nothing in common between the great commercial centre of S. Gimignano, full of small aristocratic landowners and merchants and aiming at full independence, and the miserable *homines* of Rocca di Tintinnano. Nor can one assume that a contest like Anghiari's, in the

---

[58] Redon, 'Seigneurs et communautés rurales' is the basic account; for additional detail see C. J. Wickham, 'Paesaggi sepolti', in M. Ascheri and W. Kurze (eds.), *L'Amiata nel medioevo* (Rome, 1989), 133–7; P. Cammarosano, 'Comune di Abbadia', ibid. 65–77; O. Redon, 'La divisione dei poteri', ibid. 183–95. One should compare here the analogous disputes in the late 13th cent. in the Trivio, a community in the mountains at the head of the Tiber: G. Cherubini, *Una comunità dell'Appennino* (Florence, 1972), 91–109.

[59] M. Modigliani, 'Anghiari', *Archivio storico italiano*, 4 ser. 6 (1880), 225–61; see now, for Anghiari and other *comuni di castello* in the Aretino, J.-P. Delumeau, *Arezzo. Espace et sociétés, 715–1230* (Rome, 1996), 1225–52.

[60] E. Fiumi, *San Gimignano* (Florence, 1961), 17–28.

mid-twelfth century, was fought out in the same socio-political frame-work as S. Casciano's, a century later. And, as for their typicality: Redon has only found eleven charters of franchise to communes from lords surviving among the thousands of documents for the whole Senese up to 1311, seven of them for Monte Amiata—that is to say, the furthest and the most signorial part of the territory—and I doubt that they are significantly more frequent anywhere else in Tuscany.[61] Unlike in the Veneto, or in northern France, franchises are sufficiently rare in Tuscany for them to be no guide at all to the development of rural communes. And although this fact tells us nothing in itself about the way communes were organized, it does at least underline that they were not, in them-selves, seen either as taking away from the rights of lords or as in need of the latters' recognition. The common signorial context of most Tuscan communes does not, then, prove consistency in their opposition to signorial power. Most communes in Tuscany crept into existence, in the Fiorentino, as in the Lucchesia (as we have seen in earlier chapters), and elsewhere; they opposed lords when they needed to, which was not seldom, but for the rest of the time conducted their own affairs for their own reasons. They undoubtedly appeared inside the territorial framework of the signoria, in every case that we know about, save the exceptional Sei Miglia Lucchese, where their territorial basis was that of the parish (the only parallel to this being probably the Arno valley closest to Pisa[62]); nevertheless, they were not formed *against* the signoria, but only inside its framework, just as we saw for Moriano. And the differences we have already seen between communes indicate that their major purposes could be highly diverse; these purposes are what we should be most concerned to study.

This argument does not in itself disprove the emphasis on opposition to the signoria common in north Italian historiography. Tuscany was unlike the Veneto in the relative weakness of its signorial rights, and, where it was not, as on the Amiata, Veneto-style franchises duly appear. But there were rural communes throughout Tuscany by 1200, and their internal structures were not on the whole, however various from place to place, different in type from those of the Po plain. What these Tuscan examples do is displace the signoria from its centrality, for too many historians have depicted it as *the* cause of the aggregation of the rural commune. It was only one reason among many; other processes than

[61] Redon, 'Seigneurs et communautés rurales', 149–96; this list of franchises includes statutes and a court case.
[62] Garzella, 'Cascina', 80–2, 102–3; cf. Volpe, *Pisa*, 103–6.

opposition to lords could produce the same result. What, then, were the reasons why communes developed, and the purposes they served, if they were not simply set up to oppose the signoria? Tuscan studies do not generally ask this question any more than do those for Lombardy and the Veneto (though many of the communes I have just cited do not, it should be recognized, have enough documentation for us to answer it). Perhaps the major exception to this in Tuscany is the work of Volpe, whose Pisan survey, like his more general city analyses, stresses above all the 'associative movement' of local élites and rural society in general. This sort of movement can sometimes seem a bit generic, but in Volpe's individual examples he does show how it worked in practice, in a variety of ways; I will return to this issue.[63] Otherwise, however, the answer must be that communes did not, anywhere, appear for any single reason. It was more complicated than that. Indeed in each village a whole group of processes were in operation, all of which contributed to communal development. If the foregoing empirical discussions tell us anything, it is how variable the major features and interests of rural communes are; and each new set of characteristics points us to a new set of causes.

We can best see this by means of a simple list, an extension of that already made on p. 191. Rural communes, whether in Italy or elsewhere in Europe, can be established by lords, or against them; or they can gradually crystallize, whether (as most usually) inside the organizational framework of the signoria, or else inside some other territorial structure, such as the parish. They may continue to serve the interests of lords, or turn against them, or peacefully replace lordship altogether. They may be supported by cities (or, beyond the Alps, kings and princes) against lords, or opposed by them if the lord is a citizen or at least a city ally. They may focus on the defence of a castello, or on the organization of common land, or on the control of a market. They may develop in villages with long-existing collective organizations, or in villages newly coherent as territories, or in newly founded centres, castelli or *villenuove* or clearance villages. They may develop in silvo-pastoral areas, with a high degree of economic organization, or in areas of collectively organized agriculture, or in grain- or vine-growing areas with a very individualist agrarian system. They may be controlled by local military aristocrats, or non-military property-owning notables, or (in villages entirely owned by lords) the richest tenants. They may be strong or weak; have many powers devolved from lords (justice, military organization, tax-raising) or few; be based on

[63] Volpe, *Pisa*, 50; and, more generally, 18–123.

concentrated or on dispersed settlement; be large, indeed mercantile and quasi-urban, or small and strictly agricultural.

We must not stop here, however; for, if we do, all we are saying is that everywhere is different, which does not get us very far. Once we have isolated such a daunting set of variables, taken apart the machine as it were, we must put them together again, or else all we will be left with is bits. The crucial necessity is to work out ways in which the elements on this list can be turned into a set of concrete analyses of causation. The best way to do it, it seems to me, is to regard the list as a matrix of explanations, whose elements recombined in different ways; each analysis of a specific case takes a different group of variables from the matrix and sets them together in different causal relationships. The precocity of Pisan communes, for example, may be the result of several of them working in the same direction: the relative fragility of signorial powers, which were either already weak in 1150, or else associated with figures (like the archbishop) heavily committed to the expansion of the authority of the city commune; the tendency for Pisan *incastellamento* to have produced a group of little castelli, with *milites* who were not too important to be interested in local affirmation; and the early legal and institutional development of the city commune itself. On the Amiata, the sharpness of the opposition between lords and communes derived not only from the unusually strong local power of lords by Tuscan standards, which, in an area far from the complex tenurial patterns associated with cities, was based on signorial rights and landownership combined, but also from the unusually complete concentration of all settlement into castelli, which thus could be strong enough to oppose their lords when circumstances permitted. My discussions of the various types of Lucchese communes have been set out with the same sort of matrix in mind: around Lucca, communes formed as a way of restructuring local society in a time of relatively disorganized political power, both in the city and in the countryside; but, against a background of unusually weak signorial relationships, and an unusually recent development of a consistent territorial identity for villages (and even then not one with a particularly important economic role), it was local élites who were able to choose whether or not their new communal organizations would be strong and active. By contrast, in Castile, the long history of active village communities, while not in any way ensuring the continuance of local autonomies in the face of the ambitions of local military élites and signorial decentralization, at least produced a stable array of local 'councils' with their own franchises, that would remain a real focus for village politics in the future. All these cases, and others, put the emphasis on a multiplicity of causal processes inside a single village or region. It seems to me that, instead of looking for *the* cause of the rural commune, these sorts of combinations produce the kind of analyses which, when more local areas have been adequately studied, will produce the most fruitful results.

I will conclude by stressing two general contexts for the appearance of rural communes that are not always set out as clearly as they could be. This we can see through the reposing of a problem that has recurred, on and off, throughout the book. Despite the immense variability of the rural commune, the moment of its appearance, in Italy at least, was almost always the twelfth century, or else shortly before or shortly after. Is it possible to explain why it developed in this period, without falling back into legalistic generalization about institutions, or without simply employing a circular argument such as 'communes appeared in the twelfth century because the twelfth century was the period in which communal movements developed'? The two contexts through which I will look at this problem are those which were most forcefully put into relief by my analyses of the Lucchesia: the behaviour of local élites; and the reasons for the development of local territorial identities. These two issues will have to be brought out against the grain of the Italian and European local studies described above, not all of which show any interest in them at all. But something can be said, none the less.

v. Clienteles and communities

Every study of local élites has to proceed by individual example, so let us look at one more, which I have already briefly mentioned: Borgnolino of Passignano, fl. 1173–1203, documented in the archive of the monastery of Passignano and studied in Johan Plesner's classic work on the village. What was his social world? Essentially, as I have said, he and his family were local landowners. They lived in the castello of Passignano in the early twelfth century, renting their house from the monastery as part of a monastic castle-populating programme similar to that of the bishop of Lucca in Moriano two centuries earlier (see above, pp. 62–3), and they kept the house thereafter (though by the end of the century they also lived in a house of their own at Vignola, a kilometre south of the castello). They were medium landowners, with a substantial and ever-changing array of tenant houses—as well as large numbers of single fields—either owned outright or leased from others (usually from the monastery but also from laymen); they were rich enough to accumulate lands from others on credit, and were even creditors of the monastery on a small scale. Their relations with the monastery were ambiguous. Borgnolino was described as a *homo* of the monastery in 1193, when the latter represented him at court against a local aristocrat; but he and his family very rarely appear as monastic witnesses, no more often in fact than they did for local laymen (they probably witnessed because of their local public standing, that is to say, rather than as monastic clients). Conversely, as appears in a court case between Borgnolino and the abbot from the mid-1190s, the former (at least allegedly) refused to pay rent and signorial dues for some of his lands for decades, had occupied monastic tenant houses, and on one occasion had burned down a hut of the monks and stolen an ox. This sort of tension was temporary; it did not revive again until 1244, and then again, more seriously, from the 1260s. But it is clear that Borgnolino and his family were no longer looking for advancement from the monastery of Passignano.[64]

Now, Passignano was surrounded by lay lords with signorial powers, based on a wide array of nearby castelli large and small, some of which had a close (although once again often acrimonious and competitive) relationship with the monastery, and are as a result well documented through the monastic archive. It would have been natural enough, perhaps, for Borgnolino to attach himself to them. Moro di Petruccia did so in Marlia a century or so earlier (see above, pp. 31-4). In the Casentino in the Aretine Appennines, too, in the eleventh and twelfth centuries, aggressive medium landowners sought to attach themselves to the local military aristocracy, as their followers and imitators, and sometimes in the twelfth century, as at Partina and Frassineta in the 1160s, occupied local castelli and demanded signorial dues as if they were petty lords themselves.[65] Borgnolino's 'misdeeds' were on a smaller scale than that; but also, and more importantly, he is never seen associated with any of these local lords either. It is in this context that it is significant that he was a consul of Passignano's commune in 1173; for Borgnolino, the alternative to being a *fidelis* of the monastery, which in Passignano was by no means a privilege (it extended to all Passignano's dependants, including, perhaps especially, its *manentes* or *coloni*), was not to be a client of the local aristocracy, but to lead the local population as a consul. It is impossible to say, or even to guess, whether Borgnolino had any choice about this:

[64] See Plesner, *Emigrazione*, 77-8, 90, 98-9, 135-6, 148-50; E. Conti, *La formazione della struttura agraria* (Rome, 1965), i. 265-90 (284-5 for the 1193 case); ASF Passignano 30 lug. 1130, 11 ago. 1132, 13 febb. 1142, 4 febb. 1170, 12 ott. 1173, 27 sett. 1190, '1193' (3 texts, to which must be added '12..n. 31'), 'sec.XII, n. 14', 27 magg. 1198, '11..n. v', 30 genn. 1201, 7 nov. 1202, 2 sett. 1203, 22 lug. 1205, 7 dic. 1205, 30 dic. 1225, '12..n. 20'.
[65] Wickham, *Mountains*, 325-30.

whether, that is, he avoided the clienteles of the local aristocracy or whether he was excluded from them. But it is certain that he did not *become* an aristocrat; he is not even referred to as a *miles*. Significantly, his son Ristoro, who did gain the title by 1233, one of four or five out of seventy-odd family heads in Passignano who did so, did it in a rather different context, as a 'miles pro comune Florentie'. This family is indeed one of Plesner's principal examples of rural élites who moved into the city of Florence. By the 1260s they were Ghibellines in urban politics, and their renewed tensions with the monastery were a consequence of this; in the 1290s the latter bought them out and they left Passignano altogether.[66]

This pattern replicates that which I have proposed for the Lucca plain, but develops it somewhat, following the leads offered in some of the French and Iberian examples discussed earlier in the chapter. In the Lucchesia, I argued that in the twelfth century the all-pervasiveness of aristocratic clienteles weakened, at least in the countryside, and men sought status and power through associating with—and dominating— their neighbours inside the framework of the commune, rather than by following the great. At Passignano such clienteles certainly still existed, but maybe they were less attractive for medium landowners such as Borgnolino and Ristoro; they did not, at least, by now hold out for them the hope of becoming aristocrats themselves. One could argue that local power was by this time most easily available *through* the rural commune; only when Florence made its influence felt in the early thirteenth century did it become possible to choose a third alternative, and join the city. One may contrast Partina, my Casentino example, whose élites continued to aim at the aristocracy for rather longer; here, the commune is not documented any earlier than 1257. In this area, the late affirmation of the commune coincides with an equally late concentration of settlement into local castelli, headed by these élites; here, they did not emigrate to Arezzo.[67] The pattern is also similar to that which I have guessed at for Castile, and to that which is documented reasonably clearly in Bourin's study of Béziers (see pp. 197–9), which can thus provide a model for explaining it: it is not just that early rural communes were controlled by local notables (who else would control them?), but that these notables were from precisely that stratum of local landowners or tenants which had just given up the attempt to become the lowest rung of the aristocracy.

---

[66] Santini, *Documenti*, 403–5 (*a*.1233); Plesner, *Emigrazione*, 148–50. Plesner, *Emigrazione*, 78, notes that the family were not documented as consuls after 1173, and indicates that he thinks the monastery prevented them from serving.

[67] Wickham, *Mountains*, 336–40.

Why they had given up will have varied. Maybe it was because the aristocratic and military stratum had closed; or maybe because they simply were not rich enough to sustain the expense; or maybe because they did not, for unclear reasons (sometimes, perhaps, factional oppositions; sometimes because they were in some ways too grand) have access to the military clienteles that did still exist—for a militarized aristocracy always needs men-at-arms with little status, to constitute its armies, and some of these can sometimes rise quite far. When they gave up will have differed too: the social history of aristocratic access fluctuates quite a lot across place and time in Europe. When they did give up, they may well have still wished to lord it over their poorer neighbours; but they would have to do it with their neighbours' consent, rather than from above and by coercion. This pattern, which can be found, to a varying extent, over much of at least southern Europe, underlies a good deal of the force of the early rural commune and its analogues, as also beneath its variation, and its varying date. Vertical social relationships were replaced, at least in part, by the only other type available: horizontal ones. Communes in this respect (and it is only one of their meanings) were not about egalitarianism, or the affirmation of the people against the signoria, but about *control*: though by non-aristocrats rather than aristocrats (cf. my remarks about England above, p. 205), and through horizontal ('communal') rather than vertical ('feudal') bonds. It is not enough, none the less, just to point to the existence of this control; it has to be asked *why* it became both necessary and possible to do it by 'communal' rather than 'feudal' means. One way is through reconstructing the careers of local notables, as they follow lords, rule communes (thus, sometimes, defying lords), or, in the end, leave for the city, as I have done for Borgnolino, and, previously, for several people in the Lucca plain. Another way is to look at the development of communal relationships as a concept.

On one level, the development of the idea of communal bonds is the hardest of all issues to study: we simply cannot get sufficiently inside the mentalities of any group of people in our period, except a restricted set of aristocrats and churchmen, to see what they thought about social relationships. We can tell that a social link of some kind lay behind a land sale, for example, but not, in any consistent way, how it was constructed and imagined at the time. What the *dramatis personae* of this book, Rodolfo di Andrea in Moriano, Fiorentino in Tassignano, Cortafugga in Paganico, Borgnolino in Passignano, thought about the world, and their friends and enemies, we will never know. But it is arguable that we can get closer to twelfth-century attitudes to society (in contrast, say, to those of the ninth and tenth centuries) by widening the focus rather more; it may indeed be the only way of saying anything more at all.

The Carolingian world was one in which the overarching patterns of power were dominated by public relationships: counts in their circumscriptions, aided by local notables called *scabini* (or, later, *boni homines*), ran public life, in particular the army and the lawcourt. There was no sharp boundary between a military aristocracy and the poor free, for everyone owed military service, at least in principle, and there was no legally defined nobility of blood; there were just status gradations between the rich and the poor, and people were given further status by official position. This is the classic model. It never existed in this pure form, even in Italy, except maybe in the minds of Carolingian legislators. Private clienteles abounded; plenty of people regarded themselves as an élite by birth;[68] the poor did not really do army service; office was worthless unless backed up by land and armed men, and very often served only as a means of grabbing more of these latter. But however much this is true, the principles of the Carolingian political system lasted a long time, and were widely accepted even as they were broken. One could simply say that the very fact that they were thought to be broken gave them a certain moral force; the dues owed to developing signorie, for instance, were still regarded as illegal after 1000 in most places. The rules of political life remained those of the public arena: these were the formal structures of power. Private relationships, however powerful, were informal.

As the Carolingian world order went into crisis in the tenth century, and recomposed itself in what has been called the 'feudal mutation' of the eleventh, in some cases (Catalonia, for example) after civil war, these ground rules altered.[69] Since the work of Schmid and Duby in the 1950s,

---

[68] As with, for example, the legally privileged great lineages of early medieval Bavaria, or Thegan's categorical statement that no king could make Archbishop Ebbo of Reims *nobilis*, given his servile origin. On Thegan, see J. Martindale, 'The French Aristocracy in the Early Middle Ages', *Past and Present*, 75 (1975), 5 ff., for a good discussion. In general on the Carolingian nobility, see H.-W. Goetz, '"Nobilis"', *Vierteljahrschrift für Sozial- und Wirtschaftsgeschichte*, 60 (1983), 153–91.

[69] Bonnassie, 'Du Rhône à la Galice'; J.-P. Poly and E. Bournazel, *La Mutation féodale* (Paris, 1980), e.g. 482–92. [There is now a substantial debate on whether the 'feudal mutation' or 'feudal revolution' ever actually occurred: see D. Barthélemy, J.-P. Poly, and E. Bournazel in *Annales ESC*, 47 (1992), 767–77, and *Révue historique de droit français et étranger*, 72 (1994), 401–12, 73 (1995), 349–60; and the parallel English-language debate between T. Bisson, D. Barthélemy, S. D. White, myself, and T. Reuter in *Past and Present*, 142 (1994), 6–42, 152 (1996), 196–223, 155 (1997), 177–225. It seems to me that the period did indeed mark a distinct shift from Carolingian patterns, although the exact protocols of that shift need considerable nuancing. I stand by my statements in the main text of this book, and defend them in the above-mentioned debate.]

we have recognized how the self-identification of the aristocracy became much more rigid in the period, with male-line and exclusive lineages replacing the more open *Personenkreise*, overlapping networks of family relationships, that had existed in 900 or so. Whether or not family structure really changed in content, it certainly became far more rule-bound.[70] The boundary between aristocrat and non-aristocrat became more explicit in the eleventh century, too, all over Europe.[71] And so also, as public circumscriptions and the remnants of their authority collapsed in many places into the realities of private property and private clienteles, did signorial powers. By 1100 at the latest, all these had developed into a coherent set of vertical relationships that were, now, formally defined.

Horizontal relationships, those of collectivities, have been seen by historians since the beginning of this century as developing in opposition to vertical ones from 1100 or so onwards. But it may well be that they are only products of the same sort of development. Élite families, effective class differences, influential local political-juridical networks certainly existed in practice in the ninth century; it is these *de facto* realities that crystallized into the strong and coherent vertical power networks of the eleventh century. But horizontal relationships already existed in practice too. There were villages, even if they did not have clearly defined boundaries; there were local circumscriptions dominated by *boni homines*, even if these latter were in some sense public officials; there were informal local customs and collective practices. Sometimes these too were explicit, as with the fairly exclusive village identity envisaged by *Lex Salica*, or maybe with the *fabula inter vicinos*, the sworn agreement between neighbours, mentioned by Rothari in seventh-century Italy.[72] (We do not have to fetishize the concept of the *vicinia* into a legally defined institution to recognize that villagers could co-operate pretty systematically under certain circumstances, in 700 as in 1300.) In certain areas this was particularly common, such as in the Catalan Pyrenees, both a mountain and a frontier region, with its early-developing formal collective structures; there could well have been others, scattered on a larger or smaller scale all across western Europe. And, even though we must recognize that,

---

[70] K. Schmid, 'Zur Problematik von Familie, Sippe und Geschlecht', *Zeitschrift für die Geschichte des Oberrheins*, 105 (1957), 1–62; G. Duby, *Hommes et structures* (Paris, 1973), 395–422; though see the criticisms in K. Leyser, 'The German Aristocracy', *Past and Present*, 41 (1968), 32–9, 47–53, and, implicitly, in C. Violante, 'Quelques caractéristiques des structures familiales', in G. Duby and T. Le Goff (eds.), *Famille et parenté* (Rome, 1977), 87–147.

[71] E.g. Keller, *Adelsherrschaft*, 342–79.

[72] *Pactus legis salicae*, cap. 45; *Edictus Rothari*, cap. 346—and n.b. caps. 279–80 for a more seditious version.

usually, horizontally organized social groups, whether strong or weak, were informally structured or else (at least in theory) patterned along public lines in the Carolingian world, we should not doubt that it was once again these realities that were the ancestors of the crystallizing local communities of the twelfth century. That is to say: communities, like clienteles, had to formalize themselves, to give identity to society as a whole in the more localized political environments that replaced the Carolingian world order. It is only because communities were a hundred years or so slower to crystallize than clienteles had been that we see them simply as a *reaction* to the latter; in reality, both have roots that go far back into the past in a less organized form.[73]

The common element in the formalization of both vertical and horizontal relationships was that of the development of boundaries (*encellulement*, as Fossier calls it), to give society some sort of coherence in the new post-public world: boundaries between noble and non-noble, or, on the ground, the territorial definition of the signoria, *and* of the parish, *and* of the village, *and*, in the end, of the rural commune. These linked territorializations, particularly when they had the same boundaries, were often overdetermined; they laid down newly defined environments, that constituted the social worlds of (among other people) peasants, in ways that were far less avoidable than two or three centuries earlier.[74] Toubert commented in his study of Lazio how much more easily the church, through its (newly developed) parish structure, could set about influencing local social norms when people were all assembled in their (equally new) concentrated castelli. Signorial domination was easier too; but so was social and economic co-operation between peasants, which could often produce active rural communes (as, for example, to take the closest Tuscan example, on the Amiata).[75] *Incastellamento* along the lines of Lazio was at one extreme, that of a fully overdetermined local territorial identity; but territorialization and newly formalized collective relationships existed at the other extreme, in the fragmented and unsignorial villages of the Lucchesia, as well. Moriano and Tassignano needed to develop local identities in the crisis of the public world, just as Rocca di Tintinnano did, and they did so. This is what Volpe was talking about when he discussed the new

[73] I have already argued along these lines, more sketchily, in *Mountains*, 5–6, 330–6.
[74] Fossier, *Enfance de l'Europe*, 288–601, *passim*; see further C. Violante, 'La signoria "territoriale"', in W. Paravicini and K. F. Werner (eds.), *Histoire comparée de l'administration* (Munich, 1980), 333–44; C. J. Wickham, 'Frontiere di villaggio in Toscana', in J. M. Poisson (ed.), *Castrum 4* (Paris, 1992), 239–51.
[75] P. Toubert, *Les Structures du Latium médiéval* (Rome, 1973), 729–30; for communes, Carocci, *Baroni di Roma*, 255–61, 283–91.

twelfth-century 'associative movement', and its new capacity to give form to hitherto unstructured social relationships[76]—though he regarded these unstructured, informal patterns as the product of fragmentation and crisis, whereas I would see them as *functional* to the public world of the Carolingian past.

In this context, we can revalue the importance of the signoria. The commune had a common root with the signoria in a need for organization at the level of the locality that was new in post-Carolingian Europe. Like the signoria, it was based on local interpersonal relationships first, public/formal/institutional ones only after. On the other hand, it need not be denied that it was helped in its development in some places by common signorial oppression, and indeed pre-existing signorial territorialization, as Violante has pointed out.[77] I would add that the local organization of the signoria, which was almost inevitably largely in the hands of peasants, itself created frameworks for co-operation, competition, and control, that were themselves part of the movement towards the commune. These patterns could be found throughout Europe, and unify our Iberian and French examples with our Italian ones. Now, however, we can perhaps see more clearly the role of the relationship between lords and peasants in the formation of rural communes. Signorial oppression certainly stimulated the development of local political structures; but the date of this development, the way in which it occurred, and above all the strength (or the weakness) of the new commune which resulted from it, depended for the most part on the nature of social relationships *inside* the village. Furthermore, even in the context of the relationship between the village and the outside world, signorial power was not the only relevant element; in the local world of the twelfth century, there were other reasons to develop political structures.

One could say much the same for the trends of macro-economic development. Population growth (in cities, large castelli, and the countryside), the growth of the city economy and of the prosperity of citizens, the new possibilities for the systematic exploitation of common woods and pastures, the resultant pressure on land (both communal and individually held) and the need to organize its exploitation more tightly, the commercialization of the land market: all these led to a new need to organize collectively. They have been considerably stressed in the most wide-ranging European syntheses that discuss our theme, such as those of

[76] Volpe, *Pisa*, 18–51; and see also his classic 1904 article on the commune in his *Medioevo italiano*, 87–118.
[77] Violante, 'Signoria "territoriale"'.

Fossier and Reynolds (however different their other conclusions).[78] Indeed, in individual contexts, I have stressed them too. If I have given less space to specifically economic pressures in this book, it is because they do not seem to me particularly homogeneous in type: the profit-orientated land sales of the twelfth-century Sei Miglia Lucchese and the expansion of the transhumance routes in the Appennines can certainly be related to each other inside a macro-economic model of development, but the ways each of them contributed to the formation of the rural commune (as each of them did) were very diverse indeed. I would say, for that matter, that the ways that different economic trends contributed to that formation have in every case to be understood through social relationships: for economics does not ever cause social change—only people do that. But I would be the last person to deny an underlying role for economic change in all historical analysis; beyond doubt, in the matrix of causes for communal development, it must have an important place.

The last element that must be emphasized, in a book about Italy, is once again the city. Cities in north-central Italy were developing their own collective practices in the direction of the commune in 1100. They were always politically powerful; and they were the powerhouses of the economic trends referred to in the previous paragraph. They were dangerous for local villages, in their economic and political rapacity (although the full extent of this danger may not have been obvious until citizens began to buy up land, and city taxation spiralled, around 1200). But they were also models for collective organization that villages sought to copy, in Italy as in France (following the major urban franchises) and Castile (following the largest *concejos* with their developing urban institutions and their wide territorial circumscriptions). In Italy, too, the relative professionalization of law perhaps allowed the process of institutionalization to move faster than elsewhere. In this way, public power could come to constitute itself again from scratch, in the countryside as in the city, in the twelfth century, to form the institutions of the late Middle Ages, which have lasted up to our own time.

And, this time, returning to a specifically Italian context, it may be possible to see why the moment was the twelfth century. For that century was, in many ways, the low point of all public power in Italy. Counties and residual royal rights lasted, as an overarching structure, right up to the civil wars of the Investiture Dispute. It was only after that that cities were forced to develop their own forms of government, and those, as I

---

[78] See above, n. 24.

have already suggested for Lucca (above, pp. 181–3), were uncertain, still relatively informal, based on incoherent and virtually private 'institutions', and regarded even by their rulers as not fully legitimate, until they were tested successfully against Barbarossa's attempts to turn the clock back. Early city communes were politically and economically powerful; but institutionally and ideologically they were still weak. In some senses, the true analogue of the 'feudal crisis' of the early eleventh century in France is 1080–1150 in Italy, the period not only of the moves towards the city commune but also of a great number of local wars, far more than in the preceding century. The city commune thus has a paradoxical role in the affirmation of the rural commune. Its twelfth-century institutional weakness was the very moment at which the construction of the rural commune was possible, and indeed necessary, to fill the local vacuum of legitimacy. Its presence, however, provided the model for the communal form that Italian villages began to take. And, finally, in some places, not least Lucca, its continuous power as a political and economic drawing-point could be the cause of the relative weakness and the relative informality of rural communes themselves. All these three contradictory processes could happen simultaneously, and often did. But their joint effect points firmly to the particular environment of the twelfth century as the moment at which it was most logical that rural, as well as city, communes should appear. Just at the moment at which village élites, excluded from access to the aristocracy, were forced back on trying to lead the society of their local communities, socio-political changes were favouring the crystallization of communities that were sufficiently structured *to* lead.

The huge complexity of rural society, in the twelfth century as any other, resists synthesis in any easy way. I have been focusing on the rural commune, however, not just for its own sake, but as an attempt to make some sense of this wider complexity. As I argued at the start, communes can act as a guide to this variation, precisely because they can be so different in content (as illustrated in the list on p. 229), while still remaining similar, or at least comparable, in form: the different purposes communes had can be used as direct guides to the differences between their social structures. I have been comparing Lucca with northern Italy, France, and the Iberian peninsula, with this in part in mind. In this way, it may be possible to give some order to the multiplicity of variables inside our matrix. Systematic comparison between rural communes can, when carried out effectively, mean that in our characterization of this multiplicity we are not merely *reduced* to lists.

All that needs to be added by way of a conclusion is that these considerations are only valid for the earliest stages of the development of the Italian rural commune. In the late twelfth century and into the thirteenth century, communes changed. They developed proper institutions, for the first time, following the example of the city, and indeed encouraged by the city, which needed to collect taxes and keep the peace in its sphere of influence; but their original social basis began to weaken as well, as cities regained their own public identity and capacity to dominate territorially, as citizens bought land in the countryside, and as rural élites realized that the alternative to aristocratic clienteles and local communities was, quite simply, the city itself. Communes became *merely* local institutions, the lowest level of city government. They could focus community identity, action, and opposition; indeed, their present-day descendents still do. But their moment of affirmation had passed.

Appendix 1
Guide to Main Archival Sources

Lucca has three archives with substantial medieval material, the Archivio Arcivescovile, the Archivio Capitolare (both of these housed in the same archive in the Arcivescovado), and the Archivio di Stato. These provide all the documentation used in this book, except for a few references to the *fondo diplomatico* of the Archivio di Stato di Firenze (ASF), which I cite for comparative purposes —and also because a handful of Lucchese charters have ended up there, mostly in the fondo Strozziane-Uguccioni. The comments that follow relate mainly to the period 1050–1225, the focus of this book.

Archivio Arcivescovile (AAL)

This archive has retained its identity as the documentary record of the bishop's affairs. Its *fondo diplomatico*, containing single-sheet parchments and parchment rolls, is the richest in all Italy up to 1000, and remains rich until the early fourteenth century. It is most systematically introduced in D. J. Osheim, 'The Episcopal Archive of Lucca', *Manuscripta*, 17 (1973), 131–46. It has four *fondi*, *, +, ++, and A. There are editions of most of its documents up to 1073.

Barsocchini.   D. Barsocchini (ed.), *Memorie e documenti per servire all'istoria del ducato di Lucca*, v. 2, 3 (Lucca, 1837–41) is the basic edition of documents from 774 to 1000. (L. Schiaparelli (ed.), *Codice diplomatico longobardo*, i, ii (Rome, 1929–33), replaces it for the years 700–74.)

Bertini.   F. Bertini (ed.), *Memorie e documenti per servire all'istoria della città e stato di Lucca*, iv (Lucca, 1818–36) is an earlier selection of texts, including some twelfth-century documents used in this book. It is technically very inferior.

AAL ii and iii.   The AAL is publishing all its eleventh-century documents in modern scientific editions. The first two volumes are: G. Ghilarducci (ed.), *Archivio Arcivescovile di Lucca. Carte dell'XI secolo*, ii. Dal *1018 al 1030* (Lucca, 1991); L. Angelini (ed.), *Archivio Arcivescovile di Lucca. Carte dell'XI secolo*, iii. Dal *1031 al 1043* (Lucca, 1987).

Other AAL documents between 1023 and 1073 are published in *tesi di laurea* of the Department of Medieval History, University of Pisa. I list them all, for I used them all before the appearance of AAL iii; I cite them in the text after the *fondo* reference. The editors are L. Marchini for the years 1023–9 (*anno accademico* 1966–7), G. Mennucci for 1030–4 (*anno accademico* 1964–5), E. Isola for 1035–40 (*anno accademico* 1964–5), M. G. Nesti for 1041–4 (*anno accademico* 1967–8), M. G. Pianezzi for 1045–50 (*anno accademico* 1967–8), P. Bertocchini for 1051–5 (*anno accademico* 1969–70), for all of whom Professor C. Violante was the *relatore*; and L. Gemignani for 1056–73 (*anno accademico* 1956–7, *relatore* Professor O. Bertolini). Gemignani's huge task, an edition of over 300 texts, led her to miss a few, which have been listed in Cecilia Angeli's more recent *tesi* (*anno accademico* 1985–6, *relatore* C. Violante: see bibliography); she was kind enough to show me her own registers of them.

Frat. Cap.   The *fondo* of the Fraternita dei Cappellani Lucchesi, kept separately in AAL. I cite these according to the brief Italian register by S. Andreucci, 'I regesti delle pergamene della fraternità dei capellani lucchesi sec. XI–XII', *Actum luce*, 2 (1973), 201–16.

Libro della Croce. Privilegia ad episcopatum lucanum spectantia. A late fourteenth-century book of formal episcopal documents; where the copies can be compared with surviving originals, they can be seen to be reasonably accurate.

AAL contains the documents for the parts of the Lucchesia where the bishop had interests. Moriano, Marlia, Compito, Guamo, Sorbano del Vescovo, S. Maria a Monte, and Fucecchio are particularly well represented. (For Guamo, see D. J. Osheim, *A Tuscan Monastery and its Social World: S. Michele of Guamo* (Rome, 1989).) Outside the Sei Miglia, apart from the areas of the Valdinievole and the Versilia documented in the Capitolo and Pozzeveri archives (see ACL below), AAL is usually our only source.

*

Archivio Capitolare (ACL)

The archive of the cathedral chapter, or Canonica. ACL also includes the archive of the rural monastery of Pozzeveri, founded in 1056, the most substantial rural archive for the whole of the Lucchesia in our period.

RCL.   P. Guidi and O. Parenti (eds.), *Regesto del capitolo di Lucca*, 4 vols. (Rome, 1910–39), contains the ACL documents up to 1200. Although a register rather than a full edition, in practice it is as good as an edition. It is the most reliable research tool for the Lucchesia in the period, and has an excellent index.

ACL.   For documents from the main archive after 1200, I cite the *fondo* numbers, which are arranged by single letters of the alphabet, thus: F109 (*a*.1209).

Fondo Martini.   A separate *fondo* inside the ACL *diplomatico*; up to 1150 it is edited in a Pisan *tesi di laurea* by M. N. Guidoni (*anno accademico* 1971–2, *relatore* C. Violante), which I cite; after 1150 I cite documents by their archival marking, which is simply a date.

A+1. The first surviving notarial register from Lucca, dating to 1220–5 and 1236, for the notaries Benedetto and Ciabatto. A+2 and the long series of LL registers continue Ciabatto's career from 1226 into the 1260s. The uncontrollable wealth of documentation in these registers is the best reason to keep one's researches strictly to the period up to 1225. From the start, they are on paper. A. Meyer, 'Der Luccheser Notar Ser Ciabatto und sein Imbreviaturbuch von 1226/1227', *Quellen und Forschungen*, 74 (1994), 172–293, edits an early volume.

Archivio di Stato (ASL)

ASL i, ii.   G. degli Azzi Vitelleschi (ed.), *Reale archivio di stato in Lucca. Regesti* 1, i, ii (Lucca, 1903–11). A register in Italian and Latin of all the *fondi* then existing in the ASL *diplomatico* up to 1155. It is not a very adequate register; not much detailed work on these documents can be done without looking at the originals.

S. Giustina, S. Ponziano, etc.   Single-sheet documents from the twenty-five or so *fondi* of ASL *diplomatico* from 1156, further identified by date. ASL Guinigi, a family archive, has pre-1156 documents not registered in ASL i or ii.

SMCO, SMFP   Parchments from, respectively ASL S. Maria Corteorlandini and ASL S. Maria forisportam.

Estimo. Fourteenth-century (and later) tax records from the Lucchese contado.

ACL and ASL documents, which, like AAL, are essentially the archives of churches, are overwhelmingly for the city and the Sei Miglia. Different *fondi* tend to focus on different villages, reflecting the tendency for members of individual communities to be linked to one specific urban (or, more rarely, rural) church: so, Brancoli documents tend to be found in ASL Spedale and SMFP, S. Concordio di Moriano in ASL Archivo de' Notari, S. Margherita in *RCL*, and so on. But the fit is never complete; landowning was too complex in the Lucchese Sei Miglia to permit the exclusive village allegiances to an ecclesiastical community that can be found in more rural areas of Tuscany (see, for example, C. J. Wickham, *The Mountains and the City* (Oxford, 1988), 204–15). Although we have a great many documents from many villages—over a hundred for the twelfth century alone in several cases—arguments from silence have to be constructed with an awareness of these patterns of distribution in mind.

Where I use dates in the text, I have as far as possible made sure, by checking indictions, that they follow modern *anno domini* dating, with the year starting on 1 January. Where I simply cite documents, such as AAL ++D21 (*a*.1102), or ASL S. Ponziano 7 febb. 1202, I have left them as they are listed in the archives, for these are their collocation numbers, and it would be pointless to correct them.

Lucchese documents normally, fortunately, begin the new year on 25 December, leaving relatively few ambiguously dated texts in the last week of the modern year; the main exceptions are documents from the Valdarno (including S. Maria a Monte), which often follow the Pisan style, which began the year '1150' on 25 March 1149 by our dating.

For other published editions, see the bibliography.

Appendix 2
Two Documents

I publish here two hitherto unedited documents, the first from AAL, the second from ASL, of particular relevance to the argument of the text (they are summarized above, pp. 101, 140-3). The first is published with kind permission from AAL's archivist, Mons. G. Ghilarducci; the second with *permesso* no. 2383-V/9 from the ASL. I have resolved abbreviations in each text, and modernized punctuation but not spelling. Words added interlineally are marked so: * sint *. I am grateful to Enzo Matera for his help with these editions.

Breve of the commune of Moriano, c.*1170*. AAL ++A98, 'sec. XII'

For the date, see above, Ch. 4 n. 33. The text is a thin offcut, 52 × 13 cm., with 54 lines. It is written in a careful and trained twelfth-century roundhand, with more grammatical errors and interlineal additions than are by now normal in a formal document. It has no formal authentication, whether date, signatures, or notarial marks. On the dorse: 'Moriano' in large letters, sec. XII; 'Foedus initum inter homines Moriani', sec. XVII.

In Christi nomine. Breve ad memoriam habendam vel retinendam qualiter homines de | toto districto de Moriano. Ita iuramus nos homines de toto districto de Moria | no sicuti circumdatum est ad fossam et a carbonaiam ad castrum de Moriano, quod nul | lus homo de toto distro non sit ausus, subter istud sacramentum, ferire de ferro, vel | de ligno, vel de petra, vel in aliquo modo irato animo manum mittere in | personam in castrum sicuti designatum est ad fossam et a karbonariam. Et illi | hominies quod hoc sacramentum faciunt vel facient et postea fregerint et non ob | servaverint, consules sunt tenuti cum toto populo de stricto[1] de Moria | no non eum dimittere habitare in toto tempore vite sue, in alico[2] | loco de toto districto de Moriano. Et si aliquis homo vel hominis mitteret | manum ad spadam vel spiedum vel ad cultellum vel ad lignum vel ad pe | tram vel ad aliqua arma, *in castrum vel in eius confinibus,* illi homines quod hoc sacramentum faciunt vel faci | [e]nt et consules sciverint in rei veritatem; consules sint tenuti | cum toto populo XX solidos tollere, et non reddere neque[3] reddere facere. | Et insuper iuramus quod deinceps inantea non erimus in consilio vel | infacto vel in aliquo ordinamento per aliquum ingenium; illi homines | quod hoc sacramentum faciunt vel facient sint tenuti per bonam | fidem sine *omni* fraude ubicumque[4] sint. *Et sint* tenuti subter istud sa | cramentum quod

---

[1] For 'de districto'.   [2] There follows 'modo de', cancelled.
[3] There follows 'f', cancelled.   [4] There follows 'e', cancelled.

non sint percussum neque innaveratum vel mor | tuum. Et si ipse vel ipsi sciverint sint[5] tenuti facere | remanere; et si non possint facere remanere debet | dicere consuli vel cui rem debuisset evenire. | Et si aliquis homo de districto *de* Moriano exisset de | stricto[6] prius vel postea, et voluisset facere offensi | onem ad illis hominibus quod hoc sacramentum fecerunt, debent | inter se adiuvare per bonam fidem sine[7] fraude. | Et si aliquis homo quod hoc sacramentum faciunt vel fa | cient, et non observaverint, consules *sint* tenu*ti* | tollere solidos centum, et non reddere per aliquot | ingenium, vel peiorare. Et hoc totum sit | in potestate consulum *addere vel minuere* cum consilio de | quadraginta bonis hominibus, excepto sacra | mentum de crastro[8]; quod semper sit firmum | et ratum usque imperpetuum. Et si aliquis | homo de stricto[9] de Moriano fuerit in | tradimentum de populo de Moriano, con | sules cum populo sint tenuti non eum dimit | tere habitare in aliquo loco de | districto de Moriano. Rolandinus | Ildibrandinus atque[10] Gualfredus, | nos ita sumus tenuti in tempore de nostro | consulatu ita firmiter tenenere[11] | et observare per bonam fidem sine fraude, | et facere iurare ad alios[12] *nostros* sucesso | res consules, et illi consules ad aliis, | et omnes alios consules ad alios. | Et hoc totum sit salvo honore | sancti Martini et domini episcopi.[13] | Et subtus istud sacramentum populo de | Moriano et de eius districto quod | si aliqua compagnia esset inter eos sive[14] ali | quid sacramentum, debent destruere, et de | inceps inantea non facere. Unde populus | [. . .]sset[15] dividi[. . .][16] de m[. . .]no.

*

Court case between the commune of Tassignano and the church patrons of Tassignano, 1206. ASL Archivio de' Notari, 14 novembre 1206

The text is a large rectangular parchment, 63 × 32 cm., with 81 lines. It is written in a standard early thirteenth-century notarial hand. A dorsal note of the late sec. XIV reads: 'XVIII januarii de 1396, curie maxime sindici et. [. . .] presenti, sex mensis de 1394'.

In Christi nomine amen. Causa seu lis que vertebatur inter Florentinum consulem de Tassignano litigantem ab una parte pro consulatu et comuni ipsius loci et vici | nie et universitate, et Albertinum Soffreduccii respondentem ab altera parte, delata coram infrascriptis consulibus per sententiam diffinienda, talis erat.

---

[5] Literally, 'sint(us)'. [6] For 'de districto'. [7] There follows 'm', cancelled.
[8] For 'castro'. [9] For 'de districto'. [10] There follows 'Gra', cancelled.
[11] For 'tenere'. [12] There follows 'suos', cancelled.
[13] From here to the end, the ink is different and more faded, though the hand is the same.
[14] My reading of 's' with an abbreviation sign.
[15] I would guess at '[n(on) e]sset'; there is space for about two letters. Alternatively, '[fui]sset', if the sentence be taken as a clause modifying 'sacramentum'. The grammar here is particularly haphazard.
[16] After the lacuna, a white space of about 2 cm.

| Petebat siquidem predictus Florentinus pro consulatu et comuni ipsius loci et vicinie et universitate a predicto Albertino ne inbrigaret predictum comunem et con | sulatum et viciniam et universitatem eligere consules et habere consules et facere iurare eos consulatum qui pro tempore electi fuerint, seu potius permitteret ipsos consules | presentes et futuros officium consulatus exercere et consules et guardianos eligere vel facere eligere et ponere et facere iurare secundum quod modo iuratum ha | bet et secundum quod inantea eorum sacramentum ordinatum fuerit comuni consilio consiliariorum qui pro tempore fuerint. Et hec omnia petit salvo honore et iure civitatis, dicens predictam viciniam | sive predictam comunem habuisse consules ab antiquo tempore usque hodie per annos centum et ex compositione civitatis respondendo consulibus et eorum missis civitatis quotiens | civitas mittebat edictum de honeribus civitatis, sive de personalibus honeribus sive de patrimonialibus. Albertinus nisi interfuerit ipse vel aliquis de domo sua in ca | pite scilicet frater vel aliquis eorum descendentium a predicta facienda et etiam ad sacramentum conputandum vel unus seu duo de consortibus suis pro se et aliis et nisi iu | raverint honorem ecclesie et suum et suorum consortum et nominatim sicut continetur in sacramento quod fecerunt presentes consules se teneri suprascriptis petitionibus, opposita prima e | ceptione ex persona agentis et quod non pro comuni vicinie et universitate neque pro maiori parte faciunt nec eorum voluntate et facere negabat. Sacramento calump | nie facto, sexsto kalendas madii.

Dicebat Florentinus quod ipse cum duobus suis sociis eorum voluntatem facit hanc causam et sunt consules predicti loci in quantum est | vicinia Sancti Stefani. Albertinus confitetur. Dicebat Florentinus quod fuerunt et steterunt consules in illa vicinia per annos centum et quod illa vicinia stetit sub | consulatu et habuit consulatum per quadraginta annos. Albertinus confitetur quod predicta vicinia habuit consules per annos quadraginta. Dicit Florentinus | quod consules qui pro tempore fuerunt ibi semper habuerunt guardianos sive camparios et quicumque eos elegit voluntate et parabola consulum elegit. Albertinus ne | gat. Confitetur tamen quod per quadraginta annos fuerunt ibi guardiani in predicta cappella seu vicinia. Dicit Florentinus quod placet et placuit | hoc anno consulibus civitatis ut Florentinus et socii essent consules predicte vicinie. Albertinus confitetur quod cum esset discordia inter ipsum Alber | tinum ex una parte et consortes et vicinos ex altera pro factu consulatus, consules maiores[1] cum voluntate ipsius Albertini et licentia miserunt ibi | consules vel castaldi eorum mandato salva omni ratione Albertini et consortum et aliter negat. Quod Florentinus negat, et confitetur Florentinus quod erat | inde discordia quando consules fuerunt ibi missi hoc anno per castaldum fuit dictum salva ratione Albertini et consulum et vicinie. Dicit Floren | tinus quod maxima utilitas est habere consules civitatis et populi lucani in Tassignano et in aliis villis, ut respondeant honeribus civitatis | personalibus et patrimonialibus cum fuerit eis indicta a civitate et eius missis. Albertinus non respondit quia non credit pertinere ad causam. Dicit Al | bertinus

---

[1] i.e. of Lucca.

quod iam sunt anni quadraginta et plus quod pater suus fuit ad eligendum consules cum aliis hominibus in predicta cappella de Tassignano et non elige | bantur sine sua licentia. Florentinus negat. Dicit Albertinus quod antiquitus omnes rustici erant manentes seu servi de predicta villa excepto de uno | casamento nisi esset ibi aliquis avena[2] et nominatim de ecclesia et de patronibus. Florentinus negat ultra medietatem de eorum qui ibi abitabant essent manen | tes illorum vel ecclesie. Dicit Florentinus quod iam sunt transacti quadraginta anni quod de sex partibus quinque partes fuerunt et sunt franchi homines in illa | vicinia. Albertinus negat dictum eius set de quanto recusat.[3] Dicit Albertinus quod homines de Ponthano de super et de subter fuerunt sui manentes et consor | tum suorum et de ecclesia. Florentinus confitetur set dicit quod de quibusdam hominibus essent liberos a viginti annis hucusque. Dicit Albertinus quod presentes con | sules qui modo sunt in Tassignano non iuraverunt sacramentum consulatus usque dum non interfuerunt Albertinus vel frater vel consortum suorum vel aliquis | pro eis. Florentinus negat. Item dicit Albertinus quod nominatim interfuit ibi quando consules iuraverunt esse pro factu consulatus et interfuit ibi sicut con | suevit et sua voluntate et asentimento fecerunt sacramentum et quicquid fecerunt[4] et non aliter fecissent et hoc quando presentes consules iu | raverunt. Similiter petitione facit Florentinus a Bandino ut fecit ab Albertino per omnia ut dictum est superius. Bandinus respondit et negat ut fecit | Albertinus. Sacramento calumnie facto, quarto kalendas madii.

Florentinus eodem modo allegat et dicit contra Bandinum sicuti fecit contra Albertinum | per omnia et Bandinus allegat et negat et respondit ut fecit Albertinus per omnia, et tanto plus quod dicit quod fuit consul cum Ildebrandino et sociis et fecerunt mitti fo | vea de ysola et posuerunt passagium in via et recoligerunt passagium et de superfluo que remansit fecerunt inde commestionem et interfuit ibi tunc Bandinus | sicuti alii consules. Florentinus negat de fovea quod Bandinus fecisset mitti illam, confitetur tamen concordia populi et patronorum fuit missa. Dicit Florentinus | quod eo anno quo dicta fovea fuit missa Aldibrandinus et Bernardus et Detisalvi et Toringhellus qui stat modo ad Sanctam Margaritam erant consules de Tas | signano et Bandinus erat consul patronorum et suorum consortum. Bandinus confitetur quod erat consul cum predictis et quod erat ipse adhuc consul patronorum et a | liter et alio modo negat. Dicunt Albertinus et Bandinus quod omnes homines de Tassignano singulariter solvunt et dant expensas huius cause et nominatim solverunt et | dederunt illos de tenuta. Florentinus negat quod Bandinus fuisset consul de Tassignano, de aliis negat dictum eius, confitetur tamen quod consules colligerunt | hab eis quos solverunt pro tenuta et colligerent pro expensis huius cause.[5] Florentinus negat, confitetur

---

[2] For 'advena'.

[3] My reading for 'R', here and elsewhere in the text; see, for a parallel, RCL 1652. An alternative reading would be 'respondet', but the meaning is, in any case, 'denies', or 'replies negatively'.

[4] There follows 'fecerunt', crossed out.

[5] At least one sentence seems to be missing at this point. From 'Florentinus', the notary is writing with a new pen, and may have omitted a portion of text while copying.

tamen quod quando iuravit, Paltonerius fuit ibi quia sedebat cum aliis hominibus, | uterque confitetur quod dictus Paltonerius iuravit primo. Dicit Albertinus quod omnes alii consules iuraverunt sicuti iuravit Paltonerius. Florentinus confitetur quod iura | virunt,⁶ set ad breve iuraverunt et ad eundem breve iuraverunt idem unus quod alter. Albertinus confitetur. Dicit Albertinus quod in breve super quo iuraverunt con | tinetur quod iuraverunt honorem patronorum et ecclesie Sancti Stefani. Florentinus recusat. Dicit Albertinus quod cum discordia esset inter consules de Tassignano et patrem suum vel | ipsum Albertinum seu fratrem vel consortes seu homines de Tassignano et haberent scriptum alter quam consuetum fuit, scissum fuit breve et nominatim fece | rut secum concordiam seu pactum, et statuerunt quod ab inde in antea non debebant habere consules nisi Albertinus esset ibi vel unus de suis consortibus pro se et aliis, | et sine illo non debebant habere consules nec ipse sine eis nec camparios seu guardianos cum etiam Albertinus misisset consules sine ipsis et qui non iurarent | honorem ecclesie et patronorum et etiam obtentum est usque hodie. Florentinus confitetur quod fuit scissum breve set fecerunt illud facere iterum. Et confite | tur quod pater Albertini vocavit Aldibrandinum in consulem set ille fuit cassatus et non habuit bailiam et ita dicit. Dicit Florentinus quod ubi superius dixit | de quadraginta annis quod fuerunt consules et guardiani in Tassignano modo dicit de centum. Albertinus confitetur de quinquaginta et non plus. Set | dicit quod non fuerunt ibi pro villanis inmo pro suis consortibus et patronis; quod Florentinus negat. Dicit Florentinus quod quandoque in nummero trium consulum | fuit unus de patronis set non iam sunt anni quadraginta. Albertinus negat. Dicit Florentinus quod in is proximis quadraginta annis sepe cum consilio | quorundam qui eligebantur a consulibus et consiliariis fuit mutatum breve ad quod consules postea iurabant quod aliquit adebatur et aliquit minuebatur. Albertinus negat dictum | eius; inmo dicit quod consortes eius et pater fecerunt iurare et faciebant prout placebat eis et sicut videbant eis bonum. Dicit Florentinus quod in predicta vicinia non sunt ibi modo | quinque manentes neque decem cum in veritate sint ibi octuaginta tres familie in illa vicinia sive cappella. Albertinus negat. Dicit Florentinus quod quando patroni elige | runt Aldibrandinum in consulem tunc erant ibi tres consules, et vicini cassaverunt dictum Ildebrandinum ita quod nullo modo tenuerunt eum per consulem, et ille non ammini | stravit nec cum consulibus qui ibi erant neque sine illis in illo anno, et hoc iam sunt anni decem parum plus vel minus. Albertinus respondit ut supra. Et dicit Florentinus⁷ | quod Ildebrandinus aministravit in toto tempore sui consulatus et semper postea fuerunt ibi quactuor consules de voluntate et adsensu patronorum cum primo non essent | nisi tres. Dicit Florentinus quod post quam Burgum Sancti Genesii fuit reedifficatum⁸ vicini predicte vicinie fecerunt breve sine exenplo hostensum consulibus, ad quod consu | les postea iuraverunt et solunmodo eorum arbitrium fecerunt illud breve. Albertinus confitetur quod fecerunt cum sua voluntate fieri et presbiter ecclesie

---

⁶ The text says, 'iuravirrunt': a dot under the first 'r' denotes an erasure.
⁷ An error for 'Albertinus'.   ⁸ 1199 (see above, Ch. 6 n. 14).

scripsit et aliter | negat. Quod Florentinus negat excepto quod confitetur quod presbiter scripsit. Uterque confitentur quod non sunt duo anni quod Soffreduccius pater Albertini obiit.[9] Dicit Florentinus | quod patroni elegerunt guardianos cum primo essent ibi guardiani pro populo, unde vicini ita fecerunt quod nullam guardiam fecerunt in illo anno et sic vicini habuerunt | illos pro cassatis, quorum nomina sunt hec: Martius Guarinus et Bongiadore. Albertinus confitetur quod predictos vocavit ipse et pater suus et alia et omnia negat. Floren|tinus negat quod ipse vel pater vocasset eos. Dicit Florentinus quod quando castaldiones de civitate fuerunt in Tassignano ad hoc ut constituerentur ibi consules | dixerunt tunc Lucani castaldi ut fierent ibi consules salva ratione et patronorum et hominum de Tassignano. Albertinus confitetur quod castaldi dixerunt salva ratione | omnium hominum.

| Quam litem, secundum quod spectat ad petitiones quas suprascriptus Florentinus pro comuni et universitate de Tassignano faciebat adversus suprascriptum Albertinum, et secundum quod spectat ad alias | similes petitiones quas idem Florentinus pro suo comuni et vicinia seu universitate faciebat a suprascripto Bandino fratre dicti Albertini, nos Federigus iudex et Bovarius quondam Ghislimi|eri et Birrus filius Cristofani in dei nomine Lucensium causarum et foretanorum consules in ecclesia Sancti Alexandri Maioris residentes taliter per sententiam habito consilio quamplurium sapi|entum virorum diffinimus. Videlicet suprascriptum Albertinum et suprascriptum Bandinum eius fratrem ab omnibus presentibus petitionibus factis a iamdicto Florentino ut suprascriptum est absolvimus. Salvo eo quod | consules de Tassignano qui pro tempore fuerint possint facere electionem de consulibus eorum successoribus et facere eos iurare officium consulatus, ita tamen ut ipsi consules vel ille persone | qui predictam electionem facere debent seu possunt habeant secum unum de patronis ecclesie Sancti Stefani de Tassignano qui pro tempore fuerit consul seu capitaneus patronorum dicte ecclesie | pro inveniendis novis consulibus et trovandi eos in iandicta villa; quibus inventis consules debeant eligere sibi successores. Quod si dictum capitaneum seu consulem patronorum habere non | potuerint, vel si patroni dicte ecclesie non haberent consulem vel capitaneum de suis consortibus inter se quando dicta electio de consulibus fieri debet, nichilominus tamen ipsi con|sules de Tassignano possint facere electionem de consulibus dicte ville, et facere eos iurare officium consulatus, facta prius denuntiatione per duos dies dicto capitaneo patronorum | si inveniri potuerit Luce vel in villa de Tassignano aut in eius confinibus. Quia sic nobis constat pactum intercessisse inter patronos et consules dicte ville ut superius in hac sen|tentia continetur ubi dicitur salvo eo quod consules et cetera. Iterum non obstante ac sententia comuni et universitati seu consulibus de Tassignano quominus possint eorum ar|bitrio sine consensu alicuius patroni eligere et facere guardianos et iurare illos facere ad utilitatem et bonum et salvitatem hominum de Tassignano et comunis et univer|sitatis. Acta

---

[9] i.e. 1204.

sunt hec in suprascripta ecclesia, presentia Panfollie causidici et Cremonensis
iudicis et Viviani Sciocte et Rainerii quondam Borgogni. Anno nativitatis domini
millesimo | ducentesimo sexsto, octavodecimo kalendas decembris, indictione
decima.

| Martinus inperialis aule iudex et notarius his omnibus interfui et hec omnia
in publicam scripturam redegi et meo signo et nomine publice confirmavi.

Bibliography

1. Primary Sources

ANGELINI, L. (ed.), *Archivio Arcivescovile di Lucca. Carte dell'XI secolo*, iii. *Dal 1031 al 1043* (Lucca, 1987).

BARSOCCHINI, D. (ed.), *Memorie e documenti per servire all'istoria del ducato di Lucca*, v (3 parts, Lucca, 1837–44).

BERTINI, F. (ed.), *Memorie e documenti per servire all'istoria della città e stato di Lucca*, iv (Lucca, 1818–36).

BONAINI, F. (ed.), *Statuti inediti della città di Pisa dal XII al XIV secolo*, i (Florence, 1854).

BUTLER, H. E. (ed.), *The Chronicle of Jocelin of Brakelond* (Edinburgh, 1949).

CAFFARO, *Annali genovesi*, i, ed. L. Tommaso Belgrano (Genoa, 1890).

Edictus Rothari, in F. Beyerle (ed.), *Leges Langobardorum 643–866* (2 edn., Witzenhausen, 1962).

ENRIQUEZ, A. M. (ed.), *Le carte del monastero di S. Maria in Firenze (Badia)*, ii (Rome, 1990).

FABRE, P., DUCHESNE, L., and MOLLAT, G. (eds.), *Le Liber Censuum de l'église romaine* (Paris, 1910).

FICKER, J., *Forschungen zur Reichs- und Rechtsgeschichte Italiens*, iv (Innsbruck, 1874).

FONT RIUS, J. M. (ed.), *Cartas de población y franquicia de Cataluña*, i (Barcelona, 1969).

GHILARDUCCI, G. (ed.), *Archivio Arcivescovile di Lucca. Carte dell'XI secolo*, ii. *Dal 1018 al 1030* (Lucca, 1991).

GIUSTI, M., and GUIDI, P. (eds.), *Rationes decimarum Italiae nei secoli XIII e XIV. Tuscia*, ii (Rome, 1942).

GUIDI, P., and PARENTI, O. (eds.), *Regesto del capitolo di Lucca*, 4 vols. (Rome, 1910–39).

—— and PELLEGRINETTI, E. (eds.), *Inventari del vescovato della cattedrale e di altre chiese di Lucca* (Rome, 1921).

IMPERIALE DI SANT'ANGELO, C. (ed.), *Codice diplomatico della Repubblica di Genova*, ii (Rome, 1938).

KEHR, P. F., 'Die Minuten von Passignano. Eine diplomatische Miscelle', *Quellen und Forschungen*, 7 (1904), 8–41.

MANARESI, C. (ed.), *I placiti del 'regnum italiae'* (Rome, 1955–60).

MARAGONE, BERNARDO, *Gli annales pisani*, ed. M. Lupo Gentile, in *Rerum italicarum scriptores*, 2nd edn., vi. 2 (Bologna, 1930).

MEYER, A., 'Der Luccheser Notar Ser Ciabatto und sein Imbreviaturbuch von 1226/1227', *Quellen und Forschungen*, 74 (1994), 172–293.

MGH, Heinrici IV diplomata, ed. D. von Gladiss (Weimar, 1952–3).

MGH, Friderici I diplomata, ed. H. Appelt (Hanover, 1975–90).

MURATORI, L. A., *Antiquitates italicae medii aevi*, ii (Milan, 1739).

Pactus legis Salicae, ed. K. A. Eckhardt, in *MGH, Legum*, iv. 1 (Hanover, 1962).

RANGERIO, *Vita Anselmi lucensis*, ed. E. Sackur, G. Schwartz, and B. Schmeidler, in *MGH, Scriptores*, xxx. 2 (Leipzig, 1934), 1152–1307.

SANTINI, P. (ed.), *Documenti dell'antica costituzione del comune di Firenze* (Florence, 1895).

——(ed.), *Documenti dell'antica costituzione del comune di Firenze. Appendice* (Florence, 1952).

SANTOLI, Q. (ed.), *Liber censuum comunis Pistorii* (Pistoia, 1915).

SCHIAPARELLI, L. (ed.), *Codice diplomatico longobardo*, i, ii (Rome, 1929–33).

SERCAMBI, G., *Le croniche*, i, ed. S. Bongi (Lucca, 1892).

STUMPF-BRENTANO, K. F., *Die Reichskanzler vornehmlich des X., XI., und XII. Jahrhunderts*, iii. *Acta imperii adhuc inedita* (Innsbruck, 1865–81).

Tholomei Lucensis Annales, ed. B. Schmeidler, *MGH, SRG*, NS 8 (Berlin, 1955).

VOLPINI, R., 'Placiti del "Regnum Italiae" (secc. IX–XI)', in P. Zerbi (ed.), *Contributi dell'Istituto di storia medioevale*, iii (Milan, 1975), 245–520.

WINKELMANN, E., *Acta imperii inedita*, 2 vols. (Innsbruck, 1880–5).

2. Secondary Sources

ABULAFIA, D., *The Two Italies* (Cambridge, 1977).

ALFONSO, I., 'Poder local y diferenciación interna en las comunidades rurales gallegas', in R. Pastor (ed.), *Relaciones de poder, de producción y parentesco en la edad media y moderna* (Madrid, 1990), 203–23.

ALVAREZ BORGE, I., 'El proceso de transformación de las comunidades de aldea: una aproximación al estudio de la formación del feudalismo en Castilla (siglos X y XI)', *Studia historica. Historia medieval*, 5 (1987), 145–60.

ANDREOLLI, B., 'Considerazioni sulle campagne lucchesi nella prima metà del secolo XIV: paesaggio, economia, contratti agrari', *Atti del convegno su Castruccio Castracani e il suo tempo* (Lucca, 1986), 277–302.

—— 'Contratti agrari e patti colonici nella Lucchesia dei secoli VIII e IX', *Studi medievali*, 19 (1978), 69–158.

—— 'I prodotti alimentari nei contratti toscani dell'alto medioevo', *Archeologia medievale*, 8 (1981), 117–26.

ANDREUCCI, S., 'Per uno studio dei comuni rurali nel territorio lucchese: Sesto di Moriano in un antico documento dell'Archivio Arcivescovile', *Rivista archeologia storia costume*, 13. 1 (1985), 3–8.

—— 'I regesti delle pergamene della fraternità dei capellani lucchesi sec. XI–XII', *Actum luce*, 2 (1973), 201–16.

ANGELI, C., 'Anselmo I da Baggio vescovo di Lucca', University of Pisa, Facoltà di lettere, *tesi di laurea* (*anno accademico* 1985–6), *rel.* C. Violante.

Archeologia medievale, 16 (1989).

AUREGGI, O., 'Ricerche intorno alle origini del comune di Chiavenna', *Bollettino della società storica valtellinese*, 12 (1958), 16–48.

AUREGGI-ARIATTA, O., 'Comunità rurali e comuni medioevali nella Lombardia montana e pedemontana avanti il sec. XIV°', *Recueils de la société Jean Bodin*, 43 (1984), 207–28.

BANTI, O., ' "Civitas" e "commune" nelle fonti italiane dei secoli XI e XII', now in G. Rossetti (ed.), *Forme di potere e struttura sociale in Italia nel medioevo* (Bologna, 1977), 217–32.

BARBERO, A., and VIGIL, M., *La formación del feudalismo en la Península ibérica* (Barcelona, 1979).

BARCELÓ, M., *et al.*, *Arqueología medieval. En las afueras del 'medievalismo'* (Barcelona, 1988).

BARSOCCHINI, D., 'Sull'antico corso del Serchio', *Atti dell'Accademia lucchese di scienze, lettere ed arti*, 14 (1853), 393–487.

BARTHÉLEMY, D., *Les Deux âges de la seigneurie banale. Coucy (XIe–XIIIe siècle)* (Paris, 1984).

BELLI BARSALI, I., 'La topografia di Lucca nei secoli VIII–XI', in *Atti del 5° Congresso internazionale di studi sull'alto medioevo* (Spoleto, 1973), 461–554.

BERENGO, M., *Nobili e mercanti nella Lucca del Cinquecento* (Turin, 1965).

BERTOLINI, M. G., 'Bonifacio', *Dizionario biografico degli Italiani*, xii (Rome, 1970), 96–113.

BISSON, T. N., 'The Crisis of the Catalonian Franchises (1150–1200)', in J. Portella (ed.), *La formació i expansió del feudalisme català* (Girona, 1985–6), 153–72.

BLAIR, J. (ed.), *Minsters and Parish Churches: The Local Church in Transition, 950–1200* (Oxford, 1988).

BLOCH, M., *Les Caractères originaux de l'histoire rurale française* (2nd edn., Paris, 1955).

—— 'Une nouvelle théorie sur l'origine des communes rurales', *Annales d'histoire économique et sociale*, 1 (1929), 587–9.

BLOMQUIST, T. W., 'Trade and Commerce in Thirteenth Century Lucca', University of Minnesota Ph.D. thesis, 1966.

—— and OSHEIM, D., 'The First Consuls at Lucca: 10 July 1119', *Actum luce*, 7 (1978), 31–8.

BOGNETTI, G. P., *Studi sulle origini del comune rurale* (Milan, 1978).

BONAZZOLI, V., *Il prestito ebraico nelle economie cittadine delle Marche fra '200 e '400* (Ancona, 1990).

BONGI, S., *Inventario del Reale Archivio di Stato in Lucca*, i, ii (Lucca, 1872–6).

—— 'Quattro documenti de' tempi consolari (1170–1184) tratti dal R. Archivio di Stato in Milano', *Atti della Reale Accademia lucchese di scienze, lettere ed arti*, 21 (1882), 217–34.

BONNASSIE, P., *La Catalogne du milieu du Xe à la fin du XIe siècle* (Toulouse, 1975–6).

—— 'Du Rhône à la Galice: genèse et modalités du régime féodal', in *Structures féodales et féodalisme dans l'Occident méditerranéen (Xe–XIIIe siècles)* (Rome, 1980), 17–55.

—— 'Une famille de la campagne barcelonaise et ces activités aux alentours de l'An Mil', *Annales du Midi*, 76 (1964), 261–303.

—— and GUICHARD, P., 'Les Communautés rurales en Catalogne et dans le pays valencien (IXe–milieu XIVe siècle)', *Flaran*, 4 (1982), 79–115.

BORDONE, R., *La società cittadina del regno d'Italia* (Turin, 1987).

—— and JARNUT, J. (eds.), *L'evoluzione delle città italiane nell'XI secolo* (Bologna, 1988).

BORTOLAMI, S., 'Comuni e beni comunali nelle campagne medioevali: un episodio della Scodosia di Montagnana (Padova) nel XII secolo', *Mélanges de l'Ecole française de Rome*, 99 (1987), 555–84.

—— *Territorio e società in un comune rurale veneto (sec. X–XIII)*. *Pernumia e i suoi statuti* (Venice, 1978).

BOURIN-DERRUAU, M., *Villages médiévaux en Bas-Languedoc: genèse d'une sociabilité (Xe–XIVe siècle)* (Paris, 1987).

—— and DURAND, R., *Vivre au village au moyen âge* (Paris, 1984).

BOYD, C., *Tithes and Parishes in Medieval Italy* (Ithaca, NY, 1952).

BRANCOLI BUSDRAGHI, P., 'Patti di assistenza giudiziaria e militare in Toscana fra XI e XII secolo', in *Nobiltà e ceti dirigenti in Toscana nei secoli XI–XIII: strutture e concetti* (Florence, 1982), 29–55.

BRÜHL, C. R., *Fodrum, Gistum, Servitium Regis* (Cologne, 1968).

BULLOUGH, D. A., 'Burial, Community and Belief in the Early Medieval West', in C. P. Wormald (ed.), *Ideal and Reality in Frankish and Anglo-Saxon Society* (Oxford, 1983), 177–201.

CAGGESE, R., 'Chiese parrocchiali e università rurali', *Studi storici*, 20 (1911–12), 129–76.

—— *Classi e comuni rurali nel medio evo italiano*, 2 vols. (Florence, 1907–8).

CAMMAROSANO, P., *Le campagne nell'età comunale (metà sec. XI–metà sec. XIV)* (Turin, 1974).

—— 'Le campagne senesi dalla fine del secolo XII agli inizi del Trecento', in *Contadini e proprietari nella Toscana moderna* (Florence, 1979), i. 153–222.

—— 'L'economia italiana nell'età dei comuni e il "modo feudale di produzione": una discussione', *Società e storia*, 5 (1979), 495–520.

—— 'I primordi del Comune di Abbadia', in M. Ascheri and W. Kurze, (eds.), *L'Amiata nel medioevo* (Rome, 1989), 65–77.

CARLÉ, M. C., *Del concejo medieval castellano-leonés* (Buenos Aires, 1968).

CAROCCI, S., *Baroni di Roma. Dominazioni signorili e lignaggi aristocratici nel Duecento e primo Trecento* (Rome, 1993).

CASSANDRO, G., 'Un bilancio storiografico', now in G. Rossetti, (ed.), *Forme di potere e struttura sociale in Italia nel medioevo* (Bologna, 1977), 153–73.

—— *Storia delle terre comuni e degli usi civici* (Bari, 1943).

CASTAGNETTI, A., 'Le comunità della regione gardense fra potere centrale, governi cittadini e autonomie nel medioevo (secoli VIII–XIV)', in G. Borelli (ed.), *Un lago, una civiltà: il Garda* (Verona, 1983), i. 33–114.

—— *L'organizzazione del territorio rurale nel medioevo* (Turin, 1979).

—— *La pieve rurale nell'Italia padana* (Rome, 1976).

—— 'Il potere sui contadini', in B. Andreolli *et al.* (eds.), *Le campagne italiane prima e dopo il Mille* (Bologna, 1985), 219–61. This article includes the text of id., *Le comunità rurali dalla soggezione signorile alla giurisdizione del comune cittadino* (Verona, 1983), except some introductory chapters and an appendix of documents.

—— *La Valpolicella dall'alto medioevo all'età comunale* (Verona, 1984).

CASTAGNOLI, F., 'La centurazione di Lucca', *Studi etruschi*, 20 (1948–9), 285–90.

CELLI, R., *Longevità di una democrazia comunale. Le istituzioni di Bormio dalle origini del comune al dominio napoleonico* (Udine, 1984).

CHAPELOT, J., and FOSSIER, R., *Le Village et la maison au moyen âge* (Paris, 1980).

CHECCHINI, A., 'Comuni rurali padovani', *Nuovo archivio veneto*, 18 (1909), 131–84.

CHÉDEVILLE, A., *Chartres et ses campagnes (Xe–XIIIe s.)* (Paris, 1973).

CHERUBINI, G., 'Le campagne italiane dall'XI secolo al XV secolo', in UTET, *Storia d'Italia*, iv (Turin, 1982), 267–448.

—— *Una comunità dell'Appennino dal XIII al XV secolo* (Florence, 1972).

CHITTOLINI, G., '"Quasi-città". Borghi e terre in area lombarda nel tardo medioevo', *Società e storia*, 13 (1990), 3–26.

CIAMPOLTRINI, G., and NOTINI, P., 'Montecatino (val Freddana, com. Lucca). Scavi 1986 nell'area del castello. Notizia preliminare', *Archeologia medievale*, 14 (1987), 255–66.

CIANELLI, A. N., 'Dissertazioni sopra la storia lucchese', *Memorie e documenti per servire all'istoria del principato lucchese*, i (Lucca, 1813).

COLLODO, S., 'Il Cadore medievale verso la formazione di un identità di regione', *Archivio storico italiano*, 145 (1987), 351–89.

—— 'I "vicini" e i comuni di contado (secoli XII–XIII)', in *Storia di Treviso*, ii (Venice, 1991), 271–97.

CONTI, E., *La formazione della struttura agraria del contado fiorentino*, i (Rome, 1965).

CORSI, D., 'Il "breve" dei consoli e del podestà del comune di Santa Maria a Monte (secoli XII–XIII)', *Atti dell'Accademia lucchese di scienze, lettere ed arti*, NS 10 (1959), 153–72.

CORSI, M. L., 'Piccoli proprietari rurali in Garbagnate Marcido: i Veneroni', in *Contributi dell'Istituto di storia medioevale*, ii (Milan, 1972), 687–724.

CUVILLIER, J.-P., 'Les Communautés rurales de la plaine de Vich (Catalogne) aux XIIIe et XIVe siècles', *Mélanges de la Casa de Velazquez*, 4 (1968), 73–105.

DAMERON, G. W., 'Episcopal Lordship in the Diocese of Florence and the Origins of the Commune of San Casciano Val di Pesa', *Journal of Medieval History*, 12 (1986), 135–54.

—— *Episcopal Power and Florentine Society, 1100–1320* (Cambridge, Mass., 1991).

D'AMIA, A., *Diritto e sentenze di Pisa* (Milan, 1962).

D'AMICO, R., 'Note su alcuni rapporti tra città e campagna nel contado di Pisa tra XI e XII secolo', *Bollettino storico pisano*, 39 (1970), 15–29.

260   *Bibliography*

DAVIDSOHN, R., *Storia di Firenze*, i (1896; Ital. edn., Florence, 1956).

DAVIES, W., and FOURACRE, P. (eds.), *The Settlement of Disputes in Early Medieval Europe* (Cambridge, 1986).

DELUMEAU, J.-P., *Arezzo. Espace et sociétés, 715–1230* (Rome, 1996).

—— 'Des Lombards de Carpineto aux Bostoli (secc. XI–XIII)', in *I ceti dirigenti dell'età comunale nei secoli XII e XIII* (Pisa, 1982), 67–99.

—— 'L'Exercice de la justice dans le comté d'Arezzo (IXe–début XIIIe siècle)', *Mélanges de l'Ecole française de Rome. Moyen âge, temps modernes*, 90 (1978), 563–605.

—— 'Sur les origines de la commune d'Arezzo', in *Les Origines des libertés urbaines* (Rouen, 1990), 325–46.

DE STEFANI, C., 'Storia dei comuni di Garfagnana', *Atti e memorie della reale deputazione di storia patria per le provincie modenesi*, 7 ser. 2. (1925).

DINELLI, G., 'Il castello di Fibbialla e il Capitolo di S. Martino', *Bollettino storico lucchese*, 13 (1941), 137–44.

—— 'Una signoria ecclesiastica nel contado lucchese dal secolo XI al secolo XIV', *Studi storici*, 23 (1915), 187–291.

DUBY, G., *Hommes et structures du moyen âge* (Paris, 1973).

—— *La Société aux XIe et XIIe siècles dans la région mâconnaise* (2nd edn., Paris, 1971).

DYER, C. C., 'Les Cours manoriales', *Etudes rurales*, 103: 4 (1986), 19–27.

—— 'The English Medieval Village Community and its Decline', *Journal of British Studies*, 33 (1994), 407–29.

—— 'Power and Conflict in the Medieval English Village', in D. Hooke (ed.), *Medieval Villages* (Oxford, 1985), 27–32.

ESCH, A., 'Lucca im 12. Jahrhundert', Habilitationsschrift, University of Göttingen, 1974, in the process of publication.

—— 'Überlieferungs-chance und Überlieferungs-zufall als methodisches Problem des Historikers', *Historische Zeitschrift*, 240 (1985), 529–70.

ESTEPA DIAZ, C., *Historia de Castilla y León, iii. El nacimiento de León y Castilla (siglos VIII–X)* (Valladolid, 1985).

—— 'Poder y propiedad feudales en el periodo astur', in *Miscel.lania en homenatge al P. Agustí Altisent* (Tarragona, 1991), 284–327.

FALCE, A., *Bonifacio di Canossa, padre di Matilda* (Reggio Emilia, 1926–7).

FASOLI, G., 'Castelli e signorie rurali', *Settimane di studio*, 13 (1965), 531–67.

—— 'Un comune rurale veneto nel Duecento: Bassano', *Archivio veneto*, 5 ser. 15 (1934), 1–44.

FILIERI, M. T., *Architettura medioevale in diocesi di Lucca. Le pievi del territorio di Capannori* (Lucca, 1990).

FIUMI, E., 'L'imposta diretta nei comuni medioevali della Toscana', in *Studi in onore di Armando Sapori* (Milan, 1957), 329–55.

—— *Storia economica e sociale di San Gimignano* (Florence, 1961).

—— 'Sui rapporti economici tra città e contado nell'età comunale', *Archivio storico italiano*, 114 (1956), 18–68.

FONSECA, C. D., *La signoria del Monastero Maggiore di Milano sul luogo di Arosio (Secoli XII–XIII)* (Genoa, 1974).

Formazione e strutture dei ceti dominanti nel medioevo: marchesi conti e visconti nel regno italico (secc. IX–XII), i (Rome, 1988).

FOSSIER, R., *Chartes de coutume en Picardie (XIe–XIIIe siècle)* (Paris, 1974).

—— 'Les Communautés villageoises en France du nord au moyen âge', *Flaran*, 4 (1982), 29–53.

—— *Enfance de l'Europe, Xe–XIIe siècles* (Paris, 1982).

—— *La Terre et les hommes en Picardie jusqu'à la fin du XIIIe siècle* (Paris, 1968).

FREEDMAN, P., 'La Condition des paysans dans un village catalan du XIIIe siècle', *Annales du Midi*, 94 (1982), 227–44.

—— *The Origins of Peasant Servitude in Medieval Catalonia* (Cambridge, 1991).

GABOTTO, F., 'Le origini "signorili" del "comune"', *Bollettino storico-bibliografico subalpino*, 8 (1903), 127–50.

GARCÍA DE CORTÁZAR, J. A., *La sociedad rural en la España medieval* (Madrid, 1988).

GARZELLA, G., 'Cascina. L'organizzazione civile ed ecclesiastica e l'insediamento', in M. Pasquinucci, G. Garzella, and M. L. Ceccarelli Lemut, *Cascina*, ii (Pisa, 1986), 69–108.

GÉNICOT, L., *Rural Communities in the Medieval West* (Baltimore, 1990).

—— *Une source mal connue de révenus paroissaux: les rentes obituaires: l'exemple de Frizet* (Louvain, 1980).

GOETZ, H.-W., '"Nobilis". Der Adel im Selbstverständnis der Karolingerzeit', *Vierteljahrschrift für Sozial- und Wirtschaftsgeschichte*, 60 (1983), 153–91.

GOLINELLI, P. (ed.), *I poteri dei Canossa. Da Reggio Emilia all'Europa* (Bologna, 1994).

GRONEUER, H., *Caresana. Eine oberitalienische Grundherrschaft im Mittelalter 987–1261* (Stuttgart, 1970).

GUIDI, L. M., 'Per la formazione delle circoscrizioni parrocchiali a Lucca: la "ecclesia sancti Leonardi pontis S. Quirici"', in *Pisa e la Toscana occidentale nel Medioevo*, ii (Pisa, 1991), 181–202.

HERLIHY, D., 'Direct and Indirect Taxation in Tuscan Urban Finance, *ca.* 1200–1400', in *Finances et comptabilités urbaines du XIIIe au XVIe siècle* (Brussels, 1964), 385–405.

—— *Pisa in the Early Renaissance* (New Haven, 1958).

—— 'Santa Maria di Impruneta: A Rural Commune in the Late Middle Ages', in N. Rubinstein (ed.), *Florentine Studies* (London, 1968), 242–76.

HILTON, R. H., *Bondmen Made Free: Medieval Peasant Movements and the English Rising of 1381* (London, 1973).

—— 'Les Communautés villageoises en Angleterre au moyen âge', *Flaran*, 4 (1982), 117–28.

—— *A Medieval Society: The West Midlands at the End of the Thirteenth Century* (2nd edn., Cambridge, 1983).

HUMPHREYS, S., 'Social Relations on Stage: Witnesses in Classical Athens', *History and Anthropology*, 1: 2 (1985), 313–69.

IRICO, N., 'Il problema della presenza signorile nei primordi del comune di Biella', *Bollettino storico-bibliografico subalpino*, 69 (1971), 449–504.

ISTAT, *11° Censimento generale della popolazione*, 3. 9 (Rome, 1974).

JARNUT, J., *Bergamo 568–1098* (Bergamo, 1980).

JONES, P. J., 'An Italian Estate, 900–1200', *Economic History Review*, 2 ser. 7 (1954), 18–32.

—— 'From Manor to Mezzadria', in N. Rubinstein (ed.), *Florentine Studies* (London, 1968), 193–241.

—— 'La storia economica', in *Storia d'Italia*, ii (Turin, 1974), 1469–1810.

JØRGENSEN, L., 'Castel Trosino and Nocera Umbra', *Acta archaeologica*, 62 (1991), 1–58.

KELLER, H., *Adelsherrschaft und städtische Gesellschaft in Oberitalien (9.–12. Jahrhundert)* (Tübingen, 1979).

—— 'Mehrheitsentscheidung und Majorisierungsproblem im Verbund der Landgemeinden Chiavenna und Piuro (1151–1155)', in H. Jäger *et al.* (eds.), *Civitatum communitas. Festschrift Heinz Stoob* (Cologne, 1984), 2–41.

KEMP, B., 'Some Aspects of the Parochia of Leominster in the Twelfth Century', in Blair, *Minsters and Parish Churches*, 83–95.

KOTEL'NIKOVA, L. A., *Mondo contadino e città in Italia dal XI al XIV secolo* (1967; Ital. edn., Bologna, 1975).

KURZE, D., *Pfarrerwahlen im Mittelalter* (Cologne, 1966).

KURZE, W., 'Monasteri e nobiltà nella Tuscia altomedioevale', in *Atti del 5° Congresso internazionale di studi sull'alto medioevo* (Spoleto, 1973), 339–62.

LANDAU, P., *Jus patronatus* (Cologne, 1975).

LE ROY LADURIE, E., *Montaillou, village occitan de 1294 à 1324* (Paris, 1975).

LEVEROTTI, F., ' "Crisi" del Trecento e strutture di inquadramento nelle Sei Miglia lucchesi', in *Pisa e la Toscana occidentale nel Medioevo*, ii (Pisa, 1991), 203–62.

—— 'La crisi demografica nella Toscana del Trecento: l'esempio delle Sei Miglia lucchesi', in S. Gensini (ed.), *La Toscana nel secolo XIV* (Pisa, 1988), 67–150.

—— 'Dalla famiglia stretta alla famiglia larga', *Studi storici*, 30 (1989), 171–212.

—— 'Gli estimi lucchesi del 1411–13', in *Scritti in ricordo di Giorgio Buratti* (Pisa, 1981), 199–222.

—— 'La famiglia contadina lucchese all'inizio del '400', in R. Comba, G. Piccinni, and G. Pinto, (eds.), *Strutture familiari, epidemie, migrazioni nell'Italia medievale* (Naples, 1984), 237–68.

—— *Popolazione, famiglia, insediamento* (Pisa, 1992) (this book collects and re-elaborates all the preceding articles).

LEYSER, K., 'The German Aristocracy from the Ninth to the Early Twelfth Century: A Historical and Cultural Sketch', *Past and Present*, 41 (1968), 25–53.

LUZZATTO, G., *Dai servi della gleba agli albori del capitalismo* (Bari, 1966).

MAGNOU-NORTIER, E., *La Société laïque et l'église dans la province ecclésiastique de Narbonne (zone cispyrénéenne) de la fin du VIIIe à la fin du XIe siècle* (Toulouse, 1974).

MAIRE-VIGUEUR, J. C., 'Comuni e signorie in Umbria, Marche e Lazio', in *Storia d'Italia*, vii. 2 (Turin, 1987), 323–606.

MARTÍ, R., 'L'Ensagrerament: l'adveniment de les sagreres feudals', *Faventia*, 10 (1988), 153–82.

—— 'Els inicis de l'organització feudal de la producció al bisbat de Girona', Ph.D. Thesis, Autonomous University of Barcelona, 1987.

MARTINDALE, J., 'The French Aristocracy in the Early Middle Ages: A Reappraisal', *Past and Present*, 75 (1975), 5–45.

MARTINEZ SOPENA, P., *La Tierra de Campos occidental* (Valladolid, 1985).

MARX, K., *Capital*. Various editions.

MATRAIA, G., *Lucca nel Milleduecento* (1843; 2nd edn., Lucca, 1983).

MEEK, C., *Lucca 1369–1400* (Oxford, 1978).

MENANT, F., *Campagnes lombardes du moyen âge. L'économie et la société rurales dans la région de Bergame, de Cremone et de Brescia du Xe au XIIIe siècle* (Rome, 1993).

MENGARELLI, R., 'La necropoli barbarica di Castel Trosino', *Monumenti antichi*, 12 (1902), cols. 145–380.

MILLER, M. C., *The Formation of a Medieval Church: Ecclesiastical Change in Verona, 950–1150* (Ithaca, NY, 1993).

MÍNGUEZ, J. M., 'Ruptura social e implantación del feudalismo en el noroeste peninsular (siglos VIII–X)', *Studia historica. Historia medieval*, 3 (1985), 7–32.

MODIGLIANI, M., 'Studi e documenti ad illustrazione degli statuti del comune di Anghiari del secolo XIII', *Archivio storico italiano*, 4 ser. 6 (1880), 225–61.

MONSALVO ANTÓN, J. M., 'Concejos castellano-leoneses y feudalismo (siglos XI–XIII). Reflexiones para un estado de la cuestion', *Studia historica. Historia medieval*, 10 (1992), 203–43.

—— 'Transformaciones sociales y relaciones de poder en los concejos de frontera, siglos XI–XIII', in R. Pastor (ed.), *Relaciones de poder, de producción y parentesco en la edad media y moderna* (Madrid, 1990), 107–70.

MONTANARI, M., *L'alimentazione contadina nell'alto medioevo* (Naples, 1979).

MORETTI, I., 'Espansione demografica, sviluppo economico e pievi romaniche: il caso del contado fiorentino', *Ricerche storiche*, 13 (1983), 33–69.

MORRIS, R., *The Church in British Archaeology* (Council for British Archaeology Research Report 47, London 1983).

MOSIICI, L., 'Documenti di lega, patti e convenzioni stipulati da comuni della Valdinievole nel secolo XIII: note diplomatiche', in C. Violante and A. Spicciani (eds.), *Pescia e la Valdinievole nell'età dei Comuni* (Pisa, 1995), 101–38.

NANNI, L., *La parrocchia studiata nei documenti lucchesi dei secoli VIII–XIII* (Rome, 1948).

NIERMEYER, J. F., *Mediae latinitatis lexicon minus* (Leiden, 1976).

NOBILI, M., 'L'evoluzione delle dominazioni marchionali in relazione alla dissoluzione delle circoscrizioni marchionali e comitali e allo sviluppo della politica territoriale dei comuni cittadini nell'Italia centro-settentrionale (secoli XI e XII)', in *Atti della VIII settimana di studio* (Milan, 1980), 235–58.

OCCHIPINTI, E., *Il contado milanese nel secolo XIII* (Bologna, 1982).

—— 'Una famiglia di rustici proprietari legati alla canonica di Sant'Ambrogio: i da Trezzano', in *Contributi dell'Istituto di storia medioevale*, ii (Milan, 1972), 747–78.

—— 'Piccoli proprietari rurali in Garbagnate Marcido: i de Vico, ibid., 727–44.

ONORI, A. M., *L'abbazia di San Salvatore di Sesto e il lago di Bientina* (Florence, 1984).

OSHEIM, D. J., 'Countrymen and the Law in Late-Medieval Tuscany', *Speculum*, 64 (1989), 317–37.

—— 'The Episcopal Archive of Lucca in the Middle Ages', *Manuscripta*, 17 (1973), 131–46.

—— 'Independent Farmers in Late Medieval Tuscany', in press.

—— *An Italian Lordship* (Berkeley, 1977).

—— *A Tuscan Monastery and its Social World: S. Michele of Guamo (1156–1348)* (Rome, 1989).

OVERMANN, A., *La contessa Matilde di Canossa* (1895; Ital. edn., Rome, 1980).

PADERI, E., 'Variazioni fisiografiche del bacino di Bientina e della pianura lucchese durante i periodi storici', *Memorie della reale società geografica italiana*, 17 (1932), 89–118.

PALMIERI, A., 'Degli antichi comuni rurali e in ispecie quelli dell'Appennino bolognese', *Atti e memorie della R. Deputazione di storia patria per le provincie di Romagna*, 3 ser. 16 (1898), 239–327.

PANERO, F., *Servi e rustici* (Vercelli, 1990).

—— *Terre in concessione e mobilità contadina: le campagne fra Po, Sesia e Dora Baltea (secoli XII e XIII)* (Bologna, 1984).

PASTOR, R., *Resistencias y luchas campesinas en la época del crecimiento y consolidación de la formación feudal Castilla y León, siglos X–XIII* (Madrid, 1980).

PESCAGLINI MONTI, R., 'Nobiltà e istituzioni ecclesiastiche in Valdinievole tra XI e XII secolo', in A. Spicciani and C. Violante (eds.), *Allucio da Pescia (1070 ca–1134)*, 225–77.

—— 'Le vicende del castello di Collodi dalle origini alla metà del XIII secolo', in *Atti del convegno: I castelli in Valdinievole* (Buggiano, 1989), 47–87.

—— 'Le vicende politiche e istituzionali della Valdinievole tra il 1113 e il 1250', in C. Violante and A. Spicciani (eds.), *Pescia e la Valdinievole nell'età dei Comuni* (Pisa, 1995), 57–87.

PEZZANO, P., 'Istituzioni e ceti sociali in una comunità rurale: Racconigi nel XII e nel XIII secolo', *Bollettino storico-bibliografico subalpino*, 74 (1976), 619–91.

PICARD, J.-C., *Le souvenir des évêques* (Rome, 1988).

PINI, A. I., *Città, comuni e corporazioni nel medioevo italiano* (Bologna, 1986).

—— *Le ripartizioni territoriali urbani di Bologna medievale* (Bologna, 1977).

PINTO, G., *La Toscana nel tardo medio evo* (Florence, 1982).

PIRILLO, P., 'I beni comuni nelle campagne fiorentine basso medievali', *Mélanges de l'Ecole française de Rome. Moyen âge*, 99 (1987), 621–47.

PLESNER, J., *L'emigrazione dalla campagna alla città libera di Firenze nel XIII secolo* (1934; Ital. edn., Florence, 1979).

POLY, J.-P., and BOURNAZEL, E., *La Mutation féodale. Xe–XIIe siècles* (Paris, 1980).

RANGER, T., 'Taking Hold of the Land: Holy Places and Pilgrimages in Twentieth-Century Zimbabwe', *Past and Present*, 117 (1987), 158–94.

REDON, O., 'La divisione dei poteri nell'Amiata del Duecento', in M. Ascheri and W. Kurze (eds.), *L'Amiata nel medioevo* (Rome, 1989), 183–95.

—— 'Seigneurs et communautés rurales dans le contado de Sienne au XIIIe siècle', *Mélanges de l'Ecole française de Rome. Moyen âge*, 91 (1979), 149–96, 619–57.

—— *Uomini e comunità del contado senese nel Duecento* (Siena, 1982).

REPETTI, E., *Dizionario geografico fisico storico della Toscana* (Florence, 1833–46).

REYNOLDS, S., *Kingdoms and Communities in Western Europe 900–1300* (Oxford, 1984).

RIPPE, G., 'Dans le Padouan des Xe–XIe siècles: évêques, vavasseurs, "cives"', *Cahiers de civilisation médiévale*, 27 (1984), 141–50.

ROMEO, R., 'La signoria dell'abate di Sant'Ambrogio di Milano sul comune rurale di Origgio nel secolo XIII', *Rivista storica italiana*, 69 (1957), 340–77, 473–507.

RONZANI, M., 'Aspetti e problemi delle pievi e delle parrocchie cittadine nell'Italia centrosettentrionale', in *Pievi e parrocchie in Italia nel basso medioevo (sec. XIII–XV)* (Rome, 1984), 307–49.

—— 'L'organizzazione della cura d'anime nella città di Pisa (secoli XII–XIII)', in C. Wickham *et al.*, *Istituzioni ecclesiastiche della Toscana medioevale* (Galatina, 1980), 35–85.

ROSSETTI, G., 'Formazione e caratteri delle signorie di castello e dei poteri territoriali dei vescovi sulle città nella Langobardia del secolo X', *Aevum*, 49 (1975), 243–309.

—— 'Histoire familiale et structures sociales et politiques à Pise aux XIe et XIIe siècles', in G. Duby and J. Le Goff (eds.), *Famille et parenté dans l'Occident médiéval* (Rome, 1977), 159–80.

—— 'Il lodo del vescovo Daiberto sull'altezza delle torri', in *Pisa e la Toscana occidentale nel Medioevo*, ii (Pisa, 1991), 25–47.

—— 'Società e istituzioni nei secoli IX e X. Pisa, Volterra, Populonia', in *Atti del 5° Congresso internazionale di studi sull'alto medioevo* (Spoleto, 1973), 209–338.

—— *et al.*, *Pisa nei secoli XI e XII: formazione e caratteri di una classe di governo* (Pisa, 1979).

SALRACH, J. M., *El procés de feudalització (segles III–XII)* (Barcelona, 1987).

SALVEMINI, G., 'Un comune rurale nel secolo XIII' (1901), now in id., *La dignità cavalleresca nel Comune di Firenze e altri scritti* (Milan, 1972), 274–97.

SAMBIN, P., *L'ordinamento parrocchiale di Padova nel medioevo* (Padua, 1941).

SANTINI, G., '*I comuni di pieve' nel medioevo italiano* (Milan, 1964).

—— *I comuni di valle del medio evo. La costituzione federale del 'Frignano'* (Milan, 1960).

SAVIGNI, R., *Episcopato e società cittadina a Lucca da Anselmo II (+1086) a Roberto (+1225)* (Lucca, 1996).

—— 'La signoria vescovile lucchese tra XI e XII secolo', *Aevum*, 66 (1993), 333–67.

SCHÄFER, P., *Il Sottoceneri nel medioevo* (1933; Ital. edn., Lugano, 1954).

SCHAUBE, A., *Handelsgeschichte der romanischen Völker des Mittelmeergebiets bis zum Ende des Kreuzzüge* (Munich, 1906).

SCHEFFER-BOICHORST, P., *Zur Geschichte des XII. und XIII. Jahrhunderts* (Berlin, 1897).

SCHMID, K., 'Zur Problematik von Familie, Sippe und Geschlecht, Hause und Dynastie beim mittelalterlichen Adel', *Zeitschrift für die Geschichte des Oberrheins*, 105 (1957), 1–62.

SCHNEIDER, F., 'Nachlese in Toscana', *Quellen und Forschungen*, 22 (1930–1), 31–86.

—— *L'ordinamento pubblico nella Toscana medievale* (1914; Ital. edn., Florence, 1975).

—— *Le origini dei comuni rurali in Italia* (1924; Ital. edn., Florence, 1980).

SCHWARZMAIER, H. M., *Lucca und das Reich bis zum Ende des 11. Jahrhunderts* (Tübingen, 1972).

SCOTT, J. C., *Weapons of the Weak: Everyday Forms of Peasant Resistance* (New Haven, 1985).

SELLA, P., *La vicinia come elemento costitutivo del comune* (Milan, 1908).

SERENI, E., *Comunità rurali nell'Italia antica* (Rome, 1955).

SETTIA, A. A., *Castelli e villaggi nell'Italia padana* (Naples, 1984).

—— 'Pievi e cappelle nella dinamica del popolamento rurale', *Settimane di studio*, 28 (1980), 445–89.

SIMEONI, L., *Studi su Verona nel medioevo*, iv (*Studi storici veronesi*, 13 (Verona, 1962)).

SIVÉRY, G., *Terroirs et communautés rurales dans l'Europe occidentale au moyen âge* (Lille, 1990).

SORBELLI, A., *Il comune rurale nell'Appennino emiliano nei secoli XIV e XV* (Bologna, 1910).

—— *La parrocchia dell'Appennino emiliano nel medio evo* (Bologna, 1910).

SPICCIANI, A., 'I prestiti su pegno fondiario durante il secolo XII dell'ospitale lucchese di Altopascio', in *Banchi pubblici, banchi privati e monti di pietà nell'Europa preindustriale* (Genoa, 1991), 643–71.

SQUATRITI, P., 'Water, Nature and Culture in Early Medieval Lucca', *Early Medieval History*, 4 (1995), 21–40.

STEUER, H., 'Archaeology and History: Proposals on the Social Structure of the Merovingian Kingdom', in K. Randsborg (ed.), *The Birth of Europe* (Rome, 1989), 100–22.

TABACCO, G., *Egemonie sociali e strutture del potere nel medioevo italiano* (Turin, 1979).

—— *I liberi del re nell'Italia carolingia e postcarolingia* (Spoleto, 1966).

—— 'Gli orientamenti feudali dell'impero in Italia', in *Structures féodales et féodalisme dans l'Occident méditerranéen (Xe–XIIIe siècles)* (Rome, 1980), 219–40.

TIRELLI, V., 'Lucca nella seconda metà del secolo XII. Società e istituzioni', in *I ceti dirigenti dell'età comunale nei secoli XII e XIII* (Pisa, 1982), 157–231.

—— 'Il vescovato di Lucca tra la fine del secolo XI e i primi tre decenni del XII', in A. Spicciani and C. Violante (eds.), *Allucio da Pescia (1070 ca–1134)* (Rome, 1991), 55–146.

TOMMASI, G., *Sommario della storia di Lucca* (Florence, 1847).

TOUBERT, P., 'Les Statuts communaux et l'histoire des campagnes lombardes au XIVe siècle', *Mélanges d'archéologie et d'histoire*, 72 (1960), 397–508.

—— *Les Structures du Latium médiéval* (Rome, 1973).

VACCARI, P., *L'affrancazione dei servi della gleba nell'Emilia e nella Toscana* (Bologna, 1926).

—— *La territorialità come base dell'ordinamento giuridico del contado nell'Italia medioevale* (2nd edn., Milan, 1963).

VIOLANTE, C., 'Pievi e parrocchie nell'Italia centrosettentrionale durante i secoli XI e XII', in *Atti della VI settimana internazionale di studio* (Milan, 1977), 643–799.

—— 'Quelques caractéristiques des structures familiales en Lombardie, Emilie et Toscane aux XIe et XIIe siècles', in G. Duby and J. Le Goff (eds.), *Famille et parenté dans l'Occident médiéval* (Rome, 1977), 87–147.

—— 'La signoria rurale nel secolo X. Proposte tipologiche', *Settimane di studio*, 38 (1991), 329–85.

—— 'La signoria "territoriale" come quadro delle strutture organizzative del contado nella Lombardia del secolo XII', in W. Paravicini and K. F. Werner (eds.), *Histoire comparée de l'administration (IVe–XVIIIe siècles) (Beihefte der Francia*, ix, Munich, 1980), 333–44.

—— *La società milanese nell'età precomunale* (Bari, 1953).

—— 'Le strutture organizzative della cura d'anime nelle campagne dell'Italia centrosettentrionale (secoli V–X)', *Settimane di studio*, 28 (1980), 963–1162.

VOLPE, G., 'Lambardi e Romani nelle campagne e nelle città', *Studi storici*, 13 (1904), 53–81, 167–82, 241–315, 369–416.

—— *Medioevo italiano* (Florence, 1961).

—— *Studi sulle istituzioni comunali a Pisa* (2nd edn., Florence, 1970).

VON DER NAHMER, D., *Die Reichsverwaltung in Toscana unter Friedrich I. und Heinrich VI.* (Aalen, 1965).

WICKHAM, C. J., 'Aspetti socioeconomici della Valdinievole nei secoli XI e XII', in A. Spicciani and C. Violante (eds.), *Allucio da Pescia (1070 ca–1134)* (Rome, 1991), 228–9, 279–96.

—— 'Documenti scritti e archeologia per una storia dell'incastellamento: l'esempio della Toscana', *Archeologia medievale*, 16 (1989), 79–102.

—— *Early Medieval Italy* (London, 1981).

—— 'Ecclesiastical Dispute and Lay Community: Figline Valdarno in the Twelfth Century', *Mélanges de l'Ecole française de Rome. Moyen âge*, 108 (1996), 7–93.

—— 'Economia e società rurale nel territorio lucchese durante la seconda metà del secolo XI', in A. Spicciani and C. Violante (eds.), *Sant'Anselmo vescovo di Lucca (1073–1086)* (Rome, 1992), 391–422.

—— 'European Forests in the Early Middle Ages: Landscape and Land Clearance', *Settimane di studio*, 37 (1990), 479–548.

—— 'Frontiere di villaggio in Toscana nel XII secolo', in J. M. Poisson (ed.), *Castrum 4* (Paris, 1992), 239–51.

—— 'Manentes e diritti signorili durante il XII secolo: il caso della Lucchesia', in C. D. Fonseca (ed.), *Società, istituzioni, spiritualità. Studi in onore di Cinzio Violante* (Spoleto, 1994), 1067–80.

—— *The Mountains and the City* (Oxford, 1988).

—— 'Paesaggi sepolti: insediamento e incastellamento sull'Amiata, 750–1250', in M. Ascheri and W. Kurze (eds.), *L'Amiata nel medioevo* (Rome, 1989), 101–37.

—— 'Pastoralism and Underdevelopment in the Early Middle Ages', *Settimane di studio*, 31 (1985), 401–55.

—— *Il problema dell'incastellamento nell'Italia centrale: l'esempio di San Vincenzo al Volturno* (Florence, 1985).

—— 'Problems of Comparing Early Medieval Societies', *Transactions of the Royal Historical Society*, 6 ser. 2 (1992), 221–46.

—— 'Rural Communes and the City of Lucca at the Beginning of the Thirteenth Century', in T. A. Dean and C. J. Wickham (eds.), *City and Countryside in Late Medieval and Renaissance Italy* (London, 1990), 1–12.

—— 'Settlement Problems in Early Medieval Italy: Lucca Territory', *Archeologia medievale*, 5 (1978), 495–503.

—— 'La signoria rurale in Toscana', in G. Dilcher and C. Violante (eds.), *Strutture e trasformazioni della signoria rurale nei secoli X–XIII* (Bologna, 1996), 343–409.

—— *Studi sulla società degli Appennini nell'alto medioevo. Contadini, signori e insediamento nel territorio di Valva (Sulmona)* (Bologna, 1982).

—— 'Vendite di terra e mercato della terra in Toscana nel secolo XI', *Quaderni storici*, 65 (1987), 355–77.

Index

Note: where villages are not ascribed to a diocese, they are in the medieval diocese of Lucca.

272 *Index*